The Asbury Theological Seminary Series in Christian Revitalization Studies

This volume is published in collaboration with the Center for the Study of World Christian Revitalization Movements, a cooperative initiative of Asbury Theological Seminary faculty. Building on the work of the previous Wesleyan/Holiness Studies Center at the Seminary, the Center provides a focus for research in the Wesleyan Holiness and other related Christian renewal movements, including Pietism and Pentecostal movements, which have had a world impact. The research seeks to develop analytical models of these movements, including their biblical and theological assessment. Using an interdisciplinary approach, the Center bridges relevant discourses in several areas in order to gain insights for effective Christian mission globally. It recognizes the need for conducting research that combines insights from the history of evangelical renewal and revival movements with anthropological and religious studies literature on revitalization movements. It also networks with similar or related research and study centers around the world, in addition to sponsoring its own research projects.

Professor Rem Edwards' study brings his long and distinguished career as an ethicist to bear upon the task of engaging the life and thought of John Wesley from the holistic perspective of how Wesley's Christian witness embodies a model for living the good life, regarded as a universal human aspiration. It is also a theme that resonates with the concern of this project for assessing movements of Christian revitalization.

Employing what he calls an axiological approach to values study, Edwards engages the primary data of Wesley's life afresh from an explicitly ethical rather than a doctrinal perspective. At the same time, it may be noted that, while his method interfaces some aspects of Wesley's thought with process philosophical thought, he explicitly sides with Wesley over Whitehead in affirming creation *ex nihilo*. The greater concern of this study is its intensive focus on "what and how John Wesley valued," including the relevance of his values for Christians today who wish to take "growth in grace" and "working out our salvation with fear and trembling" with earnestness. Our readers will find the study engaging this time honored priority of Wesley with fresh insight and relevance for Christian living and thought.

    J. Steven O'Malley, PhD
    Director, Center for the Study of World Christian Revitalization Movements
    General Editor, *The Asbury Theological Seminary Series in Christian Revitalization Studies*

John Wesley's Values – and Ours

~ ~ ~ ~ ~

Rem B. Edwards

*Asbury Theological Seminary Series:
The Study of World Christian Revitalization Movements in
Pietist/Wesleyan Studies, No. 7*

EMETH PRESS
www.emethpress.com

John Wesley's Values - and Ours

Copyright © 2012 Rem B. Edwards

Printed in the United States of America on acid-free paper
All rights reserved. No part of this book may be reproduced, or stored in a retrieval system or transmitted in any form or by any means, electronic, mechanical, photocopying, recording, scanning or otherwise, except as permitted by the 1976 United States Copyright Act, or with the prior written permission of Emeth Press. Requests for permission should be addressed to: Emeth Press, P. O. Box 23961, Lexington, KY 40523-3961.
http://www.emethpress.com.

Library of Congress Cataloging-in-Publication Data

Edwards, Rem Blanchard.
John Wesley's values--and ours / Rem B. Edwards.
    p. cm.
Includes bibliographical references (p.   ) and index.
ISBN 978-1-60947-031-9 (alk. paper)
1. Wesley, John, 1703-1791. 2. Values. I. Title.
BX8495.W5E257 2012
230'.7--dc23
                        2012015159

Front Cover
Photograph of Christ Church Cathedral, University of Oxford where John and Charles Wesley were ordained.
Used by permission.

Dedication

Dedicated to two Methodist ministers who meant much to me years ago, and still do today:

Rev. George T Shell, former minister, Crawfordville, GA Methodist Church, and

Dr. J. Hamby Barton, Jr., former minister, Allen Memorial Methodist Church, Oxford, GA

Contents

Preface. 11

Chapter 1: Value Theory, and Christian Values and Evaluations. 17
    What We Value 17
    How We Value.. 18
    Prioritizing Values and Evaluations.. 20
    Christianity and the Three Value Dimensions. 22
        Christian Intrinsic Values and Evaluations. 22
        Christian Extrinsic Values and Evaluations.. 26
        Christian Systemic Values and Evaluations.. 28
    Spiritually Significant Value Combinations.. 30
    Biblical Value Rankings. 31

Chapter 2: John Wesley's Intrinsic Values and Evaluations. 35
    God as Intrinsically Good. 36
    God's Attributes or "Perfect-Making Properties". 37
        Perfection or Supreme Goodness.. 39
        Omnipotence. 40
        Feelings or Affections. 42
        Omniscience and Eternity. 45
    People as Intrinsically Good. 50
        Is God the Only End, The Only Intrinsic Good?. 50
        Human Good-making (God-like) Properties. 57
            Our Common Image of God Properties. 57
            Wesley's Emphasis on Human Liberty.. 64
            Defending Human Liberty or Freedom of Choice. 65
    Animals as Intrinsically Good. 73
        God Cares About Animals.. 74
        God Provides for Both Animals and People. 75
        Animals are Entitled to Compensation Hereafter.. 76
        Animals Share our Good-making Properties. 77

Chapter 3: John Wesley's Extrinsic Values and Evaluations. 83
    The Extrinsic Value of the Means of Grace. 83

Overvaluing, Undervaluing, and Rightly Valuing
   the Means of Grace. 87
Valuing and Overvaluing the Things of the World. 90
   The Good Things of the World. 92
   Overvaluing Worldly Goods, and the Hierarchy of Value................ 97
      Pursuing Pleasure.. 101
      Avoiding Pain.. 104
   The Goodness of Human Bodies. 107
   The Goodness of Human Actions and Good Works. 111
   Worldliness and Original Sin............................... 116
      The Scriptural Case for Original Sin......................... 118
      The Experiential Case for Original Sin. 120
      Starting Low versus Starting High........................... 128
   Worldly Religion. 131
   Respecting and Loving Worldly People.......................... 133

Chapter 4: John Wesley's Systemic Values and Evaluations..................... 135
   Wesley as a Believer: Faith in Three Dimensions. 136
      Systemic Faith.. 138
      Intrinsic Faith.. 142
      Extrinsic Faith.. 146
   Wesley as More Than a Believer............................... 149
      Why Beliefs Have a Subordinate Place....................... 149
      Hope for Non-Christians................................. 152
   Wesley's Hermeneutics of Love.............................. 155
      Wesley's Non-literal Literalism............................ 158
      Applying Love to the Scriptures. 161
   Wesley's Own Hierarchy of Christian Values..................... 166
      Christian Zeal. 166
      The Good, and Degrees Thereof. 167
      Wesley's Own Hierarchy of Christian Value-Objects................ 169
      Ranking Doctrines Within the Hierarchy...................... 170
   Systemic Religion. 175

Chapter 5: John Wesley's Saintly Values and Evaluations. 179
   Making the Transition. 179
      Salvation is Today; Sanctification Takes Forever. 181
      Continuities and Discontinuities........................... 183
   The Good-making Properties of the Saints. 185
      Perfection, Including Power Over Sin......................... 189
      Love to and Union with God............................... 191
      Love to All Humankind.................................. 200
         The Nature of Love to Other People...................... 200
         The Scope of Love to Other People....................... 204
      The Spiritual Senses. 208
         An Inner Consciousness of God's Presence................. 212
         Intensified Religious Affections......................... 217
         Perceived Assurance............................. 219

    More Perceived Religious Affections. 221
    Enhanced Discernment of Good and Evil.. 222
    A New Appreciation for Old Beliefs. 225
An Awareness of God's Presence or Omnipresence
in All Creation. 227
    God's Metaphysical Omnipresence. 228
    The Devotional Significance of God's Omnipresence. 236
Abundant Life. 241
    Almost Heaven on Earth.. 241
    Pluralistic Goodness.. 245
    Actualizing our Good-making Properties.. 246
    Sanctified Souls are Better.. 248
    Stars in Our Crowns.. 250

Notes. 255

Index.. 283

About the Author. 291

Preface

This book evolved from a much simpler series of talks given to a large elective study class at Church Street United Methodist Church in Knoxville, Tennessee during the summer of 2009, but it goes far beyond those talks. I greatly appreciated the kindness and patience of that audience for hearing me out and allowing me to show them how to do some orderly thinking about Christian values in general and Wesleyan values in particular. This book will apply an orderly or systematic theory of value to John Wesley's values and, to some extent, more broadly to the values of Methodism or Wesleyanism.

This book centers on what and how John Wesley valued, and on how Wesley's insights can help us develop and sustain a profound spirituality for today. It presupposes a value theory, explained briefly in Chapter One and developed and defended philosophically in more detail elsewhere.[1] This is the very best theory of human values that I ever found during my long career of teaching, research, and writing about value theory on college and graduate levels. I hope that it will seem simple and obvious once readers take a look at it, though many people are oblivious to the obvious until it is pointed out to them. This theory of value was developed by my former senior colleague in philosophy at the University of Tennessee, Robert S. Hartman, though I omit a few little details with which I strongly disagree. This is the last you will hear of him here, but his work is always in the background throughout these pages. The technical name for his position is "formal axiology," (value theory), but the simpler "axiology" will be our occasional word for it. Formal axiology gives the basic grammar of value theory. In Chapter One, after briefly explaining this theory, it is then applied to Christian values in general. If the value theory itself seems a bit dull, please be patient; the applications, first to Christian values generally, then to John Wesley's values and evaluations, are much more exciting.

This theory of value affords a very different way of looking creatively at John Wesley's thought. It is a very powerful tool for organizing, analyzing, explaining, and systematizing Wesley's somewhat unsystematic theology. This is not at attempt to impose an alien "agenda" or "meta-narrative" upon Wesley. Please give it a chance. You will likely find it to be a good fit, a natural fit.

This book is philosophically informed and organized, but it is definitely not a philosophical book or written for a philosophical audience. It presents a holistic picture of what a Christian form of life would look like, given *all* the positive values that are within it, properly ordered. Launched from a Wesleyan perspective, it is an invitation to, a credo about, but not an argument for, a spiritual way of life that speaks loudly for itself. Most of us do not know how to do it, but all of us wish to live good lives, meaningful lives, worthwhile lives. Christianity definitely has something to say about that. So did John Wesley, who explained the "good life" as well as any Christian thinker ever has, and better than most. Taken in its entirety, that is, given all the positive values and evaluations that Wesley took seriously, this book outlines his view of what a really good life would be like—a life that has everything in it that could make it worth living for its own sake and for others, including God. It also identifies major obstacles to living such an abundant life. It sketches a Wesleyan, indeed a Christian, way of life that simply speaks emphatically for itself.

The title of this book, *John Wesley's Values—and Ours*, oversimplifies its contents. Both *what* Wesley valued—his values, and *how* he valued—his evaluations, are covered. Who is encompassed by "ours"? We today, obviously, but which of us today? Today's Methodists or Wesleyans will likely be its primary audience, but this book should be of great interest and relevance to all Christians who want to understand what and how Christians value. Wesley's thoughts about such issues can enlighten our path today, even if we do not always agree with him about minor details. Though not the whole story, what and how to value are major concerns of all Christians, and they are central to spiritual discernment, growth, development, and abundant living. Spiritual growth should be of immense significance to ministers, pastoral counselors, lay leaders, and ordinary church members. A worthwhile life does not just happen automatically; we must grow into it, and we need guidance for it. By focusing on the value dimensions of spiritual growth, this book aspires to assist and guide today's readers in their own personal spiritual quest and maturation. The general patterns of value analysis in this book could, in principle, be applied to any and all religious traditions, Wesleyan or not, Christian or not. Others are invited to do it for their own traditions.

Wesley's perspectives on what and how Christians value will be developed somewhat beyond where he left them. We may disagree with him occasionally, mainly about some of his now obsolete scientific assumptions. Yet, he made use of the very best "natural philosophy" of his own day,[2] which is what we now call "natural science," thereby setting a sound precedent for us in our own time and place. Most of his reflections on Christian values and evaluations are very insightful and should be highly relevant, empowering, and helpful to Christians here and now and to Christianity today.

This book is definitely not an overview of Wesley's complete theology. It covers a lot of ground, but it is not comprehensive. It takes only a minimal account of the historical background and development of his theology, and it deliberately ignores many of the fine distinctions of Wesleyan scholasticism. Much of it just focuses upon what scholars call the "mature" Wesley, or what we will call the most "plausible" Wesley. For more comprehensive accounts of Wesley's life and theological thinking, readers should go to other exceptionally thorough and thoughtful books such as William R. Cannon, *The Theology of John Wesley*[3] John B. Cobb, Jr., *Grace and Responsibility: A Wesleyan Theology for Today*,[4] Kenneth J. Collins, *The Theology of John Wesley: Holy Love and the Shape of Grace*,[5] Richard P. Heitzenrater, *Wesley and the People Called Methodists*[6] (mostly historical), Randy L. Maddox, *Responsible Grace: John Wesley's Practical Theology*,[7] and Ted Runyon, *The New Creation: John Wesley's Theology Today*.[8] Fine studies of the background, contents, and historical consequences of certain themes in Wesley's thought such as mysticism and prevenient grace area also available, for example, Robert G. Tuttle, Jr., *Mysticism in the Wesleyan Tradition*[9] and J. Gregory Crofford, *Streams of Mercy: Prevenient Grace in the Theology of John and Charles Wesley*.[10] For details about how Wesley applied his values and evaluations to urgent social issues in his day like poverty, education, slavery, and prison reforms, take a look at Manfred Marquardt, *John Wesley's Social Ethics: Praxis and Principles*.[11]

This book investigates both what and how John Wesley valued, not for their historical significance, but for their vital interest to us today. The books mentioned above explain the historical background and content of Wesley's thought, chronological changes in Wesley's own convictions, and many subtle and complex theological distinctions having such small spiritual significance that ministers are never likely to preach sermons on them. Please consult such books for more information if you are curious about such things.

This book concentrates mainly on Wesley himself, not on the secondary literature about him. It makes no claim to comprehensiveness and in no way competes with or substitutes for other books that reach for it. It focuses narrowly but intensely on what and how John Wesley valued, and on the relevance and importance of his values and evaluations for Christians today who take "growth in grace" seriously. "Working out our salvation with fear and trembling" definitely involves both getting our values and priorities straight and working with God, while God works with us. This book's emphasis on the values involved in spiritual development is probably closest to the "therapeutic" orientation of Maddox's book. All of the preceding books recognize that Wesley's was a "practical theology." The present book shows that a practical theology is values-oriented, mainly so, even if not exclusively so.[12] Just as practical philosophy is values-centered, so is practical theology. Books by other Wesley scholars *comment* on Wesley's values; this book *concentrates* on them.

Spiritual rehabilitation, healing, and growth are largely, though not entirely, matters of getting our value priorities straight. They involve getting clearer answers to: "What do (or should) I value?" and "How do (or should) I evaluate what I value?" They also involve putting those answers into practice over time and throughout our lives. Most people, even many Christians, are very confused about such things. Maybe this book will help. The following pages give many quotations from Wesley's works, selected deliberately for their current relevance and plausibility as spiritual values and evaluations for today's Christians. Sometimes, the plausible is best understood when contrasted with the implausible, so some of that will also be considered.

The present book does give some attention to historical influences, connections, and developments. For example, it compares the views of John Wesley with those of Jonathan Edwards simply because their similarities, differences, and connections are interesting, informative, and enlightening. Other scholars trace their affiliations much more extensively, especially Richard B. Steele in his excellent *"Gracious Affections" and "True Virtue" According to Jonathan Edwards and John Wesley.*[13] One reason for comparing Wesley and Edwards, suggested by Steele, is that Wesley's deep (but one-sided) indebtedness to Edwards is "a fact not generally acknowledged in the Methodist tribal literature."[14] The more limited comparisons made here bear primarily on what and how Wesley valued.

This book also compares some issues in Wesley's theology with contemporary Temporalistic Theism, which includes mainstream Whiteheadian Process Theology and Panentheism[15] as well as Open Theism,[16] Relational Theism,[17] and any others that ascribe to God real relations in and through time or process. Most Temporalistic Theologians believe that God changes in some desirable respects, does not change in other desirable respects, includes all without determining or being perfectly identical with all, and interacts with real people and other creatures in time and history, rather than from a timeless eternity. God's general nature does not change, but God's particular experiences and decisions do change as God acts on the world and its creatures act on God. God's moral and spiritual perfections do not change, but God's overall experience of value does change or increase as an endlessly creative God takes the constantly-being-created goodness and reality of all of nature, history, and every individual creature into himself to remember and cherish forever. God has real and not merely apparent relations with all of creation in space and time. Since all of God's creatures have degrees of freedom or self-creativity and responsibility, the future is partly open and does not pre-exist determinately for God to foreknow in complete detail, though God can preeminently predict probabilities and has a supreme general knowledge of what is most likely to happen. Where mainstream Process Theology excels on issues of spatiotemporality, modifications of Wesley's theology are suggested; where Wesley excels on some issues like creation *ex nihilo*, modifications of mainstream Process Theology are suggested. Again, no claim to comprehensiveness is made, and there is plenty of room for honest disagreement.

Many scholars distinguish between the "mature" and the less mature Wesley as a covert way of expressing their own value preferences. ("Late" might be less evaluative than "mature.") The import of Wesley's "maturest thoughts" is as much evaluative as it is chronological, even if Wesley himself used the expression.[18] This book will not use these terms. Instead, it goes directly and overtly to Wesley's very best, most plausible, and most defensible Christian values and evaluations. A few of his more implausible beliefs are also identified and critiqued. We need a Wesleyan spirituality for the twenty-first century that does not require us to live within the mentality of the eighteenth century—or earlier. Wesley's plausibility, not his maturity, is the real issue. Admittedly, as the author of this book, I judge what is and what is not plausible or worthy of serious consideration. Not everyone will agree, of course, but what else is new? Every author does this; but at least a strong case will be made. Please consider it. Do not hesitate to disagree with this book when you see fit; also, do not hesitate to disagree with Wesley when you see fit.

Most mainstream protestant denominations, including those of Wesleyan descent, have experienced significant declines in membership in recent decades. There are many reasons for this, but one of them is surely that spirituality, growth in grace, and the religious affections have been neglected in both preaching and practice. This author believes that the rank and file of today's Methodists, Nazarenes, and other Wesleyans know far too little about John Wesley and his profound insights into spirituality, growth in grace, the spiritual affections, and how they are constituted largely by what and how Christians value. What would happen if we go back to the best of John Wesley?

Extensive quotes to follow document *what* and *how* Wesley valued, as explained in Chapters Two through Five. Endnotes on Wesley's sermons and other writings refer to the Bicentennial Edition of Wesley's works whenever possible. Items not yet available in the Bicentennial Edition are nevertheless often available on the Internet, as indicated, or in other or earlier editions of his works. In the endnotes, the first time his sermons are listed, his titles are given, then the sermon number, then the section and paragraph numbers, then the volume and page numbers. Later references do not give sermon numbers. After specific sources are identified in the endnotes, additional relevant references are often given. Words introduced throughout to clarify or make transitions are included in brackets [ ]. The writings of John Locke, available in the public domain in many editions, are referenced by book, chapter, and section number. Endnotes for more recent sources are given as academic conventions dictate.

Thanks to Yale University Press for permission to quote from the *Works of Jonathan Edwards* and to Abingdon Press for permission to quote from the *Works of John Wesley*. In almost instances, quotes from the Bible are from the King James Version. I grew up on it, and I just like the language except for "charity" in I. Corinthians 13, but Wesley didn't like that either.

The values and evaluations involved in spiritual growth discussed in this book can actually be *measured* very effectively. I and two colleagues in the Robert S.

Hartman Institute, David and Vera Mefford, have developed a "Christian Values Profile" that does this, along with a handbook that helps make sense of the Profile's results. The CVP discloses where people are in their own spiritual development and where they need to go from here. The handbook, *Developing Your Christian Values*, guides in fulfilling these objectives. This Profile and that book are not addressed specifically to Wesleyan audiences, but they nicely complement the present book. For more information, go to: www.christianvaluesprofile.com.

Rem B. Edwards
Lindsay Young Professor of Philosophy, Emeritus
The University of Tennessee, Knoxville, TN

Chapter One

Value Theory and Christian Values and Evaluations

Applied to Christianity in general, and to John Wesley, Methodism, or Wesleyanism in particular, value theory can be very helpful and illuminating. You will need to read much further to understand and be convinced of this, but the relevance of this novel axiological approach to John Wesley should become obvious as this book progresses. We will now consider what value theory says about what we value (values, or objects of value), how we value (evaluations), and the ranking of our values and evaluations—the value hierarchy. All of this will be applied in later chapters to John Wesley.

What We Value

During every waking moment, we are constantly involved with and being bombarded by values, that is, with objects of interest that we judge or feel to be good or bad, right or wrong, moral or immoral, virtuous or vicious, desirable or undesirable, acceptable or unacceptable, correct or incorrect, beautiful or ugly, and so on. Conscious awareness is evaluative awareness through and through. Values can be either positive (good, right, moral, virtuous, desirable, acceptable, correct, beautiful, saintly, etc.) or negative (bad, evil, wrong, immoral, vicious, undesirable, unacceptable, incorrect, ugly, sinful, etc.). This book accents positive values, beginning with the meaning of "good" or "valuable." Sins and evils are revisited in later chapters, so disvalues are also covered, but less extensively. Let's start by saying that good things are desirable things in which we take a positive interest and that fulfill our expectations or standards. A more carefully formulated definition will come later. Disvalues are just the opposite.

What things, after careful consideration, do we value positively and judge to be good? To answer, we must recognize three kinds or dimensions of goodness—*intrinsic, extrinsic, and systemic.*

Intrinsically good things are ends in themselves, valuable to, for, and in themselves, valuable for their own sakes.
Extrinsically good things are useful in getting other things that we desire; they are means to ends.
Systemically good things are intellectual, mental, or conceptual values that exist in our minds and thoughts.

So, what kinds of things are intrinsically, extrinsically, or systemically good? Again, after careful consideration, we should arrive at these answers:

People (or unique conscious beings like God, angels, or animals) are intrinsically good, i.e., ends in themselves, valuable to, for, and in themselves, valuable for their own sakes.
Things (understood as perceivable physical objects, processes, and actions in public or common space and time) are extrinsically good, i.e., useful as means to ends beyond themselves.
Ideas (concepts, beliefs, doctrines, rules, principles, rituals, laws, forms, formalities, etc.) are systemically good, i.e., intellectually or cognitively desirable.

How We Value

Not only *what* we value (the good things just mentioned) but also *how* we value is important. We can relate affirmatively to any and all the good things above in at least one of three ways. Corresponding to the three basic kinds of goodness are three basic kinds or dimensions of evaluation, each of which has both a cognitive and an affective aspect.

On the *cognitive or rational level*, evaluation in each of the three dimensions involves matching the actual properties of any valued object with its ideal properties. This is what "good is concept fulfillment" means, which is axiology's formal definition of "good." Here is how it works. We, or the authorities on which we rely, must actually experience an object being evaluated to gain information about its actual qualities and relations (properties). Then on a rational level we must have or create an ideal that conceptualizes the good-making predicates that the object being valued is supposed to have. Then we must ascertain the degree to which the actual properties of the thing being evaluated correspond with the ideal predicates that we apply to it. If the match is exact, we have a good thing. If it is less than exact, then we have something that is only fair, average, poor, or virtually worthless, depending on the degree of the match. Completely good things are everything that they are supposed to be; less than good things are less complete in their good-making properties.

Evaluation is both rational and affective. Here are the three correlated *affective aspects* of evaluations in three dimensions.

Evaluating intrinsically means valuing with intense feelings—with passionate affections like intense love, compassion, consolation, consolation, empathy, forgiveness, and concentration. Its ultimate form is complete personal identification with what is being valued. Whatever we identify with, we are creating an identity for ourselves thereby. People (intrinsic values, conscious individuals, final ends) are the most natural and appropriate objects of intrinsic evaluation. However, we can also passionately love or otherwise identify with things and thoughts, with extrinsic and systemic values. Sometimes this is morally or spiritually objectionable, sometimes not, as we will see.

Evaluating extrinsically involves valuing pragmatically in terms of, or for the sake of, normal everyday practical desires, feelings, and interests. Physical or sensory things, bodies, processes, and actions in our ordinary spacetime world (extrinsic values) are the most natural and appropriate objects of extrinsic evaluation. They are normally or primarily valued because they are useful to us, because they are means to ends beyond themselves. We can also personify the things of the world and value them intrinsically, as if they were persons, and we can apply formal thought systems like logic and mathematics to them. We can also evaluate people and thoughts extrinsically, that is, for their usefulness. Sometimes this is morally or spiritually objectionable, sometimes not, as later explained.

Evaluating systemically means relating to good things with disinterested (but not uninterested) objectivity. Truth, knowledge, ideas, thoughts, beliefs, laws, rules, principles, rituals, mathematics, logic, and other formalities are the most natural and appropriate objects of systemic evaluation. We can also evaluate people and things systemically—as instances of abstractions, doctrines, beliefs, and conceptual constructs. We can also evaluate beliefs and other formalities intrinsically as if they were persons. Sometimes this is morally or spiritually objectionable, sometimes not, as indicated later.

Values and evaluations can be combined with one another to produce almost endless varieties and complexities of what is being valued and how. This can be done positively, as above, with respect to good things; but it can also be done negatively with respect to bad things. We normally relate to disvalues through aversive feelings as lacking good-making properties or as manifesting bad-making properties. Having values and sorting out their relative worth may start simply, but it can become very complicated rather quickly.

Another complication is that the paradigm instances of every type of value can be evaluated as if they were some other kind of value. All values can be evaluated in every dimension. This means that we can love people, see them as useful, and view them objectively. It means that we can see things as useful, but we can also love things, count them dispassionately, and manipulate them practically. It means that ideas and beliefs can be assessed rationally and objectively, but they can also be loved, viewed as useful, and put to use.

Prioritizing Values and Evaluations

Getting our priorities straight is very important, and people, Christians included, are often very confused about how to do this. Intrinsic, extrinsic, and systemic values and evaluations can and should be *ranked or prioritized* (judged as better or worse) in the following ways. The three kinds or dimensions of goodness fall into a *hierarchy of values*, based on different degrees of goodness. Some positively valued things have more kinds or degrees of what philosophers call "good-making properties" than others. Good-making properties are the ones that must be present if anything is good or valuable, as explained more carefully later, but the following *hierarchy of values* captures and expresses the proper ranking of the three value dimensions.

> *People (intrinsic values) are more valuable than things.*
> *Things (extrinsic values) are more valuable than ideas (symbolic tokens) of people and things.*
> *Ideas (systemic values), though very valuable, are less valuable than things and people.*
> *So, we should always put or rank people first, things next, and ideas last.*

We don't always make this ranking consciously, if at all; and since these three value dimensions often complement rather than conflict with one another, we are not constantly making choices that require that we prioritize them. However, most of our moral and spiritual problems spring from overvaluing things and ideas while undervaluing people. Since God, angels, animals, etc. are also intrinsically valuable, we can expand this hierarchy of value at a spiritual level to mean:

> *God, people, animals, and all conscious individuals are more valuable than mere things.*
> *Mere things are more valuable than mere ideas (symbolic tokens) of God, people, animals, conscious beings, and non-conscious things.*
> *Mere ideas, though very valuable, are less valuable than both conscious individuals and mere things.*
> *So, we should always put or rank God, people, animals, and all conscious individuals first, mere things next, and mere ideas last.*

God should be ranked first of all because God is infinitely more valuable than finite conscious individuals like us. God contains an infinite quantity and quality of good-making properties within himself; we have only a finite number within ourselves—and then only by God's creative grace. So God is infinitely more valuable than we are. Since God's love for and gracefulness toward us are aspects of God's infinite reality and worth, this gives us a kind of relational infinite worth that we would not have without God's love for us.

These three kinds or dimensions of value and evaluation can be and usually are *combined with one another into complex valuational wholes*, and *everything can be evaluated in any dimension, that is, in ways that are most appropriate for the objects that most naturally belong to some other dimension*. We can value every good thing in any of these three ways, that is, as if it were some other kind of value. Every good thing can be misused or abused, that is over or under valued. We can combine values from different dimensions to get new compositional wholes that are more (or less) valuable than their parts. For example, consider the value of *people* (or any other conscious individuals) *without* God's love, versus people (or any conscious beings) *with* God's love. Consider the value of *things* without God, versus things with God. Consider the value of *ideas* without God, versus ideas with God. John Wesley, we will discover, usually valued people, things, and thoughts holistically within God, not as separated from God.

Philosophical distinctions like "ends in themselves," "means to ends," and "conceptual values" are not biblical categories, but they can be applied to what we read in the Bible, to the writings of the theologians, and to all human discourse. The results can be very illuminating and fruitful. Wesley was certainly familiar with the first two of these distinctions, and he explicitly used them. Conceptual or systemic values were there all along, but, like most earlier thinkers, Wesley did not expressly recognize that they belong to a separate realm or dimension of value. Yet, in his own way he did emphatically separate systemic cognitive values (religious beliefs and opinions) from extrinsically good works and physical objects, and from intrinsically loving God and our neighbors. He definitely ranked and combined them and had many important and fruitful things to say about them and their relative worth. Anticipating later discussions, and just in case you have initial reservations about the axiological hierarchy of value, consider this quote from John Wesley, where he actually ranks the values mentioned in I. Corinthians 13.

> It is proper to observe here, First, what a beautiful gradation there is, each step rising above the other....St Paul begins at the lowest point, *talking well*, and advances step by step; every one rising higher than the preceding, till he comes to the highest of all. A step above eloquence is knowledge. Faith is a step above this. Good works are a step above that faith; and even above this, is suffering for righteousness' sake. Nothing is higher than this, but Christian love; the love of our neighbour, flowing from the love of God.
>
> It may be proper to observe, Secondly, that whatever passes for religion in any part of the Christian world, (whether it be a part of religion, or no part at all, but

either folly, superstition, or wickedness) may with very little difficulty be reduced to one or other of these heads.[1]

Note that here Wesley clearly acknowledged the relevance of value analysis to "whatever passes for religion." Later we will see how Wesley's "heads" can be reduced to our three basic dimensions of value, or to combinations of them. The following chapters apply this basic theory and hierarchy of values to Wesleyan Christianity. Before we get to Wesley, let's first consider whether Christians generally recognize these three kinds of value and evaluation, and, if so, how they rank them. Illustrations that follow will focus (selectively, as is always the case) on Biblical affirmations of value and evaluation.

Christianity and the Three Value Dimensions

Do Christians recognize and affirm intrinsic, extrinsic, and systemic values and evaluations, at least implicitly if not explicitly? They do, as explained next. The life, ministry, and teachings of Jesus affirm and rank these three dimensions of value; so does much of the rest of the New Testament beyond the four gospels; so does much of the Old Testament; so does much of Christian history and tradition, and so do most Christians today.

Christian Intrinsic Values and Evaluations

Jesus affirmed the value of God and people for their own sakes without using exactly those words for it. He manifested and commended intense positive affective involvement with God and people. This comes out in the evaluative heart of the New Testament—how Jesus responded when asked, "Which commandment is the first of all?" Jesus answered with *two* very closely related commandments. His "Great Love Commandments" identify both what we should value and how we should value them. Neither one is in the official lists of the "Ten Commandments" in Exodus 20 and Deuteronomy 5, but both of them are found in the Old Testament.

> The first is, "Hear, O Israel: The Lord our God, the Lord is one: and you shall love the Lord your God with all your heart, and with all your soul, and with all your mind, and with all your strength." The second is this; "You shall love your neighbor as yourself." There is no other commandment greater than these. (Mark 12:28–31; see also Matthew 22:36–40; Luke 10:27; Deuteronomy 6:5, and Leviticus 19:18.)

Both of these Great Love Commandments tell us *what* we should value most (first God, then people) and *how* we should value them (lovingly). Both involve the *love* of *someone* intrinsically valuable; both involve intrinsic values and evaluations. Loving God should involve us totally—all of our hearts (intrinsically), minds (systemically), strengths (extrinsically), and souls (holistically). Loving people is not far removed from this. We cannot love God fully without loving all that God loves. Unless mentally disturbed, we naturally love ourselves with great intensity, endeavor, and thought; and we are here invited, indeed commanded, to love others accordingly, even if our sinfulness and finitude make this extremely difficult.

In much of the Old Testament, New Testament, traditional Christian theology, and John Wesley's own thought, all three dimensions of value are positively valued and properly ranked without being either over- or under-valued. For example, God and Jesus are unique conscious individuals who are to be valued intrinsically (loved) for their own sakes (as ends in themselves). They are not to be valued merely extrinsically, that is, merely because they are useful to us or to God. Also, they are not to be valued merely systemically, that is, merely because they happen to fit our pre-conceptions, doctrines, or beliefs. The same is true of the proper Christian way to evaluate people, both ourselves and our neighbors. People are to be valued for their own sakes, not merely because they are useful to us or share our skin color, customs, prosperity, or practices, and not merely because they conform to, accept, or agree with our ideas, ideals, beliefs, and preconceptions.

Furthermore, Christian salvation is offered primarily to unique conscious individuals, not to non-conscious things, not to social orders, and not to ideas, ideals, or beliefs as such. We are not instructed to love things, practices, customs, societies, or doctrines with all our hearts, souls, minds, and strength. We are not told that Christ came to save material, social, or conceptual objects of value. The Good Shepherd is passionately concerned for *all* lost sheep, *each* of whom is a unique conscious individual. He knows every last one of them personally and by name, that is, as unique individuals, and not merely as instances of "humanity," "rationality," "Methodism," or "Christianity" (John 10:11–16).

Societies and human institutions are to be transformed, and thus "saved" or redeemed in some secondary sense; but this is to be accomplished mainly by redeeming and transforming conscious individuals, especially those in power who make, manage, and enforce the laws, customs, wealth, and social arrangements by which we live. Yes, societies, social institutions, and social arrangements are to be "saved" or transformed into something better (e.g., the Kingdom of God), but not for their own sakes. Redeemed social orders exist for the sake of the concrete conscious individuals living within them. They are not ends in themselves but means to other more valuable ends. Sinful social orders place terrible restraints and unjust burdens on those living within them, but only people working together with other people and with God can correct them. Better social institutions and orders, including better churches, are desirable because they benefit the individual people who belong to, express, and live their lives within them. According to John Wesley, the church and "all ecclesiastical order" exist merely for the sake of individual members, not for their own sake. Wesley asked about the purpose of the church and answered rhetorically, "Is it not to bring souls from the power of Satan to God, and to build them up in his fear and love? Order, then, is so far valuable as it answers these ends; and if it answers them not, it is worth nothing."[2] Likewise, Christian guidelines and beliefs are valuable, not in themselves or for their own sakes, but only because they play a formative, informative, and regulative role in the salvation and sanctification of unique persons. Faith, the Law, the Sabbath, the Church, and the Kingdom are made for unique conscious human beings, not the other way around.

For the philosophically inclined, the concept of "unique conscious persons" used throughout this book does not presuppose any notions of substance, non-relationality, or self-sufficiency. *We human beings are the integrated totality of all of our properties—our total property inventory*, which consists of both our inherent qualities and of those relations with significant others, human and non-human, that partly constitute our very being and identity. If we could *literally* "see our whole lives (both internal and external) flash before our eyes," we would have a momentary glimpse of who we really are. Our uniquely integrated entirety of qualities and relations is constantly being enriched by every new personal experience and personal initiative. Time is integral to our singular reality, to who we have been, are, and will become. Time makes our freedom possible. We are who we are in part through our temporally ordered causal relations with God, with those persons and natural processes that preceded us, and with those who share our own more immediate world; but in part we also create our own reality and identity through the free personal choices that we make. We are all unique persons, but we are also inherently social beings who share many properties or traits with and derive them from God, other persons, and non-human animals. Much of what we are is simply given to us by heredity and environment, but we are who we are in part because of the decisions we have made ourselves and the initiatives we have taken in the past. We are presently deciding and thereby creating, in part, who we will become in the open future.

That we are the integrated entirety of all our properties (our total property inventory) may shed some light on and help us to appreciate Wesley's understanding of and profound sensitivity to the depth of human sinfulness. We often hear the expression, "hate the sin but love the sinner," but this is almost too good to be true. It presupposes that the two can be easily and completely separated, but being a sinner is too deep for that. Sinfulness is an integral aspect of our very identity and constitution, of who we really are. If we are the integrated entirety of all our properties, this includes our bad properties as well as our good ones, both of which are inherent and integral aspects of who we really are. Wesley himself affirmed, in his own words, that we are the integrated entirety of all our properties, both good and bad, when he discussed what will be disclosed and remembered about the "whole life" of each of us on the final day of judgment.[3] He included all our good and bad works, actions, words, thoughts and "every inward working of every human soul: every appetite, passion, inclination, affection, with the various combinations of them, with every temper and disposition that constitute the whole complex character of each individual."[4] Wesley had his own version of "hate the sin but love the sinner," but he qualified this in a very significant way: "Be angry at sin...but love the sinner still" like "our Lord" who "was grieved at the sinners, angry at sin."[5] *Grieving* involves disvaluing something, but what? Jesus applied it to sinners themselves, Wesley thought, not just to their sins.

Maybe we can love part or even most of any person, ourselves included, without loving some other part, the corrupt part; but we can't just hate "sin," "sinful acts," or "sinful dispositions" in the abstract while affirming and loving absolutely *everything* about the sinner. Our souls are structured by our values and evaluations, both good and bad. Repenting means repudiating and grieving over not just our sinful acts, but the sinful parts of our souls, the sinful dispositions that are fundamental features of who we really are deep inside. Sinfulness partly constitutes our personal identity; it is not just an abstraction easily separated from who we are as "sinners." Conversion and sanctification together involve an inner and usually gradual transformation of who we are deep inside. Salvation and sanctification mean becoming new persons who are, with God's help, overcoming and transcending the undesirable aspects of who we once were. This is largely a matter of acquiring new and better values and habits of evaluation, new personalities, new identities, along with the affections and beliefs that support them and the behaviors that express them.

We must identify with the sinful parts of ourselves to the extent that we honestly recognize them as our own, as integral parts of our personal identity, of our entire reality, in order to disassociate ourselves from, repent of, grieve over, and overcome them, that is, in order to disvalue and disown them (repent) and make room for the positive moral and spiritual values of saintliness. We can and should identify with (face up to) our own personal sinfulness as our own, but only with reservations, regrets, guilt, grief, and repentance. In giving up our sins, we are giving up integral aspects of our former selves.

One great theological advantage of thinking of both God and Jesus as sinless[6] is that identification spirituality enables us to understand how the man Jesus fully identified with God without reservations, and how God fully identified with the human Jesus without reservations. At least in this very important sense, Jesus was both fully God and fully man. All the rest of us hold back somewhere. Jesus so fully identified, not only with God, but also even with people who are and do evil, and with those who suffer and are downtrodden, that he bore within himself all the sins and sufferings of the world. Jesus wept; Jesus suffered and died for and with us. *Ideally*, Christians identify so fully with Jesus that they can say with St. Paul that "I live not, but Christ liveth within me" (Galatians 2:20). They strive to have within themselves not only the mind or thoughts of Christ, but also his holiness, his virtues, his affections and tempers, and his faith that worketh by love.[7] They value what he valued (God, every person, every creature) and as he valued them (lovingly and completely).

Christian Extrinsic Values and Evaluations

Within creation, the values of, in, and for individual souls matter the most, but they are not the only good things that matter to Christians. The world also matters, but its goodness should not be overvalued or undervalued. The things of the world can be and often are overvalued at the expense of people or souls, as in worldliness. They can function as great temptations. Yet, Christianity affirms the goodness of the world. The world, yes; worldliness, no. Worldliness puts the things of the world first, but Christians put God first, then people, and only then comes everything else that is important to them. The good things of the world can be valued and used rightly as well as wrongly. Christians try to understand, use, and appreciate them rightly.

Extrinsically valuable things are the physical or material objects, processes, practices, and activities that exist in public space and time and are given to us in ordinary sense experience. Extrinsically good things include our own bodies, the actions or deeds that we perform with them, and the social practices and roles that we act out through them. Their most important goodness or value to us is their usefulness to us and to others. Extrinsically valuable things are good as means to ends beyond themselves. We need and want material or physical resources like property, healthy bodies, food, water, shelter, heaters, and coolers in order to preserve and sustain our lives, for comfort and enjoyment, and to share with others. Many of our actions, social practices, and social roles appropriately address such physical needs. We have a hierarchy of needs, values, goals, and terminal ends. All of our moral and spiritual ends presuppose our survival, either here or hereafter. For the time being, we will concentrate on the here and now. The hereafter comes later and is entirely in God's hands.

This world is good, and the things of the world are good. They should be valued neither too much nor too little. Worldly people value them too much. Christians presumably value them just right. Ideologists, dogmatists, and "absent-minded professors" tend to value them too little. Fairly early in the history of Christianity, Christians encountered and responded to a competing worldview called "Manicheanism." Manicheanism was rejected, especially its claim that matter as such is bad and only spirit is good. This view of the physical world flies in the face of the first chapter of the book of Genesis, according to which the world (including its materiality and pre-human life forms) was "good" from the start, even before human beings were created. After God created human beings, the creation story adds, God saw the world as "very good" (Genesis 1:25, 31). Christianity went with Genesis, not with Manicheanism. The physical world and its particular contents, extrinsically good things, are indeed good, but some highly desirable things (e.g., people) are even better. Our physical environment was, is, and will be good for us. Being responsible for taking care of it, having "dominion" over it, means keeping it that way. Human sinfulness can ruin anything—even the physical environment that sustains us. Birds can unknowing foul their own nests; we do it knowingly and have no excuse for it.

The positive value of physical or extrinsic goodness is further affirmed in the Christian doctrines of the incarnation and the resurrection of the body. In the incarnation, God "became flesh and lived among us" (John 1:14). Christians are to value their own bodies as temples of God. Our souls and bodies exist in indissoluble unity. We use our bodies to do the works of mercy, love, justice, and piety. Christian survival after death takes an embodied form, not the form of disembodied minds. When consistent with the teachings of the New Testament, which they have not always been, Christians reject the Greek notion that only completely disembodied minds or spirits survive after death. Christian survival after death involves the resurrection of the body, yes a transformed body, as St. Paul taught (I. Corinthians 15), but a body all the same. Finally, the most powerful metaphor for the church that Paul could find was "the body of Christ." Bodies are good!

So, what is a body? On this, philosophers almost universally agree, and so did Wesley: "All bodies are spatially extended," or, as Wesley put it, "It may be observed of them all, that they are extended, solid, divisible, figured, and capable of motion. We cannot conceive any body that is not extended, or composed of several parts."[8] This and later quotes from it come from Wesley's *A Survey of the Wisdom of God in the Creation: A Compendium of Natural Philosophy*. Wesley's survey, originally published in 1763, was largely an abridgment of Charles Bonnet's, *The Contemplation of Nature*, but Wesley was a heavy-handed editor who deleted, altered, or re-wrote almost everything with which he disagreed; and he republished only what he personally affirmed, only what he believed to be true. Thus, this and the following citations from the *Compendium* are here attributed to Wesley, as authorized by Wesley's own words from his "Preface": "I have found occasion to retrench, enlarge, or alter every chapter, and almost every section. So that it is now, I believe, not only pure, containing nothing false or uncertain."[9]

Bodies are by definition perceptual things that are spatially extended, said highly influential Descartes, and Wesley agreed. This means that all bodies, by definition, have spatial properties like size, shape, motion, resistance, weight, and efficient causal efficacy (energy). Christians affirm that spatially extended perceptual objects and processes are good, not bad. Thus, transformed resurrected bodies, to be bodies at all, must have some kind of size, shape, motion, resistance, weight, and efficient causal efficacy; and they must exist in a wider spatiotemporal environment (heaven—or a transformed earth) in which they co-exist and communicate with other individual resurrected embodied souls. Living bodies exist to be used by living souls, here and hereafter. Extrinsic values, including human bodies, are useful spatiotemporally extended objects and processes that exist in public spacetime and are given to us through the external senses. They can be very good as means to desirable ends beyond themselves. Embodiment is good for us, here and hereafter. The things of the world are good for us evaluated properly, not too much, not too little, but just right.

Christian giving can take place in all three dimensions of value. We can give of ourselves, of our physical and social resources, and of our ideas, thoughts, and beliefs. Christians definitely share their extrinsically valuable properties and physical resources, e.g., their money, with one another and with their human and non-human neighbors. Money is good; only the love of money, the overvaluation of money, is bad. Many Christian "means of grace," (e.g., the water of Baptism and the bread and the wine of the Eucharist) are extrinsically good things combined or imbued with systemically valuable beliefs and ritual forms and practices. When they work properly as means of grace, they lead us into intrinsic identification with God and the intrinsic communion of the saints. When the means of grace work properly, they are holistic extrinsic/systemic/intrinsic value combinations.

Christians definitely affirm the goodness of the world, that is, of extrinsically valuable things, processes, and activities. Christians also definitely affirm the ordinary ways that we evaluate them, our normal practical everyday thoughts about, desires for, feelings about, and emotional responses to them, so long as they do not become inordinate or obsessive. Jesus taught us to pray for our daily bread (Matthew 6:11 and Luke 11:3), but he cautioned that we cannot live by bread alone (Matthew 4:4). He said that God knows that we have physical needs for food, drink, clothing, and the basic necessities of life (Matthew 6:25), but he cautioned that we should not value them first, that we should not treasure them more highly than the inner Kingdom of God, the Kingdom of Love (Matthew 6:31–33), which, as St. Paul said, is not meat and drink (Romans 14:17). Extrinsically valuable things definitely have a place in the Kingdom of God, Jesus taught, for after we seek that Kingdom first, such things of the world will then be "added unto us."

Human behaviors or actions are extrinsically good things. Christians do good things, good works, good deeds. They do the works of love, mercy, justice, and piety. God as Loving Creator worked and works. Christ as Servant and Savior worked and works. God as the Holy Spirit worked and works in us today. Godlikeness, Christlikeness, requires us to work, to act as the God of love and mercy would act, to do what Jesus would do, to follow in his steps, to live in his spirit, to express our intrinsic and systemic values and evaluations extrinsically, to practice what we preach.

Christian Systemic Values and Evaluations

With a firm basis in biblical religion, Christians should and often do evaluate systemic values very positively and highly—again not too much, not too little, but just right in relation to other Christian goods. Recall that systemic goods are conceptual entities like truth, knowledge, ideas, thoughts, beliefs, doctrines, laws, rules, principles, rituals, mathematics, logic, and other formalities. Positive evaluations of such systemic goods are found in many places in both the Old and New Testaments.

In the Old Testament, for example, the ninth commandment requires that we speak truthfully and not bear "false witness" against our neighbors (Exodus:20:16). Here the value of truthfulness is combined positively with the value of people; more specifically, the disvalue of not being truthful is seen as harming people—our neighbors and ourselves. What Jesus regarded as the "First Commandment" is not one of the Top Ten, but it does occur in the Old Testament in Deuteronomy 6:5. Jesus added "all your mind" to it, according to Mark 12:28–31, making it more explicit than the Old Testament in this respect, though "all your soul" includes "all your mind." What is often called the "intellectual love of God" is implicitly there in this Old Testament decree and explicitly there in the words and teachings of Jesus.

St. Paul required that Christians have the "mind of Christ" (I. Corinthians 2: 16), that they be "transformed by the renewing of [their] minds that [they] may prove what is that good, and acceptable, and perfect, will of God" (Romans 12:2), and that they think about good things (Philippians 4:8). Having the mind of Christ involves thinking as Christ thought, believing as Christ believed, and using our minds both to identify God's reality, nature, and will and to distinguish between God's highest aims and goals for us and what falls short. Christians often recognize that they need evidences or proofs for what they believe and value, and St. Paul authorized the search for them. Good Christians are required to have the mind of Christ, to use their minds, do dwell on good things, to affirm the goodness of systemic values. In at least one respect, of course, we cannot share the mind of Jesus. He and St. Paul both expected the kingdom of God to come in all its glory during the lifetime of their hearers. This did not happen, so their apocalypticism cannot be a part of our minds. Innumerable predictions of the immanent "end of the world" since their time have always been wrong. Maybe only God knows, just as Jesus said (Matthew 24:35–36)! Maybe the end of the world is just the end of worldliness.

You have heard and asked the question, "What would Jesus *do*?" As it stands, this is a purely extrinsic question about *doing*, and taken by itself it is very insufficient. To this extrinsic question, a values-centered practical theology must add these systemic and intrinsic questions: "What would Jesus *think*?" and "What (or who) would Jesus *love*?" Intentional doing inevitably involves thinking and feeling. Christlike or Godlike doing and thinking inevitably involve loving and all the other Christian or religious affections.

St. Paul also taught that Christians have to live *in* the world without being *of* the world. Christians today must come to terms with this within our secular society. To live effectively in the world, Christians need to be as well educated as possible, as knowledgeable as possible, and as practically shrewd, astute, and competent as possible. Without knowledge, without systemic or cognitive development, without the capacity to assess "the facts" and competing belief claims objectively and fairly, Christians would be practically and mentally incompetent, and the works of love and mercy would never get done. Christians must know how to weigh consequences, see and assess causes and effects over the long run, and avoid ignorance, bias, short-sightedness, and stupidity. Incompetence in every value dimension is something that Christians definitely should avoid and repudiate. Christians need to be systemically or conceptually competent, extrinsically talented, skilled, and shrewd, and intrinsically committed and involved—all three. God created us in his image as thinkers, lovers, and doers. Something like this is what Jesus had in mind when he said to his disciples, "Behold, I send you out as sheep in the midst of wolves; so be wise as serpents and innocent as doves" (Matthew 10:16). Wisdom is highly valued throughout the Bible, definitely so by Jesus who grew in wisdom. Wisdom is or involves systemic values. Christians need to *know* what they are doing, believing, and loving; they need to be "as wise as serpents." They need to ask, "What would Jesus *think*?" They need to have the mind of Christ. But this is not all.

Spiritually Significant Value Combinations

Values and evaluations in all three dimensions can be combined with one another in either beneficial or hurtful ways. Some value/evaluation combinations increase goodness, some decrease goodness, some increase evil, some make little or no difference at all. Positive value combinations may have greater worth than their components considered separately, and negative value combinations may be worse than their components taken separately. Value combinations have holistic or organic value-effects that go beyond mere addition or subtraction. This will be illustrated and explained next by considering a few positive value combinations that increase value. Innumerable spiritually and morally significant value/evaluation combinations occur in the Bible. Here are a few familiar examples from biblical religion and from Christian living and practice.

A systemic/intrinsic combination: "Delighting in the law of the Lord" as in Psalm 1: 2. This is the intrinsic evaluation of (delight in) a systemic value, "the law," made immensely more significant as united with its intrinsic source, "the Lord"—the ultimate reality to which all spiritual symbols point. This value combination is even more valuable than delight in the abstract law apart from God, or the mere concept of God apart from the law or from delight.

An extrinsic/intrinsic combination: "The heavens declare the glory of God," as in Psalm 19:1 (King James translation). This combines something extrinsically finite and empirical, the starry heavens above, with something of infinite intrinsic worth, God or God's glory. That combination has greater worth than the heavens alone (considered without God) or God alone (considered without the heavens). A God who is creative only in the abstract or only potentially but who never actually creates anything (e.g., the heavens and the earth) would be less valuable, less perfect, than a potentially creative God who also actually creates a whole universe, all the starry heavens, the earth, and all else within the universe. God without the world would be less valuable than God with the world. The world without God (an atheistic lawful spacetime universe—a merely systemic/extrinsic universe) would have less value than a world with God—a systemic/extrinsic/intrinsic universe. God plus the actual world is a value-enriched creative synthesis, a holistic combination of good things having far more worth, many more good-making properties, than God as only potentially creative. It has all its actualized good-making properties plus what God and the actual world contribute to one another. Value combinations can make a lot of difference!

An extrinsic/systemic/intrinsic combination: "Preaching the Gospel," as in Mark 16:15—even if it wasn't in the original Mark. This value combination is somewhat complicated. Just "thinking or believing the Gospel, the good news" is different from "preaching the Gospel." Thinking or believing the Gospel dispassionately would be internally valuing a systemic value (the good news) systemically or objectively (disinterestedly). But preaching the Gospel involves more than just internal thinking and believing. It involves external doing, acting with one's body, actually speaking the relevant words and gesturing to an audience of real people. Effective preaching is also quite passionate, not dispassionate; it requires the preacher's intense intrinsic affective involvement. It is more than just thinking or believing the words "with the top of one's head." Effective preachers must speak the words "from the bottom of their hearts." Effective preaching is eloquent, cognitive, and informed (systemically good); it is also spoken, often with gestures, thus bodily expressed (extrinsically good). At its best, it involves a passionate commitment of the whole messenger (intrinsic goodness); it addresses the moral and spiritual needs of real intrinsically valuable people; and it evokes an intrinsic holistic response from them.

As this book progresses, many value combinations will be considered, some positive, some negative, and some that may not matter much one way or the other.

Biblical Value Rankings

Christians highly value things that are systemically good, extrinsically good, and intrinsically good, but do they ever rank or prioritize such good things? Do they ever judge that some of these good things are more valuable than others? If required by circumstances, would they sacrifice any of these for the sake of the others? If the Bible is to be their guide, the answer to these questions must be, "Yes." If axiology or value theory is to be their guide, the answer to such questions is also, "Yes." But how well do biblical and axiological rankings coincide?

All "better than" or "worse than" judgments are value-rankings. Positive values can be very good, yet some better than others. Negative values (disvalues) can be very bad, yet some worse than others. Biblical religion constantly tells us that some things are better or worse than others. If one thing is better than another, this means that it has more goodness, more good-making properties, than the other. If one thing is worse than another, it either lacks more good-making properties or abounds in more bad-making properties than the other. "Better" and "worse" judgments are plentiful in Biblical religion. We will consider just a few.

Most of the laws, commandments, and action-guiding rules in the Old Testament are given along with specific penalties for violating them. *These penalties differ in seriousness.* The seriousness of the penalties to be inflicted upon violators indicates the ranking or relative worth of the laws themselves, that is, the degree of goodness provided and protected by the laws, and the degree of badness or harm inflicted in violating them. Some penalties have more serious bad-making properties than others; some punishments are definitely worse or more undesirable than others. Read the twenty first through the twenty third chapters of Exodus and you will see what this means. Also, in the Old Testament, the Ten Commandments are taken more seriously than other Biblical laws, which means that keeping them is better than keeping some of the others, and breaking them is worse than breaking some of the others. As Wesley believed, the ceremonial laws may have less significance than the moral laws, and in the New Testament the ceremonial laws of Judaism are largely set aside.

In the New Testament, Jesus clearly ranked intrinsic over systemic values when he proclaimed that the Sabbath was made for man, not man for the Sabbath. Both people and the Sabbath laws are good, but people are better than, have more value than, rules, principles, rituals, and regulations. Here, "Sabbath" is a metaphor that stands for all of God's beneficial laws, not the fourth commandment alone. Jesus meant that all of God's laws and ordained practices exist for the sake of us human beings, that is, for our benefit, and that we do not exist for the sake of God's laws and practices. Scholars indicate that God is the focus of the "first table," the first three of the Ten Commandments, and people are the focus of the "second table," the remaining seven. The first three are spiritual duties to God; the rest, including the Sabbath law, as Jesus indicated, are moral duties to people. "Man" (males) instead of "people" is now seen as antiquated and paternalistic. The essential idea is that God benefits when the first three laws are obeyed and is hurt or disvalued when they are disobeyed, so some laws were "made for God," including "You shall love the Lord your God with all you've got," to paraphrase a bit. "Made for God" indicates that God is better off (pleased, honored, enriched, respected) when the first three commandments are obeyed and worse off (hurt, dishonored, diminished, disrespected) when they are disobeyed. The last seven were "made for people;" both males and females, are better off when they are obeyed and worse off otherwise.

Some theologians think that nothing that people do, and nothing that happens in the world, can affect God one way or another, that is, for better or for worse, for God is changelessly perfect with or without the world, and although God acts on the world, the world never acts on God. God needs nothing, so God does not need the world, and the world adds nothing of value or disvalue to God. We will deal with that non-biblical dogma later when we see what John Wesley thought about God's attributes or perfect-making properties, especially his understanding of God's "eternity." For now, we should recognize that this is a Greek philosophical but not a biblical perspective on God, one that many historically influential Christian thinkers mistakenly adopted.

"Made for people" indicates that people are better off when the relevant laws are obeyed and worse off when they are disobeyed. Our *not* being "made for the Sabbath" (or for the laws in general) means that laws are not ends in themselves, not intrinsically good; we are. Considered by themselves, rules, principles, ritual forms, and laws are only systemically good. Considered as directing actions that benefit God and/or us, God's laws are systemically/extrinsically/intrinsically good. Everything can be valued in every dimension, so action-guiding rules like those expressed in the Ten Commandments can be valued systemically or dispassionately, but they can also be valued in more intensive ways. Without ceasing to be systemically good, they can also be valued extrinsically, that is, because they are useful, helpful, or beneficial in guiding our behaviors. Without ceasing to be systemic goods evaluated extrinsically, they can also enter into even more complex valuational wholes—into intense moral or devotional responses having intrinsic worth. Such a holistic value combination would be: loving-the-commandments-as-benefitting-God-and/or-us—as celebrated by Psalm 119.

In another context, Jesus clearly ranked people (intrinsic values) over things (extrinsic values). Jesus said that God knows that we need food, drink, clothing, and the extrinsic necessities of life; but we should seek first the Kingdom of God, then, the extrinsic necessities of life will be "added unto us" (Matthew 6:25, 31–33). God's knowing that we need them and they will be "added unto us" clearly affirm the goodness of those extrinsic things that are necessary for our survival and physical flourishing. That we should nevertheless put something else before them means that something else is even better—the Kingdom of God, the Kingdom of Mutual Love, the realm of intrinsic ends united in love. Not all very good things are equally good. Kinds of goodness can be compared and ranked. Some good things are better than others. One thing (food) can be less good than another (individual persons) without ceasing to be very good.

Consider one more significant example of value-ranking in the Bible. In chapter twelve of I. Corinthians, St. Paul discussed different spiritual gifts that exist "for the common good" (I. Cor. 12:7), all of which are very good. Specifically, he considers wisdom, knowledge, faith, healing, working miracles, prophecy, discerning the spirits, speaking in tongues, interpreting tongues, helping, administering, etc. Some of these are social roles or functions. Considered as enacted bodily, all of these are extrinsically valuable and useful gifts that contribute to "the common good." All of them also have systemic components; they involve cognitive beliefs, thoughts, and concepts. Paul was keenly aware, however, that all of these gifts can be used, given, or expressed without love or even in non-loving ways. No matter how good (or worthless) they are without love, there is something even better. His chapter twelve ends with the promise to show us a "more excellent way," (I. Corinthians 12: 31). "More excellent" also means "better."

Almost all of the thirteenth chapter of I. Corinthians develops and explains this more excellent way. It is the most axiologically significant whole chapter in the Bible. The more excellent way is the way of love, the intrinsic gift. Without that, the extrinsic/systemic gifts covered in chapter twelve are of little or no value. Just how little St. Paul valued them when not combined with love is expressed in the first few verses of chapter thirteen. Words or thoughts without love are like "a noisy gong or a clanging cymbal" (13:1); prophecy, knowledge that understands all mysteries, and faith strong enough to move mountains are "nothing" without love (13:3). Giving away all of one's property, even sacrificing one's own body, "gain nothing" without love. St. Paul may have exaggerated a bit, but systemic and extrinsic values clearly have very little real value, if any, in the absence of intrinsic values and evaluations. After explaining love, St. Paul wraps it all up with, "Faith, hope and love abide, these three, but the greatest of these is love" (I. Corinthians 13: 13). "Greatest" is clearly a value ranking word, as is Paul's phrase "a more excellent way." Christians do judge that some good things are better than others. Christians also judge that some bad things are worse than others. Christians *rank* both goods and evils. Think about it!

Can you think of additional examples of value rankings in the Bible or in your own spiritual life? Here are some further questions to consider. What values (systemic, extrinsic, and intrinsic) are present in typical Sabbath worship services? Though all may be good, are some better than others? Are some just means to ends beyond themselves? Are some valuable for their own sake? The following chapters will address questions like these in dealing with John Wesley's convictions about what and how Christians value.

Chapter Two

John Wesley's Intrinsic Values and Evaluations

What (or who) were John Wesley's intrinsic values or value-objects? What were the primary objects of his most passionate moral and spiritual affections? What, if anything, did Wesley regard as intrinsically good, as valuable for its own sake?

Wesley did not ask these questions, but the concept of "intrinsic goodness" was very familiar to his way of thinking. Wesley knew quite a bit of philosophy. While at Oxford, he taught courses in Aristotelian logic,[1] and in 1756 he wrote and published *A Compendium of Logic*.[2] With philosophical empiricists like Charles Bonnet, Peter Browne, and others influenced by John Locke's *Essay on Human Understanding*, Wesley accepted experience as the only foundation of all natural human knowledge. After he finally read Locke's *Essay* around 1781, he wrote a short critique of Locke's nominalism, his theory of personal identity through time, and his repudiation of Aristotelian logic.[3] Contrary to Locke, Wesley insisted that we are the same person from birth to death, whether conscious of it or not, that real universal (repeatable) properties, essences, geniuses, and species exist in nature itself and not just in our words or names, and that by using logic we can actually prove some conclusions to be true. Wesley frequently cited and astutely contested the views of both philosophers and theologians on rational grounds. Significant for present purposes, he was quite familiar with the philosophical distinction between intrinsic and extrinsic values, between what he called "ends" and "means," and he frequently used these concepts in his sermons and other theological writings. This will now be documented and explained. First, consider this prime example: "He sees...that this is the end of man: to glorify Him who made him for Himself, and to love and enjoy Him for ever. And with equal clearness he sees the means to that end, to the enjoyment of God in glory; even now to know, to love, to imitate God, and to believe in Jesus Christ whom He hath sent."[4]

Wesley identified many familiar features of religion as means to more valuable spiritual ends beyond themselves, especially systemic beliefs, rituals, laws, and their implementation in extrinsic communal or social practices.[5] He taught that God is an end in himself who should not be treated or regarded merely as a means to our ends;

rather, we should love God "for His own sake."[6] Yet, he did not apply the concept of intrinsic goodness only to God. He also said quite explicitly that our own spiritual growth is intrinsically good; as he put it, the development of our own holy dispositions and religious affections is "intrinsically and essentially good, and acceptable to God."[7] He assigned intrinsic worth to the faith of Christians, writing, "How desirable Christian faith is, even on account of its own intrinsic value."[8] He cast widely (but indefinitely) the net of "intrinsically good," describing Adam and Eve before the fall as "embracing nothing but good, and every good in proportion to its degree of intrinsic goodness."[9] The context suggest that "its intrinsic goodness" applies by degrees to animals as well as human beings, or at least to some of their valuable properties, even if they do not have the "capacity for God" properties that human beings have. Wesley's claim that only God should be valued for his own sake is in tension with his affirmation that aspects of human beings (and animals?) are intrinsically good, so we must explore these issues in greater depth.

Wesley clearly recognized that our extrinsic behaviors are truly good or most valuable only in value combinations, that is, only when combined with holy love. As he said, "All our actions...even those that are indifferent in their own nature, may be made holy, and good, and acceptable to God by a pure and holy intention. Whatever is done without this is of no value with God; whereas whatever outward works are thus consecrated to God are in His sight of great price."[10]

So, what were Wesley's intrinsic values? What did he value for its own sake? What were his terminal value-objects? What were their intrinsic-good-making properties? What are the proper objects today of Christian love and compassion, of Christian intrinsic evaluation? We will consider God, people, and animals as his answers to these questions.

God as Intrinsically Good

"For the LORD is good; his mercy is everlasting; and his truth endureth to all generations" (Psalm 100:5). Actually, God is better than just good; God is perfect, and we are to become perfect, like God (Matthew 5:48). Perfection is the ultimate form of goodness—the best of the best. These themes resonate loudly and often in John Wesley's preaching, writing, and teaching.

We must consider the concepts of "goodness" and "perfection" before looking at how Wesley applied them to God. Obviously, these are value concepts. "Formal axiology," the value theory presupposed in this book, defines "good" in a formal way. We will begin with this, then define "perfect" in a formal way, then see if and how these definitions help us to understand Wesley.

In formal axiology, "good" means "concept fulfillment." This probably doesn't mean very much at first. Initially, this definition doesn't "ring a bell," so it needs further explanation. It means that things are good when they fulfill our expectations, when they actually are as they ideally ought to be. It means that good things actually have the properties or attributes that they are supposed to have, that their factual or existing properties match up one-to-one with the ideal conceptual predicates or criteria that we apply to them. Good things fulfill the ideal conceptual standards by which we measure them, and this is what "good" as "concept fulfillment" means. Our ideal expectations or standards for anything name or identify its good-making properties, its qualities and relations that fulfill our ideal expectations for it. If a good person is a loving person, then "loving" is one conceptual standard by which we measure a person's goodness. People who actually love fulfill that standard; non-loving persons don't. Of course, any person's goodness is much more complicated than that, but this illustrates the essential point. A good anything fulfills its concept, that is, it exemplifies the ideal norms or standards that we apply to it in judging its worth. It actually has the properties (qualities and relations) that it is supposed to have. Ideal standards can be fulfilled by degrees, so some things are good, some are only fair, some are just average, some are poor, and some are no good at all—depending on the degree to which they fulfill our criteria, standards, or concepts.

"Perfect" in theology is like "good," except that it refers to the very highest conceivable goodness, supreme goodness. A merely good God might fulfill very high expectations, but a perfect God would fulfill our very highest expectations. As St. Anselm said, God is "that being than whom none greater [i.e., better] can be conceived." Without quoting Anselm directly, Wesley affirmed that the nature of God "necessarily includes all good."[11]

But what do we ideally expect of God, and where do we get our expectations for supreme goodness? How would Wesley answer such questions? As Albert Outler indicated, Wesley got his theological concepts, beliefs, and norms from four sources—Scripture, Tradition, Experience, and Reason. Wesley thought that all four *work in harmony* when rightly understood, used, and fully or properly developed. All four both condition and correct one another in the ongoing process of Christian reflection. Outler (not Wesley) called these four sources of spiritual and moral beliefs and norms "the Wesleyan Quadrilateral."[12] Wesley probably regarded Tradition as the least reliable of the four. He was certainly very selective about it. When he revised the Church of England's "Thirty Nine Articles of Religion" for the churches in America, he *deleted fifteen* of them and revised or modified several others. Anyway, he meant mainly *Protestant* traditions, principally *Anglican* traditions, plus the earliest traditions of primitive Christianity.[13] Many other religious traditions like Romanist "Popery"[14] and Calvinist predestination and election were excluded on scriptural, rational, moral, or experiential grounds.

God's Attributes or "Perfect-Making Properties"

"Perfect-making properties" are the ones that anything of absolute value, anything having the highest possible or conceivable goodness, must have or exemplify.

"Good," when applied to God, means "Perfect." These are value concepts, so "God" is both a value concept and an ontological concept. It refers to the highest or *best* conceivable *reality*. In our concept of "God," "being" comes together with "the true, the beautiful, and the good." Ideal perfection *exists* in a Perfect Being, we believe. God is the Christian's supremely valuable and valued reality. God deserves to be supremely valued or loved by us because God is ultimate perfection, supreme goodness. God necessarily has to the highest degree all the attributes that any ultimate reality must have in order to command and deserve our supreme love, devotion, and worship.

We will now consider some of the most basic perfect-making "properties" or "attributes" of God, as Wesley understood them. Wesley discussed God's nature and goodness in many sermons and writings. One of the most helpful is his treatment of the meaning of "Our Father" in the Lord's Prayer. He did not number them, as done below, but in his "Upon Our Lord's Sermon on the Mount, VI," Wesley said that God is entitled to be called "Our Father" because he has the following perfect-making attributes. God:

1. is "good." This means that he
2. is "loving to His children...willing to bless,"
3. is "our Creator: the Author of our being;...the Father of the universe, of all the families both in heaven and earth,"
4. is "our Preserver, who day by say sustains the life he has given,"
5. is "the Father of our Lord Jesus Christ" through whom he
    a. "justifies us 'freely by his grace'" and
    b. creates "us anew in Christ Jesus,"
6. "Loveth all that he hath made,"
7. is transcendent, "'in heaven'—high and lifted up; God over all, blessed for ever,"
8. exists "from all eternity, from everlasting to everlasting,"
9. knows everything, is omniscient, "whose eye pervades the whole sphere of created being,"
10. is omnipotent, "strong and girded about with power, doing whatsoever pleaseth thee! The Almighty, for whensoever thou willest, to do is present with thee,"
11. is immanent, omnipresent. God is everywhere, "'in heaven'... But not there alone; for thou fillest heaven and earth, the whole expanse of space,"
13. is holy, unexcelled in "purity and holiness." "'Hallowed be Thy name,'"
14. is "Trinity in Unity and Unity in Trinity."[15]

God's ideal attributes are God's "good-making" or "perfect-making" properties. This list is not exhaustive, but these are the main ideal or conceptual criteria by which we, with Wesley, conceive of, define, and measure God's perfection. Since

God in himself actually measures up to or fulfills these criteria, God is a perfect being, worthy of our supreme and complete devotion.

Perfection or Supreme Goodness

Importantly, the list above begins with a value concept—God's supreme goodness. Values are built into our very concept of God. This is our starting place for understanding God. Wesley begins with God's goodness, then offers a more detailed account of the properties that make God good. He often called them God's "perfections."[16] Though incomplete above, this list incorporates Wesley's most basic understanding of who God is ideally, of the properties that God must and does have in order to be supremely good or perfect, thus supremely worthy of our absolute love and devotion. This list expresses the "concept" of God that a supremely good and really existing God actually "fulfills." Again, as Wesley insisted, "The nature of God...necessarily includes all good."[17]

Wesley affirmed, with Charles Bonnet, that *we build our concept of God* out of "the works of the visible creation," more specifically out of the values or "perfections" that we first find in ourselves as human beings. "This we do," he said, "in the best manner we can, by removing from him all the imperfections of the creatures, and attributing to him all their perfections, especially those of our own minds."[18] These good-making properties are attributed to God only analogically rather than literally because they apply to us finitely, and in God they are infinite. From the very outset, all of our language about God is analogical or metaphorical, not literal.

> The sum is this. We have no idea of God, as he is in himself. For want of one, we frame the best conception we can, by putting together the perfections of the creatures, particularly those we observe in ourselves, to stand for his perfections: not grossly inferring, That God is in effect, such an one as ourselves; but concluding, that our greatest excellencies are the aptest representations of his incomprehensible perfections...[which] infinitely transcend the most exalted of what are in any created beings, and are far above, out of the reach of all human imagination.[19]

Thus, our concept of God is both analogical (non-literal) and value-laden from the very outset, and our understanding of God's goodness is constructed out of our understanding of our own good-making properties—expanded to infinity.

To naturalistic atheists like Sigmund Freud who claim that our concept of God is nothing more than a projection of our own values upon the cosmos, the honest and successful reply is that God has so designed us that we can this is how he expects us to create a correct idea of what he is like by doing just that! This is one reason why the topic of this book is so important. To understand God *successfully* we must understand our own values successfully! Whether we know it or not, all concepts of God are value-laden. We must understand God, as St. Anselm indicated, as that Being than whom none greater or better can be conceived. Value projection is God's way, not the naturalistic atheist's way!

Given Wesley's value-laden concept of God, we must ask if we agree. Do we agree that those listed above actually are the perfect-making properties God must have in order to be "'all good,' supremely good, perfect"? If so, do we agree with how Wesley interpreted these attributes? What must God be like in order to count as supremely good? Traditional accounts of God's "attributes" or "perfections," including Wesley's, offer answers to this question, but *we must also answer it for ourselves*. This is not as easy as it might seem. We must think carefully about such things. God's perfect-making-qualities or supremely desirable attributes, must be both *identified*, and defined, explained, or *interpreted*. Value notions and intuitions related to our own "perfections" must guide us, Wesley thought. A careful look at *a few* of God's attributes will show just how value-laden they are and how they have been interpreted in many ways, depending largely on the values of their interpreters. Our concept of God as supremely good depends ultimately on what and how we value, and our concepts of God may differ because our values differ. To agree about God, we must agree about what is ultimately good or desirable. We aren't there yet!

Omnipotence

God is said to be all powerful or omnipotent, but there are many ways to interpret both the meaning and the goodness of God's "*power*." Human experience discloses many different kinds of power over self and others, some better than others, some worse. Persuasion, for example, is better than coercion, but both are powers that may get results. Wesley thought that God is all-powerful, but how did he interpret the meaning of God's power? What did he mean by "omnipotence" or "sovereignty," as it was often called in that day? What values entered into his interpretation? What form of divine power over us would be best?

Wesley's interpretive or hermeneutic values differed immensely from those of his Calvinistic opponents (e.g., George Whitefield). For Calvinists, God's sovereignty consists in sheer power as such, like that of an absolute monarch, unqualified by other perfections such as love, mercy, justice, and truth. As absolute sovereign, they thought, God has an absolute right to elect or select only a small remnant of humankind for salvation and heaven, and to destine the "great bulk of mankind" to hell. The choice was God's to make for utterly inscrutable reasons, that is, for no reason at all, other than the sheer exercise of arbitrary power or sovereignty. Predestinationists separated God's sovereignty or power from, and value-ranked it far above, all other divine attributes.

For Wesley, the goodness of God's power or sovereignty did not stand alone, could not be separated or isolated from God's other desirable attributes or perfections, and it could not be ranked in value totally apart from or over them. Wesley saw God's power or sovereignty as inescapably related to, qualified by, and combined with God's justice, love, mercy, and truth.[20] A just, loving, merciful, and truthful God, Wesley thought, would never arbitrarily use his power in inscrutable ways to do unjust, unmerciful, and unloving things like predestining most people for hell. Any God who would do such things "is not the God of the Christians."[21]

The Christian God would never *arbitrarily* choose to send *anyone* to hell, much less *almost everyone*. Wesley was a *universalist* who held that "The God of love is willing to save all the souls he has made...But he will not force them to accept of it."[22] Without forcing it upon anyone, a just, merciful, and loving God would (and does) make salvation available to absolutely *everyone*, not just to *an elect few*. A perfect God would, and did, create people having their own power of originative or creative choice that enables them freely to accept or refuse God's universal offer of salvation. Thus, everyone can have it, but not everyone will take it. A good, loving, merciful, and just God would have *the power to limit his own power* and create responsible creatures with their own power or liberty to originate their own choices for or against goodness, for or against their own salvation, and for or against God. A loving God would elect everyone, not just an arbitrarily chosen few, but he would also give everyone the power to make their own decisions, thereby to reject or accept saving grace. Salvation is thus universally available, but we are at liberty to take it or leave it. The God of the Calvinists loves and offers grace to only a small saving remnant of humankind, but a truly good God would both love and offer saving grace to every creature, not just the elect few. Such a God would also respect the nature he gave and restored to every creature, including liberty or free choice. A truly loving God would gracefully offer salvation to everyone and would give everyone the power either to refuse that grace or to accept it and work together with God to nurture or work out that salvation and grow in that grace.[23] Wesley viewed grace as a core spiritual value and a principle attribute of God. God's grace in *us* is something "to work out," "to grow in," as well as something "to value."[24]

Wesley was convinced that God made human beings or "man" with "a power of choosing for himself, a self-determining principle,"[25] understood as "the power of choosing either to do or not to do"[26] and "a power of choosing what was good, and refusing what was not so."[27] According to Wesley, God has both the power and the will to share his own originative or creative power or agency with us, and this is where he departs most decisively from Calvinists and all predestinationists. In his view, God is "willing that all men should be saved, yet not willing to force them thereto;" and God treats us "as reasonable creatures, endued with understanding to discern what is good, and liberty either to accept or refuse it."[28] As he explained, God would be "the only proper agent in the universe; unless so far as he imparts a spark of his active, self-determining nature to created spirits,"[29] but that is exactly what God does. Without liberty of choice, we would not be responsible agents at all, for "He that is not free is not an *agent*, but a *patient*."[30] God created us to be responsible agents.

Thus, the very meaning of God's "power" is qualified by other values, by other good-making divine properties or attributes, and it must be so construed or interpreted. Wesley argued that a God who arbitrarily exercises all power in unloving, unjust, and unmerciful ways would not be God at all but a devil, as is the

God of Calvinism and predestination. A moral God of love, mercy, and justice who exercises power by sharing power would be more worshipful, more valuable, more perfect than a God who arbitrarily exercises power in isolation from all other divine attributes, that is, apart from moral goodness and love. God's power, Wesley insisted, is compatible with and in harmony with God's love, justice, mercy, and truthfulness, as well as with human freedom and responsibility. In a truly good and worshipful God, "All his attributes are inseparably joined."[31]

The basic choice here is between the value of omnipotence understood as *omnicausality* (but without the power to share it), or as involving *the power to share power, creativity or originative causality, and responsibility*. Which is best? Which most harmonizes with love, justice, and mercy? Which way of conceiving of God's power would most entitle God to be loved with all our hearts, souls, minds, and strength?

God's power manifests itself, Wesley thought, far beyond relating to us in loving, just, merciful, and truthful ways. God's power also coherently combines with and is expressed within many other perfect-making properties or attributes, such as Creator, Supporter, Preserver, Governor, and Redeemer.[32]

Feelings or Affections

All divine attributes or perfections are heavily value-laden and attributed to God because they are judged to be good—or withheld from God because they are judged not to be good. Are feelings or affections perfect-making properties? Wesley's values entered into his interpretation of what it means for God to be "loving, to His children...willing to bless"—the third attribute in the preceding list. Christian theologians prior to Wesley usually assigned the attribute of "impassability" to God. In doing so, they affirmed the values of Plato, Aristotle, and Plotinus, but not the values of the Bible. In its most extreme and influential form, God as "impassible" means that God has *no real feelings* about anything whatsoever, not just no painful, uncontrollable, or undesirable feelings, but none at all. Greek Philosophers, but not the writers of the Bible, believed that *all* feelings (emotions, moods, attitudes, and desires) are undesirable imperfections, unworthy of God, even if a few well-controlled feelings are desirable in people.

In classical Judaeo-Christian theology, beginning with Philo and Tertullian, who were much influenced by the Greeks, "patripassionism," the claim that God *does* have feelings, especially negative ones (pain and suffering), was for centuries rejected and condemned as a heresy. Classical Christian theologians were so desperate to deny that God suffers that they denied that God has any feelings at all, good or bad. St. Anselm, like Athanasius, said that when Jesus suffered on the cross, only his human nature suffered, not his divine nature.[33] In other words, while Jesus suffered, God felt absolutely nothing. Anselm also taught that God's being "compassionate" can't mean that God actually feels anything at all when we creatures suffer. It means only that we experience God *as if* he has compassionate feelings, but *in himself, he does not*.[34] Most classical theology before Wesley interpreted God's attributes of love, mercy, and compassion as involving no feelings whatsoever, because *all feelings were judged to be bad or unworthy of God*.

So how did Wesley evaluate feelings? How much did his theology of the religious affections resemble that of Anselm, Aquinas, and most medieval and other protestant theologians? When Wesley said that God is loving, merciful, compassionate, and just, did he really mean that we experience God as if he were that way, but he really isn't? Or did he really mean what he said?

We can make a strong but not an unequivocal case for the claim that Wesley returned to a more Biblical and un-Greek way of interpreting the meaning of God's love, mercy, compassion, consolation, and equality of regard for us. For the Methodist church in America, John Wesley extensively revised the Church of England's "Thirty Nine Articles of Religion," reduced them to twenty four, and modified the wording of others. The American version omitted one significant phrase from Article I, which originally said, "There is but one living and true God, everlasting, without body, parts, or passions." The American version omitted the "without...passions" phrase. That Wesley himself made this omission is somewhat controversial. Kenneth J. Collins[35] suggests that he did; John B. Cobb, Jr.[36] and Randy Maddox[37] say that he did not. According to Cobb and Maddox, the omission was made by the American church, not by Wesley himself.

No matter who made the omission, Wesley's position on God's feelings is admittedly ambivalent. In his sermon on "The Unity of the Divine Being," where he comments on a number of the Church's "Articles of Religion," he explicitly says that God does not have "such parts, or passions, as men have."[38] Here he may have meant to express unqualified agreement with Article I that God does not have any feelings at all, but he may have meant only that God does not have the *undesirable* feelings that human beings have, or that God's feelings are infinite, not *finite* like those that "men have." In "On Grieving the Holy Spirit," Wesley said, agreeing with William Tilly who wrote this sermon originally, "There is not anything of what we call passions in God. But there is something of an infinitely higher kind: Some motions of his will, which are more strong and vigorous than can be conceived by men; and although they have not the nature of human passions, yet will answer the ends of them."[39] The rest of this sermon literally teems with affective language about God. His reservations about passions in God seem only to reflect Wesley's conviction that all of our human language about God is at best analogical, not literal, because our human-like good-making properties are infinite in God, not finite, as they are in us. Wesley's position on whether God has real feelings may be unclear, but *we* must still make up our own minds and try to be clear about it.

There is strong additional evidence, however, that when Wesley spoke of God as loving and compassionate, he really meant it—but even more emphatically so than human words can ever express. To begin, *Wesley did not judge that all feelings are bad!* Some feelings are bad, he thought, like those involved in the moral and spiritual vices; but some feelings, the moral and spiritual affections or tempers, are good, desirable, and perhaps even worthy of God, like those involved in real joy, love, mercy, compassion, consolation, and justice. According to Wesley, Christians "do not desire to extinguish any of the passions which God has for wise ends implanted in their nature. But they have the mastery of all."[40] Wesley often applied his positive evaluation of human feelings to God's feelings, to their infinite counterparts in God. Recall that we construct our understanding of God's infinite perfections out of our own finite good-making properties, Wesley thought. He proclaimed, "Love existed from eternity, in God, the great ocean of love. Love had a place in all the children of God, from the moment of their creation."[41] Thus, we were made in that image. According to Charles Wesley, God in Jesus is "all compassion, pure unbounded love"—really, and not just the human side of his nature! John has God say, "My compassions fail not."[42]

The best evidence that Wesley attributed real feelings to God is found in his understanding of the "image of God." Our "affections," along with many other Godlike human properties, are consistently and explicitly said to manifest that image.

> God has entrusted us with our *soul*, an immortal spirit, made in the image of God; together with the power and faculties thereof—understanding, imagination, memory; will, and a train of affections, either included in or closely dependent upon it; love and hatred, joy and sorrow, respecting present good and evil; desire and aversion, hope and fear, respecting that which is to come.[43]

Thus, even God has religious affections or tempers, and being created with "various affections" is one of the most important ways in which we exist in God's "natural image."[44] "For he created man in his own image: a spirit like himself; a spirit endued with understanding, with will or *affections*, and liberty."[45] Most importantly and specifically, human beings were created in the image of, and with the affections of, love and all the virtuous dispositions that go with it. Originally, "Man was what God is, Love. Love filled the whole expansion of his soul; it possessed him without a rival,"[46] and "In this [moral] image of God was man made. 'God is love:' accordingly, man at his creation was full of love, which was the sole principle of all his tempers, thoughts, words, and actions. God is full of justice, mercy, and truth: so was man as he came from the hands of his Creator."[47] Yes, God's affections of love, mercy, compassion, etc. are infinite and ours are only finite, so they are ascribed to God only analogically or metaphorically. But the proper analogy involves *infinite feelings*, not *no feelings at all*.

Maddox agrees that Wesley definitely affirmed that God has real feelings or affections,[48] so we will go with that option. This presumes that not all feelings are bad or unworthy of God. Most of the time Wesley assumed that God is *with passions,* because, as he judged, *some real feelings or affections are good-making properties*, not bad-making properties; and we exist in the image of God's affections and other desirable properties. The religious affections or tempers exist just as much in God as in the saints, even more so, infinitely so. Wesley would never tell his followers (as St. Anselm did his readers) that God in himself really isn't loving, merciful, and compassionate, even though we experience him as if he were that way. Imagine preaching or listening to that sermon on Sunday morning! Compassion, by definition, means actually suffering with those who suffer. Here is Wesley's clearest affirmation of real suffering in God; speaking of "the Lord Jehovah," Wesley wrote, "Trust in him who suffered a thousand times more than ever you can suffer! Hath he not all power in heaven and earth?"[49]

Omniscience and Eternity

Knowledge is a very good thing; supreme knowledge would be a supremely good thing (systemically). Knowing everything knowable would be better than knowing just a few things. Perfection involves completeness. God's supreme goodness includes his knowing not only us but absolutely everything that there is to know, according to its appropriate mode of being. God is that being unto whom all hearts are open, from whom no secrets are hid, and to whom all facts about the universe and its creatures are revealed. God knew what he was doing when he designed and created the universe. God knows what he is doing as he sustains and governs the universe. God knows what he is doing as he forgives and redeems the world. God knows what he is doing when he loves not only the universe in general but us human beings in particular, along with all other creatures great and small. God has both abstract systemic or conceptual knowledge and direct, immediate, experiential knowledge of all that is. Omniscience is definitely a good-making or perfect-making property. But how does God's knowledge apply to a universe that is unfinished in time? How much of *time* is included in "all that is"? Does God know the open future just as decisively as he knows the closed past and the closing present? Just how we answer this depends in part on what we consider to be intelligible and in part on what we judge to be valuable.

God's omniscience is logically intertwined with other divine attributes, especially "eternity." In theology, "eternal" has had two quite distinct meanings. The first is "beginningless and endless in time," that is, "having no temporal beginning or end." The second is "all time all at once," the *totum simul* of the medieval theologians, according to which God's knowledge includes the past, present, and future of the entire universe simultaneously and changelessly in one grandiose "present." The first is the basic biblical understanding of God, who is "from everlasting to everlasting." The second is a Greek concept that was for centuries accepted by and superimposed upon the biblical understanding by most classical theologians.

Respecting tradition too much, perhaps, Wesley himself opted for the classical *totum simul* view of "eternal" and dismissed all temporalistic discourse about God as non-literal, that is, as a merely human but totally inaccurate and misleading way of thinking about God's ultimate nature and reality. The Greeks got it right, not the Bible, most theologians (including Wesley) assumed, prior to the advent of modern

Temporalistic Theology, which accepts only the biblical "from everlasting to everlasting" understanding of God's eternity. John B. Cobb, Jr., whose book on Wesley is mentioned in the Preface, is one of our finest examples of a Christian Process or Temporalistic Theologian. He is also a lifelong Methodist. (He also taught me my first course in philosophical Ethics at Emory University and got me hooked on value theory!) There are also many other excellent Process and Temporalistic Theologians, but that is not our present concern.

Here is how Wesley explained his own understanding of the classical view of eternity as "all time all at once."

> When we speak of God's *foreknowledge*, we do not speak according to the nature of things, but after the manner of men. For, if we speak properly, there is no such thing as either *foreknowledge* or *after knowledge* in God....All time...being present with him at once, he does not know one thing before another, or one thing after another, but sees all things in one point of view, from everlasting to everlasting. As all time with everything that exists therein, is present with him at once, so he sees at once whatever was, is, or will be to the end of time. But observe: we must not think they *are* because he *knows* them. No; he knows them because they are.[50]

Notice that here Wesley identifies the meaning of "all things in one point of view" with "from everlasting to everlasting," but they are very different concepts. Aside from mindlessly perpetuating a questionable tradition, how theologians understand "eternity" largely boils down to what they happen to value or disvalue. Greek philosophers, and the classical theologians (like Wesley) who were bamboozled by them, judge that all time and change are bad, or at least unworthy of God. Biblical writers and Temporalistic Theologians did not and do not agree with them. They assume that time itself and some temporal changes are very good, even if other kinds of change are undesirable. It was Plato, not the Bible, who argued that any change from or within perfection would be a change for the worse. Temporalistic Theologians disagree with Plato, and so tacitly did the Bible. Reconciling "all time all at once" with the Bible necessitates dismissing practically everything it says about God's actions in history and his interactions with historical individuals as totally misleading metaphorical speech. Wesley himself emphatically dismissed all temporalistic biblical language about God as merely human, figurative, metaphorical, or "speaking after the manner of men."[51] But why isn't thinking of God as "timeless" also just "speaking after the manner of men"? After all, the Greek philosophers who promoted timelessness as a theological value were also men, and "timeless" is just as much a human concept as "time." Why assume that the Greek philosophers "speak after the manner of God" whereas the Bible only speaks "after the manner of men"? It's ultimately a question of values.

Temporalistic Theologians say that God can be changeless in certain *desirable* ways while still being unchangeable in other desirable ways. It all depends finally on what is judged to be desirable or valuable, versus what is deemed undesirable or disvaluable. In his general *moral goodness or righteousness and faithfulness*, and in other desirable ways (the other attributes, properly understood and evaluated), God ideally ought to be changeless. Viewed in context, this is all that is asserted by the two Bible verses that affirm God's changelessness (Malachi 3:6 and James 1:17). Yet, some divine perfections like *creativity, sensitivity, responsiveness, love, and compassion* require changes and passive receptiveness. God's perfect abstract nature does not change, but his concrete experiences and decisions definitely do, so there is no "all of time all at once," says Temporalistic Theology. God's everlasting love and creativity are temporally expressed moment by moment in God's concrete changing experiences of and responses to what is happening in and what people are doing in the world. God's changeless love can be affected and activated again and again by new individuals who are loved as they come into existence and live and act in time. God's general capacity to know everything according to its appropriate mode of being or reality can grasp the actualities of the past and present in their full definiteness while knowing future decisions that have not yet been made only as indefinite possibilities and probabilities. God learns the specifics about actual free decisions and the concrete consequences thereof only as they get made and unfold in time. The open future does not have the definiteness of the past and the present, even for God. God cannot know what is not there to be known.

No purely static account of perfection can accommodate or account for God's love for and interaction with people and other creatures as they freely choose for or against God and goodness in time and history. This is what biblical religion is all about. Not God's existence, nature, or general attributes, but God's *experiences and choices* change as God creates and interacts with created individuals who make free and unpredictable decisions; and such divine experiential and volitional changes are highly desirable. That God's experiences and decisions change as God interacts with concrete individuals within history, time, and space is a perfect-making property, not an imperfection. Concrete experiential changes in God's actions, decisions, and responses are perfections, not imperfections. The best way to conceive of God's eternity is in terms of everlastingness, the biblical way, not as all time all at once, the Greek way. In some sermons, "everlasting" is the only meaning that Wesley gave to "eternal," and he often used "everlasting" in describing God's eternity. He defined it to mean, "as there was no beginning of his existence, so there will be no end."[52] Often enough, however, he gave it a very different meaning, namely, "all time all at once," which implies that all things, including future decisions that have not yet been made, are always changelessly present to God's knowledge. Sometimes he gave both definitions in the same paragraph and equated their meanings, so perhaps he was not aware of their profound difference.[53] Yet, this gives us a Wesleyan basis for disagreeing with Wesley! At times, maybe we should thank God for Wesley's ambiguities!

Wesley well understood that eternity is logically connected with the attributes of omniscience and omnipotence, but he did not construe God's omnipotence as omnicausality, given human freedom. He thought of our freedom, our limited self-causality, as a genuine and valuable gift from God, as God sharing his power with us. Given "eternity" as "all time all at once," "omniscience" has to mean knowing everything (all of time) all at once. This implies that God learns or experiences nothing in and from time and history themselves. Wesley recognized the difficulty of reconciling free human decisions for or against God with God's knowing everything changelessly and atemporally. He tenaciously defended human freedom on the grounds that we would not be responsible or accountable for our thoughts, words, feelings, decisions, or actions if God from eternity knew and *caused* all of them to be exactly as they turn out to be. If predestination is true, "The man does not act at all; He is only acted upon by the Creator, and *must* move thus, being irresistibly impelled."[54] Being responsible presupposes that our decisions *originate* with us, not with God.[55] But could we be responsible for our free decisions if God eternally and changelessly *knows* them to be exactly as they turn out to be in time? Doesn't knowing everything from eternity imply that everything just exists from eternity, and nothing ever gets settled or decided by us in time?

To meet this problem, Wesley advanced a very clever argument. God's *foreknowing* the future (including those who would and would not be saved), he said, is not the same thing as *causing* or determining the future (including our final destiny), *any more than knowing the past amounts to causing or determining it*. "We must not think they are because he knows them," he said, for "He knows them because they are;" and "Yet what he knows, whether faith or unbelief, is in no wise caused by his knowledge."[56] Thus, God can *know* all future free decisions without *causing* them.

The main problem with this clever argument is that the past is fully definite and determinate, whereas the open future seems not to be, and it could not be in a universe that allows for genuinely free choices. Jonathan Edwards, the most astute critic of human liberty or free choice who ever wrote on the topic, insisted, to the contrary, that God could not eternally foreknow all future human volitions infallibly unless they are "necessary events," meaning that if they are known necessarily from eternity they must exist necessarily from eternity, could not be otherwise, and thus could not originate contingently and freely in time.[57] If anything is known by God from all eternity, it is impossible for it not to be; it could not be otherwise. The opposite of necessity is contingency, which means "might or might not be." Necessity, by contrast, means "not possible not to be." Thus, everything known by God from eternity is necessary, not contingent; it could not be otherwise. Free choices are contingent; they could be otherwise; so they could not be known from eternity. Of course, Edwards drew the opposite conclusion: free choices could not be known from eternity, so there are no free choices.

Today's Temporalistic Theologians are persuaded by Edwards' claim that everything changelessly eternal would be necessary, so to avoid predestination they re-conceive of God's relation to the future and all of time. "Omniscience" really means that God knows everything according to its proper mode of being —actualities as actualities, and possibilities only as possibilities. Future decisions that have not yet been made do not yet exist as actualities and thus cannot be known as actualities; so, in advance, God knows only probabilities and only what people *might* decide in the future, not what they *actually will* decide. He learns about actual free decisions only when they happen, when they are made, but not in a timeless eternity. Wesley himself came very close to the insight that "knowing things that do not yet exist" makes no sense at all. He wrote, "But what are the *eternal relations* of *temporal* things? Of things which did not exist till yesterday? Could the relations of these things exist before the things themselves had any existence? Is not then the talking of such relations a flat contradiction? Yea, as palpable a one as can be put into words."[58] He may have been talking only about human knowledge, but is this any more intelligible when applied to divine foreknowledge? Not only must we *value* the divine attributes, we must also be able to *make sense* of them; and "free contingent choices in time that pre-exist eternally and necessarily" just does not make sense. Temporalistic Theologians simply disagree with Wesley and all other classical theologians about how to conceive of God's "eternity" in an intelligible and valuable way. They opt for everlastingness, not for all time all at once, as the best and most intelligible way to reconcile God as everlasting with free and creative human choices.

God has many other attributes that contribute to God's goodness, but this should suffice for now to show that our concepts of God's attributes or properties are - value-laden. Wesley gave little attention to the attribute of *necessary existence,* so favored by many theologians, just as he gave little attention to the classical arguments for the existence of God, but in one place he did refer (with Charles Bonnet) to God as "necessarily existing,"[59] and, as we saw, he insisted upon God's necessary possession of all goodness. The attribute of *omnipresence* will receive special attention in the last chapter, but Wesley linked God's omnipresence, his being everywhere and in everything, with his omnipotence and omniscience. In order to know and to influence everything everywhere, God has to be present everywhere, he argued.[60] (Correspondingly, to know and influence everything everywhen, God would have to be present everywhen; but maybe there is no everywhen all at once before anything and everything ever or actually happens.) All of God's attributes are coherently interrelated in the sense that they presuppose and involve one another logically, ontologically, and valuationally. There is a complex unity in God's diversity of perfections, not undifferentiated unity and simplicity, and not unqualified sovereignty.

Attributing *any given property* to God as a "perfection" involves a value judgment with respect to its ultimate goodness in God and the worth of its counterpart in us human beings. So does the way in which such properties are interpreted or construed. Human beings made in the image of God have many good-making Godlike properties, as next explained. These image of God properties reflect the good-making properties of God himself, but only in finite ways.

People as Intrinsically Good

Angels would come between God and human beings in the "golden chain"[61] of being to which Wesley subscribed, but we will concentrate on people. What kind of goodness, if any, do people have, according to Wesley? Wesley's answer was complicated by and intertwined with his views on such things as original sin, human nature, and different kinds and degrees of grace. Let's consider next whether Wesley thought that human beings have intrinsic worth, and if so, why so?

Is God the Only End, The Only Intrinsic Good?

Are people intrinsically valuable, or is God alone the only proper end-in-himself or intrinsic good in the whole realm of reality? Affirming intrinsic worth for human beings on Wesleyan grounds is complicated because *Wesley never explicitly said that unique human persons have intrinsic worth*, and because he insisted that *God alone is the only proper end* of true religion. Wesley never explicitly applied phrases like "intrinsically good," "ends in themselves," or "good for their own sake" *to individual people*, though he did so to *God* and to *human qualities*. This is not because he was unfamiliar with the philosophical distinction between extrinsically good things as means to ends beyond themselves and intrinsically good things as ends in themselves, valuable for their own sake. He definitely used such terminology in evaluating God, but he applied it only *to aspects or properties* of human beings, e.g., our moral and spiritual properties. He never clearly and explicitly said that *individual people* as such are ends in themselves, or that we are morally and spiritually obligated to value or love individual human beings "for their own sakes." Yet, some of his expressions come very close to affirming this. Slightly different words may add up to saying the same thing, and we often approach the precision of many ideas by making gradual approximations to them.

Wesley claimed that we should value and love people and their happiness *for God's sake*, but *never for their own*. His position somewhat resembles that of St. Augustine, who held that God is the only being valuable for his own sake, and everything else has only "use" value, that is, extrinsic value.[62] However, Wesley's own position was clearly different. Unlike Augustine, Wesley definitely applied the concept of "intrinsic goodness" to things in the world, to created things, to attributes of people, and not just to God. For example, he described Adam and Eve before the fall as "embracing nothing but good, and every good in proportion to its degree of intrinsic goodness."[63] Here it is unclear whether he had unique humans and animals in mind when he wrote this, or merely some of their desirable properties or attributes. Usually he meant only the latter.

Wesley held that *our* supreme good is happiness, properly understood; but the trouble is, happiness is only an abstract feature of our total individuality. Wesley insisted that we should seek happiness, even though it is only a small aspect of our complete human reality. He did say explicitly that our religious virtues and affections are intrinsically good; yet, these also are only aspects of or "good for" properties of whole persons. Only God (as a whole spiritual reality) is valuable for God's own sake. To quote Wesley, "Any temporal view, any motive whatever on this side of eternity, any design but that of promoting the glory of God, and the happiness of men *for God's sake*, makes every action, however fair it may appear to men, an abomination unto the Lord."[64] (*Italics added.*)

Can loving people for God's sake and loving people for their own sake be reconciled? Perhaps so, if we believe *that God loves individual persons for their own sake*. Acting to make people as such happy (in morally and spiritually compatible ways) can be reconciled with acting for God's sake if God aims at human happiness or well-being in morally and spiritually desirable ways, that is, if "God's sake" somehow includes "our sake." But happiness can be only part of the story, as later explained.

On Wesleyan grounds, a strong indirect case can be made for the intrinsic worth of unique concrete human persons in the fullness of our attributes and individuating properties (and not just for those abstract human properties named by Wesley above). Perhaps Wesley implicitly regarded individual human beings as valuable for our own sakes (but within God's positive evaluation of them) for the following reasons, with which he would probably agree.

1. We are made in "the image of God," and thus we have many of the same good-making properties that God has, even though infinitely inferior in degree; and God is valuable for his own sake or as an end because he has those properties.

2. We are to love God with all our being and becoming, but loving God involves loving all that God loves, including all of us as individual persons. Thus, loving God for his own sake and loving us for our own sake are not incompatible. God is love; God is loving; and we are to be Godlike.

3. God created us and our world out of love for us and all creation, not just out of love for some of our abstract properties.

4. God loves us individually, like a good shepherd who seeks every last lost sheep and knows them all by name.

5. We are to love one another as we love ourselves, which seems to involve "for our own sake" extended to others "for their own sake."

6. Christ came to save us, each and every one, individually. As Wesley insisted in describing Aldersgate, and repeatedly thereafter, "I know he 'hath loved *me*, and given himself for *me*'. He 'hath reconciled *me*, even *me* to God.'"[65] (Italics his.)

7. The Holy Spirit of God lives and acts within the souls of individual persons, whose unique bodies become "temples of God."

8. God gives embodied immortality or everlasting life to complete and unique persons.

9. Many of our properties, such as our religious affections and virtues, are explicitly said to be intrinsically good, so the concept does not apply to God alone.

10. God wants each and every unique person to be happy and fulfilled in morally and spiritually acceptable ways.

11. Individual persons are capable of fellowship with God—forever.

12. God is a universalist who wills to save absolutely everyone, not just an elect few.

This may not be the whole case, but it seems sufficient to claim on Wesleyan grounds that unique persons have intrinsic worth, not just extrinsic or systemic worth, though we have that too. This should become clearer as the discussion progresses, but for now consider Wesley's claim that Christian happiness involves an intense awareness that God is "presiding over the whole universe as over a single person, so watching over every single person as if he were the whole universe," and "This all-powerful, all wise, all-gracious Being, this Governor of all, loves me.... And I love him."[66] Although he did not explicitly say that individual souls have intrinsic worth, indirectly he came very close to doing so. He said that "One soul is of more value than all the world beside."[67] Also, individual souls could have a relational infinite worth by virtue of their relationship with God: "Man is not only a house of clay, but an immortal spirit; a spirit made in the image of God, an incorruptible picture of the God of glory; a spirit of infinitely more value than the whole of earth; of more value than the sun, moon, and stars put together; yea than the whole material creation."[68] Thus, individual souls have a special kind of worth (here technically unnamed) that far exceeds that of extrinsically valuable objects.

There is a significant difference between having intrinsic worth and having infinite worth, even if the infinite includes the intrinsic and the finite. As generations of theologians have insisted, we are finite beings, and God is an infinite reality, so in and of ourselves, we could never have infinite worth, even if we are valuable in, of, and for ourselves, even if we are intrinsically valuable ends in, for, and to ourselves. The reason is that as finite beings, we could never have within ourselves an infinite number of good-making properties, as God does. However, if an infinite God loves and cares for us, that gives us a kind of relational infinite worth in addition to our inherent finite intrinsic worth: the value combination "God loves *me*" has infinite worth, for here the infinite includes the finite. Wesley seemed sensitive and open to this possibility.

Before proceeding further, perhaps we should ask how anyone determines whether anything has intrinsic worth or is desirable for its own sake, in, to, and of or for itself. The only method that philosophers have ever discovered for doing this was named "the method of isolation" by G. E. Moore, the philosopher who influenced Twentieth Century ethical theory more than anyone else. Moore was not the first to discover and use this method. It was and is clearly used by Plato, Aristotle, and many others since their time. But Moore was the first to name it and clearly describe it.

According to Moore, to find out if anything is valuable in itself, we must ask "what value we should attach to it, if it existed in absolute isolation, stripped of all its usual accompaniments. And this is, in fact, the only method that can be safely used, when we wish to discover what degree of value a thing has in itself."[69]

To elaborate a bit on Moore's "method of isolation," to find out if anything is intrinsically good, we must isolate it in our thoughts, experiences, and imaginations from everything else with which it is normally associated, including its causes and effects; then, under those conditions, we must intuitively judge fairly, impartially, objectively, or disinterestedly (but not uninterestedly) whether it is still desirable, or whether it is really desirable only as a means to or symbol of something beyond itself. This method has great relevance to the main themes of this chapter, and certainly to understanding John Wesley's value judgments.

Using this method should disclose that we unique persons have intrinsic worth in our full definiteness and concreteness, not just that some of our abstract properties do. Wesley should have understood one crucial thing: happiness, faith, religious virtues and affections, and any other good-making properties he identified or regarded as intrinsically good are actually mere abstractions when considered only in and by themselves. In applying "intrinsically good" only to aspects or properties of persons but not to individual persons as such, Wesley was in the company of most value philosophers through the centuries. Where did they go wrong? Abstract properties like reason, knowledge, happiness, and the moral and spiritual virtues really do not have intrinsic worth "in themselves" or "for their own sakes." They are actually good only "in us" and "for us." They cannot even exist, much less be considered, merely "in themselves" or in complete isolation from conscious individuals. They exist and can be considered only within concrete conscious individuals like *you or me*, but not entirely by themselves. Their goodness cannot be assessed in total isolation, apart from us, because they can exist only in us, and we are always there assessing their worth. Their real goodness is not in, of, for, and by themselves, abstracted or isolated from conscious individuals, but in being "good for" unique, individual, concretely existing, conscious beings like people, animals, and God.

Wesley did talk philosophically about "properties" and make philosophical distinctions between intrinsically good things (good for their own sake, good as ends in themselves) and extrinsically good things (good as means to ends beyond themselves). God is infinitely valuable and should be valued "for his own sake." To love God, he tells us, "is to desire God alone for his own sake; and nothing else, but with reference to him."[70] We are "to love nothing else but for his sake and in subordination to the love of him."[71] Wesley paraphrased the first great commandment as, "Thou shalt love God alone for his own sake, and all things else only so far as they tend to him."[72] What this means was best explained when Wesley discussed avoiding idolatry and having no Gods other than the real one.

> The one perfect Good shall be your one ultimate end. One thing shall ye desire for its own sake,—the fruition of Him that is All in all. One happiness shall ye propose to your souls, even an union with Him that made them, the having 'fellowship with the Father and the Son,' 'the being joined to the Lord in one Spirit.' One design ye are to pursue to the end of time—the enjoyment of God in time and in eternity.

Desire other things so far as they tend to this. Love the creature—as it leads to the Creator. But in every step you take be this the glorious point that terminates your view. Let every affection, and thought, and word, and work, be subordinated to this. Whatever ye desire or fear, whatever ye seek or shun, whatever ye think, speak or do, be it in order to your happiness in God, the sole End, as well as Source, of your being.[73]

So, can we reconcile the axiological claim that we are valuable "for our own sake, ends in ourselves" with Wesley's claim that "One thing ye shall desire for its own sake," namely God, who is our "sole End"? Perhaps we can by considering his qualifications that we should "love nothing [else] but for His sake"[74] or "but with reference to Him," or "only so far as they tend to him," or "in subordination to the love of him." For God's sake, we can love (intrinsically evaluate) all that God loves (intrinsically evaluates). Loving only God as our ultimate End is not incompatible with loving other things "with reference to Him" or "as it leads to the Creator," as long as "subordinated" to him.

Put another way, what Jesus called the "First Commandment," namely, "You shall love the Lord your God with all your heart and soul and mind and strength" is not incompatible with the "Second Commandment," which is, "You shall love your neighbor as yourself." Some people (e.g., St. Augustine)[75] actually saw a conflict between the two. After all, how could we love God with *everything* that is within us and still have *anything left over* for our neighbor? The answer is that truly loving God, "Him that is All in all," involves or includes loving all that God loves. Thus, if God loves people and animals intrinsically, we should too, for otherwise we do not love God completely or in the fullness and likeness of God's own love. Wesley made it perfectly clear that loving God as "the only object of our love" does not "exclude his creatures from a subordinate share of it" because "'The Lord rejoiceth in his works; and consequently man, made after his likeness, not only may, but ought to imitate him therein, and with pleasure to own that 'they are very good.'"[76] "Very good" is not exactly "intrinsically good," but it comes very close. Wesley further explained, "There are many of the works of his hands which God expressly commands us to love," and "We cannot suppose any love forbidden by God which necessarily flows from this love of him."[77] Also, we are to love one another both *because* and *as* God has loved us.[78] But what does the "as" mean? It means that our love should be like God's love.

If our loving God means that we value God for God's own sake, then his loving us should mean that he values us for our own sakes, even if we are unworthy of such "love divine, all loves excelling." Wesley often and emphatically proclaimed that we should love God *because* God loves us. God actually loves us *first*, before we love him, and while we are yet sinners. In his *Explanatory Notes Upon the New Testament*, commenting on I. John, 4:19, Wesley wrote, "We love him, because he first loved us," and, he announced, "This is the sum of all religion, the genuine model of Christianity. None can say more: why should any one say less, or less intelligibly?"[79] Here the "us" is all inclusive, as is "our neighbor." God loves everyone, even non-Christians. Because God loves everyone, we should also love "all mankind without exception," even our enemies, even God's enemies! Wesley took the "enemies" thing one step beyond Jesus. Where Jesus said that we should love *our* enemies, Wesley added that we should even love *God's* enemies.[80]

Loving God "because he first loved us," could mean (1) "*prior to* our existence," or it could mean (2) "because *we benefit* from God," that is, merely as a means to our own salvation and ultimate happiness. The first is most compatible with prevenient grace, one meaning of which was to precede or "go before."[81] The latter, loving God as a mere means, is incompatible with loving God "for his own sake." It looks too much like loving God, not for God's sake, but for what he can do for us. In reducing Jonathan Edwards' twelve "signs" of true religion to only nine, Wesley omitted the second sign—that our religious affections for God should be grounded in "the transcendently excellent and amiable nature of divine things, as they are in themselves; and not in any conceived relation they bear to self, or self-interest."[82] Edwards did affirm that we should love and be grateful to God because of God's benefits to us,[83] but he insisted that this should not be our *primary* motive or reason for loving God. Primarily, we should love God for God's own sake, for God's own inherent and intrinsic excellencies, because God is "lovely and amiable in himself,"[84] said Edwards. But wasn't Wesley saying the same thing when insisting that we should desire God alone for his own sake, yet, we may love other things, ourselves and our neighbors, as they "tend to this," or "but for His sake," or but "with reference" to God"?

According to Richard B. Steele, Edwards and Wesley disagreed about "the possibility of serving God from purely 'disinterested' motives."[85] Was he right about this? Yes, Wesley omitted the "second sign" from his edited version of Edwards' *A Treatise Concerning Religious Affections*, and he insisted that we should love God because he first loved us. However, when discussing God, not ourselves, as the *only* proper end of all true religion, he certainly sounds a lot like Edwards! God is to be loved for *his own* sake.

We must not confuse loving anything intrinsically with loving it idolatrously. Loving anyone or anything for its own sake *apart from loving God* would be idolatrous, Wesley thought. As he recognized, some philosophers and theologians try to base intrinsic goodness or religion itself on "another foundation," such as "grounding religion 'on the eternal *fitness* of things', on 'the intrinsic *excellence* of virtue', and the *beauty* of actions flowing from it—on the *reasons*, as they term them, of good and evil, and the *relations*, of beings to one another."[86] Actually, he did not rule these out[87]—so long as not done idolatrously, so long as they "coincide with the scriptural." In "Upon Our Lord's Sermon on the Mount, VI," presumably because it "coincides with the scriptural," Wesley himself said that our *moral virtues and affections* are *"intrinsically and essentially good."*

> In the preceding chapter [Matthew 5] our Lord has described inward religion in its various branches. He has laid before us those dispositions of soul which constitute

real Christianity: the inward tempers contained in that holiness 'without which no man shall see the Lord'—the affections which, when flowing from their proper fountain, from a living faith in God through Christ Jesus, are intrinsically and essentially good, and acceptable to God.[88]

Wesley also spoke expressly of *faith* as *intrinsically good*, writing, "You see clearly how desirable Christian faith is, even on account of its own intrinsic value."\[89] So, Wesley definitely understood and used the concept of "intrinsic value," and he did not apply it to God alone. The trouble is, he expressly applied it only to certain abstract properties of people like faith and the religious affections, but not to individual people themselves in their wholeness. Most philosophical value theorists through the centuries have done this, even those who seem to say otherwise. For example, Immanuel Kant said that we should respect and treat all persons as ends in themselves and never merely as means to ends, but when he explained what he meant by this, valuing persons as ends meant nothing more than valuing the abstract moral law within us.

Wesley said that religious forms or ceremonies (systemic goods) are definitely not intrinsically valuable, even though they have other kinds of worth or goodness. "Rites and forms," he said, "are good in their place; just so far as they are subservient to true religion...," but "Let no man dream that they have any intrinsic worth."[90] As for extrinsic goods, Wesley explained that *actions*, "even those that are indifferent in their own nature," are made "holy and good and acceptable to God, by a pure and holy intention," though without this they are "of no value before God. Whereas whatever outward works are thus consecrated to God, they are, in his sight, of great price."[91]

Wesley clearly regarded aspects of persons (tempers, virtues, faith, and maybe consecrated actions) as intrinsically good, but, although he came close, he never said explicitly that individual persons as such have intrinsic worth. This book clearly upholds the intrinsic worth of unique concrete persons as such, not just some of our abstract moral and spiritual qualities. Yet, the intrinsic worth of individual persons may be implicit in Wesley's overall outlook, as now explained. Is regarding *individual persons* as such as intrinsically good stretching Wesley too far? If he didn't think individual persons are intrinsically good, he should have! "Human dignity" often expresses our intrinsic evaluation of persons, and Wesley himself used this phrase.[92] However, it is not *generic humanity* that has intrinsic worth; only *individuated* human (or conscious) beings really count. Unique conscious beings are the real ends in themselves, the real intrinsic-value-objects; but their overall goodness is enhanced or enriched by the presence of many "good for" and "good-making" properties, such as those to which we now turn.

Human Good-making (God-like) Properties

Speaking of human qualities and relations as "properties" seems very philosophical, but Wesley himself frequently talked that way. He knew a great deal of philosophy and was very astute philosophically, even though philosophy was not his primary concern. Systemic values were not his primary values. He explicitly said that "The omnipresent God sees and knows all the properties of all the beings he hath made."[93] He also discussed in detail the "properties" of love[94] and the "properties" of ideas,[95] among other things. The value perspective of this book says that properties can be either "good-making" or "bad-making" (or neutral). Properties are good-making if they fulfill the positive ideal standards that we apply to them. Good things, by definition, fulfill their ideals, their normative concepts; they have all the properties that they are supposed to have, those contained in our prescriptive expectations for them. Things considered as wholes are good by virtue of their combined ingredient properties, not their isolated properties, but they may have much more value than the mere sum of the goodness of their ingredient parts.

In application, we unique persons are good intrinsically in all our unified complexity; we are ends in ourselves, by virtue of our total set of integrated properties. So, what are we like? What our good-making properties? This question is important even if our properties are made available to us only through God's prevenient grace and not simply "by nature" in total detachment from God. Being intrinsically good is not the same thing as being morally or spiritually good. People can be intrinsically good, valuable for their own sakes, even though they are sinners and fall immensely if not infinitely short of moral or spiritual perfection. The good news is, says Christianity, says Wesley, that God can and does love us for our own sakes while we are yet sinners, while we lack moral and spiritual goodness, while we are yet lost sheep, while we are spiritually asleep.

Our Common Image of God Properties

Wesley carefully considered the value status of human properties, many of which were included explicitly in his understanding of our being made "in the image of God." For him, our human good-making properties are our desirable God-like properties, those through which we manifest God's image or likeness. Through God's prevenient grace, all people have many Godlike but finite properties. Having them "naturally" means that God created us to have them, so everything "natural" is also "supernatural" by prevenient grace. Our image of God properties are corrupted by sin, Wesley thought, but they were partly restored to everyone without interruption by God's prevenient grace. We will consider "restored" more carefully later.

So, what are our common human good-making image of God or Godlike properties? A good place to begin to answer is with Wesley's sermon on "The General Deliverance," where he tell us,

Now, 'man was made in the image of God.' But 'God is a Spirit.' So therefore was man. Only that spirit, being designed to dwell on earth, was lodged in an earthly tabernacle. As such, he had an innate principle of *self-motion*. And so, it seems, has every spirit in the universe; this being the proper distinguishing difference between spirit and matter, which is totally, essentially passive and inactive, as appears from a thousand experiments. He was, after the likeness of his Creator, endued with *understanding*, a capacity of apprehending whatever objects were brought before it, and of judging concerning them. He was endued with a *will*, exerting itself in various affections and passions; and lastly, with *liberty*, or freedom of choice; without which all the rest would have been in vain, and he would have been no more capable of serving his Creator than a piece of earth or marble; he would have been as incapable of vice or virtue, as any part of the inanimate creation. In these, in the power of self-motion, will, and liberty, the natural image of God consisted.[96]

Here and in other sermons[97] Wesley identified *five essential Godlike properties of all existing human beings*, all of which are aspects of our being created in God's image. First, we are *immaterial spirits*, though embodied. Second we are *self-moved*, which means self-changing, self-starting, or self-initiating, in all sorts of internal and external ways, including actively repositioning ourselves in space. Third, we have *understanding*, the ability to know and judge. Fourth, we have *wills*, equated here with having feelings—desires, feelings, affections, moods, emotions—especially love. Fifth, we have *liberty* (free choice), a capacity for originating and making our own decisions, which is the essence of "self-determination." That we really have this last property was denied in Wesley's day by Calvinistic predestinationists like Jonathan Edwards and George Whitefield and by philosophical determinists like Lord Kames and David Hartley.

Note carefully that Wesley usually distinguished between willing and choosing. He believed in freedom of choice, not freedom of will. He defined "will" in terms of feelings, that is, of "various affections and passions." Having feelings is an essential and desirable aspect of our existing in God's image, so God, too, has feelings. Most significantly, having the affection of love is the very heart of our existing in the image of God. Wesley is one of the very few theologians who affirm explicitly that love is the core image of God in us![98]

When comparing our universal human properties with those of non-human animals in "The General Deliverance," Wesley emphasized *reason or understanding,* but not to drive a wedge between us and them. We share reason by degrees with animals, he thought, contrary to what most philosophers and theologians had said and still say today. Reason, working with experience, makes natural knowledge possible for us. Through rational reflection on experience, we can acquire an elemental natural knowledge of God, self-knowledge, knowledge of others, and knowledge of our common world.

In the preceding quote, Wesley omitted several very significant universally human Godlike properties or "attributes" that he added and heavily emphasized elsewhere, either later in "The General Deliverance" or in other writings—namely, *sentience, consciousness or self-consciousness, conscience, imagination,* and *memory.*[99] In these ways also we resemble God, even if they are not "officially" included in the "Image."

Sentience, having the five "external" senses, is something that we share with non-human animals. It is not the same thing as "sensual" or being dominated by sensory experiences and pleasures. Sentience is a good thing; sensualism is not, Wesley thought.[100] Our organs of sense are gifts from God,[101] and Wesley apparently agreed with Newton that space itself is God's own sensory organ, the "divine sensorium;"[102] so even in this respect we reflect or resemble God. Wesley held that God actually had to be present everywhere and everywhen in order to know (directly experience) what is going on in all time and space.

Wesley often emphasized our godly or Godlike capacities for both *consciousness* and *conscience*. In "The Witness of Our Own Spirit," Wesley says of *consciousness* that

> God has made us thinking beings, capable of perceiving what is present, and of reflecting or looking back on what is past. In particular, we are capable of perceiving whatsoever passes in our own hearts or lives; of knowing whatsoever we feel or do; and that either while it passes, or when it is past. This is what we mean when we say, man is a 'conscious' being: he hath a 'consciousness' or inward perception, both of things present and past relating to himself, of his own tempers and outward behaviour.[103]

Wesley often used "tempers" as a synonym for "affections" such as feelings, desires, and emotions. What Wesley here calls "consciousness" is what most people call "self-consciousness." It is more than just being awake, alert, and externally focused (minimally conscious). It is being internally focused. It is direct wakeful awareness or "inward perception" of what is going on within our own souls, whether perceiving, reflecting, feeling, or doing. To this, he should have added choosing, which he did include elsewhere.

Conscience, Wesley promptly added, is not the same thing as consciousness, though conscience is conscious by degrees. Conscience has a moral or axiological function. It tells us the difference between good and evil, right and wrong. God has a conscience in this sense, though Wesley never said this explicitly, but this is a Godlike human property. Some philosophers of his day (e.g., Frances Hutcheson) called conscience the *"moral sense,"* but Wesley said that he preferred the more common and scriptural word "conscience." Wesley agreed with the "moral sense" philosophers that conscience involves pleasant feelings of "approbation," that is, approval of or taking pleasure in what is right, and unpleasant feelings of "disapprobation" or disapproval of what is wrong.[104] He defined conscience as "a faculty or power, implanted by God in every soul that comes into the world, of perceiving what is right or wrong in his own heart or life, in his tempers, thoughts, words, and actions."[105] Since it is possessed by "every soul that comes into the world," it functions independently of and does not depend on scriptural knowledge; many morally good and conscientious people in the world have never heard of the Christian Scriptures. His sermon "On Conscience" defined it as: "That faculty whereby we are at once conscious of our own thoughts, words, and actions, and of their merit or demerit, of their being good or bad, and consequently deserving either praise or censure. And some pleasure generally attends the former sentence, some uneasiness the latter. But this varies exceedingly, according to education and a thousand other circumstances."[106]

Wesley classified conscience as a *natural* property "because it is found in all men," but in another sense it is a *supernatural* property, "a supernatural gift of God, over all his natural endowments."[107] Just what this qualification accomplished is not at all clear because *all human properties are gifts of God* and thus ultimately of supernatural origin. So is everything else that exists. Drawing a line between natural and supernatural human properties is not a neat and easy task. In another sermon, Wesley claimed just the opposite: conscience is *not a natural property* because it is a gift of prevenient grace, from whence all natural or universal image of God properties derive. If all natural properties are gifts of grace, how do they differ from supernatural properties as gifts of grace?

> No man living is entirely destitute of what is vulgarly called 'natural conscience'. But this is not natural; it is more properly termed 'preventing grace'. Every man has a greater or less measure of this, which waiteth not for the call of man. Every one has sooner or later good desires, although the generality of men stifle them before they can strike deep root or produce any considerable fruit. Everyone has some measure of that light.[108]

The expression, "vulgarly called natural conscience,"[109] indicated that "natural" was not how Wesley preferred to think or talk about it. The problem is, human properties given by prevenient grace are empirically indistinguishable from those belonging to universal human nature as such, which we also have only by the grace of God. Thus, all natural properties are prevenient properties, and all prevenient properties are natural properties! Universal human nature and preveniently restored human nature are empirically indistinguishable. Human nature never was or is without prevenient grace.

Natural or not, Wesley clearly thought that all human beings have distinctively moral values and make distinctively moral judgments. All people everywhere can discern the difference between moral good and evil, right and wrong, can generalize this discernment into universal moral laws that are "written in their hearts,"[110] and can apply these laws critically and thoughtfully to concrete situations. Everyone by degrees develops attitudes and habits (dispositions of soul) for goodness (the virtues) or for badness (the vices). The trouble is, all too often we go for what is much less than the best, even though we know better. We find the directives of conscience all too easy to stifle, ignore, or forget. We suppress the still small voice within.

Our universal human properties are relevant to our intrinsic human worth to the extent that they fulfill our concept of "intrinsic human worth," but how do or should we frame this concept? What intrinsic-good-making-properties are common to all individual persons? The following can be abstracted from Wesley's own writings. We are or have:

1. embodied spirituality or ensoulment,
2. self-motion, self-initiation, or being self-starting,
3. reason or understanding, the ability to inquire, think, and know,
4. will, that is, desires, feelings, affections, emotions—especially love,
5. liberty (free choice), a capacity for making and originating our own choices,
6. imagination,
7. memory,
8. sentience, our five "external senses,"
9. consciousness (awareness) and self-consciousness (inner awareness),
10. conscience, the capacity for discerning good and evil, right and wrong,
11. moral laws "written in our hearts,"
12. moral and spiritual sensitivities, affections, dispositions, and virtues, in various degrees of activation or actualization, and
13. a "capacity for God."

Each of us shares these properties by degrees with all other human beings, but they are uniquely configured and employed within and by every individual person, and every concrete individual has many other properties as well, including some individuating properties not possessed by anyone else. So both universals (common or repeatable properties) and uniqueness are relevant and synthesized to make our intrinsic worth.

Is our human "capacity for God," the last item above, a natural or common property of prevenient grace, or is it a "supernatural" property of special saving grace? To some degree, Wesley thought, everyone has a limited capacity for God, thanks to prevenient grace. Wesley drew a line, admittedly fuzzy, between universal *human nature*, restored or sustained by God's prevenient grace, and *saintly nature*, available only through the saving grace of God and our willful cooperative response to it. Yet, those who are not saints and are yet sinners, those who fall far short of maximal moral and spiritual goodness or perfection, those who depend on God's prevenient grace for all of their common human goodness, still have the above universally human good-making properties. Most philosophers and theologians think that these are just the kind of properties that add up to or constitute intrinsic worth. The presence within us of such properties (plus our unique existence) makes us valuable as final ends, not as mere means to something else beyond ourselves.

True, our universally human good-making properties do not equal the highest spiritual worth of saintliness. Human dignity or inherent worth just consists in having exactly the sort of good-making properties that we have, like those above, and perhaps a few others. Yes, we have them only by God's prevenient grace, but from "day one" (whenever that is) they still need a lot of development. Some if not all of these good-making properties are the very ones by which our intrinsic goodness itself is usually defined or identified. They are the essential components or good-making properties of our very concept of intrinsically good realities, but in every person they are uniquely configured and applied, and they never exist apart from concrete uniqueness and individuating properties. They function as the conceptual norms or standards by which we measure our actual intrinsic worth. All human beings fulfill this set of norms by degrees; thus we are ends, and not *mere* means to anything beyond ourselves, because we actually have just such good-making properties, because we fulfill that concept, because our natural (universally human) properties measure up to those standards or criteria.

From a comprehensive spiritual perspective, by *prevenient grace* we have basic *intrinsic worth* because we are largely made of such good-making properties—uniquely configured; but we can achieve even greater *spiritual worth* as *special saving grace* gives us additional or enhanced moral and spiritual qualities. We can have this special grace by freely accepting what God is ready at every moment to give to us, and by working or cooperating with God to cultivate our initially rudimentary moral and spiritual gifts. Wesley definitely thought that the "new birth" properties acquired through saving grace during conversion and sanctification further enrich our overall goodness. Only in such sanctification-enriched properties do we find real happiness, complete fulfillment, and a truly abundant life, he believed. Saintliness, sanctified personhood, is much richer in good-making properties than the basic intrinsic human worth, dignity, or personhood, common to all. Just what these saintly properties are is a story for the final chapter.

Another comment about prevenient and saving grace is now in order. Wesley officially or theoretically accepted the Protestant view of *total human depravity*, according to which, through sin, we have absolutely *no goodness or good-making properties at all*. Perhaps none of its defenders ever really meant "total." This doctrine was actually nothing more than an abstract conceptual construct for Wesley, as other scholars have indicated.[111] All his talk about total depravity was little more than lip service to Protestant orthodoxy because, as Wesley conceded, *no actual people like this have ever existed*. As he said, although "All the souls of men are dead in sin by *nature*, this excuses none, seeing there is no man that is in a state of mere nature," because of prevenient grace.[112] All human beings have always existed under prevenient or universal grace. All of our natural or common good-making properties, though theoretically lost completely in the fall, were, by God's prevenient grace, immediately or instantly restored to all human beings as unearned and undeserved gifts of God. There was no time gap between the fall and prevenient restoration, not even a brief moment. Wesley's practical doctrine of prevenient grace completely undercuts his theoretical lip service to total depravity. Do all Wesley scholars understand this and its implications? Some do. As early as 1936, Umphrey Lee wrote, "For Wesley, the "natural man" is only a logical fiction. In this world man exists as a natural man plus the prevenient grace of God."[113]

Wesley and today's scholars take Wesley's theory of "restoration" very seriously,[114] so seriously that they seldom question its presuppositions—a once-unblemished Adam and Eve, and the original perfection of all of creation. But what sort of work does "restored" actually do in light of the fact that all people everywhere *now live under and always have lived under* prevenient or common grace. Like "original perfection," the concept of "restored" seems to be little more than a vacuous theoretical construct. Descriptively, it would be much more accurate to say that God has always gracefully and *continuously* provided, in diminished form, all the "natural" (universally human) good-making properties of God's image that make us valuable for our own sakes. *Wesley's theory of "restoration" is empirically indistinguishable from the Catholic view of the "continuation" of our desirable human properties in diminished form.*

Are not ALL *restored* properties *natural* properties because "found in all men," just as Wesley said of conscience? Though theoretically distinct, "restoration" is empirically equivalent to and indistinguishable from "preveniently universal" or "natural," meaning "always common to all." In infancy, these common human properties are mostly latent. "Total depravity," according to which all human good-making properties were completely lost through the sins of our ancestors, is a distinctively Protestant belief that is usually qualified in some way even by its ardent defenders. It is definitely not a biblical or a universal Christian belief. Roman Catholic thinkers usually hold that our good-making properties were *diminished* by the fall, but *not totally demolished* thereby. Wesley acknowledged that by God's prevenient grace our diminished or undeveloped capacities for reason, conscience, will, choice, desirable affections, etc., have always existed *continuously* in every person everywhere and at all times. So, what sense does it make to say that they have been *restored* from a state of absolute zero when there never was an absolute zero? Wesley's own view of preveniently natural or *universally restored minimal human goodness* is empirically identical with the Catholic view of *continuing, though diminished, human goodness*. Perhaps even the concept of a "diminished image" should ultimately be replaced by that of "undeveloped Godlike potencies."

Not just reason and conscience, but all *ongoing or sustained* human properties are in one sense supernatural properties, that is, gifts of God, because everything, (the whole of creation, all of nature itself, even human nature), is a gift of God. All natural properties are gifts from and created ultimately by God, even if indirectly dispensed through secondary causes. Thus, all natural properties are in this sense supernatural properties. More about special saving grace later, but Wesley recognized that *nothing* exists in a mere "state of nature" apart from God. Naturalists, atheists, and skeptics insist that we don't need God because the world exists and functions perfectly well without God. Their "without God" claim is question-begging, however. There is no such thing as "the world without God." We cannot observe a well-functioning world "without God" because no such world exists! Ours, the only world we can observe, is a world with God, and that is why it exists and works so well! Correspondingly, there is no such thing as "totally depraved human nature without God." Human nature and its good-making properties exist and are sustained if not restored by the prevenient grace of God. *All* that we are and have, including our "natural" properties, are gifts of God. We should thank John Wesley for insisting on that.

A Wesleyan view of ongoing and naturally or universally present prevenient grace has great significance for many theological disputes of long standing. For example, is there a valid "natural theology" or "natural religion"? Wesley definitely thought so, as long as "natural" is construed as "prevenient." The contents of a natural theology would be acquired by using our universally human God-given properties of reason, conscience, and experience. As Randy L. Maddox pointed out, the seemingly interminable Protestant dispute over whether there is a valid natural (rational, conscientious, experiential) knowledge of God usually take place within a conceptual framework that Maddox calls a "polarization of 'nature' and 'grace'."[115] This means that those rejecting natural theology *falsely assume that nature, specifically human nature, exists entirely apart from God and God's prevenient grace.* Wesley effectively annulled that assumption. This is why he could affirm the validity of a limited (but unsaving?) natural theology, just as Catholic thinkers have done. Given depravity as an abstruse construct, that is, given human beings totally without God, there can be no natural theology. But the real world with real people in it is never totally without God, so a limited natural theology is possible. There is no nature without grace; nature is always with grace. No totally depraved, utterly incompetent, and completely grace-less human beings have ever existed. Thus, from a Wesleyan perspective, the Protestant dispute over natural theology without grace never gets off the ground. In another context, Wesley claimed that viewing *anything* as totally without God is a kind of "practical atheism" because God is in everything everywhere.[116] If so, the limited effectiveness of universal human reason, conscience, and experience cannot be completely denied without repudiating God's own universally available presence and effectiveness, that is, without denying God's prevenient grace. That is indeed a kind of "practical atheism."

Wesley's Emphasis on Human Liberty

All of our commonly human image of God properties deserve careful attention, but human liberty in particular demands very special notice. It was one of Wesley's and Methodism's most influential yet controversial motifs. "All that we are is a gift of God" includes, among all else, our human capacity for making free choices. This was Wesley's Arminian way of avoiding determinism and predestination and making a place for human freedom, responsibility, accountability, and cooperation with God. If and only if we are the authors or originators of our own choices can we be responsible and accountable for them, Wesley insisted.

Although our general capacity for liberty of choice depends on and is a gift of God, the precise way we use it depends on us. Our particular choices are self-determined, not God-determined. We are empowered by God to choose to cooperate with God, or to refuse so to do. We are absolutely dependent on God for our power of self-direction or self-determination, thus for not being absolutely dependent on God! All of our gifts, our intrinsic good-making properties, including liberty of choice, are God-given, but we can freely use or abuse any of God's gifts. Such is "the greatness, the excellence, the dignity of man," as Wesley put it discussing the image of God in us.[117] Human dignity does not exist simply in or by itself; it exists from, under, and within God, who is All in all. A loving God gives life, love, and liberty to all. God also gives holiness to those who choose to respond to and cooperate with his "all love excelling." With our God-given freedom, we may or may not initially accept, or later mature toward, the salvation, spiritual development, sanctification, and ultimate happiness that *God offers* to everyone universally.

Wesley's God is a universalist who wills that *all* be saved, unlike the God of the Calvinists who wills only that *the very few elect* be saved. *We* may not be universalists, may not include ourselves, and may judge others to be doomed, but that is our problem, not God's. Some of us may freely refuse God's offer to all. In explaining "God worketh in you; therefore you *must* work," Wesley cited St. Augustine, who said, "He that made us without ourselves, will not save us without ourselves," meaning, Wesley thought, that we must constantly choose to labor together with God.[118] Salvation isn't a totally free lunch. We don't have to pay to be admitted to the stadium, but thereafter we do have to play the game or participate somehow according to our talents, many of which may be greatly underdeveloped. We must freely cooperate with God, grow in grace, and work out our salvation with fear and trembling. Otherwise, we backslide or fall by the wayside; many do "turn again to folly," but there is always hope of restoration.[119]

Defending Human Liberty or Freedom of Choice

Many objections were raised against the view of human freedom that Wesley accepted and defended. Jonathan Edwards knew very little about John Wesley and cared even less, but he wrote the most powerful book ever written against the sort of Arminianism to which Wesley subscribed. Wesley knew a lot about Edwards, but the reverse did not hold. Wesley read Edwards' treatise on the *Freedom of the Will* (and many of his other writings) and tried to reply to it, but he did not include this book in his Christian Library. Richard B. Steele suggests that Wesley's reply to Edwards was relatively "superficial."[120] Maybe so, maybe not, but if so, we may have to go beyond Wesley in replying to Edwards and to later generations of determinists who echo but do not improve upon his arguments. Here are his main arguments and some plausible responses to them.

1. Edwards *may* have argued that *there is no free will because choice and will are identical, because will and the affections are indistinguishable, and because all affections have determinate causes.*[121] This way of putting it is forcefully argued by Steele, who seems to regard it as an almost insurmountable objection to Wesley's theory of free choice. According to Steele, Jonathan Edwards subscribed to

a "two-faculty soul," consisting of will (the affections) and understanding. Wesley needed (but apparently did not have), Steele says, a "three-faculty soul" consisting of understanding, will, and the affections. Steele complained that "instead he gives that role to "liberty" itself. So in order to refute Edwards' contention that the will cannot be self-determining, Wesley invents a faculty of self-determination *different* from the will....But," Steele asks, "Why should we regard the will as free if freedom is not a quality of the will but a faculty separate from it?"[122]

Steele's difficulty springs from his unwillingness to acknowledge that Wesley really did have a "three-faculty soul," (or at least a five and maybe even a thirteen or more faculty soul) where will (feelings) and "liberty" (our capacity for making choices) are *not* identified with or collapsed into one another. Wesley believed that unified and integrated persons consist (in part) of (1) reason or understanding, (2) will, identified with feelings, desires, emotions, affections, and (3) liberty, "a power of choosing for [ourselves], a self-determining principle."[123] Our capacity for making choices was not just arbitrarily "invented." Feeling and choosing really are very different. We know we have the capacity to choose because experience repeatedly discloses that we can and do make choices. We regularly make choices with respect to what we understand, desire, and have feelings about. Furthermore, these choices are free or self-created; they are not necessarily determined in advance by either our intellect or our affections (will). Showing this requires further arguments. Those of us who, like Wesley, believe not simply in making choices but in making *free* choices are convinced that our choices originate with and are created or "self-determined" by our own unified and integrated self as a whole.

To explain, recall three of the thirteen intrinsic good-making image of God properties of human persons previously identified. These were:

3. reason or understanding, the ability to inquire and know,
4. will, that is, desires, feelings, affections, emotions—especially love,
5. liberty (free choice), a capacity for making and originating our own choices.

Wesley actually *agreed* with Jonathan Edwards that "will" and the "affections" (our desires, feelings, and emotions) *are identical*. He further agreed that they are *not free*. He did not, strictly speaking, affirm *free will*, even though that is the way *we* often express what he meant by "liberty." Instead he affirmed *free choice*. We should take Wesley's word "liberty" with utmost seriousness. He clearly distinguished our capacity for liberty, for making or originating our own choices, from our feelings, desires, and emotions—our will. As he explained, "There can be no moral good and evil, unless they [we] have liberty as well as will, which is entirely a different thing. And the not adverting to this seems to be the direct occasion of Mr. Edwards's whole mistake."[124] It is also Mr. Steele's whole mistake.

Wesley affirmed freedom of choice, but not freedom of will. He usually identified will with the affections, as did Jonathan Edwards; but, unlike Edwards, he did not identify liberty of choice with will, thus understood, (though occasionally he identify choice with will, understood differently). This is where Steele makes his big mistake. To his question, "But why should we regard the will as free if freedom is not a quality of the will but a faculty separate from it?" Wesley's answer would be: The will is not free; our capacity for choice is free, and it is indeed a "faculty" separate from will—though only in the sense of being a distinct capacity exercised by the unified self, not as something that functions on its own in complete independence of the unified self as a whole. Wesley explained that *liberty* "is very frequently confounded with the *will*, but is of a very different nature. Neither is it a property of the will, but a distinct property of the soul, capable of being exerted with regard to all the faculties of the soul, as well as all the motions of the body. It is a power of self-determination..."[125]

Wesley thus did not identify what we will with what we choose. We will (desire, feel attracted to or repelled by) many things, but these feelings and affections are often in conflict. We have conflicted wills, not free wills. However, we do make free choices to resolve these conflicts. We exercise what Wesley called "liberty," i.e., we make self-originated or "self-determined" choices among the many conflicting things that we will or have desires and feelings about.

2. Edwards argued that *our choices are not free because they are always determined or caused by our strongest desires, or the strongest set of our cooperating desires.*[126] In this argument, even Edwards himself distinguished between desiring (willing) and choosing, although he sometimes equated them. Even our decision to be or become Christians is determined by our strongest desire(s), Edwards thought. Yes, "Whosoever will may come," but under what conditions can anyone will to come? Under what conditions can anyone ever make this choice, Edwards asked. Unless "closing with Christ" is what we *most want*, we will never be able to choose it, he argued. God gives such prevailing wants to an elect few, but not to most people. That is the basic psychology of predestination, but the general pattern applies to every choice we ever make; all our choices are determined or caused by our strongest desire(s). Edwards did not deny that we make choices; he just denied that they are free. He may have been disposed toward a "two-faculty" psychology, as Steele suggested, but he argued against freedom of choice as if choosing were a third something in its own right. His claim that all of our choices are determined by our strongest desire(s), (which at times he identified with what we think or feel to be good or best), has a great deal of initial plausibility. All of our affections have definite causes, the ultimate one being God, and they in turn produce all our choices, he claimed. But is this really true?

The main problem with his seemingly irrefutable argument is that it simply does not accord with experience. This needs some explaining. Wesley said, "I have the testimony of all my outward and all my inward senses, that I am a free agent,"[127] but what could this possibly mean? Edwards' claim that experience shows that all of our choices are determined by our strongest motive(s) draws its initial plausibility from our immediate self-awareness that most of the things we do, our actions, are indeed determined by our strongest desire(s). *Most of the time, we just do what we most want to do—but without making effortful choices at all!* And much of the time, we are not even conscious of making choices; we just act on what we most want consciously or unconsciously. Where our character, dispositions, and desires are *already settled*, we just act directly on them without having to put any further thought, creative effort, or free choice into it. We know this much about ourselves from self-experience, and this plays directly into Edwards' hands.

Determinists charge that freedom of choice would make human behaviors utterly chaotic and unpredictable. However, human behaviors are neither absolutely predictable nor absolutely unpredictable. Defenders of free choice must account for our having relatively settled and determinate characters and dispositions, for predictably "acting in character," as we usually do, while still making a place for freedom of choice. This can be accomplished, however, without undermining human freedom. Just as Edwards said, if our wicked dispositions are very strong, we just do wicked things almost effortlessly because that is who we are; if our prevailing dispositions are saintly, we just do saintly things almost effortlessly because that is who we are. The trouble is, "who we are" is never *completely* settled in advance, and especially not from all eternity. Some aspects of our *character* are always *in the making* and do not get settled until we actually choose. Many aspects of character are indeed relatively secure and predictable because our desires and habits are already fixed, and we usually just do what we most want to do, just as Edwards said.

Often, however, there is no pre-existent "what we most want to do," and our dispositions have to be created by repeatedly making free choices. That is how both virtuous and sinful habits are formed. Liberty of choice advocates can agree with the preceding account of relatively settled character, but determinists like Edwards and other Calvinists cannot account for those situations in which character is not completely formed or settled in advance. Often, character is in the process of being made or constituted by our own creative personal efforts and choices. When we are greatly tempted, as we often are, no antecedent desires are strongest. We freely choose to resist or not, to yield or to yield-not, to temptation. In many circumstances, our choices and efforts determine what will come to be desired most, not the reverse. At first, learning to walk or play an instrument requires intense personal effort, concentration, and innumerable choices, but eventually they become almost habitual, effortless, or "second nature." So it is with good or bad character. It is partly created by our choices and gradually becomes habitual or second nature. In part, this is what sanctification involves.

Most of the time, just as Edwards said, we just act from settled dispositions and strongest desires—but without any effortful choosing. Deliberate and effortful choosing is a comparatively rare thing for mature individuals. It occurs when our motives are ambivalent or unsettled and no desires (or cooperating sets of them) are in fact strongest. In such situations, choosing determines which desires (or dispositions) get to be strongest. Our strongest desires do not determine our choices because, when character is being made, no desires are strongest until we effortfully identify ourselves with those we freely select. This effortful identification of ourselves with one alternative rather than another originates with us, with our unified holistic selves. It is not programmed into us in advance or from eternity. It is the essence of that freedom of choice that Wesley called "liberty" or "self-determination."

The claim that all our choices are determined by our strongest motives assumes that our often conflicting desires always are, or somehow automatically get to be, completely resolved all by themselves, with no personal effort, concentration, attention, choice, or "self-determination" on our part. But this is not true, as experience shows repeatedly. Sometimes we have to deliberate and choose before our conflicting desires are resolved. Edwards may have assumed that deliberation itself always resolves ambiguous motivation, but this just isn't in accord with what we know about ourselves from immediate or direct experience. Very often, no amount of rational deliberation clears things up or definitively settles conflicts for us, and we just have to decide. Experiential self-knowledge reveals our free choices to us, so Wesley was right that "I have the testimony of all my outward and all my inward senses, that I am a free agent."

Wesley developed his own astute experience-based reply to the objections that we always do what we most want to do or what we believe to be best, and that our desires are thus not susceptible to originative self-control or creative self-determination. Wesley responded to these claims, as formulated by David Hartley, not Jonathan Edwards, while noting that his remarks also apply to "the two gentlemen above-mentioned," one of whom was Edwards. This response is well worth considering, and it is far from being superficial.

> Let us take this boasted argument in pieces, and survey it part by part:
> 1. "Motives are not under our power." This is not universally true: Some are, some are not. That man has a strong motive to run his neighbor through, namely, violent anger; and yet the action does not necessarily follow. Often it does not follow at all; and where it does, not necessarily: He might have resisted that motive.
> 2. "In all cases the choice must be determined by that motive which appears the best upon the whole." This is absolutely false. It is flatly contrary to the experiences of all mankind. Who may not say on many occasions, Video meliora [Ovid's "I see and approve the better; I follow the worse."]?—"I know what I do is not best upon the whole."
> 3. "Man is passive in receiving the impressions of things." Not altogether. Even here much depends on his own choice. In many cases he may or may not receive the impressions; in most he may vary it greatly.
> 4. "According to these his last judgment is necessarily formed." Nay, this too depends much upon his choice. Sometimes his first, sometimes his last, judgment, is according to the impressions which he has received; and frequently it is not.
> 5. "This the will necessarily obeys." Indeed it does not. The mind has an intrinsic power of cutting off the connection between the judgment and the will.

6. "And the outward action necessarily follows the will." Not so. The thing I would, I do not; and the thing I would not, that I do [cf. Rom. 7:19]. Whatever then becomes of the chain of events, this chain of argument has not one good link in it.[128]

3. Edwards also charged that *all so-called free choices would have to be "indifferent" in the sense of "totally unmotivated."*[129] The truth is, we often desire incompatible things, and we have to choose between them. Such choices are always preceded by desires, thus are not unmotivated at all. We just happen to desire incompatible things. Our souls are conflicted. The desires that eventually prevail have to be supplemented by our effortful personal identification with them, by our choices, in order to become strongest and prevail over competing motives. When motives genuinely conflict, our choices are neither unmotivated nor determined by our strongest motives. Rather, specific conflicting motives get to be strongest through and because of our self-originated efforts and choices, by our creative or originative power of self-determination, by our voluntary identification with them. Where character is in the making, there are motives, no one or set of which is strongest in advance of choosing; but there are also free choices, all of which are motivated but not determined by their motives. Here it is not choices that are determined by our strongest motives, but some motives emerge as strongest because and only after we freely choose them and effortfully identify ourselves with them. Wesley almost played himself into Edwards' hands on this issue in another work when he wrote, "Man was made with an entire indifference, either to keep or change his first estate: it was left to him what he would do; his own choice was to determine him in all things. The balance did not incline to one side or the other unless by his own deed."[130] However, this could be construed to mean, not that our choices are indifferent in the sense of unmotivated, but rather in the sense that we have to choose only when none of our conflicting motives outweigh the others. Then "His own choice" determines which motive is to prevail.

4. Edwards argued that *so called "free choices" give rise to an infinite regress of choosing, choosing to choose, choosing to choose to choose, and so on indefinitely.*[131] The proper response is, we just don't experience any such thing, and that settles it. We just choose, and that is it. This is what self-experience or immediate self-knowledge confirms. That is also *all* that self-experience confirms, and this is quite enough to refute Edwards' insistence that freely choosing would have to go on forever if it goes on at all.

5. *Edwards charged that free choices would, by definition, have to be uncaused choices.*[132] Against uncaused choices, he argued that "All events have causes." This is a rationally self-evident truth, he claimed, without which we would have no empirical knowledge whatsoever. Edwards did not deny that we make choices; he denied only that we make *free choices*, now defined as *"uncaused choices."* He failed to realize that "cause" is an ambiguous concept. Causes might be only *necessary conditions*, those in the absence of which a very specific effect cannot occur; or causes might be *sufficient conditions*, those in the presence of which only a very

specific effect can and must occur. Edwards assumed that all causal conditions are both necessary and sufficient conditions. The truth is, free choices have necessary conditions (desires) but not sufficient conditions; thus, they have causes, but they do not have causes! We cannot choose any given x unless we have some desire for or interest in x, so our choices are not totally indifferent or unmotivated, and our desires are necessary causal conditions of choosing. Yet, where motives conflict, no desire or set of desires is strong enough or necessary and sufficient enough in advance to force one particular choice and it alone to occur. Free choices have causes, necessary conditions; but they do not have causes, sufficient conditions. In this, there is no paradox. "Cause" is just a slippery concept, not a perfectly "clear and distinct idea." In the rationalistic tradition, there can be no self-evident truths without clear and distinct ideas.

6. *Being responsible and thus justly rewardable or punishable for what we choose to do presupposes only external freedom of action, not internal freedom of choice*,[133] so Edwards argued. Edwards claimed that most of the time we are free in the only sense relevant to moral accountability; and we are not free only in those relatively rare circumstances in which we are *externally constrained or restrained* (e.g., chained, threatened, incarcerated, etc.). When we are externally restrained or constrained, we are not free and are thus not responsible for what we are then forced to do or not do; but most of the time we are *free to do* what we most want to do. We have *freedom of action*, so we are indeed responsible for what we do. Responsibility requires *only freedom of action, not* inner self-initiative or *freedom of choice*, Edwards contended. When what we most want to do is bad or wrong and we knowingly do it anyway (as the "great bulk of mankind" usually does), we are just bad people who are *justly punishable* both here and in hell. When what we most want to do is good or right and we knowingly do it anyhow (as only the elect can do) we are *justly rewardable* both here and in heaven. *Responsibility* turns entirely on *external freedom of action*; nothing turns on *internal freedom of choice*, Edwards insisted. If so, God can get away with predestination without impugning his own moral goodness. God can justly punish most people eternally in hell for doing just what he predestined or programmed them to do, *if* just punishment is warranted simply for *doing wrong knowingly* and has nothing whatsoever to do with *originating our own choice* to do it.

This is the most crucial difference, not only between Edwards and Wesley, but also between all who affirm free choice and those who repudiate it. Edwards claimed that moral *responsibility* or accountability for wrongdoing has *nothing whatsoever* to do with originating our own choices to do wrong knowingly. He was what William James called a "soft determinist," or what many today call a "compatibilist," one who holds that we are totally predetermined, yet fully responsible anyway; determinism and responsibility are compatible, not in conflict, from this perspective. Wesley, by contrast, was convinced that moral responsibility or accountability for wrongdoing has *everything* to do with *originating* our own choices to do wrong or right knowingly. Without creative liberty of choice, Wesley held, there is no such thing as either human responsibility or moral good and evil, virtue and vice.[134] If God programs bad choices into us eternally, then they originate with God, and God is responsible for them, not us. This would make God a devil, as Wesley *correctly* maintained. Jonathan Edwards himself admitted that predestination makes God the author or originator of all evil as well as of all good. Wesley did not agree. Neither should we.

7. *God's omnipotence and sovereignty mean that God ultimately causes everything, including all of our human choices.* At times, Edwards completely denied that there are any "secondary causes" within the world at all and affirmed that God *directly* causes absolutely everything—including human sin, but only as a part of a greater good, like the dark shadows in a beautiful painting. Sustaining the world means recreating it anew every instant, for nothing in the world has any causal power whatsoever, and God has it all. Omnipotence means omnicausality, quite literally, so Edwards and the Calvinists held. It is the power to do anything (intelligible) that God pleases.[135] By contrast, Wesley's position was that in giving us the power and freedom to originate our own choices, God deliberately limits and shares his own power out of love and goodness. He has and exercises the power to limit his own power. This is the best, the most desirable, form of divine power over us. Calvinistic theologians like Edwards (or Whitefield) effectively deny that God has this power to share his power and creativity. They affirm that "omnipotence" is the power do *anything* that is not logically incoherent, yet, they assume that God lacks the power to share his own power and creativity. So whose position is logically incoherent?

Mainstream Whiteheadian Process Theologians acknowledge that our freedom limits God's power, but many do not agree with Wesley that God *deliberately* limits his own power. They claim that God's power is limited by creation or "creativity" as a matter of metaphysical necessity, that all creatures are necessarily free, and God could not create them otherwise. The Wesleyan view, by contrast, is that God creates free creatures as a matter of moral necessity, not of metaphysical necessity. In the abstract, God has the power to create a Calvinistic universe, but since his goodness, love, mercy, and justice always cohere with and interpenetrate his power, he would never do so. God's moral nature, not the universal metaphysical necessity of creativity as such, requires God to give us the power to originate our own choices. A morally good and loving God just wouldn't create a Calvinistic universe, though he has the abstract power to do it. God has the power to do anything that he pleases to do, but creating a Calvinistic universe is something that a morally good and loving God would never please to do, even if he could do it. Any God who would, would be a devil, just as Wesley said! Many other Temporalistic Theologians agree with Wesley that God deliberately limits his own power, some say voluntarily (or arbitrarily), while others, like Thomas J. Oord, say by the necessity of love and goodness themselves.[136] Wesley seemed to side with Oord; rather, Oord seems to side with Wesley.

When all is said and done, assigning "perfections" to God depends on what we most value. Predestinationists think that absolute and unrestrained power or sovereignty counts as a divine perfection. Arminians like Wesley think that only power constrained by and consistent with love, justice, and mercy counts as a divine perfection.

This debate over free choice could go on endlessly (and still does), but perhaps this is enough to show that and how free-choicers like Wesley can mount a viable defense against their opponents.[137]

In conclusion, given prevenient or common grace, what emerges is a surprisingly rosy or positive account of what most ordinary people are like in their pre-conversion "heathen" or "almost Christian" state.[138] By degrees, most real people have remarkable capacities for thinking rationally about many things, for knowing the sensory world, for believing, knowing, and acting on things of a moral and spiritual nature, for conscientiously discerning the difference between moral right and wrong, for understanding and acting from moral action-guiding rules or laws, for desirable (as well as undesirable) interests, emotions, feelings, and affections, and for freely choosing and acting to achieve goodness within and without. *Totally* depraved people would have none of these good-making properties, but, as Wesley thought, no one actually exists, or ever has existed, in such a totally depraved state, thanks to the prevenient grace of God. The universe that God created has never been that God-forsaken, sin or no-sin! Of course, most men and women in their common-grace natural state still lack the much more advanced good-making properties of saintliness, but ordinary people and Christians who are not yet perfected saints do not lack moral, spiritual, and intrinsic goodness altogether. No one is ever *totally* depraved, completely devoid of all good-making properties. Ordinary people are intrinsically good, valuable in, to, and for themselves, as well as in, to, and for God, even if they aren't saints. God values us intrinsically while we are yet sinners and fall short of perfection! Contrast this with Calvinistic Jonathan Edwards' theory that God disvalues us infinitely and intrinsically while we are yet sinners, even though he made us that way and does nothing about it, except for the elect few.

Animals as Intrinsically Good

Most Wesleyans today might be shocked to learn that John Wesley expected non-human animals as well as people to go to heaven or at least to find a permanent place in the renovated new world to come. Our Methodist and other Wesleyan preachers seldom mention that! William R. Cannon pointed out that Wesley expected to find his faithful horse in heaven. He also expected to find all animals in heaven, Cannon noted, and not merely because he had a sentimental attachment to or fondness for his own horse.[139] That animals as well as people have a God-given immortality and will be found in *the final new creation, as well as in heaven*, has great significance for the kind of value that Wesley attached to them, that we should attach to them, and that God does attach to them.

Wesley's evolving and complex eschatology[140] will not be examined here except for its significance in documenting the high value that Wesley assigned to non-human animals. Many people think that the main difference between people and animals is that we have immortal souls (by the grace of God), but they do not. Wesley did not agree with this at all! Animals are just as much immortal as we are, by the grace of God. They also have intrinsic worth, just as we do, though not as much because they lack our intrinsic-good-making properties by degrees and at least one of them in kind.

Wesley's case for believing that immortal animals will be present in the final "new heaven and new earth" is found mainly in his sermons on "The General Deliverance" and "The New Creation." There he argued that animals deserve to go to heaven, and they will, because:

1. God loves, is merciful to, and has "a tender regard" for non-human animals as well as people.
2. God provides for the well-being of both non-human animals and people.
3. Non-human animals deserve to be compensated for all the evils they suffer from other animals and especially from the hands of us human beings.
4. Non-human animals have *most* of the same good-making properties as human beings, not only sentience, but also ensoulment, powers of self-motion, understanding (reason), will, liberty or freedom of choice, a "shadowy resemblance" even of moral goodness, and immortality. They completely lack *only one thing* that we have, a capacity for God.

All of these radical and fascinating claims about animals require further validation and investigation, so here goes.

God Cares About Animals

In Wesley's words, non-human animals are *also* "the offspring of one common Father, the creatures of the same God of love!"[141] Again, "Nothing is more sure than that as 'the Lord is loving to every man,' so 'his mercy is over all his works'—all that have sense, all that are capable of pleasure or pain, of happiness or misery."[142] Clearly, Wesley rejected the Cartesian view that non-human animals are merely mindless and unfeeling machines. "Daily experiments show," he claimed, that they have emotions and feelings and can experience pleasure, pain, happiness, and misery; and they also have what is commonly called "sentience," that is, they have sensory experiences.[143] People are also sentient. Sentience is an intrinsic good-making property. Our external senses are good gifts from God; so are the senses of the animals.

Many recent thinkers insist that because non-human animals have sentience, feelings, and emotions, we human beings have moral obligations to them and should regard them as legitimate members of our moral communities, even if they do not have corresponding moral obligations to us because of their natural limitations. Wesley certainly thought that we are morally and spiritually bound to treat animals in loving, merciful, and Godlike ways. As he explained, the fact that animals are capable of pleasure and pain, happiness and misery,

> may encourage us to imitate him whose mercy is over all his works. They may soften our hearts towards the meaner creatures, knowing that the Lord careth for them. It may enlarge our hearts towards those poor creatures to reflect that, as vile as they appear in our eyes, not one of them is forgotten in the sight of our Father which is in heaven. Through all the vanity to which they are now subjected, let us look to what God hath prepared for them.[144]

Wesley argued in another sermon that God, as omnipresent, is just as much there in non-human animals as in us, and this makes a great difference in how we should treat them.

> God is in all things, and...we are to see the Creator in the glass of every creature;...we should use and look upon nothing as separate from God, which indeed is a kind of practical Atheism; but, with a true magnificence of thought, survey heaven and earth, and all that is therein, as contained by God in the hollow of His hand, who by His intimate presence holds them all in being, who pervades and actuates the whole created frame, and is in a true sense the soul of the universe.[145]

Would it make any difference in the way we treat animals if we believe, as Wesley did, that whatever we do to animals, we do to God, "who pervades and actuates the whole created frame"? We are familiar with the somewhat profane expressions, "Holy cow" and "Holy mackerel," but most Christians really do not view such beings as holy. Wesley did, for God is just as much present in them as in us. Increasing spiritual sensitivity (growth in grace) on our part would enable us to see God's presence in all things, especially all living and sentient things, just as Wesley did, and to view all good things as sacred. Most of us are just practical Atheists!

God Provides for Both Animals and People

As Wesley explained, because non-human animals are capable of sensory experiences as well as pleasures, pains, happiness, and misery, God

> 'openeth his hand and filleth all things living with plenteousness:' 'he prepareth food for cattle,' as well as 'herbs for the children of men.' He provideth for the fowls of the air, 'feeding the young ravens when they cry unto him.' 'He sendeth the springs into the rivers, that run among the hills,' to give drink to every beast of the

field, and that even 'the wild asses may quench their thirst.' And suitably to this, he directs us to this. He directs us to be tender of even the meaner creatures, to show mercy to these also.[146]

Wesley was convinced that Godlikeness would require us to be compassionate caretakers of, not heartless and domineering consumers and destroyers of, all creation, including non-human animals. As God provides, so should we. As God cares, so should we. As God shows mercy and compassion, so should we. As God loves, so should we. God is intent upon "creation care," and we should be also.

Animals are Entitled to Compensation Hereafter

Wesley believed that non-human animals are entitled to compensation hereafter for all the evils they suffer in this world from natural causes, from other animals, and from us human beings.[147] He believed, as educated people today may not be able to believe, that before the fall of Adam and Eve, all non-human animals actually lived in perfect harmony with one another. They were once perfectly happy and were not subject to conflict, disease, death, pain, or a natural struggle or competition for survival. Wesley lived before Darwin and knew nothing of the primordial "survival of the fittest" that we know about, but *we* have to take this into account, even though it is not the whole story when divorced from the cooperation and caring that run deep in nature. Wesley believed that before the Fall of Adam and Eve there was no natural evil, no pain or death, no physical threats, harms, or tumults—no dangerous places, storms, earthquakes, or excessive heat or cold, and no weeds or useless plants.[148] Before the Fall, all creatures lived in perfect harmony; all conflict, disease, death, and suffering, even for animals, resulted directly and only from the sin of the first human beings,[149] and so did all pain and suffering: "Had there been no sin, there would have been no pain."[150] Wesley assumed that all animals were originally tame or domesticated and that all wildness resulted from the Fall of Adam and Eve.

Today, we know the world has always been a dangerous place, and most animal species always were and still are born wild. We also know that the dinosaurs, for example, and their prey or food, existed, competed, were injured, diseased, suffered, and died for vast eons of time before human beings ever made the earthly scene, so, unlike Wesley, we cannot blame any of these evils on the sins of our earliest human ancestors. With few exceptions,[151] most Wesleyan scholars do not question Wesley's assumption of the original perfection of all creation, but they should.

Even if we cannot accept Wesley's views on the *original* idyllic state of perfectly harmonious nature, non-human animals, and human beings, we should still seriously consider what he says about their *present* state and ours, and the practical implications thereof. Today, as throughout the past, non-human animals suffer immensely from innumerable natural and moral evils, especially so in our hands. As

Captain James Kirk once said in an episode of *Star Trek*, "We are a predatory species," but, as he also indicated, we don't have to be, not today, not any day. He was talking, of course, about how people prey upon other people, but what he said applies just as well to how people treat and prey upon other animals, both wild and domestic. Wesley would have agreed, not only that nature, apart from man,[152] is "red in tooth and claw" (not his expression, but Alfred Lord Tennyson's), but also that we are a predatory species and may be even more vicious than other predatory animals. Consider Wesley's pre-Darwinian description of our vicious ways with animals.

> During this season of 'vanity', not only the feebler creatures are continually destroyed by the stronger; not only the strong are frequently destroyed by those that are of equal strength; but both the one and the other are exposed to the violence and cruelty of him that is now their common enemy—man. And if his swiftness or strength is not equal to theirs, yet his art more than supplies that defect. By this he eludes all their force, how great soever it be; by this he defeats all their swiftness, and notwithstanding their various shifts and contrivances, discovers all their retreats. He pursues them over the wildest plains, and through the thickest forests. He overtakes them in the fields of the air, he finds them out in the depths of the sea. Nor are the mild and friendly creatures who still own his sway, and are duteous to his commands, secured thereby from more than brutal force, from outrage and abuse of various kinds. Is the generous horse, that serves his master's necessity or pleasure with unwearied diligence, is the faithful dog, that waits the motion of his hand, or his eye, exempt from this? What returns for their long and faithful service do many of these poor creatures find? And what a dreadful difference is there between what they suffer from their fellow-brutes and what they suffer from the tyrant, man! The lion, the tiger, or the shark, give them pain from mere necessity, in order to prolong their own life; and puts them out of their pain at once. But the human shark, without any such necessity, torments them of his free choice; and perhaps continues their lingering pain till after months or years death signs their release.[153]

Wesley thought that adequate *compensation* to animals for the evils they suffer could only come in the final state of things, the new creation to come, for they will never get it otherwise. In the final new heaven and new earth to come, non-human animals will once again live in total happiness and harmony and be delivered from all conflicts, struggles, evils, diseases, sufferings, and death—as will human beings.[154] The lamb will lie down with the lion, and no one will study war and killing any more. Pray that it may be so! Meanwhile, pray that we may do all that we can here and now to bring about such a "peaceable kingdom."

Animals Share our Good-making Properties

Most interesting and important of all, Wesley believed, non-human animals have, in diminished degree, practically all of the good-making (God-like) properties that we human beings have—also restored or continued by prevenient grace. Here Wesley's thoughts were truly revolutionary! Most theologians emphasized our differences with non-human animals; Wesley emphasized our similarities!

We saw that the restored or continued "natural image of God" in human beings consists in such good-making personal properties as ensoulment, self-motion, understanding (reason), will, and free choice.[155] It turns out that *animals have exactly these same image of God good-making properties, plus even a "shadowy resemblance of even moral goodness," plus immortality!* That animals, too, are made in the image of God is a clear implication of assigning our Godlike natural image of God properties to animals, even if diminished in degree.

> What was the original state of the brute creatures, when they were first created? This deserves a more attentive consideration than has been usually given it. It is certain these, as well as man, had an innate principle of *self-motion*; and that at least in as high a degree as they enjoy it at this day. Again: they were endued with a degree of *understanding* not less than that they are possessed of now. They had also a *will*, including various passions, which, likewise, they still enjoy. And they had *liberty*, a power of choice; a degree of which is still found in every living creature. Nor can we doubt but their understanding too was in the beginning perfect in its kind. Their passions and affections were regular, and their choice always guided by their understanding.[156]

The important thing for us today is not whether animals originally had all of these good-making natural properties in some idyllic primeval state, but that they still do have them here and now. Wesley's view of animals was drastically different from that of Descartes, for whom animals were just unconscious, unthinking, unfeeling, mechanical devices—"automatons" or "mere machines"[157]—that are incapable of experiencing pleasure or pain, of making free choices, and have no senses, no consciousness, no memory, no self-initiative, no souls. According to Wesley, "Experiments show...quite the contrary."[158]

Wesley also clearly disagreed with the views of practically all previous Catholic theologians, best exemplified by St. Thomas Aquinas, who located our human image of God exclusively in *reason*. We are rational animals, St. Thomas claimed, following Aristotle; but non-human animals are not rational at all, so we exist in God's image, but they don't. Wesley would have none of this! Many people today think that Charles Darwin first discovered that non-human animals are rational by degrees, contrary to Aristotle and all those he swayed for centuries. However, Wesley recognized animal rationality and insisted upon it long before Darwin! As Wesley explained most clearly and emphatically, it is our capacity for God, not reason, that distinguishes us from non-human animals, for they too, by degrees, are rational animals, (and we today may even suspect that some of them have primitive spiritual sensitivities, as when other primates and elephants mourn their dead).

> What then makes the barrier between men and brutes? The line which they cannot pass? It was not reason. Set aside that ambiguous term: exchange it for the plain word, understanding, and who can deny that brutes have this? We may as well deny that they have sight or hearing. But it is this: man is capable of God; the inferior creatures are not. We have no ground to believe that they are in any degree capable

of knowing, loving, or obeying God. This is the specific difference between man and brute—the great gulf which they cannot pass over.[159]

This distinctively human "capacity for God" will be further explored later, but for now note that being "capable of God" means being "capable of knowing, loving, and obeying his [our] creator,"[160] as Wesley explained. This involves having a special "spiritual sense" or sensitivity to divine things, available most effectively to those who receive saving grace, as explained in the concluding chapter.

As for immortality, beauty, and the "shadowy resemblance of moral goodness,"[161] Wesley clearly attributed these to the "brutes" as well as to us, not only originally, but even now. Consider his views of the immortality, beauty, and primitive moral virtues of animals.

> And as a loving obedience to God was the perfection of man, so a loving obedience to man was the perfection of brutes. And as long as they continued in this they were happy after their kind; happy in the right state and the right use of their respective faculties. Yea, and so long they had some shadowy resemblance of even *moral goodness*. For they had gratitude to man for benefits received, and a reverence for him. They had likewise a kind of benevolence to each other, unmixed with any contrary temper. How *beautiful* many of them were, we may conjecture from that which still remains; and that not only in the noblest creatures, but in those of the lowest order. And they were all surrounded not only with plenteous food, but with every thing that could give them pleasure; pleasure unmixed with pain; for pain was not yet—it had not entered into paradise. And they too were immortal: for 'God made not death: neither hath he pleasure in the death of any living.'[162]

A great deal of work has been done in recent years on how human morality is anticipated in non-human animals, especially those with mirror neurons in their brains,[163] but we should definitely give Wesley credit for making a very good start with this theme, even before Darwin, and for indicating that many of the moral virtues of animals in their "original" state still remain today in shadowy resemblance—specifically (as above) such moral virtues as loving obedience, gratitude, reverence, cooperation, and benevolence. If Wesley had known what we know today about non-human animals, especially the great apes, whales, dolphins, and elephants, he could have added empathy, compassion, consolation, and identifying with others to his list of their moral virtues. Of course, except for domestic animals, such ethical virtues are expressed in non-human animals mainly (though not entirely) to members of their own species, clan, pack, or kin; but in that "speciesist" respect, they are almost exactly like us!

In sum, aside from the relevance and validity of such an aboriginal idyllic state, Wesley had many constructive ideas about non-human animals that were quite revolutionary in his day and still are even today. Wesley clearly rejected the extreme contrasts that most thinkers drew and still draw between people and animals, for example:

Only people, not animals, are rational beings, but not so according to Wesley.
Only people, not animals, have immortal souls and will go to heaven, but not so according to Wesley.
Only people, not animals, have conscious awareness of anything, including emotions and pains (Descartes), but not so according to Wesley.
Only people, not animals, are moral beings having moral virtues, but not so according to Wesley.
Only people, not animals, are made in the image of God, but not so (at least by implication) according to Wesley.
Only people, not animals, are loved by God, but not so according to Wesley.
Only people, not animals, should be loved by us as we love ourselves, but not so according to Wesley.
Only unto people, not animals, should we do as we would have them do unto us.

Wesley thought that both people and animals (by degrees) are rational beings, have immortal souls, will be present in the final new creation, are moral beings, are made in the image of God (by implication, because they too have many God-like properties), are loved by God, and should be loved by us and be treated by us as we would have them treat us. Wesleyans today should take Wesley's thoughts about animals much more seriously than they do.

Wesley indicated that non-human animals were an integral aspect of the original goodness of creation, as God himself acknowledged, according to the first chapter of Genesis.[164] He also acknowledged that even though animals have *great value* (great intrinsic worth), they do not have *equal value* (equal intrinsic worth) with human beings.[165] The best evidence for this is that (1) even though animals have most of the same good-making properties that people have, they do not have them to the same or equal degree, and (2) people have some properties (all those involved in our capacities for God, to be explored later) that non-human animals do not have. As Wesley explained, "God regards everything that he hath made in its own order, and in proportion to the measure of his own image which he has stamped upon it."[166] Here Wesley seems to say quite explicitly that non-human animals also exists in God's image, but somewhat less so than human beings.

Finally, Wesley thought, in the ultimate new creation, non-human animals will be morally and spiritually *elevated to the point where they would be capable of God*. In the great chain of being, *we* will be elevated to the stage where angels are now, and *they* will be elevated to the stage where we are now![167] Whether true or not, this certainly sheds great light on how highly Wesley valued animals, and how highly he thought that God values animals.

It would be illogical to find such immense goodness, so many good-making (God-like) properties, in non-human animals and still deny that they have any intrinsic worth, for these are surely among the defining good-making properties of intrinsic goodness itself. Yet, the typical view, before the recent flourishing of ethics and animals deliberations, was that of St. Thomas Aquinas, Immanuel Kant, and so many others who thought that animals were created only as extrinsic goods —that God made them only for our use, as means to our ends, but not for their own sakes or their own inherent worth. Many of Wesley's beliefs about animals were very a-typical and downright revolutionary, but highly plausible nonetheless, including his insistence that animals as well as people have immense worth. Of course, Wesley never said explicitly that animals have intrinsic worth, just as he never said explicitly that people have intrinsic worth, but that seems to be a fair interpretation of all else that he did say. Randy L. Maddox does not hesitate to say that for Wesley, within the great chain of being "Every species has intrinsic value and a right to exist for its own purposes."[168]

In sum, from a Wesleyan perspective, God, people, and animals are all intrinsically valuable beings—God infinitely so, people finitely so, animals somewhat less so—but still so. Wesley's perspective on the value of non-human animals, both domestic and wild, has great significance for how we ought to treat them. It should "encourage us to imitate Him whose mercy is over all his works."[169] God's eye is on the sparrow—and was on the dinosaurs, wooly mammoths, and Neanderthals, though Wesley knew nothing about them. (Wesley occasionally spoke of "fossils," but by that he meant metal ores and minerals, not the bones of pre-historic animals.)

Thus, being Godlike entails caring intrinsically about and for non-human animals. *It entails an ethics of love applied to animals.* Even in his early sermon "On Love," Wesley was saying that the scope of love extends beyond loving God and all human beings; it also extends to "many of his creatures." We are "to love many of his creatures in the strictest sense—to delight in them, to enjoy them," and to "earnestly desire all happiness to all."[170] *It entails applying "Do unto others as you would have them do unto you" just as much to animals as to people.* Wesley was convinced that everyone should learn this lesson at an early age, and that Christian parents should not allow their children

> to hurt, or give pain to anything that has life. They will not permit them to rob birds' nests, much less to kill anything without necessity; not even snakes, which are as innocent as worms, or toads, which, notwithstanding their ugliness, and the ill name they lie under, have been proved over and over to be as harmless as flies. Let them extend in its measure the rule of doing as they would be done by, to every animal whatsoever.[171]

So, the Golden Rule applies just as much between species as within the human species! The rule here would be, "*Do unto animals as you would have them do unto you.*" Each of us must work out the practical implications of this with fear and trembling! Applying the Golden Rule requires thought, imagination, perception, empathy, compassion, consolation, mirror neurons, and action. Do we regularly relate in those evaluative ways to non-human animals? Probably not, for we don't even relate regularly that way to most people!

Wesley himself was a vegetarian off and on for many years, but he advocated it only for prudential reasons, that is, for its health benefits, and we could definitely learn important lessons about eating for health from him. However, he did not insist upon it for others, did little to promote it on a wide scale, and did not explicitly affirm or practice it for moral or spiritual reasons. Yet, he could have done so on the grounds that God loves "every animal whatsoever" just as he loves all human beings, and because eating animals for food, when so many healthy vegetarian alternatives are available, is not compatible with doing unto animals as we would have them do unto us. Would we have them factory-farm us, raise us for food, or kill and eat us—preferably while still young and tender?

Our beastliness toward the beasts goes hand in hand with our inhumanity toward other human beings. Against non-human as well as human animals, most of us have greatly sinned.

Chapter Three

John Wesley's Extrinsic Values and Evaluations

Extrinsically valuable objects or entities are those things, processes, actions, and social roles and structures that exist in our public or common "external" sensory world of space and time. They are significant to us mainly because they are useful, because they serve us as means to ends or goals beyond themselves. According to our Hierarchy of Value, they are very good, but they are less good than intrinsic value-objects like God, people, and animals.

What were John Wesley's views on extrinsic values? Did he recognize that sensory/physical objects, processes, and human physical activities are useful in achieving desirable human and divine goals? Did he regard the things of the world as extrinsically good, as efficient means to desirable ends? If so, what kind of language did he use to say so? Did he regard extrinsic values as less good than other good things like people or animals? Did he actually discuss the value of physical things, processes, activities, and public social roles and orders; and, if so, how did he rank their worth in relation to God and individual human beings? Did he think that people sometimes overvalue or undervalue the good things of the world? Do people ever put otherwise good things to bad uses, or fail to recognize and use the good things available to them? These questions will be explored and answered in relation to Wesley's views on the nature and value of 1. the means of grace, 2. the world and worldliness, 3. human bodies and actions, 4. the goodness of human actions and good works, 5. worldliness and original sin, 6. worldly religion, and 7. respecting and loving worldly people.

The Extrinsic Value of the Means of Grace

As the preceding chapter showed, John Wesley definitely used the language of "own sake," "intrinsically good," "ends," and "means to ends," perhaps not as profusely or as accurately as he should have, but he was clearly acquainted with such theoretical concepts, and he did not apply them only to God. This chapter will concentrate on his understanding of *"means* to ends," that is, on what we are calling "extrinsic goods." Wesley never used the term "extrinsically good," but he dealt with all the relevant issues when discussing means to ends, as he often did.

According to Wesley, "Wisdom is the faculty of discerning the best ends, and the fittest means of attaining them,"[1] and he warned against "expecting the end without the means."[2] Of genuine religion, he wrote, "The end is, in one word, salvation: the means to attain it, faith."[3] He did not believe in magical solutions to ordinary human problems. He definitely recognized and employed the philosophical distinction between means and ends, (between what is here called extrinsic and intrinsic goods), in his discussion of the "means of grace." His treatment of this topic well illustrates the significance of *value combinations*. The physical means of grace *combined* with their proper spiritual ends have great significance, but considered alone, they have little or no worth, Wesley insisted. Expressed another way, extrinsic values considered alone have very little real value, but *combined* with systemic and intrinsic values and evaluations, they have great significance or worth. Yet, they are not always so combined in fruitful or positive ways.

Wesley effectively utilized the "means/ends" distinction in his sermon on "The Means of Grace." As he recognized, certain (extrinsic) means to (intrinsic) ends are highly valued in Christian belief and practice. He often and explicitly employed the concepts of "overvalue" and "undervalue." Some people, he thought, attach too much value to extrinsic physical means—they overvalue them; and some people attach too little value to them—they undervalue them. The trick is to get it just right, to steer a middle course—not too much, not too little, but just right! How did Wesley develop such themes?

First, he definitely affirmed that certain physical objects, processes, and activities have great Christian significance as means to ends beyond themselves—specifically, the traditional Christian "means of grace," understood as "any 'means' ordained of God as the usual channels of his grace."[4] We are now considering "means." "Grace" and "ends" are elsewhere considered. In his "The Means of Grace," Wesley identified three traditional "external" means of grace: prayer, searching the Scriptures, and receiving the sacrament of the Lord's Supper.[5] Elsewhere, he considered Baptism as another legitimate sacrament and means of grace. He also identified many other means of grace in addition to these two Protestant sacraments.

Wesley did not limit the means of grace to the two Protestant sacraments. All *works of piety* (devotional practices) and *works of mercy* (acts of love and mercy)[6] are means of grace. The "good works" involved in *works of mercy* include "feeding the hungry, clothing the naked, entertaining the stranger, visiting those that are in prison or sick, or variously afflicted,...endeavoring to instruct the ignorant, to awaken the stupid sinner, to quicken the lukewarm, to confirm the wavering, to comfort the feebleminded, to succor the tempted, or contribute in any manner to the saving of souls from death."[7] The works of mercy are the works of love, or what

Wesley called "the labours of love."[8] In addition to the Lord's Supper and Baptism, the *works of piety* include prayer, searching the Scriptures, meditating, and fasting as devotional means of grace.[9] What else? Roman Catholics recognize additional sacraments, e.g., marriage, confession, the last rites; why not think of these as reliable means of grace? Or what about good old Protestant preaching and hymn-singing? What about Sunday Services? What if we celebrate the Sabbath on Saturday instead of Sunday? The means of grace available to us may be far richer than we first imagine, though what works for some people might not work for others. None work inevitably or all of the time, for, as Wesley believed, there is no magic in them.

Wesley explicitly recognized that the means of grace exist "external" to consciousness, that is, in our common sensory world. He defined "means of grace," as "outward signs, words, or actions, ordained of God, and appointed for this end—to be the *ordinary* channels whereby He might convey to men, preventing, justifying, or sanctifying grace."[10] Such means, he said, are by definition "outward signs, words, or actions," which means that they exist in our common external sensory world. Of course, prayers and searching the Scriptures can be partly private and internal; but Wesley knew that in origin and often in practice, such works of piety are public, social, and external. They exist and are perceived in our common physical/social environment. He repeated the traditional definition of a "sacrament" as "an outward sign of inward *grace*, and a *means* whereby we receive the same."[11]

Words used in both inward private and external public prayers, and in searching the Scriptures, originate in social interactions and are communicated as sensory objects and processes. They are originally and primarily accessible to us through our external senses of hearing and sight. Prayers may be "in secret or with the great congregation;" "searching the Scriptures...implies reading, hearing, and meditating thereon;" and "receiving the Lord's Supper" involves "eating bread and drinking wine in remembrance of him."[12] Just as the Lord's Supper involves physical bread and wine (or Methodist grape juice), so Baptism involves physical water, all of which are external physical signs of and means to internal spiritual grace.

Third, these physical objects and processes are *valuable only as means* to ends and *not in themselves*, and Christians should value them only as means and never as ends. They have no inherent or intrinsic worth whatsoever. Apart from the ends they serve and with which they are fruitfully combined, they are virtually worthless. Wesley made that perfectly clear.

> But we allow that the whole value of the means depends on their actual subservience to the ends of religion; that, consequently all these means, when separated from the end, are less than nothing, and vanity; that if they do not actually conduce to the knowledge and love of God, they are not acceptable in his sight; yea, rather, they are an abomination before Him; a stink in His nostrils.[13]

> Remember also, to use all means *as means*; as ordained, not for their own sake, but in order to the renewal of your soul in righteousness and true holiness. If, therefore, they actually tend to this, well; but, if not, they are dung and dross.[14]

Thus, the two ends served by external extrinsic means of grace are: (1) the internal systemic value of knowing about God and (2) the internal intrinsic value of loving God. Such ends come about only within the inner consciousness or subjectivity of unique persons, whose souls are thereby enriched, renewed, and further sanctified. External extrinsic values should facilitate internal systemic and intrinsic transformations, values, and evaluations; otherwise they are but "dung and dross."

Wesley's two internal ends of the external means of grace need to be considered further. Consider first the *words* that are integral aspects of both prayers and religious knowledge. Words are extrinsic/systemic value combinations that originate in and for the sake of public social interactions. They are extrinsic physical sounds and marks, but they also have internal conscious conceptual or systemic meanings. They are more than mere sounds; they are symbols that convey meaningful thoughts and much more. If they meant nothing conceptually or systemically, they would be mere noises, smears, or blots. Normally, they do mean something conceptually within consciousness, so these extrinsic physical entities are imbued with systemic conceptual meanings. Words are extrinsic/systemic value combinations.

Think about the words, thoughts, and beliefs that accompany taking the bread and wine (or Methodist grape juice) in the Lord's Supper. Without those words and the concepts and beliefs that they convey, the bread and wine would be spiritually meaningless. They would be just bread and wine in very small quantities, nothing more. The accompanying words and beliefs give the bread and wine much more than a merely physical significance. They both convey systemic conceptual values and provoke an intrinsic "remembrance" of Christ. They help to make Christian intrinsic values and valuations possible and actual. They facilitate both drawing near to God in Christ and the communion of the saints. They communicate and convey God's grace to us.

Likewise, the words, thoughts, and beliefs that accompany Baptism imbue the water with more meaning than just "water." The water of Baptism is combined and thus imbued with deep conceptual or systemic spiritual meanings, and, like the other means of grace, it too may evoke profound intrinsic meanings and responses. Wesley said much the same thing about Baptism that he did about the Lord's Supper. He repeated his definition of "sacrament" but added the significant (for our purposes) word "visible," i.e., sensory. "Sacrament," he said, means "an outward and visible sign of an inward and spiritual grace;" and "The parts of a sacrament are two: the one, an outward and sensible sign; the other, an inward and spiritual grace."[15] With the *Larger Catechism*, he clearly distinguished the outer from the inner significance of this particular means of grace.

> What is the outward part or form in baptism? Water, wherein the person is baptized, "In the name of the Father, Son, and Holy Ghost". What is the inward part or thing

signified? A death unto sin, and a new birth into righteousness....For what can be more plain, than that the one is an external, the other an internal work? That the one is a visible, the other an invisible thing, and therefore wholly different from each other: the one being an act of man, purifying the body, the other a change wrought by God in the soul.[16]

The bread and wine in the Lord's Supper, like the water of Baptism, have greater value significance than as merely physical objects because they are imbued with conceptual spiritual meanings or beliefs. The means of grace have both extrinsic and systemic significance. When functioning as they should, they involve both physical elements and the knowledge of God and Christ. They further combine these extrinsic/systemic values with the love of God, the intrinsic evaluation of the Supreme Intrinsic Value-Object (who is also the Supreme Value-and-Valuing-Subject). Maybe they don't always work that way, but when they do, Wesley knew why: the Spirit of God is in them and in us. What a value combination that is! If God is not there in the means of grace, and if they do not help us to deepen our knowledge, awareness, and love of God, they are empty, pointless, futile, valueless, not worth the effort, mere dung and dross. Sometimes we just "go through the motions," or "the formalities," but at other times, we find God and the communion of the saints in the means of grace. Here is how Wesley explained this.

> We allow likewise that all outward means whatever, if separate from the Spirit of God, cannot profit at all, cannot conduce in any degree either to the knowledge or love of God. Without controversy, the help that is done upon earth, he doeth it himself. It is he alone who, by his own almighty power, worketh in us what is pleasing in his sight. And all outward things, unless he work in them and by them, are mere weak and beggarly elements.[17]

Overvaluing, Undervaluing, and Rightly Valuing the Means of Grace

Wesley clearly understood that some people overvalue the means of grace, some people undervalue them, and some people rightly value them.

People who *overvalue* them assume that the means of grace work like magic, with a mysterious inherent power of their own; but, said Wesley, "Whosoever therefore imagines there is any intrinsic *power* in any means whatsoever does greatly err, not knowing the Scriptures, neither the power of God."[18] The means of grace have no inherent magical or mystical power; their real power is only through the presence of God, not in themselves. For God's presence within them, we simply have to wait; but God has ordained the ways in which we should wait.

People who overvalue the means of grace may mistakenly use them as a form of "works righteousness" to try to *earn* their own salvation, instead of *graciously receiving salvation* as God's unconditional gift. Overvaluers "abuse the means of grace" and "rest content with the form of godliness, without the power." Without either the knowledge or the love of God, they assume that merely using the means of grace will make them Christians, "idly dreaming (though perhaps hardly conscious thereof) either that there is some kind of *power* therein whereby sooner or later (they know not when) they shall certainly be made holy; or that there is a sort of *merit* in using them, which will surely move God to give them holiness or accept them without it."[19]

Wesley rejected both the magic and the merit that others claimed for the Lord's Supper. He denied that mere participation in this external sacrament automatically and magically makes us better Christians and confers inward spiritual growth, and he denied that it earns merit for the participants. He also rejected the magic in the Roman Catholic theory of transubstantiation, according to which the bread and wine of the Eucharist literally become real flesh and blood, even though they continue to look, feel, smell, and taste just like bread and wine. "This is my body" is one of many biblical expressions that cannot be taken literally, Wesley thought. He would agree with our adage that "If it looks, acts, and quacks like a duck, it really is a duck." Wesley said that the bread and the wine of the Lord's Supper are not literally turned into his flesh and blood when consecrated by a priest or minister; they are only

> "tokens," "signs," or symbols "of the body and blood of Christ."
>
> Scripture and antiquity then are flatly against transubstantiation. And so are our very senses. Now our Lord himself appealed to the senses of his disciples: "Handle me and see; for a spirit hath not flesh and bones, as ye see me have." (Luke xxiv. 39.) Take away the testimony of our senses, and there is no discerning of a body from a spirit. But if we believe transubstantiation we take away the testimony of all our senses.[20]

External means of grace do not work or involve any kind of magic. If we just "go through the motions" when our "heart is not in it," participation in them will not do us any good. They are extrinsic means to intrinsic enrichment, but external elements and symbols as such should not be confused or simply identified with inward moral and spiritual graces.

Of the two aspects of Baptism, the outward water and the inward new birth, Wesley says, "Many indeed seem to imagine that they are just the same."[21] However, such people clearly overvalue the external sign and attribute magical powers and intrinsic properties to it that it does not possess. He recognized that many very bad people have been baptized,[22] so a new spiritual birth "does not always accompany baptism," and "There may sometimes be the outward sign where there is not the inward grace."[23]

Undervaluers make the opposite mistake. They assume that the sacraments and other means of grace do not work at all, that there is no point in participating in such vain and empty formalities, that having faith alone is totally sufficient, and nothing else is required. Christian quietists and antinomanians see the sacraments, and all works of piety and mercy, as merely futile instances of works righteousness.

We simply have to have faith and be still and wait for God to be with us, but we should *do nothing* to try to bring this about or in response to it, they claim. Wesley asked them, "But how shall we wait?" and responded that we should wait by using the means of grace! "If God Himself has appointed a way, can you find a better way of waiting for him?"[24]

Did Wesley himself undervalue the means of grace? After all, he denied that any of them have magical potency or *"intrinsic* power,"[25] and he said that the inner spiritual benefits or graces are quite distinct from the outward means. In themselves, the bread, wine, and water really are just bread, wine, and water. He also said that there is nothing inherently special about any of God's own ordained means of grace, for God could have turned anything into a means of grace, and God can give grace without using any external means at all. He wrote, "We know likewise that he is able to give the same grace, though there were no means on the face of the earth. In this sense, we may affirm that with regard to God, there is no such thing as means, seeing he is equally able to work whatsoever pleaseth him by any or by none at all."[26]

Wesley did his best to steer a middle course between those who overvalue and those who undervalue the means of grace. In doing this, he explicitly used the terminology of "overvalue" and "undervalue," as he did in discussing several other issues. He would have said of *all* means of grace what he said about *fasting* as a means of grace.

> How some have exalted this beyond all Scripture and reason! And others utterly disregarding it, as it were revenging themselves by undervaluing as much as the former had overvalued it! Those have spoken of it as if it were all in all; if not the end itself, yet infallibly connected with it; these as if it were just nothing, as if it were a fruitless labour which had no relation at all thereto. Whereas it is certain the truth lies between them both. It is not all; nor yet is it nothing. It is not the end; but it is a precious means thereto; a means which God himself has ordained, and in which therefore, when it is duly used, he will surely give us his blessing.[27]

What was Wesley's middle way between these extremes? He regarded all means of grace as historically contingent and conventional; they could have been otherwise. Nevertheless, God did in fact ordain these conventions as generally effective external signs and processes in and through which Christians regularly, though not inevitably, can find God's presence and graces. Such means can be rightly valued. They are symbols or tokens of grace, but more than that, they are means to grace ordained of God, who promised to be present in them. Thus, the Christian "continues in God's way—in hearing, reading, meditating, praying, and partaking of the Lord's Supper—till God, in the manner that pleases Him, speaks to his heart, 'Thy faith hath saved thee. Go in peace.'"[28] "God *can* give the end without any means at all; but you have no reason to think He *will*," Wesley warned; "Therefore constantly and carefully use all those means which he has appointed to be the ordinary channels of His grace. Use every means which either reason or Scripture recommends."[29]

With respect to God's ordinances, we should avoid "mistaking the means for the end;"[30] but we should also not avoid or neglect the means for the end. As indicated already, Wesley said, "Wisdom is the faculty of discerning the best ends, and the fittest means of attaining them,"[31] and we should not expect to "obtain the end without using the means."[32] Wesley did not *insist* upon any particular external means of grace, only upon their internal fruits of the spirit such as the knowledge and love of God and of "all mankind." In his great sermon on the "Catholic Spirit" he explained,

> I do not mean, 'Embrace my modes of worship'; or 'I will embrace yours.' This also is a thing which does not depend either on your choice or mine. We must both act as each is fully persuaded in his own mind. Hold you fast that which you believe is most acceptable to God, and I will do the same. I believe the episcopal form of church government to be scriptural and apostolic. If you think the presbyterian or independent is better, think so still, and act accordingly. I believe infants ought to be baptized, and that this may be done either by dipping or sprinkling. If you are otherwise persuaded, be so still, and follow your own persuasion. It appears to me that forms of prayer are of excellent use, particularly in the great congregation. If you judge extemporary prayer to be of more use, act suitable to your own judgment. My sentiment is that I ought not to forbid water wherein persons may be baptized, and that I ought to eat bread and drink wine as a memorial of my dying Master. However, if you are not convinced of this, act according to the light you have. I have no desire to dispute with you one moment upon any of the preceding heads. Let all these smaller points stand aside. Let them never come into sight, 'If thine heart is as my heart', if thou lovest God and all mankind, I ask no more: 'Give me thine hand.'[33]

The crucial thing is that all external and extrinsic means of grace move us toward inner holy faith that worketh through love, toward the intrinsic evaluation of God and "all mankind." Wesley asked no more. His view of the Lord's Supper as truly a means, but only a means, to this end is very different from the conclusion to which Jonathan Edwards eventually came (the one that got him fired from his church in Northampton), according to which the Lord's Supper is only a token or symbol of divine election and an exclusive privilege of the elect. Both Wesley and Jonathan's deceased grandfather, Solomon Stoddard, would have disagree with him about this. Both saw this sacrament as God's means of grace, not as the elect's exclusive privilege.

Valuing and Overvaluing the Things of the World

Extrinsically good things are valuable to us as means to ends beyond themselves. They include the aforementioned "means of grace," but they extend far beyond that. They are all the physical objects, processes, activities, social structures, and social roles in our common world. They belong to that domain of natural reality encountered through the "five external senses" functioning normally. We will call them "things" for short, even though "things" can be used much more broadly to cover anything and everything, whether physical and sensory, or spiritual and super-sensory. Briefly said, extrinsic goods are all the actually or potentially useful things in our common-sensory world of space and time. They constitute the natural world, and they include our bodies and behaviors as parts of that world.

We become acquainted with the extrinsically good or useful things that exist in ordinary space and time through our normally functioning "five external senses." As Wesley said of the elements in the sacraments, they are "external" and "visible." They are also accessible to all of our senses. Most of the problems that human beings and non-human animals have to solve and resolve, especially early in life, are practical problems of survival, so we are early and naturally oriented primarily toward the external sensory world, toward sensory objects, processes, happenings, and activities. Our very survival depends heavily on our ability to cope with and utilize our bodies to make the best of our natural sensory environment. Before we become social and spiritual beings who can cope with social and spiritual issues, we are first physical beings who must cope with physical survival and, at an appropriate age, with physical reproduction. Wesley did not undervalue physical necessities. Nor did he overvalue physical luxuries. He recognized that when ministering to others, we must often deal first with their basic material needs; only after that can and should we move on to their moral and spiritual needs. Of course, this temporal priority does not signify valuational priority.[34] For a modern version of this, consider Abraham Maslow's "hierarchy of needs."[35]

Every physical or material object, structure, or process is actually or potentially useful, either separately or in combination with other things. We are born *to* value and *with* values from "day one," and most people are initially and primarily oriented psychologically toward extrinsic goodness, that is, toward the attractions of the sensory world; thus by degrees they largely lack inwardness, self-knowledge, and knowledge of God.[36] Most people make few advances beyond that, Wesley thought, and then only by prevenient, saving, and sanctifying grace. Very early in life our inanimate environment, our own animate bodies, and the bodies of our caregivers command our attention. In due time, our capacities and needs for systemic and intrinsic values and evaluations kick in. The concept "extrinsically good" embraces the whole physical world of "external nature" and all its contents. In addition to our environment, it also includes our own living bodies, the bodies of other people, those of non-human animals, and the actions and social roles that are played out bodily. These actions can be moral, spiritual, or indifferent, as well as their opposites.

Some objects, processes, and activities are "extrinsically bad" and "useful" only as intentionally harmful, only as extrinsic evils, so we must also take that into account. Physical things and processes like knives, guns, cars, and mansions can be beneficial in some contexts and hurtful in others, depending on the uses to which they are put. Things put to good use are extrinsic goods; they serve as means to desirable ends. Things put to bad use are extrinsic bads or evils; they serve as means to undesirable ends, even though wicked people may desire and choose them, and some of them are more efficient for wrongdoing than others. Purely natural processes, diseases, injuries, or catastrophes can also be small or great extrinsic evils.

Animated human bodies, activities, and social roles will receive special attention later, but for now let's concentrate on the extrinsic goodness of inanimate physical objects and processes. For the most part, inanimate extrinsic values are just the "good things of the world." When theologians discuss them, they usually do so in terms of the "things of the world," "worldly prosperity," or "temporal goods." Whether physical objects and processes are extrinsically good or bad depends on how they affect us or others. Some help, some hurt. Some are within our control, some not. We like to be in control. Excessively unbalanced intellectual, dogmatic, impractical, ascetic, or "other-worldly" people may undervalue the things of the world, but most of us do not, and Wesley did not. Typically, we attach far too much value to the good things of the world. Some people may be lost or totally absorbed in worldly goods; others are just lost within the world, but lost all the same.

The Good Things of the World

Wesley clearly recognized immense goodness in the physical world, its objects, and its processes. To begin at "the beginning," he wholly agreed with the first chapter of Genesis (as he understood it) that God created a good world out of nothing, that it was good even before people were created, and it was "very good" afterwards.[37] Its goodness today consists largely in its usefulness to people and to the animals that were created even before people.[38] Wesley also recognized that the good things of the world are sensory objects, processes, and activities, saying, "Now this the great advantage that the good things of this world have: they are obvious to our senses; we see them; we hear them; we smell them; we taste them, we feel and handle them..."[39]

Wesley conceived of the physical world as "matter," understood in the Newtonian way as inherently inert and moved only by external forces like Newton's gravity or some subtle material ether, both equally invisible and equally reducible to God's activity, so Wesley thought. All the four elements (earth, air, fire and water), were inert, even fire, for "fire itself is moved by the almighty Spirit, the source of all the motion in the universe."[40] To this day, invisible and imperceptible gravity may be empirically indistinguishable from God's activity, though no one has the courage to say so. Wesley had and expressed serious doubts about Newton's gravity,[41] insisting that "it is the finger of God, and here our knowledge ends." Perhaps he did not know that Newton also eventually came to the view that gravity is identical with the exercise of God's power. Newton was as much interested in theology as in physics, as his prolific writings reveal. He identified gravity with God's omnipresent activity, saying that it "is not absolute in itself, but is as it were an emanative effect of God."[42] Wesley would have agreed with this.[43] According to Wesley, God is "the only Agent in the material world; all matter being essentially dull and inactive, and moving only as it is moved by the finger of God."[44] Wesley and Newton did not understand that matter and energy (activity) are convertible, though *we* know that, thanks to Albert Einstein. With mainstream Christianity, Wesley explicitly repudiated Manicheanism,[45] according to which matter is inherently bad. He believed that God created a good world originally, matter and all, bodies and all, and "every distinct part of the universe was good."[46]

Wesley's assessment of the goodness of the natural world was tied to a cosmology, chemistry, biology, and anthropology that we cannot accept today—as well expressed in his sermon on "God's Approbation of His Works," summarized in the next paragraph. But this makes no real difference with respect to the goodness, usefulness, or extrinsic value of physical objects and processes. Their utility is not tied logically or in any other way to the perfection of original creation or to any of Wesley's outmoded cosmological or scientific views. Of course, Wesley appealed to the very best science or "natural philosophy" of his day, and we should do the same.

Wesley's now antiquated cosmology knew nothing of the Big Bang[47] or of the vast age of the universe (about 13.7 billion years, by current estimates) as understood today. God literally created the world out of nothing in six days, he thought, and this happened around 4,000 years ago[48] (Sir Isaac Newton's estimate), or maybe 6,000 years ago[49] (Bishop James Ussher's calculation). Yet, Wesley's young cosmos was definitely not the small, simple, three-storied universe with no planets orbiting the sun of Genesis and the rest of the Bible; it was the comparatively vast and complicated universe in motion of Copernicus and Newton.[50]

To his credit, Wesley made use of the very best science of his day, but that science is not good enough for us. Wesley's chemistry, that of the Greek Philosopher Empedocles, knew nothing of the many chemical elements recognized today; its only four elements were earth, air, fire, and water, each composed of smaller and more "primitive" atoms.[51] Albert Outler claims that Wesley eventually came to recognize electricity or "electric fire" as a fifth element.[52] The atoms of all the elements were created in the finite past with the world, but, since Wesley accepted the principle of the conservation of matter (or energy, we would say), he thought that we have no reason to believe that any of them can be "annihilated" and that they will not exist infinitely into the future.[53] He knew nothing of "splitting atoms," thereby destroying them while converting them to energy or into smaller sub-atomic particles or waves.

Wesley's biology was creationist and pre-Darwinian. He assumed that all species were created separately and distinctly during the original six days of creation—four to six thousand years ago. He also assumed that all animals originally existed in perfect harmony in a world without any natural danger or physical or social conflict, struggle, natural selection, predation, death, suffering, or disease. Wesley castigated those "minute philosophers" who survey the evils of nature and say "that the world is now in the same state it was at the beginning"[54] with respect to struggle, death, disease, and natural catastrophes. Yet, the "minute philosophers" were right. The whole creation has *always* "been groaning in travail," as St. Paul put it (Romans 8:22), though Wesley thought that this obtained only after the Fall.

Today we know that struggles, conflicts, diseases, deaths, and natural perils and catastrophes have existed as long as life itself. That is the way the natural world has always been for millions of years, so we cannot blame biological or physical evils on Adam and Eve. The "paradisiacal earth"[55] postulated by Wesley never existed. Natural evils, pains, vile affections, self-centeredness, and death did not originate with Adam's sin. Natural dangers, the struggle for survival, and natural selection, balanced by many kinds and degrees of cooperation, are as old as life itself. Wesley's idyllic biblical anthropology of Adam and Eve is radically incompatible with what *we* know of early life and humanoid species, including our own hunter-gatherer *homo sapiens* ancestors. Today, even *Christianity Today* acknowledges this![56] Wesley said that we should not take the Bible literally when "it implies an absurdity,"[57] as later explained in more detail. Well, Wesley's literalistic theological anthropology and six days creationist cosmology are indeed absurdities. Still, he well understood the great extrinsic value of the physical world, and his obsolete anthropology and cosmology do not distract at all from that.

In interpreting the first Chapter of Genesis, Wesley made an illogical leap from "good" to "perfect." The two concepts may be related, but they are not identical. Today we cannot equate the original goodness of creation with its original perfection, which never was. We must conceive of the goodness of the sensory world from the beginning as being like its present goodness, that is, as extrinsic goodness, the goodness of possible or actual usefulness, not the goodness of paradise, where usefulness was unabated.

So, how should Christians today value the sensory world? Wesley himself definitely conceived of the *present goodness* of the world in terms of *its usefulness, its extrinsic worth*. He advised, "Only *use* the world, but *enjoy* God."[58] In "Upon Our Lord's Sermon on the Mount, VIII," he asked what Jesus prohibited in forbidding us to "lay up treasures on earth." He answered, first, that Jesus did not forbid us to pay others the debts that we owe them. More important for our purposes were his additional points.

> Neither, secondly, does he here forbid the providing for ourselves such things as are needful for the body; a sufficiency of plain, wholesome food to eat, and clean raiment to put on. Yea, it is our duty, so far as God puts it into our power, to provide these things also; to the end that we may 'eat our own bread,' and be 'burdensome to no man'.
>
> Nor yet are we forbidden, thirdly, to provide for our children and for those of our own household. This also it is our duty to do, even upon principles of heathen morality. Every man ought to provide the plain necessaries of life both for his own wife and children, and to put them into a capacity of providing these for themselves, when he is gone and hence is no more seen. I say, of providing *these*, the plain necessaries of life—not delicacies, not superfluities—and that by their *diligent*

labour; for it is no man's duty to furnish them, any more than by himself, with the means either of luxury or idleness.

Lastly, we are not forbidden in these words to lay up, from time to time what is needful for carrying on our worldly business in such a measure and degree as is sufficient to answer the foregoing purposes.[59]

Money is the paradigm example of a physical thing that is useful as a means for getting other things that we want and need. At least, it was once primarily physical—before the days when computers and electronics turned it into something almost purely systemic. Even then it was always combined with systemic numbering. Today's electronic symbols and numbers for money still stand for physical resources that can be used for other purposes. As Wesley knew, only misers love money for its own sake, and perhaps then only as a direct source of or means to the pleasure they get from acquiring, possessing, counting, and fingering it.[60] Most of us value money for what we can buy with it, for its usefulness, for "all that may be purchased thereby, such as ease, honour, and sensual pleasure,"[61] but misers just directly enjoy having, counting, and keeping it. Wesley defined "lovers of money" as "those that *delight in money*, those that take pleasure in it, those that seek their happiness therein, that brood over their gold and silver, bills or bonds."[62]

Wesley was not against money. Not money itself, he said, but *the love* of money, is "the root of all evil" (though not literally of *all* evil, he conceded).[63] Money itself "is an excellent gift of God, answering the noblest ends."[64] In "The Use of Money," Wesley gave three rules for "the right use of money." First, "Gain all you can" through "honest industry" and by "using in your business all the understanding which God has given you," but without harming your own or anyone else's mind, body, or soul.[65] Second, "Save all you can." This means, don't live for costly and foolish desires and pleasures. Don't live wastefully and extravagantly. Don't try to impress people with your wealth. (We would call this "conspicuous consumption.") And don't try to leave a large inheritance for your children.[66] Third, Wesley advised, "Give all you can," as a faithful and sacrificing steward of all that God has given to you.

Christian giving requires material resources, especially money. Helping others presupposes the availability of extrinsic resources. Doing works of mercy and love usually requires money or the physical resources and services that money can buy. Wesley insisted that extravagant living, costly clothes, wastefulness, and all of the above perversions of money can definitely interfere with giving all we can. He would doubtless regard our present "high standard of living," today's "materialism," as incredibly extravagant! The trick is to value the things of the world properly without overvaluing them, to value them for their extrinsic goodness without valuing them idolatrously, or as if they were valuable for their own sake, and without valuing them *above all else*.

Before we consider overvaluing the world, let's ask why intrinsically good realities like people and God are better than, have more value than, mere "things." It is because intrinsically valuable conscious beings have more and qualitatively different good-making properties than extrinsically good but non-conscious things like sensory objects and processes. Both quantitatively and qualitatively, animals, people, and God have more and different good-making qualities than material things. Wesley's understanding of universal human properties can explain this. As already noted, our God-like human properties (below) are intrinsic-good-making qualities, without being intrinsically good "in isolation" or "in and by themselves" apart from us.

1. People and God have or are immaterial souls or spirits, and not mere things.
2. People and God have self-motion, that is, they are self-starting, but not merely inanimate things.
3. People and God have will, that is, desires, feelings, affections, emotions, capacities for pleasure and pain; things don't.
4. People and God have reason or understanding, the desire and ability to inquire and know; things don't.
5. People and God have liberty (free choice), a capacity for making or originating our own choices; things don't.
6. People and God have imagination; things don't.
7. People and God have memories; things don't.
8. People have sentience, five "external senses." Wesley apparently accepted Newton's suggestion that God has space itself as the "divine sensorium."[67] But mere things sense nothing.
9. People and God have consciousness (inner awareness) and self-consciousness (inner awareness of themselves); things do not.
10. People and God have conscience, an "internal compass" for discerning good and evil, right and wrong; but things do not.
11. People have general moral laws "written in their hearts" that reflect the moral mind of God; but mere things comply only with physical laws and cannot disobey them.
12. People have desirable moral and spiritual sensitivities, affections, dispositions, and virtues in varying degrees of activation or actualization, and God completely so; but mere things have no moral feelings, responses, or moral and spiritual virtues or sensitivities at all.
13. People have a "capacity for God;" mere things do not.

Extrinsically good things lack the good-making qualities of intrinsically good things. This may explain why devotion primarily to intrinsic objects is ultimately satisfying, whereas devotion primarily to extrinsic objects is not ultimately satisfying. Mere things have no intrinsic worth, and they cannot reciprocate our love to or our desires for them. God, people, and animals can. Loving the things of the world is always unrequited love. As profoundly social beings, we deeply need requited love, reciprocated love. All thirteen of the good things mentioned above are *good for* us, but they are not *intrinsically good*—in isolation from us or other conscious individuals. Most philosophers confuse "intrinsically good" with "good for." These things are good for us; they enrich our lives; but the buck stops with us.

Overvaluing Worldly Goods, and the Hierarchy of Value

Money is good; greed is not good. Money is good; the overvaluation of money (the love of money) is not good. As Wesley said, "'The love of money', we know, 'is the root of all evil;' but not the thing itself. The fault does not lie in the money, but in them that use it."[68] Like all extrinsically good or useful things, money can be misused and overvalued. It can also be properly valued. John Wesley and most other theologians call people who overvalue the things of the world "worldly." Yet, the world is good. Worldliness is not good, not because it values the things of the world, but because it overvalues them in relation to other good things like people and God. It ranks extrinsic goodness higher than intrinsic goodness. Wesley never said so, of course, but *hoarders* of *things* (as on today's TV shows) as well as of *money* (misers) carry the intrinsic evaluation of extrinsic value objects to ridiculous extremes!

Worldliness is a relatively enduring evaluative orientation, a sinful disposition of the soul. Specifically, *worldliness is the disposition to value the extrinsic things of the world more than systemic realities like thoughts and beliefs* (which isn't necessarily bad) *and more than intrinsic realities like people, animals, and God* (which is always bad). All sinful people have this idolatrous tendency, but in worldly people it is pronounced and enduring. Sinfulness is a persisting state of the soul that most values non-divine things; it is not a single act or set of acts. Worldliness is the most common manifestation of enduring sinfulness. It is the mind-set of those who strive to gain the world but thereby lose their souls.[69]

The axiological hierarchy of value says that intrinsic values, i.e., unique conscious beings like animals, people, and God, are more valuable than extrinsic values, i.e., useful physical sensory objects, processes, and actions.[70] Now we know why this is so. Worldly people get it backwards. To them physical objects and process are more valuable than animals, people, and God. Spiritually viewed, loving things as if they were God is sheer idolatry; and the worldly man or woman, Wesley said, "loves, that is, worships, the world."[71] Anything other than God that any people love with all their heart, soul, mind and strength is an idol.[72] Worldliness involves more than occasional thing-affirming acts; it is a powerful and enduring bent or disposition to sin in very specific immoral and idolatrous ways. Worldly people value extrinsically good but mindless things in the way in which they should value intrinsically good conscious realities; and they value intrinsically good conscious realities as if they were only mindless extrinsic goods. They love things; they use people; but they should love people and use things. They value things as if they were people and people as if they were mere things. They are axiological materialists, and this makes them both immoral and idolatrous. Christianity is an affront to the world because it overturns the value priorities of worldliness. Instead of loving the things of the world most of all and merely using people and God, the saints consistently love people and God most of all and merely use things. This is one thing that makes them saintly.

Intrinsic evaluation takes many forms such as love, empathy, compassion, consolation, intimacy, concentration, and identification-with. We can love good things belonging to all three value dimensions. Sometimes we love in perverted or inordinate ways. We can love people and God most, as do the saints; we can love ideas most, as do ideologists, dogmatists, and many intellectuals; or we can love the things of the world most, as do men and women of the world. According to Wesley,

> We think of what we love; but we do not love God; therefore, we think not of him. Or if we are now and then constrained to think of him for a time...we drive [such thoughts] out as soon as we can, and return to what we love to think of. So that the world, and the things of the world—what we shall eat, what we shall drink, what we shall put on; what we shall see, what we shall hear, what we shall gain; how we shall please our senses or our imagination—takes up all our time, and engrosses all our thoughts. So long, therefore as we love the world, that is so long as we are in our natural state, all our thoughts, from morning to evening, and from evening to morning, are no other than wandering thoughts.[73]

The scripts that we run through our minds most regularly are clues as to what we love most, and we naturally or typically think most about the things of the world. Worldliness is our "natural state," Wesley proclaimed. Not money, but the love of money, is the root of great evils. Not the world, but the love of the world, is the root of most exceedingly great moral evils. Worldly people love, thus idolize, material possessions, sensual processes, and social dominance with all their heart, soul, mind, and strength. They are ultimately concerned about and think most about the mindless or soulless things of the world, not about mindful, conscious, and ensouled animals, people, and God. They subordinate and sacrifice God, people, and animals to their selfish materialism and sensuality. They seek pleasure and happiness primarily from owning, controlling, and experiencing sensory objects and processes. They use people, that is, try to manipulate and control them, in order to get what they value most—merely mindless things. The greatest moral atrocities in human history spring from extrinsic worldliness, with systemic ideology not far behind. No real people are totally worldly all of the time, thanks to prevenient grace, but many if not most people live for the world, not for souls or God, most of the time.

Wesley had a great deal to say about worldliness, mostly negative. As he observed, "This is the sum of worldly happiness—to dress, and visit, and talk, and eat, and drink, and rise up to play."[74] Wesley advised his hearers, "Examine yourselves," to find "the ruling principle in your soul." "Is it," he asked, "the love of God? Is it the fear of God? Or is it neither one nor the other? Is it not rather the love of the world? the love of pleasure, or gain? of ease, or reputation? If so,... you are but a heathen still."[75]

Several quotes will illustrate Wesley's understanding of worldliness. This theme occurred over and over again in his sermons and writings. Consider his description of it in "Upon Our Lord's Sermon on the Mount, IX," where the issue was: What is involved in "serving mammon" or wealth?

> And, first, it implies, the *trusting* in riches, in money, or the things purchasable thereby, as our strength, the means whereby we shall perform whatever cause we have in hand; the trusting in them as our help, by which we look to be comforted in or delivered out of trouble.
>
> It implies, the trusting in the world for happiness; the supposing that 'a man's life consisteth (the comfort of his life) 'in the abundance of the things which he possesseth'; the looking for rest in the things that are seen; for content, in outward plenty; the expecting that satisfaction in the things of the world which can never be found out of God.
>
> And if we do this, we cannot but make the world our end; the ultimate end if not of all, at least of many, of our undertakings, many of our actions and designs—in which we shall aim only at an increase of wealth; at the obtaining pleasure or praise; at the gaining in larger measure of temporal things, without any reference to things eternal.
>
> The serving mammon implies, secondly, loving the world; desiring it for its own sake; the placing our joy in the things thereof, and setting our hearts upon them; the seeking (what indeed it is impossible we should find) our happiness therein; the resting with the whole weight of our souls upon the staff of this broken reed, although daily experience shows it cannot support, but will only 'enter into our hand and pierce it.'
>
> To resemble, to be conformed to the world, is a third thing we are to understand by 'serving mammon'; to have not only designs, but desires, tempers, affections, suitable to those of the world; to be of an earthy, sensual mind, chained down to the things of the earth; to be self-willed, inordinate lovers of our selves; to think highly of our own attainments; to desire and delight in the praise of men; to fear, shun, and abhor reproach; to be impatient of reproof, easy to be provoked, and swift to return evil for evil.
>
> To serve mammon is, lastly, to obey the world, by outwardly conforming to its maxims and customs; to walk as other men walk, in the common road, in the broad, smooth, beaten path; to be in the fashion; to follow a multitude; to do like the rest of our neighbors; that is, to do the will of the flesh and the mind, to gratify our appetites and inclinations—to sacrifice to ourselves, to aim at our own ease and pleasure in the general course of both our words and actions.
>
> Now, what can be more undeniably clear than that we 'cannot' thus 'serve God and mammon'?[76]

Agreeing with his brother, Charles,[77] John Wesley taught that worldly people are very insensitive and confused, *almost asleep* morally and spiritually, and they need to wake up. Expressed axiologically, they do not value extrinsically good things extrinsically, that is, as mere means to ends; instead they value them intrinsically as ends in themselves or for their own sake. They are totally absorbed, thus lost, in the things of the world; they identify with *things* so closely that they make up most of their personal identity. As Wesley said above, worldliness involves "loving the world; desiring it for its own sake."

Worldly men and women tend to confuse valuing good things intrinsically as ends in themselves or for their own sake, with valuing them extrinsically as mere means to their own largely selfish and short-sighted pleasures. For them, valuing sensory objects and processes as means to worldly happiness and pleasure is the same as valuing them for their own sakes. They may not be good at making conceptual distinctions. Pleasures are inner realities, but worldly people are hardly aware that enjoyment is something inner and subjective, so bound are they to objective or sensory externals. They do not distinguish between loving the external world "for its own sake" and seeking their own inner happiness in worldly ways. Wesley well understood that some people confuse loving sensory things "as a means to or source of pleasure" with loving them "for their own sake." He said that "gaining the world" means "to gain all the pleasures which the world can give."[78] Confused and externally oriented worldly people collapse external means (sensory objects and processes) into internal ends (pleasant feelings) and fail to distinguish between insentient external things and agreeable conscious internal feelings. They may not be aware of it, but worldly people tend to be practical or practicing hedonists with a fixation on "low pleasures." Wesley used this term[79] but he did not explicitly use its familiar counterpart, "higher pleasures." However, he did speak of "nobler enjoyments,"[80] which amounts to the same thing. Wesley never condemned the positive evaluation of pleasure or of the things of the world. He only condemned their overvaluation and idolization when they "uncenter" us from God and our neighbors.

As for the positive value of *things*, with the New Testament, Wesley affirmed the value of "the body," e.g., the resurrection of the body, but he rejected the values of "the flesh" as supreme human values and as adequate sources of true happiness. In the New Testament, "body" and "flesh" sometimes mean the same thing, as when we are told that the "logos" became "flesh" and dwelled among us; but often these words have very different meanings. Wesley well understood this and explained that when St. John speaks of "the desire of the flesh," this expression refers not to just one of the senses but "to all of the outward senses. It means the seeking happiness in the gratification of any or all of the external senses; although more particularly of the three lower senses, tasting, smelling and feeling [touch]."[81] Worldly people tend to identify and confuse inner pleasures with external things, and their primary values are the extrinsic goods of "the external senses."

Make no mistake, Wesley vigorously defended the importance of human happiness, but he did not identify it or its sources with sensory pleasures, and he did not confuse the internal with the external. Christians are happy and joyful people,[82] Wesley repeatedly affirmed, but they find their happiness primarily in loving God and their neighbors rather than in loving the things of the world.

Did Wesley subscribe to a hedonistic understanding of "happiness" as consisting by definition of "the most pleasure and the least pain possible over time"? John Locke understood "good" to mean: that which increases pleasure or decreases pain, the "that which" being the means, and hedonic happiness being the end. Or did Wesley subscribe to an eudaimonistic or pluralistic understanding of "happiness" as a more inclusive kind of "well-being," made up partly of pleasure, joy, and delight *along with many other* desirable internal and external qualities and relations? The case for Wesley as a non-hedonistic eudaimonist will be made later. For now, note that one of his definitions of "good" centers on "happiness" but also includes "peace" and "goodwill among men."[83]

Without being a hedonist, *Wesley did not hesitate to meet hedonists on their own grounds*. He affirmed the "nobler enjoyments" of morality and religion, and he spoke of "the pleasure of loving" as an enjoyment that does not spring from self-love.[84] We can and should take pleasure in God: "One design you are to pursue to the end of time—the enjoyment of God in time and eternity."[85] *Wesley argued that the "nobler enjoyments" of the moral and spiritual life are more pleasant than the sensory pleasures of the worldly life, and that the worldly pursuit of pleasure is riddled with frustration and pain.* This warrants more careful consideration.

Pursuing Pleasure

As noted, extrinsic values are means to ends beyond themselves. Primarily, they are the sensory objects, processes, actions, and social structures, classes, and roles of the world. The things of the world are useful in many ways. They have survival value, and they are enjoyable; they are external means to inner pleasures. They can also be means of grace and/or works and objects of piety, mercy, and love. They can be experienced as purely secular entities, but they can also manifest the presence of God.

Wesley affirmed and never denied the goodness of pleasure as such. He wrote that "We no more affirm pleasure in general to be unlawful than eating and drinking."[86] But, he thought, most people go about pursuing pleasure/happiness in the wrong way; worldly people live mainly to experience the world and its pleasures. They do not live to enjoy or be enriched spiritually by grace, piety, mercy, and love for conscious creatures or for God. To this theme he gave much attention. He divided the pursuit of worldly pleasures into three groups, *pleasures of sense* ("the desires of the flesh"), *pleasures of the imagination* ("the desire of the eye"), and *pleasures of social class or status* ("the pride of life").[87] Our sensual appetites (e.g., hunger and thirst) are gratified immediately by the presence of their objects (food and drink), and worldly people live mainly for such sensual gratification. Even when sense objects are not immediately present to us, they can be there in our imaginations, which are titillated especially by "grand, or new, or beautiful objects, whether of nature or art,"[88] including "pretty or elegant apparel, or furniture," or "new clothes, or books, or... pictures, or gardens."[89] In our time, their word for such things is "amazing."

Wesley did not think in terms of "social status," as do modern sociologists and anthropologists, who say that people with high social status usually have much greater access to physical resources and sensory pleasures than persons with lower social or economic status. The prosperity-seeking and status-seeking aspects of worldliness are intimately related. Exalted social status, cherished by both rich and poor, is valuable largely for materialistic reasons. Wesley called high social status and glory the "pride of life." Its pleasures come from "reputation," "renown," "honor," "glory," and "praise"—all of which depend on the attitudes and opinions of others. Some people, he said, "applaud themselves for their love of applause!"[90] He defined "vanity" as "the love and desire of being admired and praised."[91] Worldly people live for possessions, wealth, and status, not merely because such things give pleasure and satisfy their basic appetites, but also because they think that others will applaud, admire, honor, and defer to them if they are prosperous and "high-class."

Wesley's most sustained objection to the pursuit of "low" worldly or sensual pleasures was that they are all fleeting, transient, disappointing, and ultimately unsatisfying. Enduring happiness, he argued, can be found only in what he called "the pleasures of religion," specifically, pleasures derived from "the love of God, and of all mankind," and from the more enduring joy, delight, comfort, peace, gratitude, and rejoicing that such love brings.[92] He regarded these pleasures as much more lasting and deeply satisfying. He called them "nobler enjoyments," nobler than sensory pleasures.[93] His considered advice was, "Singly aim at God...Pursue one thing: happiness in knowing, in loving, in serving God."[94]

Wesley insisted that the things of the world do not ultimately satisfy us and make us happy. "None of them bring happiness," and the world itself acknowledges with its commonplace, "No man upon earth is contented."[95] Said Wesley, "You cannot find your long-sought happiness in all the pleasures of the world...which may amuse, but cannot satisfy."[96] Only loving God with all our heart, soul, mind, and strength and loving our neighbors as ourselves can make us truly happy. In axiological terms, the intrinsic evaluation of intrinsic values (loving people, God, and animals), but not the intrinsic evaluation of extrinsic values (loving mere things), can make us truly happy. Nor can the intrinsic disvaluation of intrinsic values (despising or resenting others), or the extrinsic disvaluation of intrinsic values (misusing and exploiting others), or the systemic disvaluation of intrinsic values (constantly running negative thoughts or scripts about others through our minds) make us happy. Conscious individuals can love us back; mere things cannot. Conscious individuals can hate us back; mere things cannot. Mere things have no thoughts or feelings, no matter how intensely we feel for and think about them. Mere things cannot reciprocate; God and our neighbors can.

In truth, we are born with a great need for profound *social bonding*, something that goes much deeper than being admired by others or using others merely as means to our own selfish ends. We are by nature social animals, and our social needs go much deeper than the egoism of reciprocal altruism and self-interested social contracts. Worldlings realize that they depend on other people for many of they things that they want, so they may practice what today is called "reciprocal altruism." This is a fancy name for long-range egoism: "If you scratch my back, I'll scratch yours." Or, "I won't hurt you, if you won't hurt me." Even psychopaths and "social contract" philosophers comprehend that much morality! Reciprocal altruism is nothing more than "enlightened" or "long-range" egoism or selfishness. It only confirms the suspicions of theologians that most apparent unselfishness is really sinful selfishness in disguise. This "altruism" is really egoism! Its wording is very misleading. It is not Christian love, or even the natural unselfish altruism of innately social animals.

Wesley was definitely not against "the pursuit of happiness." He did not use that exact phrase, but he did write of "they that pursue happiness,"[97] and of "Pursuing happiness, but never overtaking it."[98] He was all for happiness, understood as composed of pleasures. He defined "happiness" in these words: "And, first, without love nothing can so profit us as to make our lives happy. By happiness I mean, not a slight, trilling pleasure, that perhaps begins and ends in the same hour; but such a state of well-being as contents the soul, and gives it a steady, lasting satisfaction."[99] He recognized that intellectual (systemic) types pursue "happiness in *learning*...whether it be in history, languages, poetry, or any branch of natural or experimental philosophy; yea, we must include the several kinds of learning, such as geometry, algebra, and metaphysics."[100] Most people, however, seek happiness in riches and worldly possessions and success rather than in intellectual delights. Wesley believed, though, that neither the intellectual nor the worldly roads to happiness would ever get us there; such pursuits of happiness will never overtake it; only the moral/spiritual way can succeed. Neither ideas nor things can love us back. As Wesley emphasized, "It is wisdom to aim at the best end by the best means. Now the best end which any creature can pursue is happiness in God. And the best end which a fallen creature can pursue is, the recovery of the favor and image of God."[101] But that image is love, not of the world for its own sake, not of the world for its pleasures, not of others merely for what they can do for us, but of God and everyone loved by God for God's own sake, to which must be added—and also for our neighbors' own sakes—so long as such loves are "subordinated to God." Worldly people and ideologists may be lovers, but they love the wrong objects— things that are not inherently satisfactory or satisfying, ephemeral things, mindless things that cannot reciprocate or love them back. Christians are happy people, but they find their happiness in loving God and people, not in loving things or intellectual abstractions.

Wesley's own explanation of why "sensory pleasures" cannot, but "religious pleasures" can make us happy is very powerful and insightful. Unlike sensory objects, the nobler pleasures inherent in moral and spiritual virtues, affections, and practices are *inherently satisfying, enjoyable, and abiding*. The moral/spiritual intrinsic bonding inherent and expressed in meekness, gentleness, patience, kindness, honesty, and love are integral and essential to "the truest happiness...the greatest happiness of which we are capable."[102] Wesley's position can be supported further: the qualitatively distinct pleasures associated with moral and spiritual virtues, affections, and practices are practically and logically unavailable to us apart from their "sources."[103] There are no such pleasures simply "as such." They are bound inextricably to their distinctive objects. Without those objects, we don't have and can't get them.

A moral and spiritual life is a happy life, but that does not mean that it contains no pain, suffering, or unhappiness. Christian happiness is not pure or unmitigated bliss; it is always mixed with pain and suffering. All suggestions to the contrary are misleading and naive. Christians do deny themselves and carry crosses.[104] Wesley defined "A cross," as "anything contrary to our will, anything displeasing to our nature."[105] For example, overcoming worldliness (sacrificing or dethroning worldly desires and pleasures, delaying gratification, controlling our passions) is contrary to our natural will; actually doing so may be very distressing, thus displeasing to our basic human nature, at least temporarily. Even the pleasures of compassion, of suffering with those who suffer, or what Wesley called "sympathizing sorrow," are mixed with pains of soul; but, he contended, they are still worth it! "These are 'tears that delight and sighs that waft to heaven.'"[106] Through the best and the worst of times, the Christian "has learned to be content, to be easy, thankful, joyful, happy."[107] Christians do carry crosses, bear one another's burdens, console one another, and suffer with those who suffer. Christians, like Christ, are also suffering servants; yet, even in that they find great and enduring happiness. The pleasures associated with compassion, love, gratitude, and other Christian virtues are very "noble" or high quality pleasures, and they are available to us in no other way.

Avoiding Pain

Hedonistically conceived, both avoiding pains and procuring pleasures are integral aspects of the pursuit of happiness. The higher or nobler pleasures of soul inherent in the moral and religious virtues and affections are profoundly fulfilling, Wesley argued. Correspondingly, the moral and religious vices of sinfulness are profoundly frustrating, and the worldly approach to happiness is largely miserable and self-defeating. These claims deserve more careful consideration.

Worldly people value and take pleasure in sensory objects and processes, but not in people or God, as their primary ends or goals in life. They usually regard and treat people as if they were mere things, and mere things as if they were real people. They do not respect and value other people as ends in themselves; instead, they abuse, exploit, and use others merely as means to their own selfish and sensory pleasures, prosperity, and social aggrandizement. Other people get the worst of it if they stand in the way, or if they are perceived as useless "nobodies." Indifference is the sinful vice of perceiving other souls as nobodies. Worldly vices range from indifference to envy, greed, pride, domination, exploitation, snobbery, anger, hatred, and revenge toward rivals for this world's goods. For such vices, worldly people expect, amazingly enough, to be admired, praised, and honored. Sometimes, they are! Worldly people do admire, respect, envy, and emulate other ruthless but successful worldly people. We often admire and imitate our oppressors!

Wesley also argued that the specific *vices or "vile affections"* that usually accompany the worldly pursuit of status and sensory objects, processes, and pleasures *are inherently miserable*. According to Wesley, "All unholy tempers are unhappy tempers. Ambition, covetousness, vanity, inordinate affection, malice, revengefulness, carry their own punishment with them, and avenge themselves on the soul wherein they dwell."[108] The first quote below specifically mentions anger, fretfulness, revenge, ill-will, malice, envy and "any other temper opposite to kindness." The second quote identifies additional miserable vices.

> The more opposite tempers—anger, fretfulness, revenge—prevail, the more unhappy you are. You know it; you feel it; nor can the storm be allayed, or peace ever return to your soul, unless meekness, gentleness, patience, or in one word, love, take possession of it. Does any man find in himself ill-will, malice, envy, or any other temper opposite to kindness? Then is misery there; and the stronger the temper, the more miserable he is. If the slothful man may be said to eat his own flesh, much more the malicious, or envious. His soul is the very type of hell, full of torment as well as wickedness....Yet there is a Spirit ready to help his infirmities...[109]

> No wicked man is happy. The reason is plain: all unholy tempers are uneasy tempers. Not only malice, hatred, envy, jealousy, revenge, create a present hell in the breast; but even the softer passions, if not kept within due bounds, give a thousand times more pain than pleasure....All those general sources of sin, pride, self-will, and idolatry, are, in the same proportion as they prevail, general sources of misery.[110]

Worldly people are disappointed, angry, and frustrated, thus miserable, both when they do and when they do not get what they want when they want it. When either circumstances or people actively thwart or do not cooperate with their acquisitiveness and social aspirations, they become angry and frustrated, but these are miserable emotional states. They envy the possessions, social position, and honors of others, but envy is a miserable emotional state, and others are not likely to appreciate or admire it. They hate people who jeopardize their worldly ambitions, and they demand revenge or retribution when it happens. They are malicious toward anyone who threatens their prosperity and power over others. Yet, hatred, revenge, and malice are miserable states of soul. And so it goes! Wesley agreed with St. Augustine that God made us for himself, and we are restless until we come to rest in Him. As Wesley put it, "Nothing short of God can satisfy your soul."[111] He did not rest his case for this merely by citing Augustine's authority. He also appealed to "universal experience, both our own and that of all our friends and acquaintance."[112] Wesley identified despair or hopelessness, the "want of hope," as another utterly miserable feeling, one to which backsliders are especially prone,[113] but they are not the only ones who despair.

Since genuine or spiritually advanced Christians are free from all these vices, they are also free from all of these miseries, Wesley said.[114] The "avoiding pain" part of the hedonistic agenda is best fulfilled by living as a Christian, especially so with respect to emotional or affective pains. Unlike some weird Christian thinkers, Wesley never commended or regarded either suffering just for the sake of suffering, or the dark night of the soul without God, as positive Christian values. He was all for avoiding them.

In bondage to sentience, to the five external senses, worldly people are little attuned to the reality or worth of intrinsic personal, moral, and spiritual good-making properties, whether in themselves or in others. They take little or no joy from them or in them. As identified earlier, these include embodied spirituality, self-motion (being self-starting), will (desires, feelings, affections, emotions), liberty (free choice—the capacity for making or originating our own choices), reason or understanding, (the ability to inquire and know), memory, (recall of past events), imagination, (anticipation and fanciful recombinations), consciousness (awareness), self-consciousness (awareness of one's own inwardness), conscience (the capacity for discerning good and evil, right and wrong), general moral laws ("written in our hearts"), moral and spiritual sensitivities, affections, dispositions, and virtues in various degrees of actualization, and a capacity for God. Worldly people have and use all of these internal capacities to a small degree, but they find it difficult to use them, pay attention to them, derive much happiness from them, or attach much value to them; their primary focus or orientation is external—on the world, on extrinsically valuable things. They are weak in inwardness; they have very little direct self-knowledge or soul-knowledge. They have superficial values, and they are superficial people. For the things of the extrinsic world, they lose, or never find, their intrinsic souls. Yet, no one is purely worldly. Worldly people subordinate but almost never entirely suppress their intrinsic value capacities. No one is entirely devoid of prevenient grace.

Worldly people judge their own worth and the worth of others mainly in terms of external wealth and social rank, or what Wesley regularly called "honor," but not by their inner qualities of soul. By identifying almost completely with extrinsically valuable things, they thereby create a worldly self-identity for themselves. Even if somewhat attuned to their own intrinsic good-making properties, they regard or value them mainly as useful means to external ends, not as inherently worthwhile, and not for growing in soul and inner richness of good-making properties. They extrinsically value their own intrinsic properties. They are selfish, but without much of a self. They lack inwardness; their self-awareness is dim. As selfish as they are, they really do not know themselves very well. To themselves, they are mainly just their bodies and adornments. Their self-awareness is largely body-awareness. Their self-concepts are largely body-concepts.

Worldly people tend also to be oblivious to the intrinsic good-making properties of other unique people, animals, and God—especially God. They do not identify with intrinsic goodness and make it a part of themselves. They derive no happiness from it. Animals exist to be used in any way they see fit, they assume, but so do other people. They have little or no awareness either of what they or other people or animals feel, think, choose, and are internally. With little empathy, compassion, or awareness of the "insides" of others or themselves, they may not care how much they hurt others, make them to suffer, violate their beliefs, frustrate their feelings, or thwart their choices—so long as they can get away with it. But getting away with it is a big part of their problem; the other part is that their vices are inherently miserable. They can't get away with it; their life-style is self-defeating and frustrating; and other people can "see through them." They extrinsically evaluate the intrinsic worth of others. They have little or no place in their souls for genuinely unselfish love, empathy, and compassion—the things that truly make life meaningful and happy. For all their vaunted wealth, prestige, and high class, they live value-impoverished lives. Once they "have it made," they are not nearly as happy as they expected to be. They are disappointed with success and prosperity.

Abundant living comes with abundant loving, the real thing, not with reciprocal altruism, mere egoism in disguise. Abundant living requires maximal reciprocal intrinsic loving, not minimal obedience to a merely reciprocal social contract. Moral and spiritual happiness or abundance is not just for tomorrow or the hereafter; it is also for today, here and now. As Wesley said, it is for "here and hereafter."[115] One of the most striking features of Wesley's theology is his insistence that the benefits of Christian existence become increasingly available to us here and now as well as later. In this life we can grow into them more and more abundantly as time passes, and this growth will extend endlessly into the hereafter.

The Goodness of Human Bodies

Matter is good, not evil; our human bodies are good, not evil. The Word made flesh was good, not evil. Human bodily actions, properly motivated and guided, are good, not evil. The "flesh" (as worldliness) is not good, but our bodies have a wisdom and goodness of their own. However, human bodies and physical actions as such are only extrinsically good, not intrinsically good. Human souls are embodied in this world and will be in the world to come. Wesley accepted all of these judgments. To explain, we will begin with the goodness of the human body, then move on to the value of good works, bodily performed.

For many converging reasons, Wesley positively valued human bodies. They are integral parts of the overall goodness of the original creation of the universe. They were originally free from all imperfections, he believed. He rued their present imperfections (that resulted from sin, he thought), but not embodiment itself. Only since the Fall have human bodies been "corruptible" and "pressed down on the soul."[116] In future resurrected bodies, all physical imperfections and hindrances will be removed. The goodness of our bodies consists in their usefulness to our souls—their extrinsic worth. Soul and body are intimately united, for "not only the memory, but all the operations of the soul, (including thinking, though many suppose otherwise[117]) are now dependent on the bodily organs, the brain in particular."[118] "Man at his creation was a compound of matter and spirit; and...it was ordained by the original law that during this vital union neither part of the compound should act at all but together with its companion; that the dependence of each upon the other should be inviolably maintained; that even the operations of the soul should so far depend upon the body as to be exerted in a more or less perfect manner, as this was more or less aptly disposed;"[119] and "Indeed at present this body is so intimately connected with the soul that I seem to consist of both. In my present state of existence I undoubtedly consist of both soul and body. And so I shall again, after the resurrection to all eternity."[120] Finally, we have Christian duties to take care of our own bodies and to give aid to the bodily needs of others. Spiritually viewed, our bodies are temples of God and God's instruments (extrinsic goods) within the world, and membership in the body of Christ is the best way to understand the Christian Church.

Wesley affirmed the goodness of human bodies, but not without qualifications. He most valued human bodies in their original, immortal, uncorrupted, innocent state before the fall of Adam and Eve. In that state, human bodies were an integral part of the overall goodness of perfected creation itself. Originally, human bodies were problem-free, for there were no such things as death, disease, pain, negative affections, weakness, or infirmity of any kind, not even in the non-human world, Wesley thought. He was convinced, as we cannot be, that human sin brought all death, disease, pain, toil, vice, weakness, and infirmity into the world. We now know that animals and our earliest pre-human ancestors suffered death, disease, pain, weakness, and infirmities of many kinds before any members of our *homo sapiens* species evolved, so we can no longer blame any of these things on the earliest human beings. We cannot specifically identify any real and flawless Eden or Adam and Eve, much less blame stuff on them. Infirmities, conflicts, struggles, suffering, and death have always plagued all living creatures. Plants draw their nourishment mainly from the soil and the sun, but all other living things must kill and eat other living things to survive. Death even creates the organic matter in the soil that nourishes plants. So life has been finite and a struggle from the beginning.

Yes, human bodies are good, but they are best when they are healthy and problem free. With that, it is hard to disagree. In this world, our bodies are very serviceable, but they are far from being problem free. That is a brute fact, of which Wesley was well aware. He positively valued human bodies, but he disvalued our bodily problems and infirmities. About our physical limitations, illnesses, and troubles in this life, he observed:

> The best thing we can say of this house of earth, is, that it is a ruinous building, and will not be long before it tumbles into dust; that it is not our home – we look for another "house eternal in the heavens," that we shall not always be confined here, but that in a little time we shall be delivered from the bondage of corruption, from this burden of flesh, into the glorious liberty of the sons of God. What frail things

these bodies of ours are! How soon they are disordered! To what a troop of diseases, pains, and other infirmities they are constantly subject! And how does the least distemper disturb our minds, and make life itself a burden! Of how many parts do our bodies consist! and if one of these be disordered, the whole man suffers. If but one of these slender threads, whereof our flesh is made up be stretched beyond its due proportion, or fretted by any sharp humor, or broken, what torment does it create! Nay, when our bodies are at the best, what pains do we take to answer their necessities, to provide for their sustenance, to preserve them in health, and to keep them tenable, in some tolerable fitness for our soul's use![121]

Wesley anticipated the eventual restoration of the human body to its "original" trouble-free state, actually, to something far better. The definitive mode of survival after death that he affirmed was not that of the Greek philosophers—the immortality of disembodied souls. However, as a mind/matter dualist, he allowed for temporary disembodiment between death and the final day of resurrection and judgment. Wesley thought that those who die do not go immediately to heaven or hell. Instead, all go to an intermediate place where the saved and the unsaved are separated by an impassible gulf. He called the locus of the saved "paradise," which is "not heaven" but is "the antechamber to heaven"[122] where redeemed souls have a foretaste of heaven. Within their own disconsolate antechamber, unsaved souls have a foretaste of hell. In a temporarily disembodied state, all souls await the *one* general and final Day of Resurrection and Judgment. His sermon on "The Good Steward" and his late sermon "On Faith" develop his ideas about "disembodied spirits" in paradise and describe their highly appealing functional capacities.[123] Wesley definitely carried his Platonic/Cartesian dualism (discussed later in more detail) into "paradise" with him, and the reader of these two sermons may wonder if disembodiment is not a permanent and highly desirable condition of the soul.

In "On The Resurrection of the Body," Wesley affirmed with its original author that death "divides us, indeed, from this body awhile; but it is only that we may receive it again more glorious."[124] Instead of a *final* state of disembodiment, he affirmed the quite contrary—the Christian mode of survival after death, the God-given everlastingness of *embodied* souls, the *resurrection of the body*. Here, he affirmed with its original author that resurrected spiritual bodies would be healthy and problem-free, but they would be bodies all the same. In his commentary on I. Corinthians 15:42–44, which he definitely did write, Wesley explained that the resurrection body is

Utterly incapable of either dissolution or decay. It is sown in dishonour - Shocking to those who loved it best, human nature in disgrace! It is raised in glory - Clothed with robes of light, fit for those whom the King of heaven delights to honour. It is sown in weakness - Deprived even of that feeble strength which it once enjoyed. It is raised in power - Endued with vigour, strength, and activity, such as we cannot now conceive. It is sown in this world a merely animal body - Maintained by food, sleep, and air, like the bodies of brutes: but it is raised of a more refined contexture, needing none of these animal refreshments, and endued with qualities of a spiritual nature, like the angels of God.[125]

In "The Great Assize," which Wesley also definitely wrote, he said that our incorruptible resurrected body will be "so changed in its properties as we cannot now conceive."[126] Transformed or not, bodies, by definition, are spatially extended perceptual objects having some kind of size, shape, motion, resistance, weight, and physical energy or causal effectiveness.

One of Wesley's most definitive statements was, "In my present state of existence I undoubtedly consist both of soul and body. And so I shall again after the resurrection to all eternity."[127] That he decisively affirmed the finality of the resurrection of the body, and regarded disembodiment as only as an intermediate condition, is powerful evidence that he positively valued embodiment as such. The *kind of goodness* that he attributed to trouble-free human bodies was expressed in his resurrection sermon (even if someone else originally wrote it) and in many other sermons that he definitely composed himself. It was extrinsic goodness. Our bodies, whether here or hereafter, are "for our soul's use." Their goodness consists in their usefulness. Our resurrected bodies "will be spiritualized, purified, and refined from their earthly grossness; then they will be fit instruments for the soul in all its divine and heavenly employment."[128] The goodness of even our resurrected bodies is thus extrinsic; they are means to the soul's intrinsic ends. Like the material means of grace, bodies have no inherent or intrinsic worth, but they have immense extrinsic worth as means to non-material or spiritual ends. Combined with our souls, they are essential parts of our total personal reality and worth. Extrinsic and systemic values can be taken up into or included within intrinsic values. Here or hereafter, a complete answer to "Who am I?" must include my body and its properties. The goodness of bodies is instrumental to, yet finally inseparable from, the soul's intrinsic existence and goodness. At a spiritually advanced level, we can evaluate bodies both intrinsically and extrinsically, both as temples of God and as indispensable and desirable houses for our own souls.

Wesley's positive evaluation of bodies as extrinsically good instruments of souls was expressed in several other ways. He insisted on the intimate mutual relatedness of bodies and souls and their significant powers to affect each other.[129] Minds and bodies interact, and their relations are so intimate and indissoluble that Wesley almost treated them as identical, thereby nearly overcoming his Cartesian mind/matter dualism. His medical book, *Primitive Physick*,[130] written mainly for the desperate poor of his era, went through many editions and was the most widely read book that he ever wrote. Though primitive indeed by today's medical standards, he offered detailed practical instructions for taking care of our bodies, through which we do the "works of our calling." He warned, "Yea, the body may sometimes be afflicted too much, so as to be unfit for the works of our calling. This also we are diligently to guard against; for we ought to preserve our health, as a good gift of God."[131] He repeatedly expressed concern for ministering to the bodily needs of other people as well as to their spiritual needs. Of the Christian "peace-maker," he wrote:

> He doeth good to the uttermost of his power, even to the bodies of all men. He rejoices to 'deal his bread to the hungry,' and to 'cover the naked with a garment.' Is any a stranger? He takes him in, and relieves him according to his necessities. Are any sick or in prison? He visits them, and administers such help as they stand most in need of. And all of this he does, not as unto man, but remembering him that hath said, 'Inasmuch as ye have done it unto one of the least of these my brethren, ye have done it unto me.'
>
> How much more does he rejoice, if he can do any good to the soul of any man! This power indeed belongeth unto God. It is he only that changes the heart, without which every other change is lighter than vanity. Nevertheless it pleases him who worketh in all, to help man chiefly by man; to convey his own power, and blessing, and love, through one man to another.[132]

Wesley viewed our bodies not only as *our* instruments, but also as *God's* instruments. God works through us to take care of human bodies as well as human souls. God does *his* good works among us "chiefly" through *our* good works. This theme was repeated more than once in Wesley's sermons. To those who argued that doing good to sinners was pointless and we should just let God deal with them, he responded, "I answer, (1), whether they will finally be lost or saved, you are expressly commanded to feed the hungry, and clothe the naked. If you can, and do not, whatever becomes of them, you shall go away into everlasting fire. (2). Though it is God only changes hearts, yet he generally doeth it by man"[133] and "It is God alone who can cast out Satan. But he is generally pleased to do this by man, as an instrument in his hand..."[134] Doing good works is essential to Godliness or God-likeness, Wesley insisted, "For, first, God works; therefore you *can* work. Secondly, God works; therefore you *must* work."[135]

Now are we prepared to consider ourselves, our bodies, and our deeds or actions as instruments of God, who does much of his work in our social world in and through us. Our hands should be and often are God's hands.

The Goodness of Human Actions and Good Works

Merely thinking about it is internal, Wesley recognized, but actually doing good and avoiding evil are *external*. That is, they involve bodily actions in our commonsensory world. He noted, "Thus, to do no harm, to do good, to attend to the ordinances of God...are all external."[136] These are the three most fundamental behavioral rules for all Methodists, as given and explained in Wesley's "General Rules" for the church.[137] And they are worth nothing if separated from their internal intrinsic spiritual counerparts.[138]

As Wesley well understood, good works are done with our bodies, and we should use our bodies to do good. We are "To glorify him therefore with out bodies as well as with our spirits, to go through outward work with hearts lifted up too him, to make our daily employment a sacrifice to God, to buy and sell, to eat and drink, to his glory."[139] In the language of value theory, good works are extrinsic goods, actions in public perceptual space and time, and they are properly valued as means to intrinsic ends beyond themselves. Yet, even the extrinsic can be made holy when combined with the intrinsic, when dedicated to the glory of God.

Protestants strive earnestly, but sometimes with confusion, to make a significant place for the value of human works without lapsing into "works righteousness." This can actually be done rather easily, and Wesley did it quite successfully. As he repeatedly affirmed, we cannot save ourselves through our own good works. Only the grace of God saves us, and then it works through faith and love within us. God's salvation from our sinful state is an absolutely free and unearned (by us) gift. Christ earned it for us; we cannot earn it for ourselves. We can do absolutely nothing to save or justify ourselves. Many people try to save themselves and mistakenly assume (as Wesley says he did before Aldersgate) that they must *first do or be something worthy of salvation* before God can or will help them, love them, or have mercy upon them. Many prominent Anglicans in Wesley's day maintained that good works as well as repentance and faith are essential *conditions* for salvation.[140] After Aldersgate in 1738, Wesley affirmed salvation by faith alone and repudiated all forms of works righteousness; yet he still emphatically affirmed the value and importance of good works. How can these motifs be reconciled?

Some people wonder, "What is the point of being good or doing good if good works have no bearing whatsoever on our being saved or damned?" This conundrum has a perfectly clear and logical solution, and Wesley found and frequently expressed it. Good works do have a bearing, but not a saving bearing. Works righteousness "has the cart before the horse." Good works are not the *cause* of our salvation, justification, and new birth. Rather, good works are the *effects* of our being saved and reborn, and of our growth in love, holiness, and Godliness. Good works are the consequent *fruits* of spiritual soul-transformation and sanctification, not their antecedent necessary conditions or *roots*. As Wesley insisted, "Good works follow this faith."

> We are, doubtless, 'justified by faith'. This is the corner-stone of the whole Christian building. 'We are justified without the works of the law' as any previous condition of justification. But they are an immediate fruit of faith whereby we are justified. So that if good works do not follow our faith, even all inward and outward holiness, it is plain that our faith is nothing worth; we are yet in our sins.[141]

Thus, we do the works of love out of love, the works of mercy out of mercy, the works of justice out of justice, or *because we have been saved, not in order to be saved*. We *first* accept God's gifts of salvation and soul-transformation, knowing that we have not earned or merited them. Then, out of newborn gratitude, compassion, and other tempers and virtues that express and culminate in holy love, we do the works of love, mercy, justice, and moral virtue. Salvation and ongoing sanctification transform us into persons with vital spiritual tempers or religious affections and dispositions. Good works do not cause us to have faith; they are caused by our having faith; so are many other Christian virtues and dispositions. They and the holy tempers from which they flow are the fruits, not the roots, of grace. Love expresses itself in doing, or it is not love at all. Good works *express* salvation; they do not *earn* it. Loving people just do loving things. Inward holiness is necessarily expressed in outward holiness, for "It is his will that we should be inwardly and outwardly holy; that we should *be good and do good* in every kind, and in the highest degree whereof we are capable."[142]

Wesley conceded that before people undergo the inner transformations of new birth and progressive sanctification, they may do many good things that are in one sense, "good works." They are "good and profitable to men." They may do things that are very beneficial to others, things that are means to desirable ends. However, these do not count as truly Christian good works because they are not properly motivated; they are not done out of Christian faith and love, for such things only "*follow after justification*."[143] Yet, they do indeed follow. Christian light does shine; Christian salt does savour.[144]

Wesley argued that good works done before conversion have no worth or value at all because they are not properly motivated, but do we agree? To get to the bottom of this, and to decide if we agree, we must make some distinctions. It is quite possible for something to be good in one sense but not in another. *The moral goodness or virtuous character of a person is different from the moral goodness of actions or of action-guiding rules like the Commandments.* Their good-making properties are logically quite distinct and can be independently fulfilled. Recall that "good" axiologically means "fulfilling our concepts or standards." Our ideal expectations for "morally good person" are quite different from our ideal expectations for "morally good act" or "morally good rule." Thus, acts and rules can be morally good or valuable even when the persons who either conform to them for the wrong reasons, or intentionally violate them, are not good and are without virtue. As Wesley recognized, such actions can be "very beneficial to others" even when they are "not properly motivated."

The ideal good-making-criteria for our concepts of "morally good act" and "morally good rule" might be:

1. God commands them,
2. Enlightened conscience approves of them, and/or
3. They are likely to have "beneficial to others" consequences.

These good-making features are not necessarily in conflict. Presumably God commands actions and gives us action-guiding rules that are likely to be beneficial; and presumably God has so constituted us that our consciences, properly enlightened, approve of such things. Good acts and good rules or guidelines are truly good if they fulfill just these standards. But in this sense bad people can do good things.

The ideal good-making-criteria for "morally good or virtuous persons" are quite different. They revolve around internal motives or dispositions rather than external consequences. Some good people (those with virtuous motives) do bad things (bring about undesirable consequences), and some bad people (with vicious motives) do good things (bring about good consequences). For example, good people who do not know all the relevant facts or who do not understand what is required of them might still conscientiously follow good rules and do unselfish, compassionate, and loving things that turn our badly. And those acting beneficially for selfish reasons (e.g., reciprocal altruism) may do good things and follow good rules that turn out well for others. The moral goodness of persons is different from the moral goodness of the consequences of their acts and guidelines. Let's say that morally good persons are those who have the following virtuous motives and dispositions and act from them.

1. love,
2. conscientiousness,
3. unselfishness,
4. compassion,
5. humility
6. faith, etc.

This list of good-making properties could be extended indefinitely to include every human virtuous desire or disposition and exclude every human vice. Persons who are so disposed and motivated would be good persons, and, by degrees, their acts would be virtuous and meritorious acts that deserve respect, praise, and rewards, even if they turn out badly. By degrees, people who lack these motives, or who have contrary motives, would be bad people, even if they sometimes do helpful things. Since the standards we apply to them are different, bad people could do good things and follow beneficial rules, but there would be no moral merit in it. Wesley was right about that. However, if their acts and rules fulfill relevant good-making-criteria, they do not cease being morally good just because the people who act upon them are morally bad.

Considerations of "merit" are complicated, however. In denying that beneficial acts performed before conversion have any value, Wesley may have meant they have no merit in the eyes of God because they are not performed from *virtuous motives*.[145] Being meritorious might also mean *deserving rewards*. Making this an issue seems strange for someone who, like Wesley, repudiates works righteousness. Or perhaps Wesley here equated merit with *optimal virtue* or perfection. Thus, before conversion, a person could be highly conscientious and beneficent, follow the rules, and do those works that are likely to have the best consequences—yet all of this could have no merit because they are not *maximally* loving and faithful or otherwise absolutely perfect. But merit for what? And why insist on "entire" perfection rather than lesser degrees of goodness? Does the goodness of prevenient grace count for nothing? Surely merit is not to earn salvation, for that is a gift of grace, and merit has nothing to do with it. So what was Wesley's point? The answer seems to be that he actually thought that rewards could be earned *after* conversion, but *not before*. In heaven, some people will have more "stars in their crowns" than others, depending on their merits or good works after conversion, as further explained near the end of this book.

Some Christians in Wesley's day, especially the Moravians, held that being a true Christian is a purely inward thing that finds no expression at all in outward actions, not even in attending church, using the means of grace, praying, reading the Scriptures, actively helping others, or otherwise obeying the commandments.[146] Some antinomanians think "that faith in Christ entirely sets aside the necessity of keeping his law,"[147] so faith just becomes a license to sin boldly. Some quietists think that inner religion is everything, and it never expresses itself outwardly. Wesley warned, "'Beware of 'Moravianism'—the most refined antinomanianism that ever was under the sun."[148] As such "quietists" or "antinomanians" were described by Wesley,

> Many eminent men have spoken thus: have advised us 'to cease from all outward action'; wholly to withdraw from the world; to leave the body behind us; to abstract ourselves from all sensible things—to have no concern at all about outward religion, but 'to work all virtues in the will', as the far more excellent way, more perfective of the soul, as well as more acceptable to God.[149]

To those quietists who reject everything but inwardness and who think that we should just wait passively on God, Wesley offered a twofold response: "I shall endeavor to show," he wrote, "first, that Christianity is essentially a social religion, and that to turn it into a solitary one is to destroy it; secondly, that to conceal this religion is impossible, as well as utterly contrary to the design of its author."[150] The Moravians and other antinomanians seemed to think that there is no place for systemic and extrinsic values and virtues in the Christian life. "Some of these, in order to exalt the value of faith, have utterly depreciated good works."[151] By "having faith" these Moravians may have meant being internally trusting of, confident in, and loving to God in Christ, rather than merely assenting to doctrines, which would be systemic. Faith is total inward intrinsic perfection all at once, they assumed; but their perfectionism made no place for systemic knowing and extrinsic doing. These know-nothing and do-nothing quietists aspired to be neither in nor of the world, and they would not cultivate the mind of Christ. Their sins were primarily those of omission (extrinsic and systemic) rather than commission.

Wesley thought, to the contrary, that we should be very much in and well informed about the world, without being of it, without being worldly. We should live knowingly and lovingly in the world and *practice* obedience to God's will and commandments. We should not withdraw from the world or assume that a sentimental antinomanian faith alone, with no practical knowledge of or obedience to the law, is a saving faith. Some antinomanians believed that since Christ set them free from the law, they didn't even have to obey the Ten Commandments, much less the laws of love. Wesley vehemently disagreed. *Being saved from the law means being forgiven and thus saved from its condemnation and guilt; but it does not mean being excused from learning about it or being exempted from obeying it.*[152]

Jesus told us how to separate the "sheep" from the "goats," the barren fig trees from the good ones: "By their fruits you shall know them" (Matthew 7:20). This means that *real Christians practice what they preach*. As Wesley put it, "See that your practice be in all things suitable to your professions."[153] That is how to recognize and identify true Christians. Although they disagreed very strongly about predestination and free choice, Jonathan Edwards very much influenced John Wesley's thinking on many important issues. Edwards also heavily emphasized good works, not as earning salvation, but as expressing it once salvation becomes available to the elect. In his *Christian Library*, Wesley re-published highly edited and censored versions of five of Jonathan Edwards' books, including his *A Treatise Concerning Religious Affections*.[154] In that treatise, Edwards identified twelve "marks" or "signs" of "true religion," but Wesley shortened them to nine. The last mark, the most definitive, the most difficult-for-the-devil-to-counterfeit, and one which Wesley preserved, was the perseverance of the saints in good works, in godly and righteous living. According to Edwards, "As the Scripture plainly teaches that practice is the best evidence of the sincerity of professing Christians; so reason teaches the same thing. Reason shows that men's deeds are better and more faithful interpreters of their minds, than their words."[155] His final and most definitive "mark" of true religion was: "Gracious and holy affections have their exercise and fruit in Christian practice."[156] With this, Wesley agreed wholeheartedly.[157] He highly valued extrinsic values without overvaluing or undervaluing them. According to Wesley, "love is productive of all right actions," and "it constrains [Christians] to do all possible good, of every possible kind, to all men."[158] Both Edwards and Wesley believed that the saints would persevere in godly and righteous living. The perseverance of the saints was destined, inevitable, and eternally secure according to Edwards. For Wesley, it requires constant vigilance and innumerable voluntary renewals to avoid backsliding.

Worldliness and Original Sin

Wesley identified original sin mainly with self-centeredness, combined with worldliness, that is, with the selfish overvaluation of extrinsically good things. We value mainly the things of the world, and we want them mainly for ourselves. We must now take a fresh look at original sin, at our universal and natural *bent* to sinning, our *enduring dispositions* to overvalue extrinsically good things in greedy ways.

By nature, most people fall far short of saintliness, largely because they are ultimately concerned about and with the things of the world. By nature, most people are evaluationally absorbed in the things of the world and too little concerned about unique conscious beings, including God and their own souls. Original sin may manifest itself in other forms of idolatry, in other ultimate concerns and overvaluations like systemic dogmatism and authoritarianism, but its primary or most prevalent manifestation is in worldliness and self-will.[159] Most people are, by nature, in selfishly bondage to the world. They inordinately love what Wesley called "*undue objects*." Worldly people are capable of loving; they just love the wrong stuff, material stuff, extrinsically valuable stuff; and they love too few intrinsically valuable people, if any at all. They love God hardly at all, except when and to the extent that they think God might make them prosper and succeed. They respond warmly to the "prosperity gospel." As Wesley explained to the natural sinner, "Thy affections are alienated from God, and scattered abroad over all the earth. All thy passions, both thy desires and aversions, thy joys and sorrows, thy hopes and fears, are out of frame, are either undue in their degree, or placed on undue objects."[160] He also called them "worldly objects."[161] These "undue objects" are the material things and processes of the external or sensory world, extrinsic goods, not intrinsic goods. Wesley further described this worldly "idolatry" in these words:

> I mean *love of the world*, which is now as natural to every man as to love his own will. What is more natural to us than to seek happiness in the creature instead of the Creator? What more natural than the desire of the flesh? That is, of the pleasure of sense in every kind?...Sensual appetites, even those of the lowest kind, have, more or less, the dominion over him. They lead him captive, they drag him to and fro, in spite of his boasted reason. The man, with all his good breeding and other accomplishments, has no pre-eminence over the goat. Nay, it is much to be doubted whether the beast has not pre-eminence over him![162]

Now we understand what worldliness is, but what about the currently unpopular notion of *original sin*, with which worldliness is strongly linked? Wesley understood sin to be a willful violation of the laws of God, especially the laws of love, and original sin to be an enduring state or disposition of the soul that distracts or prevents people from loving God and all the creatures God loves. It ranks or values non-divine things over divine things; thus, it is always some kind of idolatry. It makes us treat God, people, and all of God's sentient creatures as having less value than they actually have. We are in its grips, in bondage to it, in bondage to the world.

Original sin as a doctrine is largely out of vogue today, just as it was in Wesley's day. As he said, "It is now quite unfashionable to talk otherwise, to say anything to the disparagement of human nature; which is generally allowed, notwithstanding a few infirmities, to be very innocent and wise and virtuous."[163] Perhaps, however, we can make a contemporary case for it in a roundabout way. Wesley appealed to *two independent sources of evidence* for original sin, first, to the Scriptures, next, to our own experiential knowledge of ourselves and our fellow human beings. At least one of these is still very viable today, possibly both if some things are not taken too literally.

The Scriptural Case for Original Sin

Wesley's first case for the reality of original sin *appealed first to the Scriptures*, to the anthropology of the book of Genesis, taken quite literally. He was not a dogmatic scriptural literalist, but he did not have a Twenty First Century critical perspective on the book of Genesis. Wesley repeatedly reaffirmed uncritically what Genesis said about Adam and Eve, summarize as follows.

Once upon a time, Wesley thought, the very first humans actually existed as immortal beings in a physically, morally, and spiritually perfect, harmonious, and idyllic Garden of Eden. Just how they could be morally and spiritually perfect when they did not yet know the difference between good and evil, right and wrong, (when they had not yet eaten of the fruit of that tree), Wesley never explained. Wesley acknowledged that "the tree" of which Adam and Eve eventually ate was "the tree of the knowledge of good and evil."[164] Occasionally, however, he just mentioned "the tree" and its "fruit" without calling it "the tree of the knowledge of good and evil." He conveniently ignored the important complication that arises if Adam and Eve had not eaten of "the tree." How could a morally perfect being not know the difference between good and evil? Doesn't their not knowing the difference between good and evil before the fall conflict with Adam and Eve's moral perfection, with Wesley's assumption that "God made man upright"?[165] Morally good people would surely have to know the difference between moral good and evil, right and wrong. Thus, as morally perfect from the outset, Adam and Eve definitely must have eaten of "the tree of the knowledge of good and evil" before the fall, before they could choose evil. In his commentary on Genesis 2:17, Wesley tried his best to avoid this issue, writing, "What is good? It is good not to eat of this tree: what is evil? To eat of this tree. The distinction between all other moral good and evil was written in the heart of man; but this, which resulted from a positive law, was written upon this tree."[166] So Wesley thought, despite the words in Genesis, that Adam and Eve actually did know the difference between good and evil in their hearts before they ate of the tree of the knowledge of good and evil; they just did not understand the one very special "positive law" that this tree, in particular, was forbidden fruit. Irenaeus' account of Adam and Eve (explained shortly) clearly assumed the moral ignorance and innocence of the earliest humans, but not Wesley's. Irenaeus took not having eaten of the tree of the knowledge of good and evil much more seriously than Wesley.

Anyhow, according to Wesley, after they disobeyed God ("Eve made me do it!" claimed Adam[167]), God threw Adam and Eve out of the Garden and imposed the penalties of struggle, toil, conflict, death, disease, and suffering upon them, their descendants, all animals, and all other life forms, in perpetuity.[168] Before they sinned, nothing in the whole of nature had ever died, been sick, had to struggle, or experienced pain, Wesley thought. Somehow, though no one, including Wesley by his own admission, really seems to know how, our universal disposition to sin is derived from Adam and Eve. Wesley accepted the anthropology of Genesis taken quite literally, but educated people today may find it hard to swallow. Original sin is now largely out of vogue for many reasons, but let's not give up on it quite yet, even if we have doubts about Adam and Eve, taken literally.

Genetics or "inheritance" does have something to do with our propensity to sin. Even if we inherited our "human nature" from our hunter/gatherer ancestors rather than from a literal Adam and Eve, we still "by nature" have powerful propensities toward selfish acquisitiveness, aggressiveness, social dominance and competitiveness, libidinous pleasurable indulgence, pain avoidance, revenge, nepotism, and egoistic reciprocal altruism—any or all of which can incline us to think, feel, and act in unloving ways, which is the very essence of sinfulness. There is something to the highly defective "natural man" (and natural woman) of the theologians, but that is not the whole story. Reformed Theology and Social Darwinism greatly exaggerate our independence, selfishness, callousness, aggressiveness, and other antisocial traits. By nature (or prevenient grace) we are also social beings with a conscience and capacities and needs for cooperation, justice, mercy, love, compassion, consolation, forgiveness, and intense identification with others. We are born conflicted and undeveloped but not totally depraved.

Wesley was acutely interested in and well informed about the natural science of his day, which was then called "natural philosophy." He wrote extensively about it, abridged and republished the best available scientific works, and tried to integrate what he knew of it into his worldview and religious beliefs.[169] For example, unlike Luther and Calvin, he definitely accepted the unbiblical Copernican theory, according to which the earth is not the center of the universe; instead, the sun is the center of our solar system, and the earth rotates around it, as do the moon and the other planets.[170] The "three-story universe" Biblical picture knew nothing of other planets orbiting the sun, or even that our earth is a planet, much less that our earth revolves around our sun. Wesley lived in and shared the assumptions of an era that was largely pre-critical with respect to Biblical studies and primitively scientific with respect to cosmology, physics, chemistry, biology, and anthropology.

Today we know that physical nature has always been both dangerous and supportive, and that animals suffered pain, were often injured or diseased, viciously competed, and were regularly killed or died naturally long before our human ancestors evolved, so we can no longer blame any of that stuff literally on Adam and Eve. Our earliest ancestors lived in struggling hunter/gatherer social orders that were never idyllic, none of them or their precursors were ever completely non-aggressive or at all death-free, and none of them were at the top of the scale of moral and spiritual development. They did not "fall" from such a perfect state *because* they were never in it in the first place. No one can be literally "restored" to such a state for the same reason, but by degrees everyone can be elevated (sanctified) toward perfection.

Educated Twenty-first Century Christians can never start exactly where Wesley started. Our main problem is *whether a deep spirituality is possible for us today that does not require us to live in yesterday's world.* Wesley lived before Darwin; we do not. Can we make a case for original sin today without having to blame everything or anything on a literal Adam and Eve? It's really very hard to blame stuff on people who never existed. Doing so really would be absurd! Yet, even without them, general and persisting human perversity is very real, and the Bible was absolutely right about that. We only need to look around us to see it.

The Experiential Case for Original Sin

This brings us to *Wesley's second line of evidence for original sin—our own current human experience.* Our own experience here and now can tell us what most people are like most of the time. What are most people (including ourselves) actually like, as we know and experience them? In our own experience, are most of the people we know saints, or are most people predominately sinful, or maybe somewhere in between? That is the central issue for us. When Wesley asked about universal sinfulness in his own day, he answered, "This account of the present state of man is confirmed by daily experience."[171] Could we, should we, get the same results today?

Wesley's own *empirical case for universal sinfulness* was actually less convincing that it might have been because in his sermon and book on "Original Sin" and elsewhere, *total depravity*[172] was assumed or verbally affirmed, with no relief from prevenient grace. Here "total" really does mean "total." In that sermon, Wesley asked of fallen humanity, "But was there not good mingled with the evil?" and he answered "No, none at all."[173] Taken seriously, total depravity is fundamentally incompatible with Wesley's own doctrine of prevenient grace, so we cannot take it very seriously. As we saw, total depravity and the totally depraved "natural man" (and natural woman) were only theoretical theological constructs, never actual empirical states, by Wesley's own admission. As Umphrey Lee said, "For Wesley, the 'natural man' is only a logical fiction. In this world man exists as a natural man plus the prevenient grace of God."[174] Prevenient grace, not total depravity, has always prevailed in the real world. God has never allowed the real world with such people in it to be totally God-forsaken. Today, we must ask whether most real people, even *with prevenient grace*, are not primarily sinful and worldly. We must answer from experience, not from pre-scientific theological anthropology or uncritical dogmatics.

Looking at the mess that the human world has always has been in and still is today, it is very difficult *not* to believe that most people most of the time fall far short of the values and evaluations of saintliness, (as these are described in a following chapter). Yet, by the grace of God, we are far from being totally depraved, by

Wesley's own admission. Considering the mess we are in today, a powerful case for almost universal human moral and spiritual inadequacy can indeed be made. Don't most of us fall far short of the mark? Here are a few things to keep in mind as you read the brief empirical case for profound human shortcomings that comes next. The "we" in this discussion definitely includes this author himself; a great deal of self-knowledge went into writing every paragraph. Also, by God's grace, there are many important exceptions to all the following generalizations, thank God. Also, here and there things may be exaggerated a bit for emphasis. Finally, remember that God loves sinners just as much as God loves saints; in fact God loved all saints while they were yet sinners!

- We live constantly and devotedly by the distinction between "insiders" and "outsiders." Insiders are people who count morally and spiritually; outsiders are people who don't count, or at least not very much. More extremely, outsiders can be bitter and detested rivals and enemies. Most people living today are outsiders to us, and we are either indifferent to them or else hostile to or resentful of them. We may love a few insiders, but definitely not any outsiders. Our supply of prejudicial concepts for stereotyping, humiliating, and degrading outsiders is almost inexhaustible, and we constantly think up new ones. Insiders are people like us—our relatives and a few friends, co-workers, close acquaintances, "our kind of people." Outsiders are "those kind of people," "strangers" as the Bible calls them. They are racially or ethnically different, foreigners, illegal aliens, poor, middle class, rich, homeless, jobless, competitors of every description, people who did us wrong in the past, people who belong to a different political party, or a different church, or a different world religion, or a different social class, even people who support or play on a different athletic team. Opportunities for pigeonholing, downgrading, and humiliating outsiders are almost endless, and most of us take full advantage of them. We are prejudiced people with limited knowledge and sympathies. We don't even want to know or to care about outsiders.
- Most people, ourselves included, have their own private and self-serving agendas and really do not care very much about what happens to others or the "common good." Just look at today's political parties! And at their members! Throughout our lives, selfishness or "party spirit" motivates our occasional moments of cooperation. Our on-the-surface cooperation and altruism are mainly just disguised egoism of the long run, reciprocal altruism. We honor the lowly self-interested social contract when we think we can't get away with cheating, but we do not honor and hardly recognize higher moral or spiritual contracts or covenants. We care little for and seldom think about the well-being of others, especially those who are different, far removed, far away. Our natural selfish drive to dominate and humiliate others, our "inferiors," is exceedingly powerful and manifests itself relentlessly in almost everything that we feel, think, say, and do socially. Despite our democracy, our manners and attitudes are haughty, snobby, condescending. We

treat "low down" people as inferiors and actually try to make them feel inferior; we humiliate them in public and face to face.

• We do not know how to make peace. We do know how to make war.[175] We study war, not peace. We are entertained (e.g., on television and other media) by war, not peace. There is no war to end all wars, for wars will never cease, given our natural human aggressiveness. In wars, "they" are always at fault, not "us." God is always on our side, not theirs; but they think so too, in reverse. Many if not most wars are fought over either religion or material resources—or both. We inevitably fight a new war in every generation, and the Twentieth Century was the bloodiest ever in all of human history. As population increases and the earth's material resources are used up, there will be more and more wars. In every war, older and well established people send young people out to do utterly horrible, unthinkable, and unconscionable things to others they have never met and have nothing personally against. Volunteer armies with no draft allow those in the "upper" social classes to avoid the hell of war. Like the Civil War, our wars today are "a poor man's fight and a rich man's war." We glorify and celebrate war and try to keep the nastiness of it out of sight and out of mind. War really is hell, and many of us and our children live constantly in such hell. So will our grandchildren. But we hide and disguise the horrors of war; we celebrate the glory and ignore the blood, guts, terror, and stench of it; we reduce intrinsically valuable people to systemic statistics. We separate "guilty soldiers" from "innocent civilians," as if soldiers cease being human once they don their uniforms. If wearing uniforms, it is perfectly OK to kill them, for they are no longer persons. Many soldiers and veterans are justly proud of their uniforms; but, on the battlefield, uniforms are a dehumanizing license to be killed and to kill. We are frustrated when our enemies refuse to wear uniforms; then we don't know who is no longer human, who we are authorized to kill, who we can kill with no qualms of conscience. We train recruits to ignore the humanity, suffering, and loss of those they are sent to kill and maim. There is no end to war. Modern technology does not help; it makes things worse; our weapons are for mass destruction. We can now destroy all life on earth. Will we?

• The rich get richer and the poor get poorer.[176] This is not an original thought! Trickle down economics is a farce; it gushes wealth up to those who already have it, and it only dribbles small bits of wealth downward, if it dribbles at all. Most of us, rich or poor, are predominantly selfish most of the time, even if we have a few unselfish moments. Greed is good, so most of us really believe, as betrayed by our actual behaviors. We pay lip service to kindness, generosity, and honesty, but that is not how we really think, feel, or live. Our actions speak louder than our words. We do not give all we can; we only get all we can; and we are too short-sighted to save all we can. We get and spend all we can—far more than we have. We live way beyond our means. Our worldly social order encourages extravagance at almost every turn, especially through ubiquitous advertising. Excessively worldly and ruthless role-models abound. We are disposed by nature and encouraged by society to be greedy. We live rich, even when we aren't rich. This happens on individual, corporate, national, and international levels. Money to pay for our current worldly prosperity is being borrowed from our great grandchildren. We definitely do not pay our own way. Our enemies no longer have to conquer us in war; they can just buy us. Sooner rather than later, our credit will run out, and our sins will find us out. Our short-sighted excessively materialistic life style is bankrupting us, but we are only doing what comes naturally. We are egocentric and care mainly about today, not theocentric and, like God, concerned for the whole earth and for all future generations. We give little thought to God and Godlikeness. We are rich in things but poor in soul.

- Worldly distractions dominate our culture and our personal lives. Perhaps they have always dominated every culture, but our human situation seems even worse today, not better. We are entertained and amused by sins of every kind and description, especially unbridled sex, hatred, cunning, and violence. Watching sinners at work and at play is great fun—they are so much like us! And we are, and aspire to be, like them! Advertising urges us to invest and spend our money on things, not on knowledge, not on people. Our social and mass media, television, movies, advertising, computers, and electronic communication devices, constantly bombard us with entertaining evils, worldly temptations, distractions, ruthless role models, and messages of *instant selfish and worldly gratification and glory*. Our children and grandchildren may never know any other world. The media incessantly reinforce our natural tendency to believe that greed, cruelty, violence, war, betrayal, bullying, revenge, and unfaithfulness are the best ways to solve our human problems and make ourselves happy. We are easily sucked in. Many talk shows are cesspools of hatred, bigotry, deliberate distortion, and misinformation. When not being amused and deceived by evils, we are utterly bogged down (lost) in irrelevant distractions and transient trivialities—as if they really matter.

- We are axiological materialists, worldly and short-sighted almost through and through. We may have degrees and moments of uneasy conscience about it, but we usually value the things of the world more than we value God, or other people, or non-human animals. Deep inside we know better, though we are not better, and we do not do better. We do what we know we ought not to do, and we do not do what we know we ought to do. We cannot and do not want to see the "big picture." We want to "have it all" for ourselves here and now, no matter what. We love and devote our lives to things that cannot love us back; and we neglect, exploit, and abuse those who can. Most of us are terribly short-sighted about almost everything. We cannot see very far into the open future. We are not naturally disposed to see very far ahead. Our ancestors had to solve mostly immediate problems, and we inherited the genes of those who were thus most successful. Like non-human animals and our pre-human ancestors, we don't see very far into the future, but we *can* do it if we really make the effort. Normally, we just don't make the effort. So we go for instant gratification, pile up debts, do not save for the future, mismanage the world, organize our businesses and lives for immediate profit, not for the long run, and devastate the environment that sustains us, our children, our grandchildren, and all future generations.

• We do not think or care much about what we are doing to nature, the environment, and other forms of life that God spent millions of years creating. We have little or no concern for future generations, human or non-human. Individuated consciousness in ourselves and in others, especially non-human others, is hidden from us; we are sensitive mainly to externals. Today, some powerful people (like the majority of the Justices on our current Supreme Court) can't tell the difference between corporations and persons! We value mainly extrinsic or systemic realities, not intrinsic realities. We are too shortsighted to grasp the results of environmental desecration. We permanently contaminate the land, the air, the rivers, the gulfs, the oceans, and the whole earth for the sake of short term gains. We overpopulate the earth beyond its carrying capacity; some religious authorities even insist that we overpopulate. We use up resources, ravish the earth, leave almost nothing for those who will come after us; and we really don't seem to notice, much less to be concerned. Creation care means nothing to us.

• Our educational systems are designed mainly to produce worldly consumers and producers, competent extrinsic and systemic evaluators—but not morally and spiritually mature souls, not experts in intrinsic values and evaluations. In budget crunches, intrinsic value education is the first thing to go—music, the arts, drama, literature, poetry, as well as basic morality, self-understanding, respect for others, human equality, and non-violent ways of solving human problems—the "soft stuff" that does not really matter. We pour money into math, science, engineering, and business education, but not into the humanities and moral education. Even the humanities, as we teach them, have and give little moral direction. They expose us to human values but give little guidance in assessing them. They are not axiologically ordered. We train only half (or less) of our children's brains, and we really don't care. This does not mean that we should breach the barrier between church and state; it means that our educational systems should give at least as much attention to intrinsic value education as to extrinsic and systemic value education, maybe even more. This is not likely to happen any time soon. Do our homes and churches do much better? Without intrinsic value education, societies and civilizations inevitably decline and fall. Will ours?

• Our knowledge, thoughts, beliefs, and prolific electronic communications manifest no depth of truth, thought, culture, insight, philosophy, morality, or spirituality. Even if they could be, are our current social media actually being used to create more loving communities of real people? Are they used to rejoice with those who rejoice and weep with those who weep? Or are they mostly just irrelevant distractions? We blog, twitter, and tweet, but we do not know how or what to think or how to critically assess anything. We are easily deceived, as our politicians know full well. Is most of our chatter just so much sound and fury, signifying almost nothing? In this respect, has the younger generation really gone to the dogs? But we were never innocent. For the most part, we have always been superficial people. We live by shallow and misleading slogans and do not think deeply about anything. We can't read much more than one short paragraph at a time. We send our young men and women off to die in wars for the sake of shibboleths and sound bites. We elect our leaders the same way. Campaign strategists know that this works. There is no truth in us or in them. Modern technology just gives us more powerful and effective ways to be superficial. There is little thought, love, or intimacy in electronic communication devices; they give no direct face-to-face contact with or interaction with real people. Only a few people seem to notice this. We have little knowledge of spirituality or its possible sources; relatively recent polls show that less than half of all Americans can name even one of the four gospels; two thirds think that Billy Graham wrote the Sermon on the Mount; and eighty percent of born again Christians believe that "God helps them that help themselves" is in the Bible.

- Our role-models constantly let us down. Our politicians sell their souls to big corporations, oil companies, banks, insurance companies, giant agribusinesses, or whoever happens to be buying souls at the moment. Our entertainment celebrities, strongest athletes, and best coaches constantly exercise and betray their moral weaknesses. Occasionally, they even get caught and only then say that they are sorry. Some ministers and priests sexually abuse our children. Some prominent televangelists assume that being at the top gives them a license to sin egregiously, especially in sexual matters. So do many of our most prominent athletes, politicians, and entertainers. They feel that they are "beyond the law," but don't we all at times? Don't we envy them, at least a little bit? Sinfulness, not prosperity, not moral maturity, not advanced spirituality, is what really trickles down from the top. *All* civilizations eventually decline from within and fall. Will we?

- We have an almost insatiable passion for revenge. If any human disposition is "intuitive" and "natural," revenge is it! If we are hard-wired for anything, it is revenge. We can't just let it go when we have been offended. We get great satisfaction from taking offense and getting even. If we can't get even ourselves, we expect the government to do it for us, so we institutionalize revenge as "retributive justice." We and others go to war for revenge. We find it almost impossible or at least impractical to forgive. "Upon Our Lord's Sermon on the Mount" means almost nothing to us, even when we hear or read the words, even when we pay it lip-service. We do not turn the other cheek or go the second mile. It's just too impractical. "Move beyond revenge" and "Forgiveness is better than vengeance" constantly fall on deaf ears. We put far more money, thought, time, and energy into getting even than into reconciling, restoring, rebuilding, and redeeming. What would the world be like if this were reversed?

- We are greatly inclined to be unhappy, restless, confused, miserable, discontented, disappointed, despondent, unbalanced. Once the basic necessities of life are met, wealthy and successful people are no happier than those who have much less. Not realizing this, we aspire to be like them and will stop at almost nothing to get there. We are unhappy over not being rich, but we would not be much happier if we were. Our conscious awareness is pervaded by shades of despair, hopelessness, depression, sorrow, anxiety, echoanxiety (over the environment), loneliness, forlornness, uncertainty, meaninglessness, guilt, anger, hatred, jealousy, envy, and resentment. We live meaningless lives, miserable lives. To drown our sorrows, we turn to alcohol and other drugs, but they just lead us deeper and deeper into crime and sin. Countless lives are consumed and wasted by them. The more prosperous our society becomes, the more drugs we consume. We live in the most prosperous and worldly civilization the world has ever known. So why do so many of us have to escape from it with drugs, both legal (e.g., alcohol, tobacco, and prescription pain killers) and illegal (e.g., heroin, cocaine, methamphetamine, and marijuana)? Something is obviously wrong with our worldly values, for they do not fulfill us. We love things more than people, more than ourselves, far more than others. Often we turn to therapists, self-help gurus, or irrelevant distractions and amusements. One way or another, we realize half-consciously that we need a lot of help, but we do not know where to find it. We are lost souls.

- We know perfectly well that we can trust very few people, especially politicians, talk show hosts, news reporters, televangelists, and maybe not even our next door neighbors. But we really do not mind lying candidates and officials, as long as they are lying for our side or cause. Where strong beliefs are at stake, even fundamentalist Christians resort to and encourage half-truths and no-truths. They isolate themselves and their children from challenging ideas. They ban or burn books. If they had the power, they would impose their beliefs on those who honestly do not agree with them and use the power of the state to do it. Whatever happened to, "Thou shalt not bear false witness"? We know that most officials, ordinary people, and perhaps even our own neighbors, will not tell us the truth, perhaps because they know that they cannot trust us either. Such things have changed very little since the days of Jeremiah (9:4-5). By example if not by precept, children learn to lie and cheat from their parents as well as their peers. With few qualms of conscience, our high school and college students plagiarize, cheat on exams, and buy ready-made term papers on the Internet. Their parents know about this, approve of it, and pay for it. (As a professor, I stopped assigning easy-to-buy term papers to undergraduates long before I retired; I gave only in-class exams and graded only what students wrote in class). You can't trust anyone under thirty; you can't trust anyone over thirty! Adults cheat as much as they can, especially when paying taxes and making profits. Our business practices are as deceptive and dishonest as we can get away with. Cheating is a way of life, along with lying, obfuscating, and denying the truth. Everyone is doing it, and we don't want to be taught any moral lessons or blocked by governmental regulations. We "spin" almost everything, but we do not know or communicate the truth that sets us free. We isolate ourselves from or try to suppress all information that challenges our narrow preconceptions. Our words are empty, misleading, deceptive, untrustworthy. Deep inside, we know that there is little or no truth in us.

- Savagery and evil dispositions galore are perfectly natural and lie just below the surface of "civilized" human consciousness. Most of us are entirely capable of incredible indifference, cruelty, and destructiveness under the right circumstances. Something deep within us easily hacks people (or animals) to death, or blows them up, or rapes them, or abuses and exploits them in ways too horrible to mention—or we mindlessly allow or require others do such things for us and reward them for it. Ideologies, prejudices, and deliberate misconceptions turn us into barbarians. We are still savages at heart and by nature, despite all the veneers of civilization. We can readily assume a "mob mentality" or "groupthink" that makes almost any atrocity easy for us. We easily go along with the crowd, no matter how vicious or mindless it is. Under slightly adverse social conditions, we eagerly participate in genocide and ethnic cleansing. "Nature" sends mixed messages, but where philosophers advise us to "Follow nature," often the best advice is, "Don't follow nature!" John Wesley suggested that worldly people "take nature, not grace, for their guide."[177] "Follow nature" is very ambivalent advice, for nature itself is conflicted.

• This jeremiad of human shortcomings could go on and on, but you get the idea. Most people are very far removed from being intrinsically or holistically oriented saints. Most people really are in bondage to sin or evil. Most are by and large self-centered, bound to the external sensory world, and have little inwardness. Many philosophers (the logical empiricists) and psychologists (the behaviorists) even tell us that there is no such thing as inwardness. Are they only speaking for themselves? Our prevailing and enduring dispositions are quite contrary to loving God with all our hearts, souls, minds, and strength, and our neighbors as ourselves. God help us!

The empirical case for original sin is really quite powerful, and we really don't need a literal Adam and Eve to make it so! *Human experience* tells us that most people have serious, enduring, and deeply ingrained moral and spiritual faults—like those just cited. It is practically impossible to say just how many of us have such problems, but we all know that the "real world out there" is *a jungle*. All of us have some of these defects, and some of us have most of them. Even if we are not as consistently bad as "depravity" suggests, these are among the most serious temptations to which almost all of us are highly susceptible. Bad societies don't help, but the romantic or rationalistic theory that we are bad only because we are born into corrupt societies is very naive, and John Wesley rightly challenged such naivete. Why are societies universally corrupt? Corrupt societies presuppose corrupt people; they do not completely explain corrupt people, even if the causal relations go both ways. People in power will not challenge or change corrupt, unjust, and inane institutions, policies, and practices because they profit immensely from them, and the "have nots" suffer the consequences.

We need a plausible current empirical explanation for *why* most of us are so deeply disposed to fall so far short of saintly beliefs, thoughts, dispositions of the heart, deeds, values, and evaluations. Traditional Christianity said that our contemporary sinful dispositions were *derived somehow* from Adam and Eve. They are indeed grounded somehow in our inherited "human nature," even if a literal Adam and Eve never existed. Theologians have offered many different accounts of exactly how transmitting sinful dispositions works. Wesley himself toyed around with several different explanations at different times in his life.[178] Yet, he was much more concerned about the fact that we are sinful than with explaining how we got that way. "I know it is transmitted," he once wrote, "but how it is transmitted I neither know nor desire to know."[179] This may be a fruitful and plausible stance for us today! Traditional explanations of how we derived our sinful nature from Adam and Eve can be of no significance to us if Adam and Eve never existed in an idyllic Eden located in a world without danger, suffering, struggle, conflict, or death. We can't blame stuff on people who never existed. Even so, we still need a plausible explanation of why we are almost universally in the moral and spiritual mess that we are in, of why our values and evaluations are so screwed up, and of how we got that way. Is there a viable alternative?

Starting Low versus Starting High

An explanation for our primitive moral and spiritual condition that *we* might find highly plausible was originally suggested by Irenaeus, a Bishop of Lyon, who lived around 130-200 CE. We may have to take his suggestion far beyond where he left it, however. If Wesley ever read Irenaeus, his theory of Adam's moral ignorance and immaturity did not seem to register with him. As Randy L. Maddox indicated, we can only "speculate what Wesley's response might have been if he had been aware of Irenaeus's alternative,"[180] but here is its essence. Explaining "Why man was not made perfect from the beginning," Irenaeus wrote:

> But created things must be inferior to Him who created them, from the beginning...Because as these things [Adam and Eve] are of later date, so are they infantile; so they are unaccustomed to, and unexercised in, perfect discipline...It was possible for God Himself to have made man perfect from the first, but man could not receive this (perfection) because as yet an infant.[181]

Wesley thought our earliest ancestors had "perfection from the beginning;" Irenaeus suggested that they did not—they were just too immature for perfection. In some translations, "infantile" above is translated as "immature." A plausible modern understanding of universal sinfulness as moral and spiritual immaturity may not coincide exactly with that of Irenaeus, but he was probably on the right track. Both of the Wesleys believed in awakening sleepers; they just didn't believe spiritual somnambulism to be primordial. Adam and Eve were not spiritual and moral sleepers; they had it all! But maybe not. Maybe they really had not yet eaten of the tree of the knowledge of good and evil. Our own profound separation from God and spiritual immaturity need not presuppose that our earliest ancestors were once connected to God in an idyllic Eden of perfect moral and spiritual maturity located in a world that had never seen danger, death, disease, struggle, toil, conflict, immorality, or suffering. Wesley believed that, but even he finally came to think that

Adam and Eve are irrelevant as far as our own sins are concerned. As Randy L. Maddox points out, Wesley eventually arrived at the view that we are responsible only for our own personal sins, not for anything inherited from our ancestors, because, through Christ's redemption, original sin is obliterated at birth in every newborn.[182]

Thus, all of us really do start almost from scratch, and an authentic Wesleyan perspective might not be far removed from that of Irenaeus. *We just start low and never get very high.* Our universal sinfulness depends on what *we* are and do, not on what *our ancestors* were and did. Even if *our ancestors* were once on the wagon and then fell off, *we* were never on the wagon in the first place. Every person "born of man and woman" inevitably starts low on the scale of moral and spiritual development. From and at "the beginning," however indefinite in the history of evolution and fetal development that might be, unborn and newborn *human babies did not and do not know anything* of God, of right and wrong, of themselves, or of anything else. Human babies are born today in ignorance, (but not necessarily in innocence with respect to all predispositions), and they were always so born. At birth, they (we) have not yet encountered the tree of the "knowledge of good and evil," much less eaten from it. As they mature, they do meet and gradually taste good and evil, they slowly learn the difference between them, and they (we) are *naturally* drawn toward both.

All of us are *born conflicted*, with both good and evil predispositions, and it usually takes us a long time to sort them all out. Most people never do, or at least not very well, and many of us get it all wrong. Given a choice between our conflicting inborn good and bad inclinations, we usually make the wrong choices. We are prone to sin; it is the easy way. Saintliness is a much harder way. When children eventually "eat of the tree of good and evil," when they come to know the difference between right and wrong, this is not a bad thing. It is a good thing, a moral and spiritual advance, a "fall upward," as someone (Hegel) once said. Starting from scratch, all of us have a long way to go in moral and spiritual development, and most people never seem to get it right, never get their priorities straight. Most people end up mainly with natural but selfish, worldly, unloving, and sinful values. Higher moral and spiritual saintly values are equally "in our genes" but largely latent and undeveloped. Activating them may require something really drastic—like an outpouring of God's special grace, and being born again.

Even when we become value experts, we usually end up as superior evaluators of inferior values, the ones that involve only sensory/hedonic good-making criteria. The temptations of the world are just too powerful for most of us to overcome or resist, even when we vaguely know better. The human nature that we inherited from our hunter/gatherer ancestors has a largely but not completely selfish and worldly bent, but this is not our inevitable fate. By God's prevenient grace, we also inherited a conscience and many other potencies, e.g., for cooperation, love, compassion, fairness, devotion, theology, etc. and for moral and spiritual growth and maturation. Activating these capacities often requires something like a dramatic conversion experience, but not always. With gracious help from God and others, we can outgrow or transcend primitive human nature, but most of us never ripen to the point of mature conscientiousness or to loving God and all other human beings holistically. There is a better way, a more mature way, but few there be that find it. Through Christ, Christians are directed toward that upward way. Others (non-Christians) may also be so directed in other ways.

Some contemporary Wesleyan theologians wonder why prevenient grace as *conscience* is not given equally to all, that is, why conscience is weaker in some people than in others.[183] The presupposition of this puzzle is that conscience is or should be given both maturely and equally to all, but that is not how it actually works. The reality is that, like all other human potencies, conscience is not given to anyone in its maturity, even if its potential is given equally to all. Many things can interfere with the equal maturation of conscience (and all other moral and spiritual qualities). For example, due to parental or primary caretaker ignorance, neglect, or abusiveness, infants may not form essential and desirable social attachment capacities during the first few weeks and months of life. Even after infancy, our dominant social role models may be morally ignorant, neglectful, abusive, or downright evil. Parents, caretakers, and social orders visit their imperfections upon the unformed souls of their children. What chance does any child or adult have in such environments? Few there be that overcome them, though it does happen.

The real empirical condition of universal human sinfulness or lack of goodness is that we all *start from the bottom* level of moral and spiritual development, not that our ancestors ever *fell from the top*. We start low, and we never get very high, partly because we are born into morally and spiritually infantile or corrupt social worlds, and partly because we start with both evil and good predispositions in wretched conflict. Wesley recognized that our human nature is "at variance with itself."[184]

Our earliest ancestors never were once perfectly well, lost it, and then ever since everyone needs to be healed. Neither we nor our ancestors were ever perfectly well. Nor were or are we ever perfectly ill or totally depraved. It's not that people once were acutely sensitive to God's presence within and without. No one ever was in the first place, especially in infancy, though everyone has a dim awareness of both goodness and God all along, and some saints do begin to approximate perfection. It's not that all people once loved God, everyone else, and all creatures great and small as they should, but not now. No one ever did originally or since, Jesus possibly excepted. No one ever had primordial perfection; so no one ever lost it; but our human situation is still quite appalling. Some saintly people make it by cooperating with God's graceful initiatives, but most of us do not collaborate. In ways too many to count, a graceful God constantly nudges or lures us in the right direction; but God's grace is resistible, not irresistible. Most of us resist and take the easy and sinful way. As Wesley explained, "No man can believe in Christ, unless God give him power. He draws us first by good desires, not by compulsion, not by laying the will under any necessity; but by the strong and sweet, yet still resistible, motions of his heavenly grace."[185] This theme would be most congenial to today's Temporalistic Theologians, who see God as actively luring us toward both himself, others, and all goodness, but not forcing them upon us.

Worldly Religion

Wesley's own definition of "true religion," repeated time and again in his writings, was primarily intrinsic. Its final intrinsic-value-objects were God and people, and its definitive mode of valuing them was intrinsic love: "True religion is the loving God with all our heart, and our neighbor as ourselves; and in that love abstaining from all evil, and doing all possible good to all men."[186] Is there a worldly extrinsic form of religion that competes with true intrinsic religion? Wesley recognized that religion itself, specifically, historical Christianity, could be worldly and corrupt, but he could have taken this theme much further than he did. In the following quote, he identified a "worldly religion" as one that is systemic/extrinsic or formal/external.

> The religion of the world implies three things: first, the doing no harm, the abstaining from outward sin—at least from such as is scandalous, as robbery, theft, common swearing, drunkenness; secondly, the doing good,—the relieving the poor; the being charitable, as it is called; thirdly, the using the means of grace—at least the going to church and to the Lord's supper. He in whom these three marks are found is termed by the world a religious man.[187]

Wesley warned that the "man" of worldly religion lacks the inwardness of Christian love, for it "is only the outside of that religion which he insatiably hungers for."[188] He identified the real difficulty with worldly religion when he wrote, "Beware of quenching that blessed hunger and thirst, by which the world calls 'religion'; a religion of form, of outside show, which leaves the heart as earthly and sensual as ever."[189] The "religion of the world" consists "either in opinions or a mere round of outward duties."[190] Extrinsic/systemic religion makes an external show of religious formalities, that is, of liturgical, doctrinal, morally conventional, and other formal patterns, but there is no heart or inwardness in it. The religious affections and the spiritual senses are lacking. The heart is still earthy, sensual, worldly; and so is worldly religion.

Wesley's concept of "worldly religion" could be taken even further, although he made a good start with the topic. He did not say so, but a religion of "works righteousness" could be construed as one of its manifestations. Those who try to make themselves worthy of God's love and forgiveness by earning them through good works have a religion of "external show." Doing, working, earning are extrinsic concepts and activities. Thus, so is a religion of works righteousness, since it is turned outward instead of inward.

The most pernicious manifestation of worldly religion is one that *uses* religion and God to promote worldly ends, "earthly and sensual" ends. Worldly people co-opt and corrupt religion and the churches by using them mainly for their own worldly purposes. *Why* do worldly people go through the external motions of avoiding the most socially scandalous sins, but not all of them? Why do they act to help others, go to church, and use the means of grace? Usually, it is not to receive or manifest God's love and forgiveness; no, it is for extrinsic, self-serving, worldly purposes. Worldly religion is a means to greater prosperity and superior social rank here and now. Going to church is good business. Church is a good place for networking. Being basically decent and helpful is a good way to impress others, to gain social respect, a better reputation, and higher social status—all of which pay off in prosperity. Not just ordinary "nominal" Christians, but even the clergy, Wesley thought, may be religious for the wrong reasons, not for saving and caring for souls, but for the sake of worldly ends: "A worldly clergyman is a fool above all fools...indolent clergymen, pleasure-taking clergymen, praise-loving clergymen, preferment-seeking clergymen."[191]

The apparent altruism of worldly people is only reciprocal altruism. They expect a payback in the end, and the sooner the better. Other people as well as God will reward them, they think, if they are externally religious. Prayer and pomposity will help them to sell more products and services, recruit more customers and followers, win more football games, triumph in more battles for success, and win more wars. God wants *me* to succeed and prosper in worldly ways, so each worldly person believes. God's ultimate function is to see that this is so; Christ died to make me rich! *God is a means* to *my* worldly ends or goals. I am much more interested in what God can do for me than in what I can do for God. That is why worldly people are at least externally religious. God endorses, sanctions, rewards, and blesses the values and practices of worldliness—prosperity and status—here and hereafter; and so do worldly churches. God (and churches) exist to make us wealthy and exalted, and to keep us that way forever, they think.

Wesley advised us to use the world and enjoy God, but, as he recognized, "half-Christians...use God, and enjoy the world."[192] Today's "prosperity gospel" is the ultimate expression of such a self-serving worldly religion. Televangelists are making a killing with it! But they promise far more than they can deliver. There is much more to his preaching and writing than the prosperity gospel, but consider these expressions of it by Joel Osteen: "We don't really stretch our faith; we don't believe for anything bigger. But God wants us to constantly be increasing, to be rising to new heights. He wants to increase you in his wisdom and help you to make better decisions. God wants to increase you financially, by giving you promotions, fresh ideas, and creativity;"[193] and "If you want to prosper in your finances, put God first. If you want to prosper in your business, put God first. When you honor God, God will always honor you."[194]

This second quote leaves us wondering what really comes first for Osteen, prosperity, or God as a means to the end of prosperity, but not as an end in Godself.

Worldly religion can co-opt and corrupt the very notion of "faith." Having faith in the worldly way consists of believing whatever you have to believe in order to get whatever it is that you want from God—namely, worldly goods and high social rank. Many televangelists like Oral Roberts, Jim Bakker, John Hagee, T. D. Jakes, and Robert Tilton preach a gospel of worldly success.[195] What we call "the American dream" is largely one of material prosperity; and, of course, God sponsors just that American dream! At its best, the American dream is far more inclusive, more intrinsic, but it isn't always at its best.

Wesley recognized that worldliness could and did at times take over the churches. He thought that this actually happened in identifiable historical circumstances. It happened, for example, when Constantine made Christianity the official religion of the Roman Empire in. In one sermon, Wesley spoke of "that evil hour when Constantine the Great called himself 'a Christian', and poured in honour and wealth upon the Christians"[196] In another, he wrote of "that fatal period when the Emperor Constantine called himself a Christian, and from a vain imagination of promoting the Christian cause thereby heaped riches, and power, and honour upon the Christians in General; but in particular upon the Christian clergy."[197] After Constantine, Wesley thought, the Church and the clergy were largely dominated and controlled by the worldly values of riches, power, and honor, more so at some times than others.[198] Is it so today? In your church? With your clergy? In his later years, as Methodism and Methodists prospered, Wesley was much concerned that increasing prosperity and worldly respect were resulting in decreasing spirituality and virtue, and greater weakness in faith, hope, and love.[199] As Wesley aged, he recognized that Methodists were prospering greatly by following his advice to "Earn all you can" and "Save all you can," while neglecting "Give all you can."[200]

Respecting and Loving Worldly People

In his sermon "On Friendship with the World," Wesley asked how godly people should relate to ungodly or worldly people. He expressed serious reservations about getting too deeply involved with them, especially about marrying them, lest godly people become corrupted by them. He still reminded godly people that worldly people are loved by God, and they too are our neighbors to be loved as we love ourselves. He asked, "What kind of friendship may we have with the world?" and answered,

> We may, we ought, to love them as ourselves (for they also are included in the word 'neighbor'); to bear them real good-will; to desire their happiness as sincerely as we desire the happiness of our own souls; yea, we are in a sense to honour them (seeing we are directed by the Apostle to 'honour all men') as the creatures of God; nay, as immortal spirits, who are capable of knowing, of loving, and of enjoying him to all eternity. We are to honour them as redeemed by his blood who 'tasted death for

every man.' We are to bear them tender compassion when we see them forsaking their own mercies, wandering from the path of life, and hastening to everlasting destruction. We are never willingly to grieve their spirits, or give them any pain; but, on the contrary, to give them all the pleasure we innocently can; seeing we are to 'please all men for their good'. We are never to aggravate their faults, but willingly to allow all the good that is in them.[201]

So, there is much good in worldly people! And Christians should acknowledge, value, and respect this. They have many good-making properties, but not enough to make them saints. Their own dominant extrinsic values are always "mingled together" with subordinated systemic and intrinsic values. No matter. We should love them as if they were saints, as if they were ourselves, as if they were equally God's creatures and loved by God—for indeed they are.

Much Christian writing and preaching rightly emphasizes God's special concern for the poor, the needy, and everyone "of low estate." Many of John Wesley's efforts and activities in applied Christian ethics were so devoted. However, if God loves all equally, then God also loves those who are successful in worldly ways. If God is not a "respecter of persons," meaning that God does not show favoritism to the high and mighty of the world, this does not mean that God loves them any less than "the least of these." Yes, God does not love the rich more than the poor, but neither does God love the poor more than the rich. Neither should we, for they, too, are our "neighbors." It might not come soon, but Wesley, the universalist, anticipated a day "before the end" when "Even the rich shall enter into the kingdom of God. Together with them will enter the great, the noble, the honorable, yea, the rulers, the princes, the kings of the earth. Last of all, the wise and learned, the men of genius, the philosophers, will be convinced that they are fools; will 'be converted and become as little children and enter into the kingdom of God'."[202]

Wesley's concluding remark about "the wise and learned" points us toward the systemic values and valuers covered in the next chapter.

Chapter Four

John Wesley's Systemic Values and Valuations

What did Wesley believe about beliefs and believing? How did he value them? Wesley highly valued knowledge, truth, beliefs, God's laws, rituals, intellectual integrity, and systemic Christian values; but he valued other Christian value-objects even more. Echoing Aristotle, he proclaimed that "The desire of knowledge is an universal principle in man, fixed in his inmost nature."[1] He said, "Knowledge is an excellent gift of God, particularly knowledge of the Holy Scriptures."[2] He insisted that Christians can and should be intellectually competent and honest. Martin Luther proclaimed that "Reason is a whore," but Wesley expressly and vehemently repudiated Luther's renunciation of reason, insisting, against Luther, that reason is our very desirable "power of apprehending, judging and discoursing."[3] According to Gerald R. Cragg, Wesley "was horrified to discover that Luther had been willing to 'decry reason, right or wrong, as an irreconcilable enemy to the Gospel of Christ'. Wesley refused to sanction any separation of faith from reason. 'I am for both', he said."[4] Wesley, who saw no incompatibility between reason and religion, wrote, "It is a fundamental principle with *us*, that to renounce reason is to renounce religion; that religion and reason go hand in hand, and that all irrational religion is false religion."[5] Reason is one of the four basic elements of the Wesleyan Quadrilateral, as previously indicated. Wesley was all for knowledge and reason, not against them, and his positive evaluation of them found many practical expressions. Unlike some theologians, e.g., Tertullian, Luther, and Kierkegaard, Wesley never thought that we should believe anything *because* it is irrational, rationally absurd, or self-contradictory.

Wesley established and generally supervised many weekday and Sunday schools for poor children and adults, who otherwise received no education at all in the England of his day. A major objective of both weekday and Sunday schools was to be able to read the Bible, the Catechism, sermons, tracts, the *Arminian Magazine*, and at least a few of the fifty books in the *Christian Library*. Even on Sundays,

Wesley's Sunday schools provided basic training in reading, writing, and arithmetic.[6] His harsh philosophy of educating children may have been somewhat flawed, but it expressed his own understanding of tough love. Like his mother Susanna, he thought that one objective in educating children was to "break their wills" (presumed to be sinful) and make them obedient to God-ordained authorities like parents and preachers.[7] This assumed that the will of every child is totally depraved by nature, but Wesley could have and should have assumed that education must respect and build upon their preveniently restored individuality, that it should cultivate the goodness that is in them, if only by prevenient grace. Though his authoritarian means were inadequate, his pedagogical intent—that everyone should be able to reason and understand—was very commendable.

Wesley made many helpful religious writings and books available to ordinary Christians and to his own ministers through his publishing house, especially his *Arminian Magazine* and his fifty volume *Christian Library*. He wanted not just his own Methodists but all people to be able to read practical books and tracts, e.g., those on health and good business, as well as religious ones. He realized that information affects the quality of the whole of life; it affects everyone's systemic, extrinsic, and intrinsic values and evaluations, we might say. He greatly valued, promoted, and insisted upon a well educated ministry, and he personally supervised the cognitive development of many of his ministers.[8] All Christians should understand and accept Christian doctrines, moral laws or guidelines, and the cognitive aspects of faith, he thought. Though he valued them highly, he still did not overvalue any systemic Christian value-objects. He ranked them properly in relation to extrinsic Christian values like good works and intrinsic Christian values like loving God and "all mankind." If doctrines had to be minimized and de-emphasized in order to express love, so be it. Now for the details.

Wesley as a Believer: Faith in Three Dimensions

John Wesley was both a thinker and a believer. No doubt about that. He highly valued cognitive values like reason, truth, knowledge, and Christian doctrines. He had great curiosity that ranged far beyond theology and evangelism. He taught Logic as well as Philosophy and Greek[9] when he was teaching at Oxford. He said, "How small a part of this great work of God is man able to understand! But it is our duty to contemplate what he has wrought, and to understand as much of it as we are able."[10] He was also acutely sensitive to the limitations of human knowledge, whether in natural science (natural philosophy) or in theology.[11] He still thought that reliable but fallible beliefs are made available to Christians through four different mutually supportive and corrective sources, the revealed scriptures, rational inquiry, experience, and tradition—what Albert Outler (but not Wesley himself) called the Wesleyan Quadrilateral. Wesley hit on three of these when he wrote, "We prove the doctrines we preach by Scripture and reason; and, if need be, by antiquity."[12] To these he often added experiences, especially those of conscience and the spiritual senses.

Keep in mind that Wesley was mainly a traveling revivalistic preacher, not a divinity school professor or systematic theologian. Wesley had only the world as his parish but no local parish of his own. Yet, Wesley was also a profound thinker and exceptionally competent scholar. As Kenneth J. Collins notes, Wesley has an undeserved reputation for being a second-rate theologian, largely because he was primarily interested in practical theology rather than systematic theology.[13] Yet, anyone who reads and digests Collins's book, or any of the books mentioned in the Preface to the present book, must come away with the firm conviction that Wesley had an intricately complex, subtle, and well integrated set of Christian beliefs and values, even if less than systematically organized. Being only human, some of his beliefs changed over time, but many remained fairly constant. Wesley was no intellectual slouch, even though he valued the heart more than the head, even though he insisted on integrating beliefs with affections and practices, and even though he never wrote a formal systematic theology. His practical theology was values-centered, with God and neighbors at the top of his scale of Christian values, but lesser values were not neglected.

Wesley doubtless regarded certain core beliefs as indispensable for Christians.[14] He had firm and well developed views about God's existence and attributes, Jesus as God made flesh, the atonement, the final judgment, the resurrection, original sin, justification by faith, the nature and proper order of salvation, sanctification, Christian perfection, the end of the world as we know it, the new creation to come, heaven and hell,[15] moral laws and guidelines, ritual forms and practices, and many other such things. Wesley thought that Christians do and should believe many things, some of which "heathens" also believe, like "the being and attributes of God, a future state of reward and punishment, and the obligatory nature of moral virtue."[16] But Christians also believe many things that are distinctively Christian; they "confess with thy mouth the Lord Jesus, and...believe in thy *heart* that God hath raised Him from the dead."[17]

Many of these beliefs are examined in various chapters of this book, but for thoroughness, take a careful look at the books by Kenneth J. Collins, Randy Maddox, and other authors mentioned in the Preface. Our present focus is not so much on *what* Wesley believed as on *that* he believed, and on *how* he valued Christian beliefs in relation to other Christian values. Wesley believed systemically, but he valued some Christian beliefs, not just systemically or dispassionately, but also intrinsically or passionately. Still, he valued them less than other Christian goods because he was far more than just a cognitive believer or assenter.

As a good Protestant, Wesley firmly believed in salvation and justification by faith, but what is faith, and how did Wesley define it? Wesley's complex understanding of "faith" requires a three-dimensional analysis that accounts for all of the systemic, intrinsic, and extrinsic values and evaluations inherent in saving faith itself. As Wesley himself put it, "We esteem no faith but that 'which worketh by love.'"[18] This formula for saving faith includes all three dimensions of value, faith (systemic), works (extrinsic) and love (intrinsic). So nothing fulfills the Wesleyan definition or concept of "saving faith" that does not involve the presence and proper ranking of Christian beliefs put to work in daily life out of love. This is also how Wesley understood "holiness" and "true religion" (in one of its formulations). Thus, faith, holiness, and true religion are basically identical, and all three elements are absolutely essential. If any one of these is isolated from the others and turned into the exclusive essence of faith, holiness, or true religion, the result is anything but Wesleyan (and Christian?) faith, holiness, and true religion, properly understood.

Systemic Faith

Systemic value-objects (beliefs, doctrines, rules, principles, ritual forms, etc.) can be combined with human evaluations in many ways—systemically, extrinsically, or intrinsically. Many people approach systemic religious values systemically, that is, with disinterestedness, fair-mindedness, and objectivity. Wesley was perfectly capable of approaching both Christian and non-Christian beliefs with rational objectivity in his more scholarly moods and moments. For example, in his debates with predestinationists, and in many other writings, he appealed to "every impartial mind" to be self-consistent and to consider his arguments impartially, calmly, fairly, and without prejudice.[19] In "The Case of Reason, Impartially Considered," he argued that we should neither "undervalue" nor "overvalue" reason. In order to value reason correctly, Wesley tried to explain "first, to undervaluers of it, what reason can do; and then to the overvaluers of it, what reason cannot do."[20] This involved carefully defining basic terms like "reason" itself. To understand "reason," we should lay aside all prejudice and weigh the matter calmly and impartially; we should be systemically rational and unbiased even about "reason." No disputes will ever get anywhere, Wesley the logician insisted, without clear definitions of key concepts from the very outset,[21] so clear and consistent thinking is highly desirable in both religion and rational philosophy.

In case you are curious about the outcome of Wesley's inquiry, he equated "reason" with "understanding" and defined it and what it can do as follows.

> It means a faculty of the human soul; that faculty which exerts itself in three ways: by simple apprehension, by judgment, and by discourse. *Simple apprehension* is barely conceiving a thing in the mind, the first and most simple act of understanding. *Judgment* is the determining that the things before conceived either agree with or differ from each other. *Discourse*, strictly speaking, is the motion or progress of the mind from one judgment to another. The faculty of the soul which includes these three operations I here mean by the term *reason*.[22]

Notice that there are no innate ideas, no intuitively or rationally self-evident truths, in Wesley's understanding of "reason." Curiously, John Locke himself,[23] others influenced by him like Thomas Jefferson,[24] and even John Wesley,[25] appealed at times to self-evident truths that were substantive or informative and not merely tautological or analytic. Wesley's own "self-evident" examples did not include any intuitively obvious moral truths, though he certainly opened the door for them; and they may have been latent in his understanding of "conscience" and how it works.

Reason, as described above, is absolutely indispensable in managing the everyday affairs of life, Wesley insisted. In all areas of human life, we must have concepts, combine these concepts into judgments, and make logical inferences with and from them ("discourses"). Is reason relevant to religion? About religion Wesley asked, "What can reason do here?" and answered, "It can do exceeding much, both with regard to the foundation of it, and the superstructure."[26] Combined with experience, preveniently effective reason gives even non-Christians a knowledge of the being and the basic attributes of God; and only by using reason can Christians understand the Scriptures and Christian truths, solve "cases of conscience," and understand and discharge our practical and moral duties.[27] Even without revelation, the "heathens" know many such things.[28] A great deal of reasoning goes on within the Bible itself; Jesus and Paul were careful thinkers, "strong reasoners;" and in "Holy Writ" we find "both our Lord and his apostles continually reasoning with their opposers."[29]

As for what reason cannot do, it alone cannot "give either faith, hope, love, or virtue...[or] happiness."[30] Christian faith, hope, love, virtue, and happiness may go beyond what unaided reason alone can deliver, but they never contradict or conflict with reason. Christian faith "is always consistent with reason."[31] In this respect, Wesley's solution to the reason versus religion problem was very much like that of St. Thomas Aquinas. Also like Aquinas, Wesley thought that reason might be able to show us that God exists, yet still not tell us very much about his essence or what God is like. Fortunately, the spiritual senses provide experiential evidence of this and add relevant information to bare reason.[32] As an avowed empiricist, Wesley thought that reason provides no content of its own. There are no "innate ideas." To have anything to reason about, any "matter to work upon," something else is required, either sensations, internal or spiritual experiences, or divine revelations.[33]

Religious irrationalist say that we should believe *against* reason, but Wesley was not a religious irrationalist. He did express some reservations, however, about the definitive adequacy of a purely "natural reason," which he once called "that blind leader of the blind."[34] Perhaps we can make some sense of this and reconcile it with his repeated affirmations of reason in the following way. Since reason supplies no content of its own, this is always derived from other sources. Reason always functions within the context of the experiences, assumptions, and values we bring with us to the process of conceiving, judging, and making logical inferences. "Natural reason" brings with it mainly worldly extrinsic-value experiences, assumptions, and biases. It has nothing else with which to work. What we might call "ivory tower reason," by contrast, is dominated by intellectualistic assumptions, biases, and systemic values. Redeemed rationality, what Wesley called "enlightened reason,"[35] by contrast, includes the extrinsic and the systemic, but it also brings godly assumptions, perspectives, experiences, and intrinsic values into the thinking, learning, knowing, and believing process. The inclusive context within which it functions is much richer in meaning and goodness than the worldly way or the ivory tower way. Wesley insisted that it is perfectly *reasonable* to love God and all our human neighbors and thus that the "religion we preach and live [is] agreeable to the highest reason."[36]

Whether we agree or not with Wesley's account of how natural and redeemed reason work, he clearly and strongly supported systemically rational, impartial, and unprejudiced inquiry and clear thinking in natural philosophy, religion, morals, and wherever appropriate. Later Methodists and Wesleyans built and have been justly proud of their (our) very fine colleges, universities, and graduate schools and of the intellectual honesty and integrity that they represent and uphold. Wesley would be proud of their (our) educational successes. Wesley was not a religious irrationalist who advocated believing in the absurd, and neither should we be. Yet, we should neither overvalue nor undervalue reason, as he well understood. Realistically, the only thing that reason and philosophy can offer is an enlightened faith. Getting our values straight comprehensively is essential to such enlightenment.

Wesley made it perfectly clear that Christian living involves much more than a merely disinterested affirmation of and attachment to either rational, philosophical, or Christian beliefs. He thought that some Christian doctrines, laws, rules, principles, and rituals go beyond (but not contrary to) reason. He further stressed that *Christian beliefs and guidelines are not to be accepted merely disinterestedly; they are also to be intrinsically valued.* Being a true Christian involves *loving* Christian doctrines, God's laws, and other systemic or formal Christian values with one's "heart," that is, intrinsically—as the author of Psalm 119 loved God's law—but not just with one's "head," that is, systemically or disinterestedly. The Christian "keeps all his commandments, loves them all, values them above gold or precious stones."[37] We are to "love and value" the law and let it be our "glory and joy."[38]

Wesley advocated both the systemic and the intrinsic evaluation of Christian systemic values. There are appropriate times and places for each. He said that Christian believing or faith "is not barely a speculative, rational thing, a cold, lifeless assent, a train of ideas in the head; but also a disposition of the heart."[39] It is also "not *formality*, the most exact observance of all the ordinances of God."[40] He personally identified whole-heartedly with and cherished his own beliefs and formal ritual practices. They became an integral part of his very being or constitution. He thought that all Christians should identify intensely and intrinsically with their carefully considered moral and spiritual convictions and ordinances. Wesley affirmed both the heart and the head. Specifically, he advocated beliefs taken thoughtfully to heart, to an informed and enlightened heart, to heart and head conjoined. He strongly disapproved of mind without feelings (cold speculation or assent), and of feelings without mind (what was then called "enthusiasm"). Wesley not only accepted or assented to basic Christian guidelines and beliefs, he loved them, and he thought that all Christians should do the same. Yet, this was not his last word on the subject, for he loved other Christian values even more, for example, actually doing the works of love, and identifying personally with others through love, empathy, compassion, consolation, mercy. He deliberately and consciously subordinated cognitive assent to doctrines to heartfelt loving and doing. He said that Methodists "hold right opinions; but they are peculiarly cautious not to rest the weight of Christianity there."[41]

The "how we value" aspect of relating to systemic faith objects can range from *disinterested* cognitive assent to fundamental Christian doctrines to *passionate love* of and involvement with such doctrines, preferably the latter most of the time, Wesley thought. Belief in systemic objects—the "what we value" aspect—clearly belonged within Wesley's understanding of "faith." He thought that we should love certain systemic value-objects, certain Christian doctrines and formalities, thus that we should evaluate them intrinsically. Wesley was a disinterested cognitive thinker and believer, but he also insisted that Christians should assent *passionately* to Christian truths, that they should be "true believers."[42] Is this what we mean today in speaking, as we often do, of Christians as "believers"?

Yes, having "true religion," Wesley thought, involves being passionately committed to certain doctrinal beliefs; but there is much more to "saving faith" than that. Doctrines are not the only proper or even the most proper objects of Christian faith. A purely systemic faith is not a saving faith. Speaking of Christians as "believers" can be misleading. It may give the mistaken impression that the sanctified soul's primary values are systemic value-objects, that being a Christian is mainly a matter of subscribing either disinterestedly or passionately to a set of doctrines about Jesus, God, and other divine things. Wesley emphatically rejected this.

Instead of calling Christians "believers," wouldn't it be just as legitimate and much less misleading to speak of us as "lovers," or as "doers," or as all three at once, as those who have faith that works through love? Each of these needs to be fleshed out with details: lovers and doers of what? Believers in what? Must the loving and doing be focused only on doctrines? Why not passionate lovers of people and God rather than, or in addition to, lovers of and believers in doctrines? Why not passionate doers of the word instead of just passionate hearers or assenters only? Is there nothing more to "having faith" than "cognitive assent," even when passionate? Wesley certainly thought so, calling "*believers*, men full of faith and love."[43] His convictions about this were so strong that he refused to recognize *a purely systemic faith* as being faith at all. Stripped of its "worketh in love" aspects, a merely cognitive assent to Christian truth is not a saving faith at all; *even the devils have it*! To his question, "What is faith?" he answered, "Not an opinion....Not an assent to any opinion, or any number of opinions. A man may assent to three or three-and-twenty creeds; he may assent to all the Old and New Testament (at least, as far as he understands them) and yet have no Christian faith at all."[44] Elsewhere he wrote, "If it contains no more than this, no more than the embracing such and such truths,"[45] it will not avail before God; it is not a saving faith. Faith involves beliefs or opinions, but it is far more. What else is it? What do authentic Christian saints have that the devils do not have? Can non-systemic value-objects like intrinsically valuable persons or God ever be its proper targets? Can it even exist without being expressed in doing and living?

Intrinsic Faith

Intrinsic faith goes far beyond believing certain doctrines or propositions to be true, though it definitely includes that. It involves not only *how* saints value but also *what* they value. It is much more personalized than systemic faith. The disinterested systemic "how" of faith moves into intrinsic faith once it becomes heartfelt and expands beyond mere cognitive assent. The "what" of faith also becomes intrinsic once it takes objective intrinsic realities rather than systemic doctrines about them as its proper objects. Wesley probably had both the *how* and the *what* in mind when in "Scriptural Christianity" he spoke of "'Christianity'; not as it implies a set of opinions, a system of doctrines, but as it refers to men's hearts and lives."[46] "False religion," Wesley said, "is any religion which does not imply *the giving the heart to God*. Such is, first, a religion of opinions, or what is commonly called orthodoxy."[47] Here Wesley calls all doctrines, "opinions," even those of orthodoxy, but at times he applied the term only to *unessential doctrines*. But by what criteria do we distinguish between the essential and the unessential? Which beliefs really support intrinsic Christian values and evaluations? Those are really crucial questions.

Wesley included doctrines in saving faith, though convinced that they are not the whole story or even the most important part of the Christian story. In "Scriptural Christianity" and elsewhere he identified what he believed to be the *essential doctrines* of the Christian's faith. The very "essence of his faith," Wesley explained, is "a divine [evidence or conviction] of the love of God the Father, through the Son of His love, to him a sinner, 'now accepted in the beloved.'"[48] Beliefs are involved here, but the beliefs refer to the reality of a person's being in a direct intrinsic relationship with a personal God, and to the reality of that person's assurance of being an "accepted" child of God. In one sermon, fundamental beliefs, or what he called the "capital doctrines," were said to be "the fall of man, justification by faith, and of the atonement made by the death of Christ, and of his righteousness transferred to them."[49] Varying somewhat in details, he summarized the doctrines that he regarded as central or "fundamental" in a number of his writings.[50]

In recognizing Christian doctrinal fundamentals or essentials, Wesley was very much like Twentieth Century fundamentalists. Some Christian doctrines are essential, Wesley thought, but the real focus of "faith" is not on fundamental doctrines as such. In this respect, he differs significantly from much Roman Catholic and Protestant fundamentalistic thought. Wesley's real focus was on the objective intrinsic *realities* to which fundamental Christian doctrines and conceptual symbols point and refer. He did not value Christian truths or biblical doctrines *for their own sake*;

he valued them because they were *good for us*, because they can help to set us free, because they point toward and can induce contact with the intrinsic realities to which they refer, because they play a role in transforming our characters into the likeness of those objective divine realities, and because they convey blessed assurance of personal salvation.[51] Beliefs *mediate* between us and the divine things to which they refer, but they should not be confused with or valued as much as those realities. Otherwise, systemic idolatry results. "Realities" is plural here because of the Trinity and all of its unified complexities.

There is a crucial difference between purely systemic and intrinsic understandings of "faith," even though Christians need both. According to the "what" of systemic faith, we assent at least disinterestedly, perhaps even passionately or intrinsically, to the truth of certain doctrines or *"propositions,"* as Wesley and many other theologians called them. According to intrinsic faith, by contrast, we assent passionately and lovingly to the *objective realities* to which such doctrines or propositions refer. This is a radical difference in emphasis. Systemic faith worships the Bible or traditional doctrines; intrinsic faith worships the loving and forgiving God of the Bible and of church traditions. Wesley's thinking about "faith" was just that radical. According to Wesley, "Christ, and God through Christ, are the proper object of it."[52] Faith is really about trust and confidence in *them,* the objective realities, the living divine persons in themselves and in us. The living reality of God's Spirit within us will be discussed later in connection with what Wesley called the "spiritual senses." Intrinsic faith in personal realities is "not a barely speculative, rational thing, a cold, lifeless assent, a train of ideas in the head; but also a disposition of the heart."[53] This disposition of the heart is toward the *objects* of Biblical and Christian beliefs, not the biblical doctrines or church teachings and traditions themselves, even if such words are practically indispensable mediators, symbols, or pointers.

Christians agree with Paul and Silas (Acts 16:31), that we must "Believe on the Lord Jesus Christ" in order to be saved, and with the author of I. John that "Whosoever believeth that Jesus is the Christ is born of God." But what does "believe on" mean? Is it just a matter of "believing that" certain doctrines, those of orthodoxy, are true? Is it merely a matter of assenting dispassionately or even passionately to the truth of propositions about Jesus? Wesley did not think so. Explaining the meaning of "faith," he said, "But it is not a barely notional or speculative faith that is here spoken of by the Apostles. It is not a bare assent to this proposition, 'Jesus is the Christ;' nor indeed to all the propositions contained in our creed, or in the Old and New Testament."[54] The "believing on" or "believing in" that saves is having a personal loving, trusting, confident relationship with the realities to which "believing that" refers. All of our words and beliefs about God and Jesus are attempts to make conceptual sense of the objective Divine Realities toward which they point.

In his sermon on "The Scripture Way of Salvation," Wesley recognized that having a personal relationship with the objective intrinsic realities of faith definitely involves beliefs, most specifically, "not only that 'God was in Christ reconciling the world unto himself', but also that Christ 'loved *me* and gave himself for me'."[55] In a temporal sense, he contended, these beliefs are the "first" aspects of faith, because they appear immediately in believers, and the other or "second" parts of faith usually take time and are not available to us without them. Yet, a much more advanced intrinsic faith is spiritually or valuationally first; it involves a *direct love for and experience of* the realities to which those beliefs refer; and it means responding to those realities with tempers of *assurance, trust, love, peace, joy, and confidence.* Since all religious affections, including these are ramifications of love, intrinsic faith is itself an expression of love, and by definition it includes love.

These spiritual tempers are also aspects of Wesley's theory of the spiritual senses, discussed later, and they are integral to his understanding of what is here being called "intrinsic faith." Through the spiritual senses, we can have a direct awareness of the *reality* of God's Holy Spirit *within us,* giving us the *assurance* that we are the loved, forgiven, and accepted children of God.[56] The spiritual senses provide the "evidence of things hoped for, the conviction of things not seen" (Hebrews 11:1). Even faith, thus understood, is based on evidence, not that of the physical senses, but that provided by the spiritual senses—a direct personal encounter with the Spirit of God. This faith is not mediated solely through teachings and doctrines; it is knowledge through immediate experience, through direct inner personal contact with the Holy Spirit of God.

In explaining "believing," Wesley added important information about the *how* of intrinsic faith. It is more than just *assent* to propositions. It also involves *trust* and *confidence in objective religious realities.* Of "the nature of this faith," he said,

> It is not (as some have fondly conceived) a bare assent to the truth of the Bible, of the articles of our Creed, or of all that is contained in the Old and New Testament. The devils believe this, as well as I or thou; and yet they are devils still. But it is, over and above this, a sure trust in the mercy of God, through Christ Jesus. It is a confidence in a pardoning God. It is a divine evidence or conviction that 'God was in Christ, reconciling the world to himself, not imputing to their former trespasses;' and in particular that the Son of God hath loved me, and given himself for me; and that I, even I, am now reconciled to God by the blood of the cross.[57]

Trust and confidence can be treated in the same systemic way belief is sometimes treated. What are the "due" or proper objects of Christian trust and confidence? Is this just a matter of "trusting the Bible" or "having confidence that traditional Christian doctrines are true?" Or is it much more than that? Do we, should we, most properly trust in the realities of the loving and forgiving God and Christ to whom the Bible and our doctrines point? What are the most proper "objects" of Christian trust and confidence?

Wesley thought that Christians having what we are calling "intrinsic faith" relate personally, individually, and experientially or "experimentally" to the personal realities of God as Spirit in Christ with *love, assent, assurance, trust, peace, and confidence.* All of these religious affections are integral to the very notion of "faith" or "believing in" properly understood,[58] intrinsically understood. Believing on or in Christ, essential to Christian salvation, involves *direct spiritual experience, assurance, deep trust and confidence, enhanced religious affections (especially love), as well as cognitive assent.* Yes, it makes use of conceptual symbols, doctrines, and biblical beliefs (which even the devils accept); but most important of all are the affective responses of trust and confidence in the objective personal loving and forgiving realities of God and Christ, as signified by those beliefs, and as applied to the believer. According to Wesley, "The true, living, Christian faith...is not only an assent, an act of the understanding, but a disposition, which God hath wrought in his heart; 'a sure trust and confidence in God that through the merits of Christ his sins are forgiven, and he reconciled to the favour of God';" and faith is "'not only a belief of all the articles of our faith, but also a true confidence of the mercy of God, through our Lord Jesus Christ'."[59]

In intrinsic faith (involving assent, assurance, love, trust, joy, and confidence) is *in or directed toward* the *objects or realities* to which our "propositions" and "articles" refer, not simply in the propositions and articles themselves, as in systemic faith. Remember that Wesley threw out fifteen of the Thirty-nine Articles of the Church of England and revised others. Intrinsic faith takes the distinction between sign and thing signified very seriously.

Intrinsic Christian faith thus involves *experiencing* a profound, personal, assuring, and trusting relationship with and confidence in the realities of God through Christ and in Christ, mediated and in-formed largely by symbols, beliefs, doctrines, and practices, but not centered on or exhausted by them. God, the Holy Spirit, and Christ as objective realities are far richer in meaning and value than anything that we can ever put into words, thoughts, or propositions. All related words or signs are inadequate attempts to interpret the meaning of those realities. Positive symbols are never as rich in meaning and goodness as the positive realities they symbolize, which is why they have less value than those objective realities.

This intrinsic understanding of "faith" also has a bearing also on very nature of Christian *revelation*. Is God's revelation to us the *person* of Jesus, or *propositions* about Jesus? This question has been much discussed and debated, and it still is even today. Systemically understood, Christian revelation consists primarily of the Bible and the truths or propositions that it contains, or at least selected "fundamentals" thereof. Wesley certainly had a mean systemic streak in him, much more so in some moods and writings than others, but there was a lot more to Wesley than that. Intrinsically understood, Christian revelation consists primarily of Jesus himself, the real person, the object and most proper referent of those "fundamental" truths, whatever they are. In intrinsic faith, the ultimate revelation of God is a person, not a doctrine. Systemically understood, "The Bible is the revelation of God" (Protestant version), or "The traditional teachings of the church are the revelation of God" (Roman Catholic version). Intrinsically understood, "Jesus Christ is the revelation of God," and bibliolatry is idolatry. Christian faith, systemically understood, consists in believing or assenting to certain fundamental truths. Christian faith, intrinsically understood, consists in having an intense intrinsic personal relation with and spiritual experience of the Spirit of the living Christlike God himself through the indwelling witness of the Holy Spirit. This is far more than anything that merely conceptual symbols, words, or doctrines could ever capture or convey. Viewed exclusively, systemic "believing that" and intrinsic "believing on" are radically different approaches to the very nature of both "saving faith" and "divine revelation;" but they can also be viewed as complementary when properly combined and ranked in value.

The most important thing about the cognitive aspects of faith, as Wesley saw it, is that they lead to and support love; cognitive beliefs are *means* to that *end*, thus primarily of instrumental significance. Faith, cognitively understood, is "still is only the handmaiden of love. As glorious and honourable as it is, it is not the end of the commandment. God hath given this honor to love alone: love is the end of all of the commandments of God."[60] Along the same lines, he wrote, "I regard even faith itself not as an end but a means only. The end of the commandment is love, of every command, of the whole Christian dispensation. Let this love be attained, by whatever means, and I am content; I desire no more. All is well, if we love the Lord our God with all our heart and our neighbor as ourselves."[61] This faith has a very minimal and simple conceptual content! When he compared and ranked the worth of (systemic or doctrinal) faith with that of love, Wesley wrote of "the superior glory of love, above that of faith," and he said, "It [cognitive faith] loses all its excellence when brought into a comparison with love."[62] Here is how he spelled out the relative, relational, or comparative value of such faith and love.

> Faith then was originally designed of God to re-establish the law of love....It is the grand means of restoring that holy love wherein man was originally created. It follows that although faith is of no value in itself (as neither is any other means whatsoever), yet as it leads to that end—the establishing anew the law of love in our hearts—and as in the present state of things it is the only means under heaven for effecting it, it is on that account an unspeakable blessing to man, and of unspeakable value before God.[63]

So, a very good thing (systemic faith/assent) can be of unspeakable value as a means, yet of much less value than something else (intrinsic faith/love). Faith, hope, and love abide, but the greatest of these is love.[64] Yet, even love must be directed to its proper objects, the realities of God and people and animals.

Extrinsic Faith

Although it may exist largely by itself or combined with systemic faith, extrinsic faith can and should be an integral part or aspect of intrinsic faith. Intrinsic faith and Christian love inevitably express themselves in works as well as words. Salvation involves a faith that works through love. Without works, saving faith does not even exist. No Christian faith and love are real without works. Intrinsic faith is not merely something internal; external expression is integral to its very essence. Having real faith, intrinsic faith, necessitates "practicing what we preach." Thus it requires and involves extrinsic faith. The pragmatist tradition in philosophy says that a "willingness to act" is the very meaning of "believing." We don't really believe anything if we are not willing and ready to live it and act on it; and if we do sincerely believe anything, we are willing and ready to live it and put it into practice. The book of James (2:17) says that "Faith without works is dead." Doesn't that mean that faith without works isn't really faith at all? Wesley definitely thought so: "For inasmuch as faith without works is dead, it is not faith."[65] Thus, "works" is an integral part of the very meaning of "faith," properly understood, and faith without works does not even satisfy the very definition of saving "faith." Being unwilling to act on our beliefs is a sure sign that our intrinsic moral and spiritual affections, our hearts, are not in them.

Consider a philosophical example of how the pragmatist's "to believe it is to live it" might work. The skeptical philosopher, David Hume, was a contemporary of John Wesley. Wesley was no fan or supporter of David Hume! Hume argued, among other things, that we have no rational grounds for believing in causation, or in any regularities or uniformities (i.e., laws) in nature, or in any of our own cognitive capacities. Yet, he admitted that he could not live by his own skeptical philosophy![66] The pragmatist would advise us not to bother with theories that we can't believe, that is, those by which we cannot actually live, for no one can "believe" such things, by definition. Amazingly, philosophers from Hume's day to our own who think of themselves as friends of natural science are also admirers of David Hume. This is almost impossible to understand, since if Hume the skeptic was right, there can be no natural science because there are no natural causes, laws, or regularities, and none of our capacities and methods for knowing are reliable. Science is quite impossible without natural causes, the uniformity of nature, the laws of nature, and our use of scientific methodology. No scientist can *practice* his trade, given Hume's skepticism. So why give it? Well, Wesley himself was no friend of David Hume!

To return to faith and practice, as Wesley well knew, we can at times do good works for the wrong reasons—for example, that others might praise us;[67] but when done for Christian reasons and out of Christian faith and love, doing the works of love is a defining property "faith" (believing) as well as of "love." Wesley well understood the inescapable cognitive and psychological links between faith, love, and works. To the "usual objection" that preaching "justification by faith only" is preaching "against holiness and good works," Wesley replied: "It would be so, if we spake, as some do, of a faith which was separate from these; but we speak of a faith which is not so, but productive of all good works and all holiness."[68] According to Wesley, "*We esteem no faith but that 'which worketh by love'*;"[69] and "Love cannot be hid any more than light; and least of all when it shines forth in action, when ye exercise yourselves in the labour of love, in beneficence of every kind;" so each Christian should be an "active lover of God and man."[70]

St. Paul's *"faith that works by love"* (Galatians 5:6), was Wesley's constant theme and his very definition of "saving faith," "true religion," and "holiness." Holiness is valuationally three dimensional, containing systemic beliefs, extrinsic actions, and intrinsic love. So is faith. So is love. So is true religion. The adequacy of any perspective on Christianity can be measured by the presence or absence of one or more of these three good-making criteria of true religion, and of the priority in which they are ranked. These basic Christian concepts are coherently interlocked. Saving faith, properly understood, is a three dimensional concept, and no one really has it unless all three value dimensions are present and properly ordered: first, a profound personal trust and confidence in the objective reality of a loving Christlike God, next, a willingness to do the works of holy love, mercy, and justice, and finally, cognitive assent to mediating beliefs that point beyond themselves. Wesley championed neither cognitive faith alone, nor uninformed love alone, but an informed "faith that worketh by love."[71] And the greatest of these is love. Wesleyans have a very profound and complex understanding of the very nature of "faith." All Christians should share that understanding.

Consider the presence of all three value dimensions in Wesley's comprehensive summary below of what is involved in being a devout Christian.

> 'What is it to worship God, a Spirit, in spirit and in truth?' Why, it is to worship him with our spirit; to worship him in that manner which none but spirits are capable of. It is to *believe* in him, as a wise, just, holy being, of purer eyes than to behold iniquity; and yet merciful, gracious, and longsuffering; forgiving iniquity and transgression and sin; casting all our sins behind his back, and accepting us in the beloved. It is, to *love* him, to *delight* in him, to *desire* him, with all our heart, and mind, and soul, and strength; to *imitate* him we love, by purifying ourselves even as he is pure; and to *obey* him whom we *love*, and in whom we *believe*, both in *thought and word and work*. Consequently, one branch of the worshipping God in spirit and in truth is the *keeping* his outward commandments. To glorify him, therefore *with our bodies as well as with our spirits*, to go through *outward work with hearts* lifted up to him, to make our *daily employment* a sacrifice to God, *to buy and sell, to eat and drink, to his glory*: this is worshipping *God* in spirit and in truth as much as the praying to him in a wilderness.
>
> But if so, then *contemplation* is *only one way* of worshipping God in spirit and in truth. Therefore to give ourselves up entirely to this would be to destroy *many branches of spiritual worship, all equally acceptable to God*, and equally profitable, not hurtful, to *the soul*.[72] (Italics added.)

John Wesley was a faith-believer, but he was far more than a systemic believer. He was also a faith-doer and a faith-lover. He thought that all Christians should be doers and lovers as well as conceivers and contemplators. His was a *faith* that *works* by *love*.

Wesley as More than a Believer

Wesley clearly value-ranked beliefs, and faith as doctrinal believing, much lower than love. He ranked the intrinsic over the systemic very explicitly and very often.

As we have seen, Wesley value-ranking love-faith higher than doctrinal-faith. He firmly believed that we are saved by faith (broadly conceived in three dimensions), but when he separated them and assessed the value or goodness of doctrinal faith in relation to the value of love, he treated systemic faith in much the same way that he treated the means of grace, namely, as way to gain a higher or more valuable end, that is, as *productive* of holy love. This comes out most clearly in his sermon on "The Law Established Through Faith, II," which makes much better sense given our threefold value distinctions.

> We establish the law...when we so preach faith in Christ as not so supersede, but produce, holiness, to produce all manner of holiness, negative and positive, of the heart and of the life.
>
> In order to this, we continually declare...that faith itself, even Christian faith, the faith of God's elect, the faith of the operation of God, still is only the handmaid of love. As glorious and honourable as it is, it is not the end of the commandment. God hath given this honor to love alone: love is the end, the sole end, of every dispensation of God, from the beginning of the world to the consummation of all things.[73]

How Wesley value-ranked doctrinal assent and *thoughts* about God and Christ should now be clear. He reflected on them dispassionately or objectively, but he also loved them. He loved Christian systemic values, especially those judged "essential," but he definitely loved them less and attached much less value to them than to the intrinsic objective *realities* of God, people, and all conscious creatures. As for truth itself, it definitely has less value than love; as Wesley said, "For how far is love, even with many wrong opinions, to be preferred before truth itself without love."[74]

Why Beliefs Have a Subordinate Place

Consider now a number of reasons why Wesley subordinated systemically valuable beliefs to intrinsically valuable persons and God.

● *God himself ranks people over beliefs.* In "On Living Without God," Wesley addressed, as follows, the concerns of those who say that no one can be saved who does not have a clear view of Christianity's "capital doctrines."

> Indeed I do not believe it. I believe the merciful God regards the lives and tempers of men more than their ideas. I believe he respects the goodness of the heart rather than the clearness of the head; and that if the heart of a man be filled (by the grace of God, and the power of his Spirit) with the humble, gentle, patient love of God and man, God will not cast him into everlasting fire prepared for the devil and his angels

because his ideas are not clear, or because his conceptions are confused. Without holiness, I own, "no man shall see the Lord," but I dare not add, or clear ideas.[75]

Here, "regarding more" means "valuing more." God values people's lives and tempers or affections more than their ideas. Here, from God's perspective, heart is ranked over head, good people over clear ideas, intrinsic values over systemic values.

- *The devils believe (James 2:19) without being saved*. One of the most poignant expressions of Wesley's low ranking of assent to doctrines is repeated in a number of his sermons—that the devils mentally believe absolutely everything in the Bible and the Apostles Creed, but they are still not Christians.[76] What do they have, and what do they lack? They have systemic faith, but systemic faith in the right doctrines is not saving faith. The devils assent cognitively to all the proper doctrines, to everything in the Bible and the creeds, but they still lack something that true Christians have. They lack three things that mere assent to doctrinal truths does not encompass: love of God, love of all mankind, and a personal appropriation of God's love and forgiveness—the application of God's love and forgiveness to themselves.[77] We, like they, can be "as orthodox as the devil"[78] and still not be real Christians.

- *Christians disagree.* Wesley clearly ranked *loving over agreeing* in doctrines and ceremonial practices, especially so in his great sermon on "Catholic Spirit," where "catholic" meant "universal Christian" rather than "Roman Catholic." All true Christians are committed to loving "all mankind" as they love themselves, Wesley explained, but to this there are "two grand, general hindrances." These are, "They can't all think alike; and in consequence of this, secondly, they can't all walk alike."[79] Yet, differences in Christian opinions (unessential and controversial doctrines) and practices or "modes of worship," he insisted, should never interfere with loving one another. These should never "prevent our union in affection."

Wesley's considered advice concerning highly controversial doctrinal issues was, "Do not spend your time and strength contending for or against such things as of a disputable nature;" instead, leave "a thousand disputable points to those that have no better business than to toss the ball of controversy to and fro."[80] Preaching from II. Kings, 10:15, Wesley argued that differences of opinion on disputed issues matter very little and should be overlooked for the sake of Christian love. "Though we can't think alike, may we not love alike? May we not be of one heart, though we are not of one opinion? Without all doubt we may."[81] "'Is thine heart right, as my heart is with thy heart?...'If it be, give me thine hand.'"[82] Agreement of heart, not of head, is what really matters. Wesley exhorted, "Let thy religion be the religion of the heart."[83] Intrinsic values trump systemic values. Disagreements and controversies among Christians who love one another are inevitable, but love prevails over opinions, controversies, and disagreements. As Wesley said, "And 'tis certain, so long as 'we know' but 'in part', that all men will not see all things alike. It is an unavoidable consequence of the present weakness and shortness of human understanding that several men will be of several minds, in religion as well as in common life. So it has been from the beginning of the world, and so it will be 'till the restitution of all things.'"[84]

Joyfully accepting differences of opinion about unessentials for the sake of loving one another is not the same as having no opinions or beliefs at all. Nor it is merely judicial or systemic "tolerance." Christians can and should actually rejoice in their differences! Wesley insisted that "A catholic spirit is not *speculative latitudinarianism*. It is not indifference to all opinions."[85] Some basic opinions and actions as well as attitudes or "religious affections" are integral to the very meaning and constitution of having hearts attuned in Christian love. Wesley's more detailed explanation in "Catholic Spirit" of what it means to "have your heart right with God," as it is often put, may be summarized as follows. It means:

1. Believing in the being and perfections of God, "His eternity, immensity, wisdom, power; his justice, mercy and truth."
2. Believing in the Lord Jesus Christ and having him "dwell in thee and thou in Him."
3. Being "filled with the energy of love" to God.
4. Being "employed in doing, 'not thy own will, but the will of Him that sent thee.'"
5. Serving God, fear of displeasing him, rejoicing, reverence, hating evil ways, and a conscience "void of offence toward God and toward man."
6. Loving "all mankind, without exception" as you love yourself, not only your enemies, but "even the enemies of God."
7. Showing "your love by your works."[86]

But "Your heart is right with God, so give me your hand," does *not* mean either "Be of my opinion" or "I will be of your opinion."[87] On many issues, Christians should just agree to disagree, or, as Wesley often put it, "Think and let think,"[88] but still love one another anyway. Love has priority over beliefs, intrinsic values over systemic values, though some beliefs are indispensable for loving or for even having intrinsic values. As Wesley explained in his sermon "On the Trinity,"

> Whatsoever the generality of people may think, it is certain that opinion is not religion: no, not right opinion; assent to one or to ten thousand truths. There is a wide difference between them: even right opinion is as distant from religion as the east is from the west. Persons may be quite right in their opinions, yet have no religion at all. And on the other hand persons may be truly religious who hold many wrong opinions...but many of them are now real Christians, loving God and all mankind.[89]

The universal agreement of all rationally and spiritually competent persons may be an ideal to which we aspire, but it is not the reality with which we live. As Wesley saw it, the important thing is to love even in the face of honest disagreements.

- *Many essential doctrines are unclear and controversial.* Christians may actually agree verbally but still disagree substantively about exactly what their "fundamental" or "essential" words or concepts mean, and this is another good reason for loving while not agreeing or even fully comprehending. We saw some of this previously when discussing various interpretations of God's attributes. The problem is clearly manifest in Wesley's treatment of the doctrine of the Trinity. Wesley firmly believe in the doctrine of the Trinity; the only problem was, he didn't know what it meant! And he doubted that anyone else did! In his sermon, "On the Trinity," he argued that we believe many things without fully understanding them, so believing in the Trinity is no different from what is already familiar to us. Also, he said, he did not insist on applying the words "Trinity" or even "Person" to God, for these words are not found in the Scriptures.[90] However, the Scriptures do talk about the Father, the Son (the Word made flesh), and the Holy Spirit, without explaining exactly how they are interrelated. So, even though we "are not required to believe any mystery,"[91] we should still believe as much as has been revealed, even if a lot has not been revealed. The upshot on the Trinity was,

> I believe this *fact* also (if I may use the expression)—that God is Three and One. But the *manner, how,* I do not comprehend; and I do not believe it. Now in this, in the *manner,* lies the mystery, and so it may; I have no concern with it. It is no object of my faith. I believe just so much as God has revealed, and no more. But this, the *manner*, has not been revealed; therefore, I believe nothing about it. But would it not be absurd in me to deny the fact, because I do not understand the manner? That is, to reject *what God has revealed*, because I do not comprehend *what he has not revealed*.[92]

Thus, the exact relations between the Father, the Word, and the Holy Ghost, though the terms are biblical, are best left "unexplained."[93] (Presumably, saying that they are "three persons in one substance" does not help very much!) Wesley's account of the Trinity may still leave *us* wondering what it means and how we can affirm it without lapsing into tri-theism. But his discussion does show how little he insisted on a belief that he regarded as so central to Christian orthodoxy. The Trinity can be and has been interpreted in many ways, some of which do successfully avoid tri-theism, but that is a story for some other book.

Hope for Non-Christians

Non-Christians can be saved. The most powerful evidence that Wesley valued people more than beliefs is this. He thought that God saves people who are not *doctrinally believing* Christians at all, as long as they are *saintly* in dispositions, affections, practices, and insights, that is, as long as they do their very best given the light or enlightenment that they have, as long as their hearts, minds, and deeds are in the right place, even if they do not believe exactly as orthodox Christians believe. *Christ's atonement is sufficient for them even if they do not know it or accept it!*

Wesley's high hopes for non-Christians comes out in several of his sermons. In "A Caution Against Bigotry," he asked whether Christians should forbid others to "cast out devils" who "followeth not us," who are "not of our party," who "differ from us in our religious opinions."[94] By "casting out devils" he meant opposing and combating evils of every kind. "A bigot," he said, "is so fond of any of these [our own party, opinion, Church, and religion], so strongly attached to them, as to forbid any who casts out devils, because he differs from himself in any or all of these particulars."[95] Wesley advised, "beware" of bigotry, and he affirmed that non-Christians as well as Christians can successfully cast out devils (combat evil), no matter if they are "a Papist, an Arian, a Socinian,...a Jew, a Deist, or a Turk."[96] (Turks were Moslems.) With respect to non-Christian fellow-workers against evil, we should " Encourage whomsoever God is pleased to employ, to give himself wholly thereto. Speak well of him wheresoever you are; defend his character and his mission. Enlarge as far as you can, his sphere of action. Show him all kindness in word and deed. And cease not to cry to God in his behalf, that he may save both himself and them that hear him."[97]

Prominent Wesley scholars acknowledge that Wesley was optimistic not only about the *goodness* of those who do not believe as Christians believe, but also about their prospects for *salvation*. Unlike the Moravians, for whom faith was all or nothing, Wesley strongly defended and emphasized degrees of faith and insisted that salvation is possible without perfect faith. In his late-in-life (1788) sermon "On Faith," Wesley maintained that there are degrees of faith corresponding to different degrees of light. God has given "a small degree of light" to *heathens* and "far more" to the *Jews*.[98] Wesley saw no faith at all in *materialists* who think that "there is nothing but matter in the universe," and very little in *deists* who are "prejudiced against Christianity." He saw some faith in *heathens* and "*Mahometans*" who fail to believe the whole truth "not owing to want of sincerity, but merely to want of light," quite a bit more in *Roman Catholics* who believe "all that is necessary to salvation," and most of all in *Protestants* who believe "neither more nor less than what is manifestly contained in, and provable by, the Holy Scriptures."[99] His most important remarks, for our purposes, were made about the "Heathens" and one "Mahometan."

> No more will be expected of them, than the living up to the light they have. But many of them, especially in the civilized nations, we have great reason to hope, although they lived among the Heathens, yet were quite of another spirit, being taught of God, by His inward voice, all the essentials of true religion. Yea, and so was that Mahometan, and Arabian, who a century or two ago, wrote the Life of Hai Ebn Yokdan. The story seems to be feigned, but it contains all the principles of pure religion pure and undefiled.[100]

In "On Living Without God," and "On Charity," Wesley insisted that we not consign to hell all heathens, Moslems, and those "not under the Christian dispensation."

> I have no authority from the Word of God "to judge those that are without." Nor do I conceive that any man living has a right to sentence all the heathen and Mahometan world to damnation. It is far better to leave them to him that made them, and who is 'the Father of the spirits of all flesh'; who is the God of the heathens as well as the Christians, and who hateth nothing that he hath made.[101]

> If the love of God flows from no other fountain than faith in the Son of God; does it not follow that the whole heathen world is excluded from all possibility of salvation...? 'He that believeth not shall be damned,' is spoken of them to whom the gospel is preached. Others it does not concern; and we are not required to determine anything touching their final state. How it will please God, the Judge of all, to deal with *them*, we may leave to God himself. But this we know, that he is not the God of the Christians only, but the God of the heathens also; that he is 'rich in mercy to all that call upon him', 'according to the light they have'; and that 'in every nation he that feareth God and worketh rightness is accepted of him.'[102]

Thus, non-Christian people who "live up to the light they have" and work rightness by virtue of God's "inward voice" can have "all the essentials of true religion" and "religion pure and undefiled." Wesley talked explicitly here about people who do not "believe on Jesus" and who do not pass through the Protestant "order of salvation." For them, there is hope. God does not hate them. Significantly, one of the "Thirty Nine Articles of Religion" that Wesley omitted was Article XVIII, "Of Obtaining Eternal Salvation Only by the Name of Christ." Wesley was definitely not a Christian exclusivist! Christian exclusivism is unloving, thus unchristian!

If *we* are to love even God's enemies, then surely *God* loves them too! And since God loves them, we should too. God's love "extends even to those who neither love nor fear him. He is good, even to the evil and the unthankful; yea, without any exception or limitation, to all the children of men. For 'the Lord is loving' (or good) 'unto every man, and his mercy is over all his works' [Psalms 149:5]."[103] God's love "is not confined" to Christians but extends to Jews, Mahometans, Gentiles, and Heathens.[104] Wesley may not have been as generous to those inside the "Christian dispensation" who reject Christianity as he was to outsiders who never heard of it.[105] But if honest, loving, righteous, helpful doubters about Christianity "live up to the light they have," why should Christians condemn them or consign them to hell? Why should God do so, if God ranks intrinsic values higher than systemic values?

Most important of all, Wesley thought that God's love, expressed through the life and death of Jesus, is quite sufficient to save non-Christians who live by the best light that they have, even though they do not know this and have never heard of Jesus. Through Christ, God's special saving and sanctifying grace extends beyond the Christian fold. God is graceful and loving to everyone, and they do not have to know it or believe it for this to be so. In his commentary on Acts 10:35, Wesley said as much.

> But in every nation he that feareth God and worketh righteousness - He that, first, reverences God, as great, wise, good, the cause, end, and governor of all things; and secondly, from this awful regard to him, not only avoids all known evil, but endeavours, according to the best light he has, to do all things well; is accepted of him - Through Christ, though he knows him not. The assertion is express, and admits of no exception. He is in the favour of God, whether enjoying his written word and ordinances or not.[106]

Similarly, in a 1748 letter to Thomas Whitehead, he wrote, "The benefit of the death of Christ is not only extended to such as have the distinct knowledge of his death and sufferings, but even unto those who are inevitably excluded from this knowledge. Even these may be partakers of the benefit of his death, though ignorant of the history, if they suffer his grace to take place in their hearts, so as of wicked men to become holy."[107]

Thus, through Christ, the good, holy, faithful, loving, righteous, and practicing people we read about in the Old Testament are also "partakers of the same salvation"[108] if they live by the best light they have, even though they knew nothing about and had no beliefs about Jesus. If you disagree with Wesley, consider this. Jesus surely expected that the Good Samaritan and many others (e.g., the central spiritual figures of the Old Testament) would be accepted by God, even though they were not orthodox Christian believers and never experienced the Protestant revivalistic order of conversion and salvation. How could Christians quarrel with Jesus? Can you imagine a sermon on the Good Samaritan that ends with, "But he is still going to hell because he was not a born-again Protestant Christian"? The eleventh chapter of Hebrews also suggests that many non-Christians had saving faith.

Wesley's Hermeneutics of Love

After reason, scripture, experience, and tradition have done their best work, and since appeals to scripture and tradition are always highly selective, and since reason and experience also leave so many theological and philosophical issues unresolved and undecided, we definitely need *an ultimate intrinsic spiritual criterion* for making practical decisions about what to believe. In Wesley's spirit, we might try to formulate *a spiritual-values hermeneutics of love* for deciding what to believe and what not to believe. Wesley's distinction between *essential and non-essential* religious opinions calls for such a criterion, formulated here as follows.

> *If any given religious doctrinal belief or interpretation that is not ruled out by other criteria such as rational evidence, coherence, and consistency,*

natural science, brute facts, personal experience (including religious experience), etc. will help us to become persons more loving of God, all humankind, all animals, all living things, and all creation, then we ought to accept that belief. If any such belief would be neutral in helping us to become more loving persons, then there is little point in adopting or fretting over it. If any such belief would hinder us in becoming more loving persons, then we definitely ought to reject it.

Wesley himself came very close to formulating and applying this criterion in discussing how to identify false prophets. Citing Jesus' "Ye shall know them by their fruits," Wesley explained that we should ask,

> What are the fruits of their doctrine as to themselves? What effect has it had upon their lives? Are they holy and unblamable in all things? What effect has it had upon their hearts?...
>
> What are the fruits of their doctrine as to those that hear them?...Have these the mind that was in Christ? And do they walk as He also walked? And was it by hearing these men that they began so to do?...If they do not effectually teach either themselves or others to love and serve God, it is a manifest proof that they are false prophets: that God hath not sent them.[109]

Applying this spiritual-values hermeneutics of love to the project of adopting (or rejecting) religious "propositions" will not be easy, and outcomes will doubtless vary from person to person, from culture to culture, from one sect and religion to another. For example, some Christians may find that it makes them more loving to think that Mary was a virgin mother; but for others, this belief may be offensive or absurd, or it may make no affective difference at all, and they should just not worry about it. Consider another example. Wesley regarded the atonement as a core Christian belief, but there are many interpretations of the atonement and how it works—the ransom theory, the substitution theory, the moral or educative theory, etc. Some people may find some of these to be more expressive of and conducive to love than others. Wesley himself favored the substitutionary theory.

Despite variations in application, the spiritual-values criterion is probably a better standard for dealing practically with competing systemic religious values (religious beliefs) and disagreements than anything else currently available. If this criterion were adopted, many of the religious "opinions" over which people dispute would be of no real consequence, and most religious bickering and bigotry would disappear forever. Many wars have been fought over doctrinal differences, but many theological debates and distinctions (as interesting as they are systemically) make no real intrinsic difference. If we did not fret over such things, we would be free from systemic obstacles to loving God and one another; we would never put doctrines and principles over God and people. We could give all our hearts, souls, minds, and strengths, to loving other people as we love ourselves—especially people who are different, outsiders and strangers who have their own distinctive opinions, traditions, cultures, practices, and life styles. We could learn to rejoice in our human differences, as God surely must! We could much more easily follow Wesley's already noted advice, "Do not spend your time and strength contending for or against such things as of a disputable nature;" instead, leave "a thousand disputable points to those that have no better business than to toss the ball of controversy to and fro."[110]

Practically applying this hermeneutics of love could go in either of two directions. It might involve *accepting all* traditional beliefs and practices that do not interfere with being and becoming more loving persons, or it might involve *accepting only* those traditional beliefs and practices that contribute directly to being and becoming more loving persons. Some people will be more comfortable with one of these options, some with the other. Some will want a leaner, some a richer, set of systemic spiritual values and extrinsic spiritual practices; and perhaps there is a middle way between the extremes. Either of these approaches might be compatible with a viable spiritual hermeneutics of love. "True religion," as defined often by Wesley, seems to require only a minimal theology, a loving God than whom none greater can be conceived; but fully understanding the depths of God's love for us requires a much richer theology, such a loving God plus Jesus.

We are all creatures of our own time and place and must find both a spiritual worldview and a community of belief and practice that are compatible with our individual historicity, upbringing, definiteness, enlightenment, and uniqueness. Some religious traditions are much more alive for us than others; a lively option for one person might not be for the next. The crucial question always is, *"Will affirming this belief in faith or in reason help me to become a more loving person?"* No spiritual community or communion of saints is going to be perfect, but as social beings we should strive to find and associate ourselves with those that tend mightily towards universal loving and reverent beliefs, practices, affections, and holiness.

Wesley came very close to formulating a spiritual-values hermeneutics of love for adopting religious beliefs when he wrote, *"No Scripture can mean that God is not love, or that his mercy is not over all his works."*[111] This raises some interesting questions about Wesley's commitment to Scriptural affirmations and interpretations. He certainly thought and said that he believed everything in the Bible, but in practice and theory he often qualified this and interpreted everything from the perspective of a given *humanly-selected set* of doctrinal assumptions and values—those of love. Jesus also selected them as "first" and "second" in true religion.

Wesley was specifically addressing election and predestination when he said, "No Scripture can mean that God is not love, or that mercy is not over all his works." He identified the *many texts* to which predestinationists appeal, which, by the way, are quite substantial. He also explicitly acknowledged that all of these texts can be and were *interpreted* as affirming God's predestination of everything, including who will and who will not be saved. His response was simply that *these interpretations are wrong*! Why were they wrong? Because predestination makes God not only unloving, but downright malicious; it turns God into a devil! Any predestinationist interpretation of any text "destroys all his attributes at once. It overturns both his justice, mercy, and truth. Yea, it represents the most holy God as worse than the devil; as both more false, more cruel, and more unjust."[112]

Wesley thought that all biblical texts that seem to support predestination should be *interpreted* to mean nothing more than that God foreknew who would freely decide to become Christians and who would not. The trouble is, not all the texts clearly say this. "Destine" has causal connotations that "knew" does not have. Wesley held that "predestine" applies only to "some men" *in general*, that is, *to the general class* of those men and women who would eventually choose to become Christians, but *not to specific individuals*. God allows all individuals to decide freely whether or not to believe and thus become members of that class. Given his understanding of God's attributes, Wesley also thought that God knows from eternity exactly who they will be, but God's knowing is not destining or determining, he argued.[113] *We* do not determine the past in knowing about it, and *God* does not determine the future in knowing about it, he claimed. This has already been discussed in some depth.

Today's Temporalistic Theologians offer another way to resolve the apparent conflict between divine foreknowing and pre-determining. They deny that God can foreknow future free decisions that do not yet exist and have not yet been made. They just aren't there to be known until they are actually made. Before they are made, God knows them as *possible* decisions, not as *actual* decisions; he does not know which possibilities we will actually choose freely until our moment of decision comes. God can calculate probabilities much much better than we can, but even God does not know all the specifics. God knows everything according to its appropriate mode of being—possibilities as possibilities, probabilities as probabilities, but only actualities as actualities. This involves a very different way of conceiving of God's relations to time and eternity—from everlasting to everlasting, not the one Wesley espoused—all time all at once. Wesley understood the evaluative force of theological twists and turns, but occasionally he may have made the wrong turns. He acknowledged that we require a theology that "is worthy of God" and "is every way consistent with all the perfections of his nature."[114] The devil (or God!) is in the details!

Wesley's Non-literal Literalism

Wesley was not literally a biblical literalist. Randy L. Maddox suggests that Wesley was a biblical literalist—as long as the language was Hebrew or Greek, and one is an expert in both; but he was not a modern biblical inerrantist, because God did not directly dictate everything in the Bible. Even for the inerrantist, everything has to be interpreted within the frame work of certain fundamental doctrinal assumptions that can be used to correct errors.[115] However, these are significant qualifications. Wesley's own "stated rule in interpreting Scripture," was "never to depart from the plain, literal sense, unless it implies an absurdity."[116] As he first expressed this rule, "This is true, if the literal sense of these Scriptures were absurd, and apparently contrary to reason, then we should be obliged not to interpret them according to the letter, but to look out for a looser meaning."[117]

Ah! "Unless it implies an absurdity!" Every self-professed biblical literalist requires such an escape clause! But this crack opens a chasm! For Wesley and for us, it opens doors to the very latest and best in biblical scholarship, the natural sciences, the social sciences, philosophical theology, and textual hermeneutics, as the next few paragraphs will explain. Of course, there is much disagreement about what counts as the "very latest and best"! More importantly, it opens the door to Wesley's values-based hermeneutics of love, to a principle of interpretation grounded in love, in intrinsic values and evaluations. Consider now a few instances where Wesley explicitly repudiated literalism, always presumably on the grounds of some sort of absurdity.

Wesley was not consistently a literalist, even if usually so, or even if he said so. He took the Bible literally when and only when nothing unloving or absurd was involved, only when he had no good reason to be suspicious, but he often identified absurdities, and he did not hesitate to say so. He frequently told his hearers and readers not to take literally what the Bible says. Here are a few good examples.

1. He said that money is not literally the sole root of *all* evil because "There are a thousand other roots of evil in the world, as sad experience daily shows."[118]

2. He said that in the Lord's Supper, "This is my body" is "not to be taken literally," as in the Catholic doctrine of transubstantiation, because what looks and tastes like bread, and is also said to be bread, really is just bread.[119]

3. He said that the "fear and trembling" cited by St. Paul "cannot be understood literally" because our master does not want us "to stand trembling and quaking before him."[120]

4. I. Chronicles 16:30 denies that the earth moves, but Copernican Wesley knew that it did. Commenting on astronomy and "those scriptural expressions which seem to contradict the earth's motion," Wesley wrote, "This general answer may be made to them all, that, the scriptures were never intended to instruct us in philosophy, or astronomy; and therefore, on those subjects, expressions are not always to be taken in the literal sense, but for the most part, as accommodated to the common apprehension of mankind."[121] This qualification is as highly significant for us today as it was for those in Wesley's day. It gives Christians access to the very best of today's natural sciences and philosophies, though none of these speak with one voice. What Wesley called "philosophy" included "natural philosophy," which today is called "natural science." Wesley thus authorized us to do for our own Darwinian age what he did for his own Copernican/Newtonian age (even if this means giving up a literal Adam and Eve and the original perfection of all creation).

5. In discussing "the books were opened" and God's judging people by what is written in them during the last day of judgment (Revelation 20:12), Wesley called this "a figurative expression, plainly referring to the manner of proceeding among men."[122] He added that the judgment "day of the Lord" will probably take several

thousand years, (not literally one day), because there will be so many people to be judged.[123] Note the temporalism here attributed literally to God!

6. He may have been on the wrong track with this one, but since he subscribed to the classical *"totum simul"* theory of God's eternity—all time all at once—he insisted that all biblical and theological language with temporal overtones like foreknowledge, afterknowledge, making plans, having purposes ordered and expressed in time, interacting with people as they exist in time and history, changing his mind in light of positive human responses (as in the book of Jonah), etc., only speaks "after the manner of men,"[124] and is thus a mere "condescension to our weakness." He asked rhetorically, "But can we possibly imagine that these expressions are to be taken literally?"[125] Regrettably, his answer was negative. With that stroke, he dismissed almost everything that the Bible says about God! Temporalistic Theologians do not dismiss such things; they *can* imagine temporalistic language about God taken literally. What counts as an "absurdity" always depends on the presuppositions we bring with us to the hermeneutic process, and on how defensible or intelligible they are. Temporalistic Thinkers insist that we should *not* classify biblical affirmations of God's temporality as totally misleading myths and metaphors. Wesley's metaphysical presuppositions about God's eternity were much more Greek than Biblical, but his values, though selective, were mostly biblical, highly plausible, and relevant to our values today.

7. Wesley presupposed that God is a disembodied or incorporeal spirit having no body or spatial or temporal properties, so when interpreting the story of God's showing only his back-side to Moses in Exodus 33:22–23, Wesley said that "hand," "face," and "back-side" were being expressed only "after the manner of men."[126] More generally, "The words, figuratively transferred from one thing to another, do not agree with the things to which they are transferred, in...their literal sense. So hands and eyes, when applied to God, are not spoke in any part of their literal signification."[127] Wesley did not say so, but this also applies to God's literal masculinity or femininity. Wesley did not get into that!

8. Wesley heavily and repeatedly emphasized being "born again," but he explicitly admitted that this must be construed analogically and not literally. He even thought that Jesus was a non-literalist who recognized this himself! How can people be "born again"? To this, Jesus answered, Wesley explained, that "They cannot be literally. 'A man' cannot 'enter a second time into his mother's womb, and be born'. But they may, spiritually. A man may be 'born from above', 'born of God', 'born of the Spirit'—in a manner which bears a very near analogy to the natural birth."[128]

9. Consider next what Wesley said about the claim made in Malachi 1:2–3 and Romans 9:13 that God loved Jacob but hated Esau.

> The assertors of this doctrine [predestination] interpret that text of Scripture, 'Jacob have I loved, but Esau have I hated,' as implying that God in a literal sense hated Esau and all the reprobated from eternity. Now what can possibly be a more flat contradiction than this, not only to the whole scope and tenor of Scripture, but also to all those particular texts which expressly declare, 'God is love'?[129]

Despite its very obvious meaning, Wesley absolutely refused to accept this text at face value when taken literally. So, to generalize Wesley's values-based objection to biblical absurdities, *no Biblical text is literally true if it is incompatible with God's love, justice, and mercy*. That would be the ultimate absurdity! Wesley's claim, "All Scripture is infallibly true,"[130] must be understood in this light, that is, with this qualification: as long as it is not absurd and unconscionable, as long as it is coherent, morally good, and loving.

10. Wesley definitely thought that all Scriptures incompatible with God's love, justice, and mercy (e.g., the predestination passages) were just plain wrong because they are unconscionable. Expressed more softly, less harshly, they were just plain non-literal. Of course, this too is a matter of interpretation, as Wesley explicitly acknowledged when he said that predestination is "grounded on such an interpretation of texts...as flatly contradicts all the other texts...," especially "all those particular texts which expressly declare, 'God is love'."[131] But that is just the problem with literalism and inerrantism; interpretations are human, they are selective, and *the selections are inevitably made on the basis of the presuppositions, including the value-orientations and priorities, of the interpreters*. This is not less true simply because Wesley's values were correct, and because non-loving and contrary-to-loving values would be both spiritually and axiologically absurd.

Thus, Wesley often told people explicitly not to take unloving biblical texts literally. His sermon on "Free Grace," preached to combat George Whitefield's Calvinistic doctrine of predestination, is the crucial one that refers everything to love as the ultimate biblical and Christian principle of valuation and interpretation. Wesley's love criterion functioned as his ultimate principle of biblical hermeneutics. We can formulate this as: No matter what the Bible says explicitly and/or literally, if it is unloving, unjust, or unmerciful, we should just not believe it, i.e., not take it literally! We should "look for a looser meaning." Wesley valued reason, conscience, love, justice, and mercy far more than biblical literalism, and far more than inscrutable divine "sovereignty" or power. Calvinists most value inscrutable divine sovereignty. Which do you value most?

In many other instances, Wesley explicitly identified scriptural language as "figurative," "analogical," or written "after the manner of men," and advised against taking the Bible literally,[132] but the ten examples given thus far well illustrate the point.

Applying Love to the Scriptures

Is everything in the scriptures equally expressive of love? How do *you* think that Wesley's value-based hermeneutics of love applies to the divinely ordained massacres of men, women, children, and animals in the book of Joshua? Or to St. Paul's affirmation of the institution of slavery, as long as masters are good to slaves, and slaves obedient to their masters (Ephesians 6:5, 9)? Or to his apparent affirmation of masculine dominance over women (Ephesians 5:22–24; compare Genesis 3:16)?

Or his refusal to let women speak or teach in Church, which clearly rules out women clergy (I. Corinthians 14:34–35 and I. Timothy 2:11–12)? Wesley acknowledged that "There are some Scriptures which more immediately commend themselves to every man's conscience," than others, thus further qualifying "All Scripture is given by inspiration of God."[133] Even if all is inspired, not all is to be equally emphasized, for "of the things contained therein has been [should be] in proportion to the nearness of its relation to what is there laid down as the sum of all—the love of God and our neighbors."[134] Wesley did not oppose judging the scriptures by appealing to conscience and love to arbitrate between contrary scriptures or interpretations. This does not mean that he always got it right.

Sadly, his commentary on the book of Joshua never indicates that he saw anything unloving about the divinely ordained massacres reported there. Although he vehemently opposed slavery, despite its approval by St. Paul, he usually had little trouble with the Pauline affirmation of male dominance over females,[135] and that may have had something to do with his unhappy marriage. Some scholars say that the oppressive words about women attributed to St. Paul do not appear in the earliest manuscripts of his authentic writings. Some were probably composed by later scribes or writers, but *they are in the Bible* whether Paul wrote them or not. *Our present concern is with the values expressed in the words that are actually there.* Whether or not we accept these biblical values makes a very significant practical difference in the way women and all others are treated in our workplaces, churches, and homes.

George Whitefield firmly believed in slavery on biblical grounds and used slaves to build and operate his orphanage in Georgia. When he died, he owned around fifty slaves.[136] John Wesley never owned any slaves and always firmly opposed slavery. Some editions of his "General Rules" for the church prohibited all Methodists from "buying or selling the bodies and souls of men, women, or children, with an intention to enslave them,"[137] so the Quakers of his day were not the only ones who saw slavery as fundamentally unchristian. Originally, most Methodists in America, including the South, opposed slavery, especially Methodist women. As anti-slavery Methodists moved into the South, they met with considerable opposition; eventually most of them compromised with that slave-holding social order and lost their moral "high ground."[138] Both sides in the Civil War could and did quote the Bible, just as Abraham Lincoln said.

Wesley defended his opposition to slavery largely on non-biblical grounds. His "Treatise on Slavery"[139] deals factually and thoroughly with the greed, villainy, cruelty, gross abuses, lies, rationalizations, and misconceptions involved in slavery, but Wesley conveniently ignored all that St. Paul and the rest of the Bible explicitly said about it, "setting the Bible out of the question,"[140] as he said. He based his opposition to slavery quite explicitly on Enlightenment insights into natural human rights, justice, and mercy—knowable through natural reason and conscience, and on widespread human motives like compassion and sympathy.[141] Wesley also defended absolute liberty of choice and conscience in matters of religion as an "indefeasible" or "inalienable" right of all rational creatures.[142] Like everyone else, Wesley knew how to read the Bible very selectively in the interests of love. In his critique of slavery, he definitely appealed also to "the God of love"[143] as well as to Enlightenment insights.

Wesley's own position on male/female relations was somewhat ambivalent. He was not completely liberated from the sexism of male dominance and female subordination, but he definitely made significant progress. Very slowly and with great reluctance, he allowed women to preach if they had an extraordinary call,[144] thus allowing them to speak in church, despite Paul's prohibition (or that of a later scribe or editor),[145] but he never allowed them to become regular salaried ministers. Some Christians, even today, take the subordination of women to men to be permanently ordained of God, referencing passages attributed to St. Paul. The Southern Baptist and other churches to this day do not allow or advocate slavery, selectively ignoring what Paul said about it, but they explicitly affirm male domination in marriage, and they do not allow women to become preachers, just as Roman Catholics do not allow them to be priests. Is there a more excellent way, a more loving way, a less systemic way, a less extrinsic way?

In his sermon "On Visiting the Sick," Wesley definitely protested against "using" women, that is, against treating them as *mere things*, mere playthings, (sex toys?), mere means, mere objects, that is, as having merely extrinsic worth. Below, Wesley takes St. Paul's most "feminist" pronouncement very seriously.

> Herein there is no difference: 'there is neither male nor female in Christ Jesus' [Gal. 3:28]. Indeed, it has long passed for a maxim with many that 'women are only to be seen, not heard.' And accordingly many of them are brought up in such a manner as if they were only designed for agreeable playthings! But is this doing honour to the sex? Or is it a real kindness to them? No; it is the deepest unkindness; it is horrid cruelty; it is mere Turkish barbarity. And I know not how any woman of sense and spirit can submit to it. Let all you that have it in your power assert the right which the God of nature has given you. Yield not to that vile bondage any longer. You, as well as men, are rational creatures. You, like them, were made in the image of God: you are equally candidates for immortality. You too are called of God, as you have time to 'do good unto all men'.[146]

Even more significantly, Wesley clearly affirmed that conscience has a vital and authoritative role to play in setting limits to the subordination of wives to husbands, that is, to "the duty of wives to obey their husbands." What would St. Paul say, Wesley conjectured, if a husband demanded that his wife cease being a Christian? "What would St Paul have said to one whose husband forbade her to follow 'this way' any more?," to which Wesley's answered, "Our own conscience gives you the answer." Conscience clearly prohibits such obedience, such submissiveness. And the consciences of St. Paul and even of "our Savior" would have given the same answer.[147] To expand Wesley's question slightly, what if a husband demands that his wife do something flagrantly immoral or unchristian, something forbidden by her own conscience? Should she obey? Anyone's enlightened conscience should proclaim that such subordination, such obedience, is just plain wrong. Even further, with wives and consciences in mind, Wesley added, "Reason and persuasion are the only weapons you ought to use, even toward your own wife and children."[148] "The *only* weapons" here has extremely broad applications. Since Wesley ruled out supererogation, i.e., going beyond the call of duty, *everything* was for him a matter of conscience and love. Wesley moralized the whole of life and submitted it all to conscience; nothing good goes beyond or above the call of saintly duty; nothing good falls below the call of saintly duty. As he put it, "There is no employment of our time, no action or conversation, that is purely *indifferent*. All is good or bad."[149] Of course, duty is to be done from love and for those loved, not for its own sake. Thus, in no circumstances would it ever be legitimate for a husband to appeal to the sheer power and authority of his role of husband in order to compel his wife to obey his will. Reason and persuasion are the *only* legitimate "weapons" that husbands can ever use. Both conscience and love rule out all other forms of power of men over women, indeed, of anyone over anyone. How could anyone ever get the total submissiveness of wives to husbands in literally "all things" out of "Do unto others as you would have them do unto you"?

Dominance/subordination and status-consciousness are nature's ways, but basic human equality is the way of moral conscience, justice, mercy, and love. Human rights affirm human equality and protect the intrinsic worth of everyone—male or female, black or white, rich or poor, whatever or whatever. Although he opposed democracy and supported monarchy on biblical grounds, Wesley accepted the equal worth of all human beings, despite his Toryism. We are all equally rational beings, equally immortal souls, equally loved by God, equally sinners before God, and have equal intrinsic worth and rights in dealing with one another, including rights of conscience. Women are as intrinsically good as men, members of one race or nationality are as good intrinsically as those of any other; the poor are as good intrinsically as the rich. Social "inferiors" are as valuable intrinsically as social "superiors." To men and women of the world, supported by worldly religion, human inequality seems very natural, and equality seems very unnatural. Domination of males by females, and by all "superiors" over "inferiors," is nature's way—thus God's way—they assume, and they can cite Scripture to proof-text their chauvinism. That's the way things are and always have been almost everywhere in both the human and animal worlds. "An eye for an eye," "a life for a life," and "topdog/underdog" are among the laws of nature written in our unredeemed hearts. To the "natural man," (and woman) both forgiveness and human equality seem very unnatural, intuitively wrong-headed, but these are still the most excellent and loving ways. Some aspects of unregenerate human and animal nature definitely need to be overcome and transcended. The Christian way often requires us to overcome and not follow nature (and not take some Scriptures literally, depending on how they are interpreted).

Finally, a Wesleyan-in-spirit *hermeneutics of love* applies much more broadly than to interpreting the Scriptures. If we omit the word "religious," we get a broadly applicable and a profoundly Christian and Wesleyan spiritual principle for interpreting any and all communications and beliefs.

If any given doctrinal belief or interpretation that is not ruled out as "absurd" by other criteria such as rational evidence, coherence, consistency, natural science, brute facts, personal experience (including religious experience), etc. will help us to become persons more loving of God, all humankind, all animals, all living things, and all creation, then we ought to accept that belief. If any such belief would be neutral in helping us to become more loving persons, then there is little point in adopting or fretting over it. If any such belief would hinder us in becoming more loving persons, then we definitely ought to reject it.

Wesley's hermeneutics of love was his ultimate corrective to both mindless "enthusiasm" and excessively mindful dogmatism; and it should be for us today. If enthusiasm is to be checked by the scriptures, as Wesley and Jonathan Edwards both believed, what we take the scriptures to say must be checked by love, in particular, by the two scriptural love commandments. Interpreting the scriptures by the scriptures, which Wesley strongly advocated, is a values-selective process. If we think we have novel personal revelatory insights and inspirations, check them all by love. When we listen to contemporary prophets, priests, televangelists, politicians, moguls, pundits, and opinion-makers of every description, check them all by love. When considering philosophical options and opinions, check them all by love. When considering national, governmental, or political policies and parties, check them all by love. When supporting or opposing all "powers and principalities," check them all by love. When tuning in to our own thoughts, beliefs, attitudes, feelings, desires, and actions, check them all by love. When tempted in any way whatsoever, check all temptations with love. When wondering which religious doctrines or beliefs to make completely our own, check them all by love.

A hermeneutics of love is definitely scripture-based—but selectively so. Many unloving things in both the Old and New Testaments could be selected instead—and often they were and are. Many churches and religious organizations devote more time and effort to telling us who to shun or hate than who and how to love. The ultimate Christian value stance is the intrinsic evaluation of all intrinsically valuable beings. In more familiar and complete terms, the primary Christian values are wholeheartedly to understand and love God, all human beings, all conscious beings, and all living beings, and to act accordingly. Christians must even love non-sentient or non-living creation, the extrinsic world, the soul-less parts of nature, the physical environment that sustains, comforts, and entertains us, for God is there also. Last comes loving the symbolical moral, spiritual, philosophical, scientific, and factual beliefs that inform us. Our moral and spiritual beliefs must be appropriate, i.e., both enlightened and loving beliefs, Godlike beliefs, Christlike beliefs, beliefs that would belong to the mind and conscience of Christ. Any beliefs that we accept (1) should not be incompatible with love, and they (2) should not be absurd, Wesley would say. If they are absurd, don't take them; if they are loving, take them. Perhaps, where relevant, they should also be interesting, insightful, beautiful, enlightened, reasonable, verified, consistent, and truthful. There should be no "false witness" in our systemic values and evaluations. Christians should be intellectually honest as well as conscientious, loving, and compassionate. The Bible tells us so!

Wesley's Own Hierarchy of Christian Values

A values-based hermeneutics that accepts only sane and love-making beliefs is very Wesleyan in spirit, even if not in every letter or detail. It is in perfect harmony with what he conceived to be the very essence of true religion and with how he ranked Christian values. Wesley explicitly ranked Christian value-objects in his sermons "On Zeal," and "On Charity," where he offered and explained his own hierarchy of Christian values. So what did he say about the nature of Christian zeal, Christian love, the good and degrees thereof, his own Christian hierarchy of values, and the place of doctrines and good works within his hierarchy?

Christian Zeal

In "On Zeal," Wesley appealed to "holy tempers" or "warm emotion or affection" in defining *zeal itself*. *Religious zeal* definitely involves the affections or passions: "When any of our passions are strongly moved on a religious account, whether for any thing good, or against any thing which we conceive to be evil, this we term 'religious zeal'."[150] More specific passions define *Christian zeal*, where the primary feeling or affection is love: "Charity, or love, is not only one ingredient, but the chief ingredient in its composition." Going "further still....For it is a certain truth (although little understood in the world) that Christian zeal is all love. It is nothing else. The love of God and man fills up its whole nature."[151] In "On Charity," Wesley expressed his regret that St. Paul's *agape* was mistranslated as "charity" in the King James or "Authorized" version of the Bible. It should have been "love," he said, as it was in many earlier English translations.[152]

Christian zeal is the passion of love, but *only in its most intense manifestations*. Feelings of love in "small degree" do not count as Christian zeal. Only the most intense and sustained feelings count (just as they mark the difference between extrinsic and intrinsic evaluation). Christian zeal "is not every degree of that love.... There may be some love, a small degree of it, where there is no zeal. But it is, properly, love in a higher degree. It is 'fervent love'. True Christian zeal is no other than *the flame of love*. This is the nature, the inmost essence, of it."[153] Having Christian zeal for anything means intensely loving it, evaluating it intrinsically, because "The properties of love are the properties of zeal also."[154] Christians should love zealously, but what should Christians love? Primarily, "God and man," as indicated already, but in "On Zeal," Wesley identified other specifics that Christians should also love—specifics that both support and express loving God and all human beings. In the real world, which particular values or value-objects belong within the Christian religion and legitimately fall within the scope of zealous Christian love, and to what degree?

The Good, and Degrees Thereof

The general theory of value presupposed by this book recognizes three basic dimensions of goodness, intrinsic (e.g., people, animals, and God), extrinsic (e.g., sensory objects, processes, and activities), and systemic (e.g., all concepts, propositions, doctrines, rules, principles, and formalities). Each of these may be evaluated intrinsically (passionately, lovingly), or extrinsically (with normal practical desires and feelings), and systemically (disinterestedly or objectively). These three forms of value and evaluation fall into *a hierarchy of value*. This means that some of these good things are better than others, depending on the quality or quantity of good-making properties inherent in them.

Expressed abstractly, the hierarchy of values says that intrinsic value-objects are better than (have more good-making properties than) extrinsic value-objects, and both intrinsic and extrinsic value-objects are better than the systemic value objects that merely symbolize them. Good realities always have more worth than the good conceptual tokens and symbols that point towards them.

Expressed more concretely, the hierarchy of values says that unique conscious individuals like animals, people, and God have more value than merely mindless things, sensory objects, processes, and actions, and all of these have more value than the ideas, belief systems, and formalities that symbolize or point towards them and through which we relate to them conceptually.

Expressed religiously, we should love God, people, and animals more than mere things and good works, and mere things and good works more than the beliefs, truths, doctrines, symbols, and all formalities that merely point to or symbolize them.

So, to what extent would John Wesley agree with this account and ranking of Christian values?

Often and ideally, the three value dimensions co-exist in mutual harmony, and we can have them all without being forced to choose between them, but sometimes we have to make hard choices in order to get our moral and spiritual priorities straight. Usually, Wesley got it right, as we will see; but in one interesting instance he may have gotten it wrong. A very familiar philosophical conundrum requires choosing between intrinsic and systemic values. It requires that we do something systemically bad in order to bring about or protect something intrinsically good.

Suppose, the dilemma says, that you have a very good chance to save someone's life by telling a lie (thus harming the systemic value of truth) to some villain who is searching for that person and asks you if you know where he is. Should you tell the truth, or tell a lie? Suppose, for example, you could save the dozen Jewish friends you are hiding in your attic by lying to the Nazis who have come by your house searching for them. Lying to them involves harming the truth, a systemic value, in order to save or protect the life or lives of intrinsically valuable persons. Most of us would probably judge, after careful consideration, that we ought to try to save our Jewish friends and lie to the Nazis when they ask if we know where any Jews are hiding.

Wesley actually considered this sort of systemic-versus-intrinsic issue in one of his sermons dealing with the goodness of truthfulness. Lying maliciously to harm someone is definitely wrong, he concluded, but what about telling an "officious lie" designed, by definition, to promote or protect goodness or to prevent even greater harm?[155] Wesley insisted that "doing evil that good may come" would *always* be wrong, no matter what. "Officious lies, as well as all others," he wrote "are an abomination to the God of truth. Therefore, there is no absurdity, however strange it may sound, in the saying of the ancient Father, "I would not tell a wilful lie, to save the souls of the whole world.""[156] Wow! But wouldn't refusing to save all the souls in the world be an abomination to the God of love? Wouldn't that be incredibly unloving? Would that be approved by Wesley's hermeneutics of love? Had he lived in that era, it seems that Wesley would just sell out his Jewish friends and tell the Nazis the truth! Usually, however, Wesley had better judgment, so let us now consider his more excellent ways.

In "On Zeal," Wesley asserts that *we should be zealous for the good, and for good things in proportion to their degree of goodness.* Knowing the good, he thought, is essential both for being a real Christian and for properly identifying the attributes of God. As we saw earlier, God's attributes are selected, interpreted, and assigned to him on the basis of their goodness. The integrated (but ever growing with time and ongoing creativity) entirety of all his positive attributes constitute God's uniqueness and overall goodness, just as the integrated (but ever growing with time and free choices) entirety of our own properties constitute our human individuality and overall worth. Likewise, the specific value-objects about which Christians should be zealous are those that really are good, in proportion to their degree of goodness. Put abstractly, good things are the basic value components of real Christianity, but what are they, and what are their degrees of goodness?

As for goodness itself, "The proper object of zeal is good in general; that is, everything that is good, really such, in the sight of God."[157] Thereby, Wesley indirectly made a place for axiology and for inquiry into the meaning and kinds of "good." Wesley next asked what the good things are that belong within "that religion, wherewith God is always well pleased." He then identified the good-making properties of a "good religion" and its various "parts" or "branches." Wesley observed that these "parts" have "comparative value." Christians want to know, "What is good in the sight of God" and "What is the comparative value of them?"[158] i.e., of the parts of "the religion wherewith God is well pleased." Wesley answered with his own Christian Hierarchy of Value.

So what are the parts of a good religion, and what is their *comparative worth*? Whatever they are, we should be zealous of them, that is, we should love them intensely, we should *evaluate* them intrinsically, we should passionately identify ourselves with them while recognizing their proper priority or comparative degrees of goodness. Christian *value-objects* are not all equally valuable. They have "comparative value," said Wesley. Though we should zealously love them all, their goodness comes in degrees, and our love for them should be so proportioned. According to Wesley, "If true zeal be always proportioned to the degree of goodness which is in its object, then should it rise higher and higher according to the scale mentioned above, according to the comparative value of the several parts of religion."[159] So, by degrees we should love good things in proportion to their degrees of goodness. But what was Wesley's actual "scale," his own Hierarchy of Christian Values? What exactly are the principal parts of a good religion, and what exactly is their comparative worth?

Wesley's Own Hierarchy of Christian Value-Objects

All the principal parts of a good religion should be valued intrinsically, that is, with zealous love, in proportion to their real comparative worth; but only God, human beings, (and other conscious and sentient creatures neglected below) are intrinsic value objects. Clearly, however, systemic and extrinsic value-objects (e.g., beliefs, ritual forms, good works, and churches) are also essential parts of a good religion. Here is how Wesley ranked all of these, from highest or best to lowest or least valuable. All should be loved intensely in proportion to their *comparative worth*, ranked as follows.

1. The love of God and Man, including
    a. All the "holy tempers" ingredient in love;
2. All "works of mercy;"
3. All "works of piety;"
4. The church or "assembling ourselves together" to further the above.

Consider how Wesley himself described this Christian Hierarchy of Value-Objects.

> In a Christian believer *love* sits upon the throne, which is erected in the inmost soul; namely love of God and man, which fills the whole heart, and reigns without a rival. In a circle near the throne are all *holy tempers*: long-suffering, gentleness, meekness, goodness, fidelity, temperance—and if any other is comprised in 'the mind which was in Christ Jesus'. In an exterior circle are all the *works of mercy*, whether to the souls or bodies of men. By these we exercise all holy tempers; by these we continually improve them, so that all these are real *means of grace*, although this is not

commonly averted to. Next to these are those that are usually termed *works of piety:* reading and hearing the Word, public, family, private prayer, receiving the Lord's Supper, fasting or abstinence. Lastly, that his followers may more effectually provoke one another to love, holy tempers, and good works, our blessed Lord has united them together in one—*the church*, dispersed all over the earth; a little emblem of which, of the church universal, we have in every particular Christian congregation.

This is that religion which our Lord has established upon earth, ever since the descent of the Holy Ghost on the day of Pentecost. This is the entire, connected system of Christianity: and thus the several parts of it rise one above another, from that lowest point, 'the assembling of ourselves together', to the highest, love enthroned in the heart. And hence it is easy to learn the comparative value of every branch of religion. Hence also we learn a fifth property of true zeal—that as it is always exercised...'in that which is good', so it is always *proportioned* to that good, to the degree of goodness that is in its object.[160]

Consider next a brief axiological analysis of the "objects" in Wesley's Hierarchy of Christian Values. We are to relate proportionally to all of them with Christian zeal or love, so all involve intrinsic evaluation by degrees, but their various "objects" belong to different value dimensions and are ranked in relational or comparative value. Arranged from highest to lowest ranking, we have:

1. The intrinsic evaluation of intrinsic value-objects, the love of God and man,
2. The intrinsic evaluation of extrinsic value-objects, all "works of mercy,"
3. The intrinsic evaluation of systemic/extrinsic value objects, all "works of piety,"
4. The intrinsic evaluation of additional systemic/extrinsic value objects, the church where we unite socially to further the above.

To summarize, Wesley thought that we should most love God, people, and conscious beings, then the works of love that serve the souls and bodies of human and conscious beings, then the works of piety that involve acts structured or ordered by systemic values such as words, thoughts, and ritual forms, then the church as a formal institution and actual social union facilitating all these goals in their proper order of goodness.

Ranking Doctrines Within the Hierarchy

So, where exactly do doctrines (systemic values) fit within Wesley's Hierarchy of Christian Values? He did not explicitly address this question, so we are left to extrapolate as best we can. He clearly ranked systemic elements (words, thoughts, truths, opinions, ritual forms, all works of piety) below extrinsic values (good works of mercy and love), which in turn were ranked below intrinsic values/evaluations (loving God and people). Doctrines belong to the systemic "parts" of the Christian religion, so they would presumably occupy the lowest rungs of this Christian value hierarchy.

Ranking doctrines at the bottom of the "parts" of the Christian religion seems compatible with the preceding *spiritual-values hermeneutics of love principle* for deciding what to believe and what not to believe spiritually. *Christians should accept only those essential informative moral and religious doctrines that support loving God and our human and animal neighbors as well as doing the works of love, compassion, mercy, forgiveness, and justice.* Wesley said that "fervor for indifferent things is not Christian zeal,"[161] but, except for his example of bickering over ecclesiastical vestments,[162] in "On Zeal" he left it largely up to us to decide what is and what is not "indifferent." As previously indicated, maybe many doctrinal disputes within Christendom, and between Christians and adherents of other religions, really are just "indifferent" or irrelevant to zealous spiritual love. Maybe some are downright incompatible with it. Maybe some religious opinions, historically Christian or not, are just *unessential.* What beliefs help us to be more loving? Which ones would make us more hateful? Which ones just make no difference at all? Are Christians the sole possessors of love-making beliefs?

This is not to say that they *all* beliefs are expendable, but *many* theological disputes and distinctions, including many with which Wesley wrestled mightily, really are irrelevant to *practical theology*, as evidence by the fact that preachers seldom if ever preach on them. In fact, they almost never preach on most of the things they learn in divinity school! Most doctrinal and scholarly distinctions make no real difference to the spiritual growth and well-being of ordinary (or even extraordinary) church members, not because they would not understand them, but because they make no intrinsic difference. Preachers decide "in the field" what really matters spiritually and what does not, and divinity schools need to pay more attention to what really matters most if they are to become serious about practical theology. Preachers may fail to communicate to their parishioners much of what they learn in divinity school because they do not want to cause controversy, or jeopardize their jobs, or tempt others to lose their faith, but one main consideration surely must be that most of it is just spiritually irrelevant. Most of it has little or nothing to do with zealous love.

However, not all beliefs or systemic theological values are practically irrelevant, even if some are, even if most are. We have no infallible list of them, but certain core beliefs are indispensable for being and becoming more loving persons. What are they, and how do we decide? Perhaps our spiritual-values love criterion for believing can help us. Think about it. Maybe Wesley can give us some additional clues, but be prepared for honest disagreements.

"Doctrines," so named, do not appear explicitly in Wesley's Hierarchy of Christian Values, but he did rank what he calls "opinions," his main example being the Roman Catholic doctrine of transubstantiation. As he said, "It follows also, from the same premises, that fervor for *opinions* is not Christian zeal."[163] Wesley at times classified *all doctrines*, including those of natural philosophy (science) and orthodox theology, as "opinions,"[164] but at other times this applied only to *unessential doctrines*. In describing "The Character of a Methodist," Wesley wrote, "But as to all opinions which do not strike at the root of Christianity we 'think and let think'."[165] So, which opinions *are* at the root of Christianity? Wesley answered emphatically, T*he two love commandments and all that is essential to their understanding and application.*[166] Just what the essentials of Christian belief are is subject to much debate, but clearly the hermeneutics of love has a bearing in answering. Recall the first principle of his hermeneutics of love: "*No Scripture can mean that God is not love, or that his mercy is not over all his works.*"[167]

In "On Zeal," Wesley said that when works of mercy interfere with works of piety, "works of mercy are to be preferred"—a clear value ranking. "Even reading, hearing, prayer are to be omitted, or to be postponed, 'at charity's almighty call'— when we are called to relieve the distresses of our neighbor, whether in body or soul."[168] Intrinsic values (souls) and extrinsic values (bodies) should prevail over systemic values (reading, hearing, prayers, etc.).

Of course, some beliefs are essential to loving—like the belief that God really exists and has all the attributes required for being supremely good or perfect, or the belief that other people really exist (are not mere illusions or automatons) and have all the intrinsic-good-making human image of God properties previously identified. For Christians, many beliefs about Jesus are also essential, though we do not agree about exactly what they are or how to interpret them, and we must recognize that many saintly and loving people exist who are not Christians at all. In his "Advice to the People Called Methodists," Wesley first acknowledged that Methodists take opinions very seriously. Then he added, "Condemn no man for not thinking as you think. Let every man use his own judgment, since every man must give an account of himself to God. Abhor every reproach, in any kind or degree, to the spirit of *persecution*. If you cannot *reason* or *persuade* a man into the truth, never attempt to *force* him into it. If love will not compel him to come in, leave him to God, the Judge of all."[169] Wesley clearly value-ranked love over doctrines in this rhetorical question, "For how far is love, even with many wrong opinions, to be preferred before truth itself without love?"[170]

Wesley's most definitive and concise ranking of Christian values appears in his sermon "On Charity," where he ranks the "gifts" mentioned by St. Paul in I. Corinthians 13.

> It is proper to observe here, first, what a beautiful gradation there is, each step rising above the other....St Paul begins at the lowest point, 'talking well', and advances step by step, every one rising higher than the preceding, till he comes to the highest of all. A step above eloquence is knowledge; faith is a step above this. Good works are a step above that faith. And even above this, is suffering for righteousness' sake. Nothing is higher than this but Christian love—the love of our neighbour, flowing from the love of God.

It may be proper to observe, secondly, that whatever passes for religion in any part of the Christian world, (whether it be a part of religion, or no part at all, but either folly, superstition, or wickedness) may with very little difficulty be reduced to one or other of these heads.[171]

All of Wesley's "heads" can be reduced to three value dimensions—to systemic, extrinsic, and intrinsic values and evaluations, or to combinations of these three, as follows. This list proceeds from the lowest in value at the top to the highest at the bottom.

1. "Talking well" or "eloquence" is a combination of systemic values (words and their meanings) with extrinsic values (acts of talking). Eloquence is meaningful talk, the systemic enhancement of an extrinsic value.
2. "Knowledge" is clearly a systemic value, though it also has its usefulness. All Christian knowledge belongs at this level.
3. "Faith is a step above this," he says. Here the purely systemic features of believing are distinguished from the extrinsic and intrinsic parts. Wesley explained that purely systemic faith is not real faith precisely to the extent that it "does not work by love."[172] Real faith does. Presumably, it is systemic faith that belongs at this level.
4. "Good works are a step above that faith," he said. Here he clearly ranked extrinsic values above purely systemic values.
5. "Above this, is suffering for righteousness' sake," he said. This involves a personal identification with (intrinsic evaluation of) righteousness so extreme as to be willing to suffer for it. But what is "righteousness" here? It could be something purely systemic (moral and spiritual laws), something systemic/extrinsic (acting in accord with laws), or, so it seems, something systemic/extrinsic/intrinsic (living profoundly in accord with those loving laws of God that benefit God and people and animals).
6. The highest value of all is "Christian love; the love of our neighbour, flowing from the love of God." The intrinsic evaluation (love) of intrinsic values (God and neighbors) was at the top of Wesley's Hierarchy of Values, just as it should have been.

Wesley's ranking proceeds from items that are purely or primarily systemic (1–3), through those that are completely extrinsic (4), to those that are predominately intrinsic (5–6). Thus, the intrinsic has comparatively more worth than the extrinsic, which has comparatively more worth than the systemic. Wesley's value insights and intuitions were usually very profound and perceptive! For Wesley, everything in Christianity rests or hangs upon the two love commandments and what they mean in our hearts, minds, and practices. These express the most fundamental and the highest or best Christian values and evaluations. All else is derived from these. They have the highest "comparative value."

Just how we rank intrinsic, extrinsic, and systemic values has a great deal of practical significance, whether we are religious or not. Some people overvalue one or more of these dimensions of value, some undervalue them. Wesley often explicitly employed the concepts of "overvaluing" and "undervaluing."

- Some "enthusiasts" and "antinomanians" so overvalue the inner emotional aspects of spirituality that they neglect either their own practical duty to help others or their intellectual duty to try to learn and understand.
- Some people greatly undervalue unique persons either in pursuit of worldly success and prosperity, or because they are obsessed with beliefs, knowledge, or ritual purity—a common failure of Pharisees, intellectuals, college professors, authoritarians, dogmatists, ritualists, and formalists.
- Some people so overvalue the things of the world, or acting in the world, that they sacrifice intimate personal relations for them, or they think that "book learning" is utterly trivial.
- Some people, e.g., "ivory tower professors," so undervalue the things of the world that they are incompetent in managing their practical affairs and are largely removed from real life.
- Some people so greatly overvalue knowledge, beliefs, and doctrines that they actually despise and may abuse or condemn other people who happen to disagree with them and do not share their intellectualism, formalism, or dogmatism. They may also be so practically incompetent that they can not or do not practice what they preach.
- Some people so undervalue systemic values that they know very little about themselves or other people. They are very unsure about what they believe, they do not understand what they are doing, and they do not know how to do it, even when they are trying to "do good."

John Wesley was very sensitive to all such value distortions and constantly preached against over and under valuation. He also preached in favor of the proper ranking and evaluation of basic Christian spiritual values, as in his sermons "On Zeal" and "On Charity." Most of the moral and spiritual problems that plague us spring from wrong-headed and wrong-hearted values and evaluations. Wesley felt that the best way to avoid such value distortions is to do what Jesus would do, think what Jesus would think, and love what (or who) Jesus would love.

The rankings above are the good-making criteria of truly good versions of Christianity, or of any religion, and they may be used to identify those perspectives which fall short of the best they could be. Yes, some religious perspectives are better than others, depending on the degree to which they fulfill the good-making properties of a good religion. Worldly religion, previously defined as ranking extrinsic values first, falls short of being a truly good religion, and so does systemic religion, next explained, which ranks formalities and believing doctrines higher than loving human and Divine persons.

Systemic Religion

Systemically religious people are dominated by systemic values. They think, feel, and act as if beliefs, laws, rules, principles, rituals, and formalities are the very essence of true religion. Such people are the dogmatists, authoritarians, infalliblists, ritualists, and nit-pickers of religion. They are profound thinkers and believers, but not necessarily good lovers or doers. Wesley repeatedly repudiated a merely systemic religion, as when he wrote:

> Whatsoever the generality of people may think, it is certain that opinion is not religion: no, not right opinion, assent to one or to ten thousand truths. There is a wide difference between them: even right opinion is as distant from religion as the east is from the west. Persons may be quite right in their opinions, yet have no religion at all. And on the other hand persons may be truly religious, who hold many wrong opinion.[173]

Wesley recognized three distinctive spiritual personality types in his threefold classification of people into *natural, legal, and evangelical states*.[174] Natural people are worldly people. Legal people are those "under the law." Evangelical people are by grace forgiven, justified, and consumed by love. Natural people are dominated by extrinsics, legal people by systemics, and evangelical people by intrinsics. In real people, "These several states of soul are often mingled together, and in some measure meet in one and the same person;" worldly people have glimpses of insight into right and wrong, and legal people have glimmerings of love, for "The legal state, or state of fear, is frequently mixed with the natural" and "The evangelical state, or state of love is frequently mixed with the legal."[175] Most of the time, one of these three value dimensions dominates the other two, but all three are always present and "mingled together." Just how they mingle is very significant! Wesley's clear recognition that the three value dimensions are present in varying proportions in almost everyone is very important and insightful. In dealing with real people, we must always take account of their valuational complexity and not oversimplify. Stereotypes exist only in our minds.

Legal-minded people at least know and respect God's laws, which worldly people scarcely grasp and care little about. However, they neglect the content of the love commandments (which are formal commandments) that direct us toward intrinsically valuable realities and intrinsic evaluations of them, precisely because they concentrate so intensely on systemic values above all else. Their wakeful moments are dominated by rule-consciousness. They know cognitively the difference between right and wrong, the permitted and the forbidden. They are excessively, perhaps even compulsively, scrupulous, like the Pharisees who sought legal and ritual purity, but little else. Their most troublesome problem is this. Although the law gives guidance, it also condemns, so they have "no peace at all," said Wesley, echoing St. Paul. Before genuine conversion, the law condemns and convicts of sin by providing standards of right and wrong, and we can know if we have violated or obeyed them. It consists of systemic standards or concepts, composed of good-making properties, attitudes, and actions, but the "legal minded" find that they absolutely do not have those good-making properties, love and benevolent practices in particular. They are works-righteous perfectionists, and they always fall short of perfection. They strive earnestly, like the ancient Pharisees, to obey the law, but no matter how hard they try, they fail. They find no remedy for falling short of what the law requires, so they live in fear. They find no peace of soul until they move on to the evangelical stage of grace, freely given by God, unearned and undeserved under the law.[176]

Wesley actually defined the "legal" state in religious terms, that is, in terms of the laws of God, whether moral or ceremonial, though the ceremonial laws of the Old Testament were of little interest to him,[177] mainly because Jesus came to abolish them, he thought.[178] Jesus fulfilled the moral laws and sets us free from them, not from their requirements, but from their condemnation and guilt. Systemic religion is Pharisaical. Systemic minded people are "under" the laws—both dominated and crushed by them. So, it may not be too far fetched to say that Wesley recognized such a thing as systemic religion, at least implicitly, just as he explicitly recognized a religion of the world. In thinking further about both, we may need to move a bit beyond Wesley.

For one thing, his analysis of the "legal state" focused rather narrowly *on laws*, but our own understanding of systemic religiosity should be expanded to cover other formalities. We saw how he subordinated *faith,* as merely cognitive assent to beliefs, to *faith* as also involving love and works, so we could profitably include exclusively systemic faith in doctrines within our understanding of systemic religion.

In some sermons, he also covered rituals and said quite specifically that true religion is not any *outward* thing like "*forms* or *ceremonies*," writing, "Let no man dream that they have any intrinsic worth."[179] Elsewhere he wrote, "'Then it [religion] is going to church and sacrament.' Indeed it is not. This may be an excellent help to religion; and everyone who desires to save his soul should attend them at all opportunities; yet it is possible you may attend them all your days, and still have no religion at all. Religion is an higher and deeper thing than any outward ordinance whatever."[180]

Thus, we have a Wesleyan warrant for extending "systemic religion" to cover not only *laws* but also *beliefs* and *ritual forms*. Rituals are formal and internal when thought and external or "outward" when imposed, recorded, practiced, or performed. Our own understanding of systemic religion should be expanded in all these directions to include all such religious formalities.

Finally, in Wesley's limited version of systemic religiosity, systemic values were *only self-applied*, mainly as the systemic disvaluation of oneself (personal self-knowledge, guilt, and repentance). Systemic religion should be extended to cover our relations to *other people* as well as to ourselves. *All* systemically dominated religious people focus on beliefs, ritual purity, and laws as the essence of true religion, and they can and do use them all to condemn or disvalue, not just themselves, but also other people who deviate. Jesus warned us against it, but systemic-minded souls are very judgmental!

Systemically religious people value beliefs, truths, ritual purity, and divine laws more than they value people and God, so much so that they shun, snob, ostracize, excommunicate, judge, condemn, vilify, and sometimes maim, torture, execute, and consign to hell, others who disagree with them or reject their rigidly systemic way of looking at things or doing things. They resent and try to undermine genuine freedom of religion and separation of church and state because they think that there is only one truth, one way, one answer—their own. They exhibit what Wesley called "the spirit of persecution," and they do not accept what he called the "indisputable truth that every rational creature has a right to worship God as he is persuaded in his own mind."[181] They have a black or white, all or nothing mentality. They tend to be very intolerant. If one small thing is wrong, everything is wrong. If other people have one small flaw, if they deviate at all in beliefs or ceremonial forms, they are doomed, beyond redemption, hopeless, unworthy of further attention or consideration, utterly lost, beneath contempt. If the scriptures have even one small flaw, everything would have to go, they argue, which is why the scriptures do not have even one small flaw, they insist. The scriptures are utterly infallible. Even if they are not, some human religious authority (e.g., the Pope) is infallible. Infallibility is all or nothing, and people are either in or out. There is nothing in between. There are no shades of gray in a systemic religion. There is no sense of, and no traces of, prevenient grace *for all*. God surely could not love *them* while *they* are yet sinners!

Intrinsic-minded Christians agree with Wesley that true religion, which he equated with real or true Christianity, "lies in one single point: it is neither more nor less than love—it is love which 'is the fulfilling of the law', 'the end of the commandment. Religion is the love of God and our neighbor—that is, every man under heaven."[182] The doctrinal elements in this true religion are minimal. Wesley took very seriously the New Testament idea that love fulfills the law—all of it, not in exact detail, but in true spirit. Comprehensively understood, the first love commandment "is all the commandments in one."[183] So, how should intrinsic-minded Christians relate to systemic-minded Christians? Lovingly! Unless they are being vicious to others, we should relate to them, their total realities, including their minds, beliefs, hearts, and practices only with rational and persuasive love. Here again is Wesley's advice for relating to those who disagree with us, especially those who do so vehemently and dogmatically.

> Condemn no man for not thinking as you think. Let every man use his own judgment, since every man must give an account of himself to God. Abhor every reproach, in any kind or degree, to the spirit of *persecution*. If you cannot *reason* or *persuade* a man into the truth, never attempt to *force* him into it. If love will not compel him to come in, leave him to God, the Judge of all.[184]

Wesley, whose spirituality was predominantly intrinsic, not systemic or extrinsic, would doubtless say about systemic-minded religious dogmatists and authoritarians what he said about worldly religious people, namely that, despite everything, there is much good in them. They have many good-making properties, but not enough to make them saints. They have prevenient grace, but not saving grace. They have intrinsic worth but not saintly worth. They love with their minds but not with all their hearts and strength. No matter. Their dominant systemic values are always "mingled together" with subordinated extrinsic and intrinsic values and evaluations. Those who are merely or mainly "wise and learned" are minimally good but not maximally good. We should love them anyway as if they were saints, as if they were ourselves, as if they were equally God's creatures and loved by God—for indeed they are.

Chapter Five

John Wesley's Saintly Values and Evaluations

Saints have kinds and degrees of goodness that sinners do not have. This is an obvious fact of experience as well as a doctrine of theology. Saints have many good-making properties that sinners do not have, and to this issue we now turn our attention. What are the good-making properties of saintliness, and how do the saints acquire them? How do saints make the transition from ordinary prevenient intrinsic goodness to the extraordinary goodness of saving grace? Are these differences of kind or only of degree? Are there any non-Christian saints?

Making the Transition

Many intrinsic-good-making human properties are made available to all human beings through God's preventive grace, but our lives can have equal intrinsic worth without having saintly worth. We can all have an intrinsically good human life without having a spiritually abundant life; we can have a preveniently good life that is not yet saintly. We can have equally valuable human lives without having equally valuable saintly lives. Prevenient or common grace is a wonderful thing, but saving grace is even better. Not only is prevenient grace common to or universally present in all human beings, but it is also preventive of something worse, and it is preparatory for something better. John Wesley often called it "preventive" grace, as indeed it is, for it prevents us from being nearly as bad as the doctrine of "total depravity" says that we are! It gives us a conscientious awareness of good and evil, right and wrong, and it prepares us for making the transition from sinful (mainly worldly) values to saintly values. This does not mean we can save ourselves, but God gave us the ability, the intelligence, and the freedom to choose and to cooperate with his saving grace and to prepare for receiving it. To a few people, saving grace may come suddenly without any preparation at all, Wesley thought; but, where time allows, God's prevenient grace allows and helps us to make preparations for it.

Wesley subscribed to a distinctively Protestant understanding of the nature of conversion and the proper "order of salvation," grounded largely in his own experiences with large-scale evangelistic revivalism. Serious Wesley scholars identify many Roman and Eastern Catholic elements in Wesley's theology, but his understanding of conversion and the new birth experience was mainly Protestant. It came both from the Scriptures and from his experiences with converts during the revivals of the Great Awakening that shook both England and America in the late 1730s and climaxed during the 1740s. Wesley was a major figure in the Great Awakening. His revivalistic views about the order of salvation evolved and softened over time.

Becoming a saintly person, Wesley thought, typically involves pre-conversion yearnings for and glimpses of God and a conviction of sin, followed by an almost instantaneous conversion or "new birth" experience, followed by a lifelong sanctifying period of growth in holy understanding and love, and the good works and practices that flow from them. Being "born again" leaves converts as mere "babes in Christ," so it initiates a lifetime of *striving* for perfection, growing gradually in grace, developing morally and spiritually, and finally (for some, he thought) achieving "entire sanctification" or complete perfection. Most people experience "entire perfection" only an instant before death, he held at one point.[1] Prior to *entire* sanctification, most Christians are involved in a dynamic *process* of sanctification, of *striving* for perfection, of *becoming* more and more holy, loving, empathetic, compassionate, forgiving, and virtuous. The text of Wesley's sermon "On Perfection" was Hebrews 6:1, "Let us go on to perfection."[2] God's Holy Spirit works with and within us every step of the way as we "go on." Here is how Wesley described the proper order of salvation and progressive sanctification in his late sermon, "On Working Out Our Own Salvation."

> If God 'worketh in you', then 'work out your own salvation.' The original word rendered, 'work out', implies the doing a thing thoroughly. 'Your own'—for you yourselves must do this, or it will be left undone forever. 'Your *own salvation*'—salvation begins with what is usually termed (and very properly) 'preventing grace'; including the first wish to please God, the first dawn of light concerning his will, and the first slight transient conviction of having sinned against him. All these imply some tendency toward life, some degree of salvation, the beginning of a deliverance from a blind, unfeeling heart, quite insensible of God and the things of God. Salvation is carried on by 'convincing grace', usually in Scripture termed 'repentance', which brings a larger measure of self-knowledge, and a farther deliverance from the heart of stone. Afterwards we experience the proper Christian salvation, whereby, 'through grace' we 'are saved by faith', consisting of those two grand branches, justification and sanctification. By justification we are saved from the guilt of sin, and restored to the favour or God: by sanctification we are saved from the power and root of sin, and restored to the image of God. All experience, as well as Scripture, shows this salvation to be both instantaneous and gradual. It begins the moment we are justified, in the holy, humble, gentle, patient love of God

and man. It gradually increases from that moment, as a 'grain of mustard-seed which at first is the least of all seeds, but' gradually 'puts forth large branches', and becomes a great tree; till in another instant the heart is cleansed from all sin, and filled with pure love to God and man. But even that love increases more and more, till we 'grow up in all things into him that is our head;' 'till we attain the measure of the stature of the fullness of Christ'.[3]

Not all Christians in his day agreed with him that "entire perfection" is available to people in this life. The Reformed or Calvinist tradition, Jonathan Edwards included, stood steadfastly against Wesley's views on actually achieving perfection in this world, and so did many Methodists. Even Wesley himself recognized that striving for perfection, going on to perfection, rather than achieving it, is what most Christians are up against for most of their lives.

Salvation is Today; Sanctification Takes Forever

Salvation was, for Wesley, something that Christians have *today*, even before perfection arrives. He passionately proclaimed with St. Paul that "Now is the day of salvation"[4] and with Jesus, "The kingdom of God is at hand."[5] Salvation is not something that happens *only at the end of life*. It is a momentous inner transformation here and now. It is definitely not just a matter of getting a free ticket to heaven when we die. As Wesley explained,

> The salvation which is here spoken of is not what is frequently understood by that word, the going to heaven, eternal happiness. It is not the soul's going to paradise, termed by our Lord, 'Abraham's bosom'. It is not a blessing which lies on the other side of death, or (as we usually speak) in the other world. The very words of the text itself [Ephesians 2:8] put this beyond all question. 'Ye *are* saved.' It is not something at a distance: it is a present thing, a blessing which, through the free mercy of God, ye are now in possession of.[6]

> By salvation I mean, not barely (according to the vulgar notion) deliverance from hell, or going to heaven, but a present deliverance from sin, a restoration of the soul to its primitive health, its original purity; a recovery of the divine nature; the renewal of our souls after the image of God in righteousness and true holiness, in justice, mercy, and truth. This implies all holy and heavenly tempers, and by consequence all holiness of conversation.[7]

Today, as in Wesley's day, many Christians seem to think that only two things of spiritual significance ever happen to Christians. First, they get converted or "saved," that is, they "accept Jesus Christ as their personal Lord and Savior." Second, they die and go to heaven with a free pass. But, they assume, nothing of any spiritual significance ever happens between conversion and death.[8] Wesley vigorously contested this "vulgar" outlook, emphasizing instead that salvation is "a present thing," something "ye are now in possession of," something that transforms a person's whole life, beginning with conversion, something that makes for more abundant living here and now. As Wesley explained, "And when we say, 'Believe, and thou shalt be saved,' we do not mean, 'Believe, and thou shalt step from sin to heaven, without any holiness coming between.'"[9] Thinking that the whole of Christian life consists only in getting saved and going to heaven overlooks the vital lifelong "in between" stage of *progressive sanctification*, of spiritual development, of becoming a saint, of growing in a faith that works in love and in all other spiritual virtues, and of living a more abundant life here and now. In this very world, mere babes in Christ must grow into mature adults in Christ. Don't overlook that, Wesley advised, or you will miss most of what Christianity is really all about. You will miss almost everything that makes life meaningful and worthwhile, both here and hereafter.

Conversion is the beginning, not the end, of the Christian's road. Emphasizing saving faith alone, Wesley recognized, could and sometimes did degenerate into an antinomanian lawlessness, according to which Christians do not even have to keep the Ten Commandments or participate in the "ordinances" (sacraments and other means of grace). Wesley eventually lost all patience with the Moravians over just this issue. An emphasis on (systemic) faith alone means that people can continue to live just as immorally as ever, once saved, because actually living morally would be nothing more than "works righteousness." For the same reason, believing that true Christianity is nothing but *systemic faith alone* can also degenerate into a kind of do-nothing quietism that never expresses love in the "labours of love." Wesley viewed Martin Luther as one who short-circuited sanctification, thus missing what is vitally important in Christian living and growing in grace here and now. Luther, Wesley thought, concentrated so intensely on salvation and justification by *faith alone* that he was left in "total ignorance with regard to sanctification."[10] Wesley insisted that if the moment of new birth or first faith is not followed by sanctification or growth in holy loving and living, in *faith that works by love*, it just isn't the real thing. Salvation bears fruit here and now, and by that fruit you shall know them. Sanctification is growth in and value-enrichment through increasing holiness.

In the Protestant order of salvation, properly understood, repentance and justification by faith come first; but, Wesley thought, these must be followed by a lifelong process of sanctification (saint-making) or growth in grace and effortful cooperation with God. According to Wesley, "Justification is another name for pardon. It is the forgiveness of all our sins....And at the same time that we are justified, yea, in that very moment, *sanctification* begins. In that instant we are 'born again', 'born from above', 'born of the Spirit'."[11] After this new birth, sanctification takes place, sometimes rapidly, usually gradually.[12] During his revivalistic years, Wesley thought that the new birth experience is always instantaneous and dramatic—so much so that no one could claim to be a Christian if he or she could not remember and identify its precise time and place. Sanctification, by contrast, is usually gradual, but "getting saved" is always instantaneous and momentous, he thought at first. In later years, as his concerns and experiences became more pastoral and less revivalistic, Wesley softened his position and allowed that both the new birth experience and the process of growth in grace might be incremental, gradual, and unidentifiable in precise time and place.[13] Jonathan Edwards definitely opposed imposing any rigid order upon the stages of Christian development,[14] and John Wesley's pastoral concerns and experiences moved him in this direction.

As we will see later, Wesley thought that growth in grace would continue even after death, so "entire sanctification," even at the very end of life, is never quite "entire." Sanctification takes forever.

Continuities and Discontinuities

Just how much continuity or discontinuity of values and evaluations exists between once-born and twice-born souls? As vitally available here and now, salvation transforms or transvalues personal values in this world, in this life, here and now. For many, but not for all, this transformation is momentous and dramatic. Reorienting value priorities and affections, whether sudden or gradual, is one of the most important things about conversion, as described by Wesley in these words:

> They know the new birth implies a great change in the soul, in him that is 'born of the Spirit', as was wrought in his body when he was born of a woman; not an outward change only, as from drunkenness to sobriety, from robbery or theft to honesty (this is the poor, dry, miserable conceit of those that know nothing of real religion); but an inward change, from all unholy to all holy tempers, from pride to humility, from passionateness to meekness, from peevishness and discontent to patience and resignation—in a word, from an earthly, sensual, devilish mind to the mind that was in Christ Jesus.[15]

After the new birth, Christian growth (in values and evaluations) is usually "by degrees,"[16] Wesley said. But *how much continuity, if any, is here between pre and post conversion values?* Do any of the significant values or good-making properties of saintliness exist by prevenient grace in "natural" or unconverted people? If the new birth brings a break in what and how we value, how sharp is the break? Are the value transformations of salvation qualitative or quantitative, or somehow both? How extensive is God's prevenient grace and the human response to it before conversion? Is there a clear line between prevenient and sanctifying grace? Things formerly valued only marginally, if at all, become a convert's dominant values, central within his or her life; but how drastic, sudden, and complete is that value transformation? Wesley's answers were not always crystal clear. He acknowledged that people could be very advanced morally without being real Christians with enlivened spiritual senses, for "Unless they have new senses, ideas, passions, tempers, they are no Christians!"[17] He conceded that in his (or "her," we should add) natural or legal pre-Christian state,

> A man may be of a compassionate and a benevolent temper; he may be affable, courteous, generous, friendly; he may have some degree of meekness, patience, temperance, and many other moral virtues; he may feel many desires of shaking off all vice, and of attaining higher degrees of virtue; he may abstain from much evil—perhaps from all that is grossly contrary to justice, mercy, or truth; he may do much good, may feed the hungry, clothe the naked, relieve the widow and fatherless; he may attend public worship, use prayer in private, read many books of devotion—and yet, for all this, he may be a mere natural man, knowing neither himself nor God; equally a stranger to the spirit of fear and to that of love; having neither repented, nor believed the gospel.[18]

Wesley no doubt meant this negatively, but it can actually be read as a quite positive concession that non-Christians can be very benevolent, compassionate, and otherwise virtuous or highly moral both internally and in practice. Even those who advocate unrevealed "natural religion" take the Second Great Love Commandment very seriously, but not the First, he recognized.[19] "Heathens" have a reliable conscience, know the basic differences between right and wrong, generally internalize and practice all the fundamental moral virtues to some degree, and can even expect "a sort of love and assistance...one from another."[20] Describing those who have only preventing but not saving grace, he wrote, as previously quoted,

> Salvation begins with what is usually termed (and very properly) *preventing grace*; including the first wish to please God, the first dawn of light concerning his will, and the first slight transient conviction of having sinned against him. All these imply some tendency toward life; some degree of salvation; the beginning of a deliverance from a blind, unfeeling heart, quite insensible of God and the things of God.[21]

On both the outside and the inside, "almost Christians" may be and look very much like real Christians. But on the inside, by degrees, if not in kind, they lack *total* love to God and to "every man in the world," even if they have such things *partly*, Wesley thought.[22] *But so do most real and imperfect Christians most of the time!* Most Christians are on the way, but they have not yet arrived. Wesley confessed that before his own transforming heart warming experience at Aldersgate, he was himself an "almost Christian" who lacked *total* love to God and all human neighbors. But why insist in all or nothing? Do all new converts instantly gain *total* love? Must all Christians have total love? If not, is there an absolute difference between Christians and almost Christians? At conversion, is *the total absence of love replaced by its total presence*? Does the "new birth" really make an abrupt, drastic, and complete change in what and how we value? To these questions, his answers were clearly negative. Salvation and entire sanctification are not identical.

Was Wesley's own transformation in love at and after Aldersgate only a difference in degree, or was it a difference in kind, or somehow both? Was he a totally unloving person before Aldersgate, and only loving thereafter? What about others who experience a new-birth conversion? Are all Christian converts totally unloving before the new birth, then loving only thereafter? There is a real difference, often a dramatic difference, in the *prevalence* of love in the human souls before and after spiritual conversion and sanctification. Does the new birth merely change which values *dominate* the soul? Are existing *degrees* of love supplanted by higher degrees of the same? Is that the real difference between the once-born and the twice-born? Do new spiritual births simply transform what and how we value by degrees and dominance?

Are all *non-Christians* totally devoid of love and other saintly affections and virtues? Maybe the natural, legal, and evangelical states—all three—really are always present or "mingled together" by degrees in all human beings. Before conversion, maybe one or the other non-intrinsic value dimension tends to prevail over intrinsics—usually the extrinsic natural state, less often the systemic legal state. Clearly, at times, even saintly persons still striving for perfection are impure and may revert temporarily to worldliness or dogmatism. Don't all human beings exist *by degrees* in the *loving image* of God through God's prevenient grace? Even worldly people are capable of loving, Wesley conceded. They just happen to love and identify themselves mainly with the world and their own status-giving in-crowd, while having relatively little truly unselfish love for most other people, animals, and God. So, is the prevalence of love and other virtuous affections always just a matter of scope, degree, and dominance?

"Babes in Christ,"[23] new converts, gradually develop into mature Christians. So, do unsaintly and unloving people also gradually shade off by degrees into saintly and more loving people? No doubt, *some* saintly people make the abrupt transitions from sinfulness to saintliness that Wesley once envisioned for *all*. The Protestant way of revivalistic conversion has doubtless availed for many, but is it really necessary for all truly loving persons? Does the Protestant pathway describe all Christians, all saintly people everywhere? Is loving holiness available only in the Protestant Christian way? What is the most loving answer we could give to such questions? Wesley's answers were not always clear. Ours should be.

The Good-making Properties of the Saints

This chapter takes a careful look at what and how saints value, no matter where they are in the conversion/sanctification process, or whether they are perfect or merely "going on" toward it. Since most readers of this book will be less than perfect, the emphasis here is on growing in grace by degrees, on sanctification as a process, not on the finished product. Our emphasis is not on what Wesley called "entire sanctification" or being "altogether a Christian." "Altogether" saintliness is the ultimate regulative ideal or end-goal toward which all Christians gradually move, but most of us, who are still real Christians, have a long way to go.

Wesley's account of the *order of salvation and progressive sanctification* was a distinctively Protestant, Methodist, revivalistic account of how Christians arrive at and grow in saintly values and evaluations, but other ways to grow morally and spiritually may be available to people in other religious traditions. How to achieve or progress in saintly loving values and evaluations may be an empirical, not a doctrinal, question. Here are the salient questions. Does anyone manifest the values and valuations of saintliness who has not lived through a distinctively Protestant and revivalistic understanding of conversion and growth in grace? Was there nothing saintly and loving about Wesley himself before Aldersgate? Are any truly loving and virtuous people found in other religious or cultural traditions? Was there nothing saintly and loving about any of the non-Christian and non-Protestant people in the Old Testament?

Jesus' two love commandments, the heart of Christian spirituality, are also in the Old Testament in Deuteronomy 6:5 and Leviticus 19:18. Don't Jews take them seriously? Are they totally unloving because they are not Protestant Christians? Are reborn Protestants the only people who can show and tell us how to become more loving, compassionate, empathetic, just, and forgiving persons? Are there any truly loving, empathetic, compassionate, and forgiving people in Roman Catholic and other Christian traditions, where dawning and developing spirituality are typically experienced as gradual growth rather than as instantaneous dramatic revivalistic conversion? Can we be born again and reoriented in our basic values and evaluations gradually, incrementally, hardly knowing it at the time?

Don't people in non-Christian religions also undergo value-transformative experiences and become much more loving, compassionate, penitent, and forgiving than they once were? Can we today honestly say that no Jews or Moslems (who reject the divinity of Jesus, the Incarnation, the Atonement, and Protestant revivalism) can be truly loving and genuinely virtuous? What about those in other world religions? Does God have sheep who are not of the Judaeo-Christian or Abrahamic fold at all? Are there any truly enlightened, loving, empathetic, compassionate, and forgiving people who do not even believe in God? Wesley suggested that Christians have more enlightenment and assurance than non-Christians, but are Protestant Christians the only people on the right road, the only ones with enlightenment and assurance? Non-Christians can be saved, Wesley thought, if they live up to the best light they have.

How to answer all these questions may be clearer after we understand better what and how saintly people value. Wesley can help us with this. Theoretically, he claimed, all our natural or universally human "image of God" properties were totally lost after the fall, then instantly *restored*, but this is not a plausible way for us to think about them today. Why not? "Restored" presupposes that our earliest human ancestors had something they never actually had—moral and spiritual perfection, complete moral and spiritual development, in an idyllic world in which there was no danger, sin, suffering, struggle, or death. No morally and spiritually perfect first-humans named Adam and Eve ever literally existed, then completely lost all their image of God good-making properties. Wesley believed in the original perfection of our earliest ancestors and the world in which they lived,[24] but we cannot. "Restored" logically entails "once possessed," but such good old days of human perfection never were. Our earliest ancestors never literally lost it because they never literally had it. Without original perfection, "restored" is only a vacuous theoretical construct. It would be much more accurate and sensible to say that our universally human Godlike good-making properties are "preveniently continued" rather than "preveniently restored." If never once possessed and then lost, it makes no sense to say that God "restored" them.

Newborn human infants have only potentials or potencies for actualizing their desirable human properties, so we should look today at what they are like to find out about the "original" state of the real Adam (man) and Eve (woman). Even better, look at unborn infants nearing birth. Wesley himself did this, not when discussing the biblical Adam and Eve, but when explaining similarities between the physically first-born and the spiritually newborn. Of the physically unborn, Wesley wrote,

> There are, it may be, some faint beginnings of life when the time of its birth draws nigh, and some motion consequent thereon, whereby it is distinguished from a mere mass of matter. But it has no *senses*; all these avenues of the soul are hitherto quite shut up. Of consequence it has scarce any intercourse with this visible world, nor any knowledge, conception, or idea, of the things that occur therein.[25]

Wesley greatly underestimated the sensitivity and alertness of infants nearing birth, but he rightly discerned that they know very little. They are not acquainted with the things of this world, with moral right and wrong, and with the great spiritual truths and values of the Christian religion or any other religion.

Recall all of the universally human and commonly shared good-making properties that Wesley identified as the natural, political, and moral images of God. Theoretically, they were all totally lost, then restored; yet, in actuality, by prevenient grace we and all of our ancestors have always had them. Presumably, saintly souls have additional or more advanced good-making properties, as soon explained. But by prevenient or common grace, everyone has many good qualities in various stages of actualization or development, previously identified as:

1. embodied spirituality or ensoulment,
2. self-motion, or being self-starting,
3. reason or understanding, the ability to inquire and know,
4. will, that is, desires, feelings, affections, emotions—especially love,
5. liberty (free choice), a capacity for making and originating our own choices,
6. imagination,

7. memory,
8. sentience, our five "external senses"
9. consciousness (awareness) and self-consciousness (inner awareness),
10. conscience, the capacity for discerning good and evil, right and wrong,
11. general moral laws "written in our hearts,"
12. moral and spiritual sensitivities, affections, dispositions, and virtues, in various degrees of activation or actualization.
13. a "capacity for God."

The last two of these are universally human, but in saintly people, all are greatly enhanced, redeemed, or renewed. "The great end of religion," Wesley wrote, "is, to renew our hearts in the image of God."[26] Good people value more comprehensively than bad people, and their valuational capacities are much more developed. The "capacity for God" of the saints includes their greatly expanded and refocused religious affections, and perhaps some new powers, insights, virtues, and tempers.

Empirically, we probably cannot tell exactly what is new in spiritually newborn and more developed saints and what is just immensely improved. Liberty is definitely greater, for there is much less bondage to worldliness, religious ideology, bigotry, and sinful or distorted feelings, desires, and dispositions. Reason works better, more clearly, consistently, logically, openly, perceptively, insightfully, inclusively, and with much less bias or prejudice. The external senses are supplemented by additional spiritual sensitivities to the presence of God, not only in oneself, but in all things, even sensory things. Consciousness is much expanded and more intense, alert, inclusive, comprehensive. Conscience is awakened, the still small voice within grows louder and clearer, and moral laws or guidelines are better understood and more easily applied to particular situations. A largely dormant spiritual sensitivity begins to function more prominently and then to dominate, and the saint's capacity for God becomes the center of his or her awareness. All of this now gets expressed in actual living and doing. Saints live and give back more abundantly. Through *prevenient grace*, all human beings have many Godlike good-making properties, Wesley thought, but salvation or conversion greatly affects and expands all of our common human capacities. Through *special grace*, born-again people have additional, or at least much more advanced, Godlike properties. More and more Godlike and Christlike properties and values arrive, persist, and tend to prevail as sanctification proceeds.

Wesley explained what the saints have (dominantly) and sinners do not have (at all, or only subordinately) in many sermons and other writings. Next we will consider the most important good-making properties that belong especially if not exclusively to gracious Godlike saints. Wesley contrasted the "political and moral images" of God in us with the minimal "natural image."[27] Instead of "restored," *we* should now think of them as "new birth" or "new creation" properties—to the extent that they actually are new in either degree or kind. The saints have it all; most people don't; but what do they have?

Spiritually advanced saints are in some sense new creations; they have Godlike or Christlike properties that no one has in infancy, and the very ones that the "once-born" tend to lack as adults. What are some of these? *What moral and spiritual properties are added or at least significantly expanded during conversion and sanctification?* This list is not complete, but a careful reading of Wesley yields at least these results. Advanced saints exemplify or move significantly toward:

A. perfection, including power over sin.
B. love to and union with God,
C. love to *all* humankind,
D. spiritual senses focused on the internal presence of God's Spirit that illuminate and expand our scriptural beliefs, our sense of moral good and evil, and our spiritual affections, assurances, and virtues,
E. a keen awareness of God's external presence or omnipresence in all creation.

Each of these invites more careful consideration. Even if they are not absolutely new creations, saintly human beings have these properties much more conspicuously or in a much more developed state than non-saints. In saintly people, such enhanced intrinsic value and evaluation properties are abundant and given higher priority. They prevail and are no longer absent, dim, or subordinated to lesser values and evaluations.

Perfection, Including Power Over Sin

After the new birth, Wesley believed, Christians have, by God's grace, a power over sin that they did not previously have, a power that tends toward mastery and perfection.[28] Are all Christians perfect and absolutely sinless after conversion and the new birth, or does some residue of sinfulness remain, to be overcome only gradually during the sanctification process that follows? Is the Christian's power over sin complete at all stages of progressive sanctification, or does it fluctuate while tending or growing toward perfection?

Are all Christians perfect and thus sinless people, while all non-Christians are not? Sometimes Wesley thought so, sometimes not. You decide, but here are some seemingly incompatible things that Wesley said in different writings about Christian perfection and ongoing sinfulness, or the lack thereof. After conversion, Wesley admitted, real Christians remain in ignorance, make unintentional mistakes, succumb to weaknesses, can be sorely tempted, and even unknowingly and unintentionally sin;[29] but do they ever actually, knowingly, and deliberately sin? Do they ever knowingly and intentionally break some of God's commandments or think, feel, or act in unloving ways? The Wesley of one mind said, "No" to such questions: "A Christian is so far perfect as not to commit sin."[30] The Christian *by definition* "'keeps His commandments': not only some, or most of them, but ALL, from the least to the greatest;"[31] and "Even babes in Christ are so far perfect as not to commit sin."[32] However, in his more realistic and seasoned sermons like "On Sin in Believers," the "Repentance of Believers," and "On Zeal," the Wesley of another mind admitted, on the basis of more experience, that sin *remains*, though it no longer *reigns*.[33] After explaining this in some depth in "On Sin in Believers," he concluded:.

> The sum of all is this: there are in every person, even after he is justified, two contrary principles, nature and grace, termed by St. Paul the 'flesh' and the 'spirit'. Hence although even babes in Christ are *sanctified*, yet it is only *in part*. In a degree, according to the measure of their faith, they are *spiritual*; yet in a degree they are *carnal*. Accordingly, believers are continually exhorted to watch against the flesh, as well as the world and the devil. And to this agrees the constant experience of the children of God. While they feel this witness in themselves they feel a will not wholly resigned to the will of God. They know they are in him, and yet find an heart ready to depart from him, a proneness to evil in many instances, and a backwardness to that which is good...
>
> Let us, therefore, hold fast the sound doctrine 'once delivered to the saints', and delivered down by them with the written word to all succeeding generations: that although we are renewed, cleansed, purified, sanctified, the moment we truly believe in Christ, yet we are not then renewed, cleansed, purified altogether; but the flesh, the evil nature still remains (though subdued) and wars against the Spirit. So much the more let us use all diligence in 'fighting the good fight of faith.'[34]

So, do Christians ever deliberately sin after conversion? Our own experience will likely be in accord with Wesley's later and more seasoned judgment, based on what he calls above "the constant experience of the children of God," that we are free from sin "only in part, in a degree" and must constantly "fight" it. For this reason, repentance, and prayers for forgiveness—as in the Lord's Prayer—must be a regular and ongoing feature of the Christian life and worship services. For those who thus practice and persevere, there is "no condemnation."

Seriously, why do Christians ever have to pray "Forgive us our trespasses" more than once? Repenting just once, at the beginning, at conversion, at justification, is never enough *because we continue to sin while striving for perfection*, as Wesley conceded also in the "Repentance of Believers."[35] The Reformed tradition always insisted on this, and eventually, based largely on *experience*, Wesley agreed. During the sanctification process, overcoming and gaining power over our sinful nature, both inwardly and outwardly, usually occurs only gradually, not instantly, and seldom if ever definitively or "altogether." At times, Wesley relaxed his rigid perfectionism. The seasoned, most common, and most plausible Wesleyan way is *striving* for perfection, *going on* to perfection, not *being perfect*.

We should agree with Wesley that overcoming our bondage to sin happens only as God empowers us without coercing us, and even then only as we freely choose to cooperate with and not resist or hinder God's work within us. God's empowerment is resistible grace, not irresistible; and it must be constantly, vigilantly, and prayerfully renewed. We have to decide time and time again to cooperate with God and to use and not impede God's gifts, but we don't do this consistently or constantly, so we sin. God gives us the freedom and the power to decide, but freely deciding for God, godliness, and goodness must be *valued, nurtured*, and *exercised* again and again with reverence, humility, and gratitude. We can always yield to temptation, backslide, and choose evil over goodness, so salvation is never an absolutely done deal. Neither is sanctification. Yet, for those who thus practice and persevere, there is "no condemnation." God assures forgiveness and reconciliation to sinners, wherever they are in the sanctification process.

Love to and Union with God

God is love, (I. John 4:7 and 16), and we are made in that image. Wesley's thinking on the topic of the image of God in us was incredibly innovative. Most Catholic theologians before Wesley said that we manifest God's image *only in one respect*: *rationality*, but *not love*. Some said *rationality and will*, but rationality was the most common view. Wesley, against this massive tradition, held that our primary resemblance to God is that of *love*. He also held that we exist in God's image in many other ways. We saw earlier that he repeatedly identified being (1) an immaterial spirit and having (2) understanding or reason, (3) self-initiated internal and external movements or actions, (4) will or the desire and affections, and (5) liberty of choice as image-of-God or Godlike properties, along with many other Godlike human attributes. Unlike most theologians who came before him, Wesley emphasized the affection of love, the root of all other religious affections, as the way we were created in the image of God. Neither the book of Genesis nor the rest of the Bible tells us exactly *how* we manifest God's image. The Bible does not specify the precise property or properties that constitute God's image in us. Picking a point or property of resemblance has always been a matter of human values, an outcome of *what theologians, ministers, and ordinary Christians themselves value most in us and in God*. Wesley most valued love.

Traditional Roman Catholic theologians, much influenced by Greek philosophers, were very systemic-minded on the *Imago Dei* issue. For most of them, systemic *rationality* is the distinctively human attribute by virtue of which we exist in the image of God. At a more popular level, worldly people assume extrinsically that we just *look like God*, that God is a big, strong, handsome, bearded, (white?) guy in or beyond the sky with a humanoid face, right and left hands and sides, masculinity, etc. However, the great classical theologians, including Wesley, always insisted that *God does not look like us* at all because *God has no body*. As Wesley put it, "God's image upon man consists in his nature, not that of his body, for God has not a body, but that of his soul. The soul is a spirit, an intelligent, immortal spirit, an active spirit, herein resembling God, the Father of spirits, and the soul of the world."[36] Of course, having no body at all implies that God could not be literally male or female, but Wesley did not get into that one!

Here are two highly influential examples from classical Roman Catholic theology that identify *only one property* as the image of God in us, *rationality*. According to St. Augustine, "God, then, made man in His own image. For he created for him a soul endowed with reason and intelligence, so that he might excel all the creatures of earth, air, and sea, which were not so gifted."[37] The same theme is echoed in St. Thomas Aquinas, who is to this day the official philosopher of the Roman Catholic Church. He wrote, "Man is said to be in the image of God, not as regards his body, but as regards that whereby he excels other animals....Now man excels all animals by his reason and intellect; hence it is according to his intellect and reason, which are incorporeal, that man is said to be in the image of God."[38] These theologians identified "the image" with the one property, reason, that we supposedly have but animals do not—and Wesley definitely did not agree with that, as we saw in Chapter Two.

A much richer understanding of "the image of God" in us was offered by John Calvin, according to whom, "By this word the perfection of our whole nature is designated, as it appeared when Adam was endued with a right judgment, had affections in harmony with reason, had all his senses sound and well-regulated, and truly excelled in everything good."[39]

Contrast these accounts with what John Wesley said quite explicitly about *love* as both the primary original image of God in us and the ultimate goal of restoration or sanctification.

> But love is the very image of God: it is the brightness of his glory. By love man is not only made like God, but in some sense one with him.[40]

> In this [moral] image of God was man made. 'God is love:' accordingly man at his creation was full of love; which was the sole principle of all his tempers, thoughts, words, and actions. God is full of justice, mercy, and truth: so was man as he came from the hands of his Creator.[41]

> Now God is love; therefore they who resemble Him in the spirit of their minds are transformed into the same image. They are merciful even as He is merciful. Their soul is all love. They are kind, benevolent, compassionate, tender-hearted; and that not only to the good and gentle, but also to the froward. Yea, they are, like Him, loving unto every man, and their mercy extends to all His works.[42]

> 'Thou, O man of God, stand fast in love, in the image of God wherein thou art made. If thou will remain in life, keep the commandments which are now written in thy heart. Love the Lord thy God with all thy heart. Love as thyself every soul that He hath made.[43]

> Let our whole soul pant after a general revival of pure religion and undefiled, of the restoration of the image of God, pure love, in every child of man.[44]

Very few if any theologians before Wesley ever said so clearly that we exist in the image of God as love! Wesley was an incredibly creative theologian in many ways, especially in his thinking about the image of God in us, which he never limited to just one or two good-making properties. Most significantly, he heavily emphasized love as the core of the image within us of God who is love, but, as we saw, there was much more.

Before considering loving our neighbors, Jesus' second "Great Commandment," we must think a bit more about what is involved in *loving God*, in fulfilling the first "Great Commandment." Wesley asked, "What is it to love God?" and answered, "to delight in him, to rejoice in his will, to desire continually to please him, to seek and find our happiness in him, and to thirst day and night for a fuller enjoyment of him."[45] In more detail, loving God takes this form.

> Now, to love God, in the manner the Scripture describes, in the manner God himself requires of us, and by requiring engages to work in us, to love him as the one God; that is, 'with all our heart, and with all our soul, and with all our mind, and with all our strength'. It is to desire God alone for his own sake, and nothing else, but with reference to him; to rejoice in God; to delight in the Lord; not only to seek, but find happiness in him; to enjoy God as the chiefest among ten thousand; to rest in him as our God and our all—in a word, to have such a possession of God as makes us always happy.[46]

"Love" is a very complicated notion. Any serious reading of I. Corinthians 13 should alert us to this, and Wesley can help us to understand it better. Wesley agreed with the person who said, "This single chapter contained the whole of true religion."[47] The very notion of "love" is incredibly rich in connotative meaning. All too often we just throw the word around without paying too much attention to what it means. Wesley did not make that mistake. Later references will further enrich our understanding of what he meant by "love," but for the moment note carefully in the above quote that our loving God properly involves and is constituted by:

1. complete devotion of heart,
2. complete devotion of soul,
3. complete devotion of mind,
4. complete devotion of strength,
5. desiring God,
6. valuing God only for God's own sake,
7. valuing all other things only with reference to God,
8. rejoicing and delighting in God,
9. finding happiness in God,
10. finding rest (peace) in God,
11. valuing God as "our all," and
12. relating to God as *our own*.

Wesley did not say so explicitly, but we might also wonder if God's love to us resembles our love to God. Could "God loves us" mean that God is totally and lovingly devoted to us, that God desires us, that God values us for our own sakes as his creatures, that God rejoices and delights in our very existence, that God finds happiness in loving and relating to us, that God yearns for reciprocated love from us, that God finds in us a kind of fulfillment and expression of his own benevolence, creativity, and Divine nature? Yes, God loves all the rest of creation too, but just how God's love to us resembles our love to God is well worth considering. Wesley's usual qualification with respect to each of God's good-making attributes is that in God they are all infinite, whereas in us they are finite. Otherwise, is God's love to us like our love to God?

Anyhow, these are the basic ingredients, elements, and defining properties of our love to God. Describing our love to God in "The Almost Christian," Wesley exulted in "Such love of God is this as engrosses the whole heart, as takes up all the affections, as fills the entire capacity of the soul, and employs the utmost extent of all its faculties."[48] Actualizing just these defining properties of love—total engrossment in and identification with God—is the objective toward which we move as we grow in grace and sanctification proceeds. Perfect Christians, "*altogether Christians*"[49] Wesley might say, would doubtless love or identify with God absolutely; but we still imperfect Christians don't yet "have it all together." Consider Wesley's definitions of Christian perfection: "By perfection I mean the humble, gentle, patient love of God and our neighbor, ruling our tempers, words, and actions;"[50] and "This is the sum of Christian perfection: it is all comprised in that one word, love."[51] Most Christians earnestly strive for perfect love, for intrinsic identification and union with God, but most have it only incompletely by degrees. Loving God with all that is in us is the final destination of the sanctification or saint-making process. Growing Christians are on this road. They have not yet reached the end of it, but God's enabling and encouraging grace accompanies them every step of the way.

Being properly related to God, loving God completely, being totally engrossed in God, fully identifying with God, is often expressed as *union* with God. As Wesley said, love makes us one with God in some sense. Union with God may happen by degrees. The sanctification process involves growing toward and experiencing the constancy of this union, but it is a *process*. Speaking of our *union* with God, Wesley wrote, "The root of religion lies in the heart, in the inmost soul; that this is the union of the soul with God, the life of God in the soul of man;"[52] and "One happiness shall ye propose to your souls, even an union with Him that made them."[53] So, what does our union with God and God's union with us mean conceptually, devotionally, and theologically?

Spiritual union, the very heart of both Wesleyan and non-Wesleyan mysticism or religious experience, is a very prominent, rich, and significant theological concept, but what does becoming "one with God" really mean? Two things can be or become one in many ways, even in religion, so the meaning of "union with God" is not immediately apparent. When a drop of rain falls into the ocean, it becomes one with the ocean, but it loses its own identity in the process. In certain mystical experiences, God and the mystics are said to become one as a matter of both religious experience and metaphysical reality. The monistic or unitive mystics say that they lose themselves in or are completely absorbed into God; but, like raindrops in the ocean, they completely lose themselves, their unique identity, in the process. Is this what Wesley had in mind? Probably not.

Christian *social* union-in-plurality as Wesley understood it is radically different from monistic or unitive mysticism, the self-obliterating variety. It is self-effacing but not self-obliterating. Wesley knew English mysticism mainly through William Law and through his own chosen successor, John Fletcher, who died very prematurely, even before Wesley himself. He was also well acquainted with the writings of early mystics like Macarius, with many later Roman Catholic post-reformation mystics, and with many German, French, and Spanish mystics.[54]

Although he was initially much attracted to the mystics, especially Thomas á Kempis, and continued to admire their holy lives and perfectionism, eventually *Wesley deliberately rejected many features of mysticism* as he knew it for a number of reasons. The mystics he criticized were a diverse lot, united more by family resemblances than by a set of common properties, but here is a summary of his main objections to them.

First, the mystics emphasize and positively value negativity, the "dark night of the soul," God's absence, rather than God's presence, assurance, peace, the atonement of Christ, and other positive moral and spiritual values.[55] Their emphasis on the dark night of the soul has no scriptural basis, Wesley insisted, for "The Scripture nowhere says that the absence of God best perfects his work in the heart!"[56]

Second, the quietistic mystics focus *almost exclusively* on inner solitude, feelings, and inwardness (enthusiasm) and make no legitimate place for extrinsic social involvement in the everyday world, for doing good works, helping others, or even for participating externally and socially in the sacraments, ordinances, and other means of grace such as reading the Scriptures.[57] Wesley thought that the mystics only love to "soar upon the wings of love."[58] They think that inner faith (believing) and love completely fulfill the law without good works, without external expression; they love inward faith and love, but not needy people.[59] He eventually realized that his own personal experiments with contemplative mysticism were drawing him into solitude and away from service. We do need to retire regularly into ourselves to converse and commune with God, but excessive solitude is not sufficient for good Christians, "Not if Jesus Christ be the model of Christianity."[60]

Third, many other mystical pronouncements are unscriptural, not just the dark night of the soul.[61] Many mystics offer *self-achieved* direct access to God without the atonement and justification by faith, and they espouse unscriptural doctrines such as a works righteousness of inner spiritual works. They offer no assurance of personal or individual salvation. They overestimate human goodness and underestimate the seriousness of sin and their own need for repentance, redemption, and

God's forgiveness; they teach that suffering, anguish, and pain are spiritually more beneficial than Christian love, joy, assurance, and peace.[62]

Fourth, the "mystical divines...utterly decry the use of reason...in religion." Yet, there is "no authority" for repudiating reason "in Holy Writ," and biblical figures and writers themselves are "continually reasoning." Persons seeking true religion should "use all the reason which God hath given them in searching out the things of God."[63]

Fifth, Wesley addressed the self-obliteration theme of such monistic or unitive mystics as Meister Eckhart[64] John Tauler,[65] and Jacob Boehme. He was deeply concerned about this because he highly valued both the social and the personal. Wesley wrote, "The mystic divinity was never the Methodists' doctrine. They could never swallow either John Tauler or Jacob Behmen [Boehme],"[66] (although Boehme did not always emphasized *total* self-loss and complete self-absorption into God).[67] Some mystics claim to experience an ecstatic union with God so complete that all awareness of self disappears. The "new age" mysticism[68] that is popular today was much influenced by Buddhism and Hinduism, with which Wesley had little familiarity. But Wesley had serious reservations about the self-obliteration theme as found in many western Christian mystics. As he explained, "*I* do not 'divest faith, either of truth or reason'; much less do I 'resolve all into *spiritual mysticism* and *ecstatic raptures*'."[69]

For monistic unitive mystics, all sense of self and the world disappears, but, oddly, so does all sense of God, as we and Wesley conceive of God. These mystics are left with nothing more than an ecstatic unified consciousness of consciousness that isn't conscious of anything—not even of love or loved-ones.[70] That isn't the Christian God. That isn't the Christian way. Many mystics, both East and West, also claim that in the most profound mystical experiences, all traces of sensory awareness, personal individuality, self-identity, and all of our good-making image of God properties, just disappear altogether—because *all* properties of everything disappear. This includes all of God's own perfect-making attributes as Wesley understood and valued them, and as we do too. Many of them think that being absolutely liberated from "self" and its prolonged existence through rebirth is the ultimate goal of religion, but they are left with nothing but the mystical emptiness of a pure consciousness that has no content whatsoever (and consequently is not omniscient or loving since there is nothing to know and no one to love). But are monistic mystics experiencing anything more than their own consciousness stripped of all content?

In many ways, some themes in the Eastern religions disvalue and aim to extinguish individuality in both us and God, along with all of our image of God properties, and all shadows and images of God within the world. All definite properties of human and divine personhood and of the sensory world just disappear in the monistic experience of mystical union, so mystics do not value such things. They do not positively value a personal God, ourselves, and our neighbors as unique individuals, or the rest of the world in its fullness; from all of them, they try to escape. All are just illusions, "*maya*," they say; but Wesley thought that all are very real. Their mystical union is not a *social* union; Wesley's was.

Wesley's own residual mysticism was definitely not of the monistic type, for it retained all the richness-in-properties of our world, ourselves, and God. His favored religious experiences were of the presence of God's Holy Spirit within us as unique individuals, as well as of God's omnipresence within the world. As Robert J. Tuttle, Jr. correctly noted, "Wesley's communion with God was not a dreamy reverie in which the soul, devoid of personality, swoons away into the unseen."[71] To a correspondent, Wesley wrote in 1772, "These [mystics] are perpetually talking of 'self-emptiness, self-inanition, self-annihilation,' and the like: all very near akin to 'self-contradiction,' as a good man used to say;" and about the mystical annihilation of the sensory created world, Wesley commented, "But they [these mystics] are dangerous too: they almost naturally lead us to deny the gifts of God. Nay, and to make a kind of merit of it; to imagine we honour him by undervaluing what he has done."[72] Note this instance of "undervaluing"!

Social union in love is a different but spiritually significant way in which two individuals can become one, yet retain their rich individual identity—expanded to include the other's rich-in-goodness-properties and uniqueness. It definitely isn't emptiness. It is fullness! The way of love transforms and fulfills us without annihilating us. United in love, we can become one with God as well as with our human neighbors in all twelve ways listed above, while retaining but enlarging our own transformed personal identities. We can become one in heart and mind and deed with others, feeling what or as they feel, thinking what or as they think, and acting in unison with them, without losing who we or they are. We become new and larger persons in the process, for "who we are" and "who they are" are transformed into something much more inclusive through oneness in love. This is a pluralistic experiential spiritual union of psychological/axiological intrinsic identification-with-others. It is personalistic not monistic mysticism.

When we devote our whole souls to others and identify our whole reality with them psychologically and evaluationally, we thereby extend or expand our own total reality. We acquire (become one with) additional good-making properties—their good-making properties. Coming to think as others think, having their minds in us, (e.g., the "mind of Christ"), enlarges us without extinguishing or diminishing our own unique consciousness. Joining our strength with that of others in common tasks and projects both expresses and increases our own energy and strength. Intensely focusing our desires on others, learning to desire what and as they desire for their own good, enriches our own desires, but it does not eliminate all desires. Experiencing their satisfactions as our own increases our own satisfactions. When empathetically feeling as others feel, we thereby expand our own selves emotionally and affectively. When valuing others for their own sake, not just for what they can do for us, we thereby take their goodness, their good-making properties, into ourselves and make them integral aspects of who we are, without losing any of our own good-making properties. When we value *things* with reference to other *people*, as when we identify our homes with our families and loved ones, or when we give gifts to those we love, we are thereby blessed by positive unions of extrinsic with intrinsic values. When rejoicing and delighting directly in others, human and divine, we thereby unselfishly increase our own joy. When we find truly satisfying and enduring happiness in others, human and Divine, we become new and better persons ourselves, but we do not cease being unique persons. We can find a peace for our souls in union with others, especially in union with God, that is almost beyond comprehension and is certainly beyond anything that we could ever have without them. We can totally identify ourselves with others, with people we encounter every day, or with strangers, and find in them a greater "all" that is far removed from the monistic mystic's "nothingness," "emptiness," or pure consciousness that isn't conscious of anything. We can totally identify ourselves with a personal God, who can be encountered every day and everywhere, thereby finding in God our greatest "all." We can belong completely to others, including God, in loving social and spiritual union, and God and others can belong to us, thereby enriching everyone without extinguishing anyone. Love, empathy, compassion, consolation, intimacy, forgiveness, and justice expand our souls, increase our own good-making properties, and transform us into new souls, richer in goodness, living more abundantly. Union in love is fullness, not emptiness. The souls of the monistic mystics become poorer or emptier in properties, by their own accounts, but the souls of united lovers become richer and fuller when "lost in wonder, love, and praise."

Social union, Wesley's alternative to *monistic mystical union*, is pluralistic and realistic. Wesley insisted, *"that Christianity is essentially a social religion, and that to turn it into a solitary religion is indeed to destroy it....It cannot subsist at all without society, without living and conversing with other men."*[73] (Italics added.) Social union presupposes *a genuine plurality of persons, human and divine, who retain their own individuality and personal identity while being united in profound ways that do not obliterate or obscure them*. People in loving social union and communion still remember who they were and know who they are and who they wish to become. They still feel as they feel, have their own special gifts, make their own responsible choices, act as they want and choose to act, have their own unique perspectives on reality, have their own personal projects and duties, and are who they are. Yet, *they belong*. They are many in one and one in many, without being absorbed into undifferentiated unity. They are one with all in the body of Christ and in the body of God, and nothing gets lost.

Christians are psychological and axiological members of one another within the body of Christ, the church, and members of the body of God, the universe. They participate intrinsically in the communion of the saints. Their union with God and with one another takes the form of a mutual communion and community of individuals; it is not total absorption into one another with complete loss of individuality and self-identity. As noted, Christianity offers salvation most directly to individuals, then to social orders for the sake of individuals. It intrinsically values individuals who, as they grow in grace, constantly amplify their identity and enrich their good-making-properties, thereby living more abundantly. Such union, such salvation, such abundance, is for "*me*," as Wesley said time and again; but every saintly "me" can say this. Christian union of individuals is essentially social, and it can transform social relations, institutions, and organizations. It has many members lovingly united in one body who retain their unique identity and value their own unique memories, histories, beliefs, interests, feelings, choices, actions, gifts, responsibilities, and good-making-properties. In self-gain, not self-loss, each person enters into social union within the inclusive body of Christ and the even more inclusive body of God—if the universe is indeed the body of God, as Process Theologians suggest.

Wesley aimed at fulfilling and enriching Christian selves, unique persons. Wesleyan union with God is an infinitely differentiated social union, not a totally undifferentiated non-social unity of absorption into emptiness. This difference between Wesleyan personalistic spirituality and monistic mystical spirituality is very profound. Wesleyan spirituality seeks for a union or intimacy with God and our fellows that expands but does not devalue or destroy individual selfhood and self-realization. What could that be? The answer is, love *between* individuals, not the utter emptiness and obliteration of everything offered by unitive mysticism. According to Wesley, "We are to retain both one and the other, the knowledge of ourselves and the knowledge of God, unto our lives' end."[74] However, we should not confuse individuality, self-identity, and self-realization or self-growth with selfishness, though they are all often called "ego." Unique conscious beings can be well aware of and grateful for who they are in their own full concreteness, grateful that salvation is "*for me*," while being united lovingly with any and with all in all. Wesley often quoted Galatians 2:20, which affirms, "I live; yet not I, but Christ liveth in me." One way to interpret this is that Christians who truthfully say this retain their full personal identity and individuality while also identifying themselves fully and lovingly with Christ. In profound love, two can be intimately one while still being two. And three can also be intimately one while still being three. Many "members" can be one "body" while still being many.

Given a broad sense of "mysticism" that includes *all* forms of *religious experience*, Wesley definitely was a mystic, for he firmly believed that we could experience God and God's Spirit within us through our spiritual senses, as later explained. But his variety of personalistic mystical union with God preserves a plurality of individual selves joined in holy love who retain their own self-knowledge, self-identity, and self-fulfillment. Monistic mystical experiences are utterly devoid of good-making properties because they contain no properties at all, or so these mystics say. None of our image of God good-making properties are present in such experiences, neither in us, nor in the One. By contrast, Wesleyan pluralistic mystical experiences can be inexhaustibly rich in good-making properties; they contain all the good-making properties of God, our neighbors, and all creation. Monistic mystical experiences are those than which none poorer in good-making properties can be conceived; pluralistic mystical experiences are those than which none richer in such properties can be conceived. Which kind of experience *has* the most value? Which kind is *of* the most value?

Wesley advocated the loving communion of the saints united in "social religion." In the final New Creation there "will be a deep, an intimate, an uninterrupted union with God: a constant communion."[75] Wesleyan mysticism or religious experience transcend selfishness, as the saints gradually become new and unselfish selves *before God,* without being absorbed absolutely *into God*. Striving for individual as well as social perfection and spiritual union are primary goals of Wesleyan holiness and Christian sanctification.

Love to All Humankind

Having explored Wesley's understand of what is involved in loving God, we now turn to his understanding of what is involved in loving other people (and animals, implicitly). Grasping what is really involved in loving our neighbors as ourselves will show us how very far short of Christian perfection most of us fall. "Love," applied to people, as well as to God, is indeed a very complicated notion. Here is how Wesley further explained it. To love "all men" as ourselves is "to desire and pursue their happiness as sincerely and steadily as our own."[76] In more detail,

> And the second commandment is like unto this; the second great branch of Christian righteousness is closely and inseparably connected therewith, even 'Thou shalt love thy neighbor as thyself.' 'Thou shalt love'—thou shalt embrace with the most tender good-will, the most earnest and cordial affection, the most inflamed desires of preventing or removing all evil and of procuring for him every possible good.[77]

We must now carefully consider what Wesley said about both the *nature* and the *scope* (the geography and chronology) of Christian love.

The Nature of Love to Other People

Let's begin with Wesley's account of the nature of love itself. The following elements or properties of love are identified in the preceding quote. They are all very important, but still incomplete. Loving other people properly involves and is constituted by:

1. tender good will toward them,
2. earnest and cordial affection for them,
3. "inflamed" desires to protect them from all evil, and
4. "inflamed" desires to procure all good for them.

Wesley's more detailed explanation of the "properties of love" in his sermon "On Love,"[78] is too lengthy to quote here, but it adds more properties involved in loving other people. To summarize, loving others further involves:

5. delighting in them, enjoying them,
6. being patient with their infirmities,
7. being a pattern to them of gentleness and meekness,
8. overcoming their evil with goodness,
9. being kind to them,
10. ardently thirsting after and desiring their happiness,
11. acting in every possible way to promote their happiness,
12. not envying them or being grieved at their happiness,
13. rejoicing in their happiness,
14. not accusing them of evil (without good evidence),
15. not being proud, haughty, or "puffed up,"
16. never harming them in soul or body,
17. not preferring yourself over them, and
18. not hating them.

Now let us reflect a bit upon Wesley's complex understanding of loving other people. Today's psychologists have a great deal to say about what they call *"identification."* Sigmund Freud was interested in the way in which children identify with their parents, thereby absorbing their beliefs, values, and practices into themselves. (More evidence that the sins (or virtues) of the parents are visited upon their children, or as Wesley put it, "The wickedness of the children is generally owing to the fault or neglect of their parents."[79]) Identification can be a bad thing, as when the abused identify with their abusers, captives identify with their captors (the Stockholm syndrome), the oppressed with their oppressors, sinners with sinners, and children with their perverse parents. Identifying with their oppressors helps the oppressed to get by, but it often turns them into oppressors of others, thus perpetuating the evils thereof.

Identification can also be a very good thing, and we will concentrate on positive instances of it. Our capacity for *identification-with-others* has great positive psychological, evaluational, moral, and spiritual significance. It is grounded physically in the mirror neurons of our brains, at least in part, but it is no less significant for having a physiological basis (as do all of our image of God capacities). Identification-with-others is the most basic manifestation of intrinsic evaluation; it is common to all other manifestations such as love, empathy, compassion, consolation, intimacy, and concentration. Love is the broadly moral and spiritual form of identifying with others. Just as loving God involves a profound sense of union with God, so loving other people involves a profound psychological and valuational union with them. When we love, we identify ourselves intrinsically with (positively evaluate) something or someone (a value-object). The differences between us and what or who we value intrinsically are still very real, but they no longer matter, and we may hardly be conscious of them. Our personal identities do not disappear, but our mutual differences are consolidated into an overwhelming experiential, evaluational, and psychological unity. Identification is like being one body with many members, except that it is one soul with many members. In more detail, here is what profound intrinsic identification spirituality[80] involves for lovers.

> 1. We feel a deep and powerful sense of empathetic union and intimacy with those (people, animals, things, etc.) being valued. "That" and "thou" are evaluationally one.
> 2. We want this union and communion to continue indefinitely.
> 3. The differences between us as valuers and those valued still exist, but they no longer matter, and we may no longer pay much conscious attention to them. We may be oblivious to "self," narrowly understood, while entering into an encompassing and more fulfilling self-other union.
> 4. We experience as our own goodness the *internal goodness* of those with whom we identify. Their good-making qualities become an integral and internal part of us, of who we are. Their goodness becomes our goodness, and we are enriched by their goodness, by their good-making properties, in unselfish ways.
> 5. We experience the *external good* things that happen to those with which we identify as happening to us. Their good fortune becomes our good fortune.
> 6. We experience the *internal evils* and moral badness of those with which or whom we identify as our own personal evil or badness. We respond to their internal sins with our own sorrow, guilt, remorse, regret, and forgiveness.
> 7. We experience the *external bad things* that happen to them as if they were happening personally to us. We may respond internally with regret, sorrow, sadness, pity, and compassion. Their bad fortune becomes our bad fortune.
> 8. We are deeply moved or motivated to respond externally as well as internally to their misfortunes and distresses, to act to help them, promote their well-being, and relieve or prevent their being harmed. We act as if we and they were one. We do unto them as we would be done unto if we were they.
> 9. We take great joy and delight in their very existence, as well as in their happiness and well-being. Their life is our life, their existence is our existence, their happiness is our happiness, their well-being is our well-being.
> 10. We experience great sorrow when they are harmed, killed, or destroyed. Their hurt is our hurt; their death is our death.

A spirituality grounded fundamentally in social-identification-union with others is profoundly Wesleyan, more broadly Christian, and even more broadly Godlike. In explaining Christian love, Jonathan Edwards nicely described the kind of *union* involved in love or "true virtue." It "consists in benevolence to Being in general....It is that consent, propensity and union of heart to Being in general, that is immediately exercised in a general good will."[81] Explaining this union further, Edwards said, "I have observed from time to time, that in pure love to others, [i.e. love not arising from self-love] there's a union of the heart with others; a kind of enlargement of the mind, whereby it so extends itself as to take others into a man's self: and therefore it implies a disposition to feel, to desire, and to act as though others were one with ourselves."[82]

John Wesley likewise emphasized the sense of union or identification with others involved in Christian love. In the truly "Christian world" of "the fullness of time to come," he wrote, people will be "'filled with peace and joy in believing', and united in one body, by one Spirit, they all 'love as brethren', they are all 'of one heart and of one soul.'"[83] Identifying with others involves imagination, empathy, and compassion. Wesley did not use the word "empathy" because it had not been coined in his day, but he often spoke of sorrow and compassion.[84] Empathy involves generally identifying ourselves with others; compassion involves identifying ourselves specifically with suffering others.

Wesley often appealed to the Golden Rule, "Do unto others as you would have them do unto you."[85] Applying it effectively requires self-identification with others. Recall Wesley's insistence that this rule should guide us just as much in our relations with non-human animals as with other human beings. Even the conscience of the "heathens" sanctions this rule. Making the Golden Rule actually work involves *action, thought, imagination, and feeling*—doing unto others (human and non-human) as you would have them do unto you, thinking of and imagining others as you would have them think of and imagine you, and feeling for and with others as you would have them feel with and for you. This means imagining yourself as having *their* beliefs, thoughts, feelings, projects, responsibilities, and commitments; it does not work if you just imagine them has having *your*s. In applying the Golden Rule, said Wesley, you must suppose "yourself to be just as he is now."[86] This is what you would want them to do in applying the Golden Rule to you. It involves imaginatively and empathetically putting yourself in their place, walking in their shoes, taking their mind, beliefs, feelings, values, outlook, and station in life into yourself. It involves "imitating" or reiterating their properties within yourself. In more biblical terms, it involves rejoicing with those who rejoice, weeping with those who weep (compassion), and thinking, feeling, and acting accordingly. It involves being so united with them psychologically, evaluationally, and spiritually that the differences between you and them no longer matter and are hardly noticed. All of the goodness that is within them becomes goodness within you—not just their moral goodness, but every valuable property about and within them—to the extent that you are able to assimilate them. Thus, you live more abundantly.

Both the "Second Commandment" of Jesus and the "Golden Rule" involve and make an important place for self-love, but not for exclusive self-love. There is no point in loving others *as* we love ourselves unless we love ourselves, and there is no point in doing unto others *as* we would have them do unto us unless we value goodness and eschew evil in, to, and for ourselves. Also, being Godlike or Christlike requires self-love or positive intrinsic self-valuation. Doesn't God love himself?

Didn't Jesus? If so, loving what and as God and Christ love requires us to love ourselves as well as all others. But in so doing we are no longer the same limited selves we once were.

The Scope of Love to Other People

Now we understand the nature of love to our "neighbors." Next, we need next to grasp its scope. Just how many other people does it cover? Where do they live? When do they live? Just who exactly is our "neighbor"? Does Christian love apply to animals as well as people? Are they our neighbors? For simplicity, we will concentrate mainly on people. Wesley consistently and repeatedly gave only one answer to this question. The "Second Commandment" covers *absolutely everybody*, no matter where or when. It covers every living person on earth. It covers every person who has ever lived, all past generations. It covers every person who ever will live, all future generations. It is all-inclusive. It knows no temporal, geographical, national, racial, cultural, ethnic, or religious boundaries, no limits whatsoever. It tolerates no distinctions between insiders and outsiders, between "us" and "them." It respects and highly values the particularity, concreteness, and definiteness of every individual and his or her local involvements, personal projects, given beliefs, specific responsibilities, and individuating properties. Consider what Wesley said about the *scope* of Christian love.

> 'Thy neighbor'; that is, not only thy friend, thy kinsman, or thy acquaintance; not only the virtuous, the friendly, him that loves thee, that prevents or returns thy kindness; but every child of man, every human creature, every soul which God hath made: not excepting him whom thou has never seen in the flesh, whom thou knowest not, either by face or name; not excepting him whom thou knowest to be evil and unthankful, him that still despitefully uses and persecutes thee. Him thou shalt 'love as thyself'; with the same invariable thirst after his happiness in every kind, the same unwearied care to screen him from whatever might grieve or hurt either his soul or body.[87]

> Above all remembering that God is love, he [the Christian] is conformed to the same likeness. He is full of love to his neighbor: of universal love, not confined to one sect or party, not restrained to those who agree with him in opinions, or in outward modes of worship, or to those who are allied to him by blood or recommended by nearness of place. Neither does he love only those that love him, or that are endeared to him by intimacy or acquaintance. But his love resembles that of him whose mercy is over all his works. It soars above all these scanty bounds, embracing neighbors and strangers, friends and enemies; yea, not only the good and gentle but also the froward, the evil and unthankful. For he loves every soul that God has made, every child of man, of whatever place or nation.[88]

Even animals get into the act in a citation that directly speaks to increasing the scope as well as the potency of love: "The man who loves God feels that 'God hath given him all things richly to enjoy.' He delights in his works, and surveys with joy all the creatures which God hath made. Love increases both the number of his delights, and the weight of them, a thousandfold. For in every creature he sees as in a glass the glory of the great Creator."[89]

Wesley definitely zeroed in on what is usually our most serious moral and spiritual problem—the *limited scope* of our loves. The most significant difference between saints and sinners is not that saints love others but sinners can't. The real difference is *that sinners love so few people*—only insiders, their most intimate acquaintances, but no outsiders—not all the rest of humankind, not all animals.

Most people happen to be predominately worldly, so Wesley and most other theologians believe, but even they have secondary systemic and intrinsic capacities and are capable of loving at least a few others. The trouble is, they love or intrinsically evaluate *mainly things*, not people, not animals, and not God; and they do so only in largely selfish or self-interested ways. They conceive of their self-interest primarily in extrinsic terms, that is, in terms of wealth, luxuries, abundant material resources, and high social standing. They do not identify with many others and thus include them within themselves. Yet, such selfish axiological materialists who love mainly material realities for themselves, are never exclusively extrinsic or selfish in their values and evaluations. They may also love at least *a few* other people and even a few animals. In everyone, the three value dimensions are "mixed," as Wesley noted. To one degree or another, everyone manifests intrinsic, systemic, and extrinsic values and evaluations. More abundant living comes with expanding their scope.

We do not possess any of our human capacities or properties inherently or "naturally" in complete independence of God, Wesley rightly thought. All of them are gifts of God's prevenient grace to all. We are and have *nothing* in complete independence of God. Whether restored or just ongoing, by prevenient grace *almost everyone is capable of loving a few real people*, in addition to loving ideologies, luxury, material prosperity, extravagance, and high social status. Even most selfish worldly people are capable of unselfishly sharing their material goods and high social standing with at least a few others—their spouses, children, close relatives, and perhaps a handful of friends and acquaintances.

Modern sociobiology touts "reciprocal altruism,"—"I'll help you, if you will help me; I won't hurt you, if you won't hurt me." Of course, this apparent unselfishness is nothing but long-range selfishness. There is really nothing genuinely altruistic or unselfish about it. If we were naming it for the first time, we probably shouldn't apply the word "altruism" to it at all. Sociobiologists do recognize, however, that many people (and many animals) are indeed genuinely altruistic or unselfish and are willing and able to make authentic sacrifices for a few others, even where there is no realistic hope of payback. At times, most people are capable of more than enlightened egoism; they can manifest genuinely unselfish thoughts, desires, and deeds; they can genuinely love a few other people. *The trouble is not that such love is almost universally impossible or unavailable; it is that such available love is almost universally so severely confined in scope.*

Jonathan Edwards identified "True Virtue" with love that is universal in scope, with love to being as such, with love of being itself, which includes every particular being.[90] He claimed that anyone who falls short of loving and "consenting to" absolutely everyone is lacking in true virtue. Almost all of us are like this, except perhaps for a very few well-advanced saintly souls. He did not claim that "natural men" under sin are total egoists with no conscience and no capacity at all for loving others unselfishly. Like Wesley, Edwards thought that by common grace people in their natural state have an inborn moral sense that distinguishes right from wrong, and all people are by nature capable of genuinely loving and sacrificing for a small handful of others. Some people, he wrote, "by natural instinct or by some other means, have a determination of mind to union and benevolence *to a particular person or private system*, which is but a small part of the universal system of being;" but this "is not of the nature of true virtue."[91] A person's natural propensity toward unity with and benevolence toward others may extend beyond mere self-love and take in "half a dozen more, and...extend so far beyond his own single person as to take in his children and family;" it may reach "further still, to a larger circle," but it still "falls infinitely short of the universal system, and is exclusive of Being in general."[92] Natural (common) benevolence and good will are "limited to a particular circle of beings." Because they are so narrow in scope, these common human virtues are radically different from the universal "true virtue" of the saints.

Wesley agreed with Edwards about almost all of this. His own account (above) of the very meaning of "thy neighbor" implicitly recognizes that most real people fall far short of loving and fully identifying unselfishly with "every child of man." Let's consider more carefully his explanation of how most people limit the scope of "thy neighbor." Implicitly, Wesley recognized many specific ways in which real people limit the scope of their love. Here we have a splendid opportunity for self-examination. To determine how far the scope of your own love for and intense identification of yourself with others extends, try this thought experiment. Most of us will find that the scope of those "we really love" ends somewhere close to the top of the following Wesleyan list. As you read, ask yourself where you draw the line.

–Do I love all my family and relatives—and only my family and relatives?
–Do I love my friends—and only my friends (plus family and relatives)?
–Do I love everyone with whom I am acquainted—but only my direct acquaintances?
–Do I love only people who are virtuous—but not sinners, not bad people?
–Do I love only those who are friendly to me—but not those who are unfriendly?
–Do I love only people who love me—but not those who are indifferent or hostile?
–Do I love only those who are kind to me—but not those who withhold kindness or act unkindly?

–Do I love only people I have "seen in the flesh"—but not those I have never met?
–Do I love only people I know either by "face or name"—but not those with unfamiliar faces and names?
–Do I love only people that are good and thankful—but not those who are evil and unthankful?
–Do I love only people who do not despitefully use and persecute me—but not those who do?

This list could be expanded indefinitely on Wesley's own terms. He insisted that our love not be "confined to one sect or party, not restrained to those who agree with him [us] in opinions, or in outward modes of worship, or to those who are allied to him [us] by blood or recommended by nearness of place."[93] Now, please consider further all the groups below.

–Do I love only those who belong to my own church, denomination, or world religion—but not those of other churches, denominations, and major or minor world religions, or those who have no religion at all?
–If "party" means political party, do I love only those who belong to my own political party—but not those who happen to be Democrats, or Republicans, or Independents, or Socialists, or Communists, or whatever is not mine?
–If "party" means social class, do I love only my social "equals," but not my social "inferiors" or "superiors?" What if "party" is understood in terms of race, gender, age, wealth, sexual preference, or however I choose to describe people who are different?
–Do I love only those who agree with my opinions—but not those who disagree with me?
–Do I love only those who worship as I worship—but not those who do it differently?
–Do I love only those who are "allied" to me "by blood"—but not non-kin?
–Do I love only those familiar people who live nearby—but not outsiders, strangers, foreigners, northerners, southerners, easterners, westerners, refugees, immigrants, illegal aliens, undocumented people without papers, etc.?
–Do I love only people who are now alive—but not those who will live in the future, or those who lived in the past?
–Do I really love *my enemies* as I love myself?
–Do I really love even *God's enemies*[94] as I love myself?

These questions about scope—about the limits or extent of our loves—could be indefinitely expanded. Two crucial considerations are relevant. First, most of us draw the line *somewhere* before we get to the end of the list; we do not love inclusively, as God does. Second, if we draw the line *anywhere* short of the end of this list, we do not love as Christians should love. Wesley said often and emphatically, our "neighbor" is "every child of man, every human creature, every soul which God hath made." If we draw a line *anywhere* between insiders and outsiders, we do not love as Christians should love. "Insiders versus Outsiders" is one of the most dangerous and sinful social distinctions that anyone could ever make! Love is most properly directed to individual souls in their full concrete individuality, not to classes of people, whether insiders, outsiders, or whatever.

Now we should know why we are all sinners who fall short of the glory of God! Growing in grace and sanctification makes the scope of who we love more and more inclusive. The scope of who and what God loves is: "All his works," and we are to grow to "resemble" God. Exclusivism is always unloving.

Another theme in Wesley's value perspective is closely related to the requirement that we love absolutely everyone. Philosophers then and now try to offer an minimal ethics for ordinary or less-than-saintly people, and in so doing they distinguish between acts that are morally required versus saintly and heroic acts that go "beyond the call of duty." Acts that are just too demanding for ordinary human beings, and any acts that moralize the whole of life—the trivial as well as the significant—are called acts of "supererogation" which, by definition, "go beyond the call of duty." Wesley was familiar with this philosophical distinction, but he unapologetically developed an ethics for saints. He insisted that for true Christians, *every good thing is required*, whether it be trivial or extreme. Nothing desirable goes beyond the call of duty; nothing desirable falls below the call of duty. As he put it, "There is no employment of our time, no action or conversation, that is purely *indifferent*. All is good or bad....There are no works of supererogation....We can never do more than our duty, seeing all we have is not our own, but God's, and all we can do is due to Him."[95] When standards of expectation are set this high—at the level of mature saintliness—everyone falls far short of the glory of God. Everyone is obviously a sinner.

The Spiritual Senses

What good-making capacities, values, and evaluations do saintly people have that non-saintly people lack, at least by degrees if not in kind? An important part of Wesley's answers would be, "the spiritual senses." What did Wesley mean by this, and how much of it can we appropriate for ourselves?

Both Jonathan Edwards and John Wesley were very much influenced by John Locke and the empiricist philosophical tradition. Empiricists hold that all of our knowledge is derived from experience, and no human knowledge is innate, intuitive, or rationally self-evident. Some empiricists exclude self-awareness and maintain that the only relevant kind of experience is *sense* experience. If we can't see, hear, taste, smell, or touch it, it isn't real, these narrow-minded empiricists say. But other empiricists operate with a much broader notion of "experience." They include internal or introspective experiences (conscious self-awareness) as well as sensory experience of the external world; both can give us information about existing realities. Which kind of empiricist was Wesley?

Consider how Wesley expressed the fundamental principle of his own empiricism: "Our senses are the only source of those ideas, upon which all our knowledge is founded. Without ideas of some sort or other, we could have no knowledge; and without our senses we could have no ideas."[96] Again, "'There is nothing in the understanding which was not first perceived by some of the senses.'"[97] Wesley repeated this principle of empiricism more than once.[98] He insisted that he had only the so-called "external senses" in mind when he claimed that we know only what the senses disclose.[99] He repeated this principle of sensationalist empiricism in "On the Discoveries of Faith," where all his illustrations were from the *external senses*, and none were from *the internal* or *the spiritual senses*.[100] We know nothing that is not derived from the *external* senses, Wesley proclaimed. Yet, this seems very odd if not downright incoherent, given all that Wesley also said about our immediate *internal* experiential awareness of consciousness, conscience, the religious affections, and the spiritual senses, none of which are identical with the external senses or with knowing by pure or blind faith.

We should not assume that Wesley first got his sensationalist empiricism directly from John Locke himself. It seems to have come to him indirectly and somewhat incorrectly from Locke through others, including "the pious and learned Dr. Peter Browne, late bishop of Cork, in Ireland."[101] Albert Outler characterizes Wesley's sensationalist empiricist formula as "Thomistic,"[102] recognizing that British empiricism had deep roots in Medieval and Ancient (Aristotelian) philosophy. Locke, by contrast, recognized *two* types of experience as legitimate sources of human ideas and knowledge. In addition to the *external senses*, Locke very explicitly recognized an *internal sense*, technically designated as *"reflection."* He defined "reflection" as "that notice which the mind takes of its own operations, and the manner of them, by reason whereof there come to be ideas of these operations in the understanding."[103] Locke's examples included our direct awareness of, and the corresponding concepts of, pleasure and pain,[104] as well as of our own thinking, believing, doubting, intending, fearing, hoping, willing, and deliberately moving our bodies.[105] Thus, Locke did not neglect the inward senses or restrict human knowledge to what we learn from the external senses, plus reasoning from and about such sensory data. Where Wesley began with "All ideas come from sensation," Locke's own empiricist principle of knowledge was, "*All ideas come from sensation or reflection*," and "in that all our knowledge is founded."[106] Wesley read Browne long before he got around to reading Locke's *Essay* (around 1781). When he did read it, he finally acknowledged that Locke "fully proved" that "all our ideas come from sensation or reflection."[107] Even earlier, he affirmed that "senses" in his basic principle of empiricism applies to both the natural and the spiritual senses;[108] so his position on sensory empiricism was quite ambivalent.

Wesley would have done better to derive his empiricism directly from Locke instead of from Browne or some other lesser empiricist authority. That way, he could have avoided contradicting himself, as he and Browne did, when they added a *second* source of knowledge, "internal sensation," to "the senses *alone*." "A second kind of knowledge," they wrote, "is that we have from self-consciousness. We come to the knowledge of things about us, by the mediation of our senses; but we are immediately conscious of any idea."[109] Thus, in a very convoluted way, Wesley ended up where Locke started.

Wesley clearly went beyond sensory empiricism in appealing to the internal senses, to "self-consciousness," but he did not go beyond Locke in appealing to inner experiences as such. His addition to Locke was *the inward spiritual senses,*[110] *not the inward senses as such.* Unlike Locke, Wesley believed that we have direct experiential or "experimental" knowledge of God and divine things. To this issue we now turn our attention.

Given a notion of "experience" broad enough to include both the internal and the external senses, we can talk meaningfully, knowingly, and empirically about direct awareness of our own inner thoughts, feelings, and choices. We can also talk meaningfully, knowingly, and empirically about hearing the "still small voice within" of conscience. Its directives have to be experienced intuitively, but they are somehow innate, fixed by nature or prevenient grace. Both Jonathan Edwards and John Wesley were influenced by this broader empiricist tradition. They agreed that from experience we can know what is going on both inside of us and outside of us, including many things of great spiritual significance. Both recognized and emphasized the spiritual senses in addition to the external senses. Both drew analogies between the physical and the spiritual senses, and both thought that the spiritual senses provide *direct* data or information about divine things, about which reason can then create concepts and make logical inferences.[111] In their time, Edwards and Wesley were not alone in appealing to the spiritual senses to warrant religious beliefs, and this possibility is still astutely defended today.[112]

Not all introspective empiricists recognize that we have special inner spiritual senses that can give us a direct knowledge of God and divine things. Locke did not go that far; Browne explicitly rejected this possibility; Wesley and Edwards affirmed it. They commend what they both called "experimental religion." Not everyone is equally attuned to their spiritual senses, they agreed, but at some point during the course of the saint's spiritual development (maybe at or just after conversion, as Wesley suggested), this latent "capacity for God" is awakened and begins to function. The spiritual senses are capacities that saintly people have and non-saintly people significantly lack to some degree.

So, *how do the spiritual senses work, what do they do, and what can they tell us?* What exactly do we experience when the spiritual senses are operating? What kind of knowledge or data do they give us? Do they put us in contact with spiritual realities? How did Wesley answer these questions?

Wesley noted in "The Great Privilege of Those that are Born of God" that before birth, a baby's physical senses hardly work at all, but after birth, "all the bodily senses" are "now awakened and furnished with their proper objects." Like-

John Wesley's Saintly Values and Evaluations 211

wise, after the new birth, a convert's spiritual senses are awakened and furnished with their proper spiritual objects. Through their awakened spiritual senses, reborn souls experience what once-born souls cannot experience. Here is a summary of Wesley's account of what the spiritual senses disclose to "those that are born of God."

- They are "*sensible*" of God and "*feel*" or have an "inward consciousness of his presence."[113]
- They are now "capable of discerning spiritual good and evil."[114]
- They can now *understand and appreciate* certain scriptural or religious *beliefs*, such as
    the "exceeding greatness" of God's power, and
    God loves "them that believe,"
    God is merciful to *myself* in particular,
    God's love is reconciling and pardoning, and
    God enlightens with "the knowledge of the Glory of God in the face of Jesus Christ."[115]
- They know "what the peace of God is,"
    "what is joy in the Holy Ghost,"
    "what the love of God" is.[116]
- They see "the light of the glorious love of God, in the face of Jesus Christ" and
- They have "a divine 'evidence of things' [like those above] not seen" by the external senses.[117]

The spiritual senses give a direct awareness of the actual presence of the Holy Spirit in our souls, giving us assurance of pardon and acceptance. They provide the "evidence of things hoped for, the conviction of things not seen" (Hebrews 11:1). Through the spiritual senses, we directly experience the reality of God acting within us, Wesley thought. The newborn soul whose awakened spiritual senses are now working "dwelleth in God, and God in him." The Holy Spirit, Wesley thought, is God's ongoing empowering presence with and within us, and the spiritual senses enable us to experience or be directly aware of the presence of that Divine reality. "The testimony of the Spirit is an inward impression on the soul, whereby the Spirit of God directly 'witnesses to my spirit, that I am a child of God'; that Jesus Christ hath loved me, and given Himself for me; that all my sins are blotted out, and I, even I am reconciled to God."[118] Here and in many related discussions, Wesley drew from St. Paul's words in Romans 8:15–16, words that describe the core of this Christian religious experience.

Four key elements or functions of the spiritual senses can be abstracted from the preceding paragraphs. Just as the physical senses have many distinctive functions and objects—sight, hearing, taste, smell, touch—so the spiritual senses also have many distinctive functions and objects, but what are they? Here is a large part of Wesley's answer. The spiritual senses give:

- A keen and highly localized or personalized awareness of God's presence.
- An immense intensification of the religious affections or tempers, especially assurance, but also others like love, peace, joy, gratitude, and hope.
- A greatly enhanced capacity for discerning the difference between spiritual good an evil.
- A greatly enhanced appreciation for and evaluation of certain fundamental beliefs that are derived from the Scriptures.

Wesley's various accounts of the spiritual senses are riddled with ambiguities, and they may raise as many questions as they answer. What exactly is being experienced? How are these "inward impressions" related to their interpretations? How are they related to their effects? Are some of their effects also perceived as "inward impressions" by the spiritual senses? Can we today affirm some of the above while having reservations about others? Let us consider each of the above derivations from the spiritual senses more carefully.

An Inner Consciousness of God's Presence

Clearly, the primary function of the spiritual senses is to give a keen, highly localized, and very particularized impression, awareness, or "inward consciousness" of God's direct personal spiritual presence and actions within the individual Christian's soul, or so Wesley believed. When the spiritual senses are awakened and begin to function, saintly souls have something immensely significant that lost souls do not have, at least not to any significant degree.

> So it is with him that is born of God. Before that great change is wrought, although he subsists by him, in whom all that have life 'live, and move, and have their being', yet he is not *sensible* of God; he does not *feel*, he has no inward consciousness of His presence. He does not perceive that divine breath of life, without which he cannot subsist a moment. Nor is he sensible of any of the things of God. They make no impression upon his soul. God is continually calling to him from high, but he heareth not; his ears are shut; so that the 'voice of the charmer' is lost to him, 'charm he never so wisely'. He seeth not the things of the Spirit of God, the eyes of his understanding being closed, and utter darkness covering his whole soul, surrounding him on every side. It is true he may have some faint dawnings of life, some small beginnings of spiritual motion; but as yet he has no spiritual senses capable of discerning spiritual objects. Consequently, he 'discerneth not the things of the Spirit of God; he cannot know them, because they are spiritually discerned.'[119]

Thus, the spiritual senses discern "spiritual objects," such as God and the "other world" which, according to Wesley,

> is not far from every one of us. It is above, and beneath, and on every side. Only the natural man discerneth it not; partly because he has no spiritual senses, whereby

alone we can discern the things of God; partly, because so thick a veil is interposed as he knows not how to penetrate.

But when he is born of God, born of the Spirit, how is the manner of his existence changed! His whole soul is now sensible of God, and he can say, by sure experience, 'Thou art about my bed, and about my path;' I feel thee in all my ways: 'Thou besettest me behind and before, and layest thy hand upon me.' The spirit or breath of God is immediately inspired, breathed into the new-born soul; and the same breath which comes from, returns to God.[120]

God is clearly the primary "spiritual object" of the spiritual senses. Through them we directly encounter God as a contemporarily active Spirit—the actively comforting and assuring Holy Spirit of God's "pardoning love."[121] The spiritual senses give an "inward consciousness of his presence." What sense can we make of this sense? What exactly is being experienced when there is an "inward consciousness of his presence"? What exactly are the *experiences or data* that are being *interpreted* as "his presence"? An insightful explanation, offered by Randy L. Maddox, is that Wesley "did not construe the Spirit's witness to be an ethereal verbal communication, but an inward awareness of merciful love that evidences our restored relationship to God. In essence, it is God sharing Godself with us to the point where we can sense Divine mercy and love in a manner analogous to our awareness of our own affections and tendencies."[122]

Perhaps we can expand this fruitful suggestion about what is involved in being "sensible of God." First, as background, we do have an immediate experiential self-knowledge awareness of our own love, mercy, compassion, acceptance, and forgiveness. Next, in the "direct witness" experience, we presumably have an immediate experiential awareness of the presence of these qualities as existing *in another self*, a divine spiritual self, God. Our self-awareness is expanded to include aspects or properties of another self within and penetrating our own selves. We directly experience our own accepting love of others, but in the "direct witness" experience, an accepting love is directly encountered that far exceeds and transcends anything that can be called our own. In this interpenetration of souls, the barriers that separate us from God break down, the veil is lifted, and qualities of loving acceptance belonging to another, a Divine Other, are directly intuited or introspected.

Questions do and should arise about all of this. Here are a few.

1. Aren't we just discussing *words or interpretations rather than experiences* here? The "direct witness" or "direct testimony" experience, as Wesley called it,[123] is expressed in words like being "sensible of God" or "inward consciousness of his presence." In this respect, however, the deliverances of the spiritual senses are no different from the deliverances of the physical senses. We have to put *all* experiences into words, but that does not mean that the words do not refer to something real beyond themselves. We name and thereby interpret what we sense, whether physical or spiritual, so "ethereal verbal communication" or "empty words" is no more applicable to one than to the other. We invent words for everything that we experience and carve out for special attention. Problems do arise when our words

for the data we externally sense or internally encounter are integrated into broader conceptual world-views; yet they always are. Then, the line between reporting and interpreting becomes less than clear, as it always is.

2. Just *how much* of God is experienced in the "direct witness" experience? The answer is: very little, but just enough. Clearly the "direct witness" experience of God's presence does not include everything there is to know about God. It gives only a small taste of God's loving and forgiving presence *with and in me*, but it is not by any means an experience of the whole of God. Yet, it is enough to evoke awe. Remember the story of Moses, who got a glimpse of a small part of God from the cleft of the rock, and who was warned that no one can see the face of God and live. The biblical context was that of perceiving God's presence, mercy, forgiveness, and compassion (Exodus, 33: 14–15, 18–23). These metaphorical images convey a great deal of wisdom. If we directly intuited the whole of God, we would just be wiped out! Our finite assimilative capacities are just not that great. So, in the "direct witness" experience, God in his wisdom gives us only a fleeting glimpse of some small aspect of himself, specifically of an assurance of his majestic loving presence in, forgiveness of, and acceptance of us in particular. We try to put all of this into words. The words name or refer to what is experienced, but they are always interpretive and inadequate to express it fully.

3. How constant or enduring is the "direct witness" experience? Like the objects of sensory experiences, the "objects" or data of the spiritual senses are only transiently experienced, but this does not mean that they only transiently exist. We assume that they exist objectively and endure when we are not looking, just as we assume that about perceptual objects. *Transience* is one of the defining characteristics of all "mystical" experiences, as William James described them in *The Varieties of Religious Experience*.[124] Nevertheless, the *effects* of experiencing God's immediate presence with and within oneself are enduring, not irresistibly so, but so. To some of these enduring effects, we now turn.

According to Wesley, the spiritual senses both receive from God and respond to, give back to, and affect God in many ways. God acts on us; we act on God.

> The same breath which comes from, returns to God. As it is continually received by faith, so it is continually rendered back by love, by prayer, and praise, and thanksgiving—love and praise and prayer being the breath of every soul which is truly born of God. And by this new kind of spiritual respiration, spiritual life is not only sustained, but increased day by day, together with spiritual strength, and motion, and sensation; all the senses of the soul being now awake, and capable of 'discerning' spiritual 'good and evil'.[125]

The "senses of the soul" affect the saint's whole being and way of life. An experiential awareness of the direct presence of God anywhere and everywhere redeems, pervades, and transforms the way sanctified souls experience and practice what Wesley called the "works of piety"—the traditional formal means of grace, and the "works of mercy"—living out and enacting the works of love and mercy every day.[126] *The spiritual senses make all things holy. They result in the intrinsic evaluation of God, of God in everything, and of everything in God.* More about this later when we consider God's Omnipresence.

4. Is the "direct witness" experience of assurance the only way in which the presence of God is perceived? Recall that the primary experience so described is the direct witness of God to our spirits that we are children of God because God loves and forgives *us* as unique individuals. Wesley did not think that this is the only kind of experience in which God's presence is directly sensed or encountered. Mystics, broadly understood, talk about many other kinds of religious experience in which the barriers between God and our finite selves break down and we sense that we are with and in the presence of a Holy God. Wesley also did this, but in a pluralistic way that preserves individuality within social spiritual union. How so?

Let's begin with a suggestion with which Wesley might not agree. Creative writers, artists, and innovators of every description frequently find that the barriers between themselves and God break down, and new revelations are given. Creative insight is often described as revelatory. As Ralph Waldo Emerson once said, "From some alien energy the visions come."[127] Maybe there are new revelations after all, though not all of them are true; so we should just stop equating divine revelations with absolute systemic certainty. Revelatory insights are the beginning-points, not the end-points, of human inquiry and knowledge, including our knowledge of God. All revelatory insights need to be interpreted and tested in light of everything else that we believe. God's ongoing disclosures to us may never cease, despite what Protestants have usually said about the finality of scriptural revelation. Wesley recognized that all religious experiences have to be interpreted and checked by Scripture, Reason, and Tradition, and other Experiences. This is the only way to avoid lapsing into mindless enthusiasm; but maybe God still wants to tell us new things about himself and some other things; maybe truthful revelations did not cease with the finalizing of the Protestant New Testament; maybe we don't already know it all. As one contemporary Process Theologian suggests, maybe Panentheistic Process Theology is a new revelation.[128] Maybe we still have a lot to learn about God and divine things. Such thoughts may be too "far out" for Wesley, but are they for us?

Wesley would agree, however, that God is present in and may be sensed in many human experiences in addition to the heavily emphasized "direct witness" experience. God's presence itself is not identical with our experience of his assuring presence, so God can be and always is there, unawares to us. God may be present in other special ways, and we may actually sense or be directly aware of that presence, Wesley believed, and so do many of the rest of us. Consider some additional possible ways.

- Ordinary Christians listen carefully for the voice of God to give them guidance for daily living, and, presumably, sometimes they get it. Wesley himself expected such inspirations but cautioned that their interpretation

always needs to be checked by other Experiences, Reason, Scripture, and Tradition.
• He also recognized a "feeling of the soul whereby a believer perceives...both the existence and the presence of him in whom 'he lives and moves and has his being,' and indeed the whole invisible world, the entire system of things eternal."[129]
• We can be in "every moment, endued with a power from on high" to triumph over sin and choose the good, and we are "thoroughly and continually penetrated with a sense of this."[130]
• Wesley spoke of having "a continual sense of his dependence on the parent of good, for his being and all the blessings that attend it. To him he refers every natural and every moral endowment."[131] This sense of dependence is in one sense absolute and in one sense not. It includes an awareness of depending on God for our limited independence, i.e., for our capacity to make the free choices that originate with ourselves.
• Wesley thought that the still small voice of God within that speaks through conscience can become louder and clearer, and our activated and aroused spiritual senses enhance our sensitivity to God's own perspective on good and evil, right and wrong.
• Wesley firmly believed that God's presence can be experienced in prayer, meditation, devotions, sacraments, all means or works of piety, and all works of mercy.
• Finally, as explained shortly, saintly souls may progress to the point where the omnipresence of God is perceived not just in "direct witness" experiences but in all experiences of all things.

Wesley was well aware of the dangers of enthusiasm, self-deception, and grandiose delusional thinking when making claims to divine illumination, inspiration, and guidance, which is why he insisted that no such claims be taken at face value. All must be tested extensively through scripture, reason, tradition, broader personal experience, conscience, common sense, Christian community dialogues, their practical and spiritual fruits,[132] and Wesley's hermeneutics of love.

5. The most serious question about the spiritual senses is this. Where exactly should we draw the line between what is actually being *experienced*, and the pre-existing beliefs that we bring with us to the *interpretation* of those experiences? How much is being "read off" of these experiences, and how much is being "read into" them? (Exactly the same problems exist with sensory experiences. Wesley well understood that none of our senses give us knowledge until some interpretive conceptual scheme is applied to them.) No doubt, Wesley interpreted inner spiritual experiences using concepts and presuppositions drawn from biblical religion. His first appeal was always to Scripture. Yet, the spiritual senses do not confirm everything in the Bible, depending, of course, on how the Bible is interpreted. Wesley was most comfortable with those biblical beliefs that lived Christian experience

tends to illustrate and confirm, especially those pertaining to love, mercy, justice, and holiness.

Most if not all spiritual-senses experiences seem to be instances of intrinsic self-identification-with-something-else, but what else? Perhaps some features of the "direct witness" experience are present in all of the above—some immediate awareness of the presence of a majestic holiness, love, compassion, consolation, justice, mercy, and empowerment that far exceeds our own. It doesn't always happen, and just when it does or will happen is an unpredictable mystery, but all of these may be *thin places* where the presence of a loving and accepting God breaks through into human awareness. Just as the physical senses can have many different objects—sights, sounds, tastes, odors, and tactile qualities, even so the spiritual senses can have many different objects—God's loving and forgiving presence, assurance, a sense of (almost) absolute dependence; and they can have many effects, e.g., augmented religious affections, a more vivid conscience, a clearer mind, less prejudice and intellectual blindness, and increased value and valuation capacities—greater knowledge of and sensitivity to right and wrong, good and evil. God can even be present to us as we walk through the valley of the shadow of death; John Wesley's last complete sentence upon his death bed was, "The best of all is, God is with us."

Intensified Religious Affections

We must now consider *how the spiritual senses awaken, disclose, compose, and immensely amplify the religious affections*. In his second sermon on "The Witness of the Spirit," Wesley clarified an important point, namely that the disclosure and intensification of *how we value* through the religious affections is *a consequence of*[133] the witness of God's Spirit with our spirits that we are loved and forgiven children of God. At first, Wesley was not clear about whether the amplification of the religious affections is a *part* of or merely an *effect* or fruit of the functioning of the *spiritual senses*. Are some effects of the "direct witness" experience also perceived only by the spiritual senses? Perhaps so, but most likely they are just perceived through normal introspective experience or self-awareness, working together with the spiritual senses.

Let's begin by comparing Wesley's thoughts about the religious affections, or "tempers" as he often called them, with Jonathan Edwards' theory of the religious affections. Both Edwards and Wesley highly valued *many* human feelings, emotions, and desires and gave them a central place in Christian spirituality. Neither believed that all feelings are inherently bad. Both agreed that feelings have a vitally significant place in true religion. Both seem to think that even God has real feelings, and this is a good thing, not a bad thing. According to Jonathan Edwards, "True religion, in great part, consists in holy affections,"[134] some of which are positive (liking, attraction, etc.), some negative (aversion, opposition, etc.). "Of the former sort are love, desire, hope, joy, gratitude, complacence. Of the latter kind are hatred, fear, anger, grief, and such like."[135] All of them can be zealous, intense, and sustained. Wesley called the religious affections "holy tempers" and their opposites "unholy tempers." Echoing Edwards, he wrote. "True religion, in the very essence of it, is nothing short of *holy tempers*."[136] Holy tempers are the fundamental constituents of true happiness, and unholy tempers are the fundamental ingredients of true unhappiness. Among the unholy tempers are hatred, bitterness, prejudice, bigotry, persecution, jealousy, evil surmising, anger, murmuring, fretfulness, discontent, impatience, idolatry, fervor for evil and indifferent things, and fervor for opinions.[137] Among the holy tempers are longsuffering, gentleness, meekness, fidelity, temperance, contentedness, and resignation to the will of God, but the foremost is love.[138]

On the primacy of love, Wesley and Edwards agreed completely. As Edwards noted, "The essence of all true religion lies in holy love; and that in this divine affection, and an habitual disposition to it, and that light which is the foundation of it, and those things which are the fruits of it, consists the whole of religion," adding, in agreement with St. Augustine, that "Love is not only one of the affections, but it is the first and chief of the affections, and the fountain of all the affections."[139] God is the most proper object of such holy love, and all other loves flow from our love to God. That love is the most basic religious affection and the source of all others, Edwards and Wesley were in full agreement. According to Wesley,

> And this universal, disinterested love is productive of all right affections. It is fruitful of gentleness, tenderness, sweetness; of humanity, courtesy and affability. It makes a Christian rejoice in the virtues of all, and bear a part in their happiness at the same time that he sympathizes with their pains and compassionates their infirmities. It creates modesty, condescension, prudence — together with calmness and evenness of tempers. It is the parent of generosity, openness and frankness, void of jealousy and suspicion. It begets candor and willingness to believe and hope whatever is kind and friendly of every man; and invincible patience, never overcome of evil, but overcoming evil with good.[140]

Occasionally Wesley spoke of "disinterested love," or "disinterested benevolence." In such contexts, he was not denying that proper love or benevolence involve intense feelings or what he called "zeal." He was denying only that they are self-interested. Here "disinterested" means "not-self-interested." In intellectual systemic contexts, it means "objective," "impartial," or "dispassionate." But the non-self-interested interestedness of love can be quite passionate or intense.

Wesley, like Edwards, viewed God as the ultimate and most proper object of the religions affections, and both agreed that love to God spills over into our affective and practical relations with our fellow creatures. Wesley wrote, "True religion is right tempers towards God and man. It is, in two words, gratitude and benevolence: gratitude to our Creator and supreme Benefactor, and benevolence to our fellow creatures. In other words, it is the loving God with all or heart, and our neighbor as ourselves."[141]

True religion consists first and foremost in the heightened functioning of the religious affections. The second part of true religion is spiritual *knowledge or belief*, the systemic "light that is the foundation of it," as Edwards expressed it. A third part is *doing* the works of love, mercy, and justice. Neither Edwards nor Wesley wanted uninformed inflamed feelings, heat without light, which was enthusiasm. Wesley warned, "Beware of that zeal which is not according to knowledge."[142] Also, neither wanted a purely internal piety that bears no good fruit, which is antinomanianism or quietism. Both wanted a true religion of enlightened feelings, heat with light, that bears fruit in good works, in service devoted to others and to God. Profound spirituality goes to the mountaintop, but it also comes back down again and lives in its light and heat. Something like what we now call the Wesleyan "Quadrilateral" was definitely anticipated tacitly by both Jonathan Edwards and John Wesley, though they did not so name it. They agreed that apart from properly informed religious beliefs, the spiritual senses could lead to groundless emotionalism, enthusiasm, error, and either to inactivity or objectionable and erratic behaviors. Wesley identified enthusiasm as involving "dreams, voices, impressions, visions or revelations." He and Edwards were both very much on guard against enthusiasm, while stoutly supporting the religious affections. They agreed that there are important safeguards against it. They would agree that we should always ask, "Is this grounded in Scripture, Reason, Experience, and Tradition?" and, "Is this likely to bear good fruits, both internal and external?"[143]

As noted, Wesley included a highly edited and shortened version of Edwards' *Treatise Concerning the Religious Affections* in his *Christian Library*. Much of what Wesley had to say about the religious affections or holy tempers was at least compatible with and probably was much influenced by Edwards.

Perceived Assurance

The spiritual senses directly produce an awakening and an increase of the religious affections or tempers. For Wesley, one of the most immediate and desirable fruits of the "direct witness" experience was the religious affection of *assurance*. Calvinists like Jonathan Edwards and Arminians like Wesley both wanted *assurance* of salvation. Calvinists wanted assurance that they were among the elect and not among the damned, and the "twelve signs" of true religion developed by Jonathan Edwards were offered mainly to reinforce that assurance. We could never be absolutely sure, Edwards insisted, but we can still have strong evidences. Wesley's approach was much more direct and not driven by a fear of not being elected.

As Wesley saw it, God's Holy Spirit dwells within the hearts of redeemed souls and gives them very direct assurance that God accepts, forgives, and loves them in particular and not just people or Christians in general. Spiritual sensation or experience involves an "inward impression on the soul, whereby the Spirit of God directly 'witnesses to my spirit that I am a child of God'; that Jesus Christ hath loved me, and given himself for me; that all my sins are blotted out, and I, even I am reconciled to God."[144] This witness is intensely experiential and personal, but it is also highly doctrinal. This experience is infused with and interpreted in the light of Christian doctrines or beliefs. It is not just a deeper appreciation for Christian truths in general or in the abstract. It is a profound personal awareness and assurance that they apply to *me*. This is much more than just doctrines about God's Spirit or cognitive assent to them. It is a profound and redeeming direct experiential awareness of the actual personal presence of God's Spirit within—vouching for the doctrines and manifesting God's reality. More than that, it is an immediate awareness of a forgiving love that is similar to, yet distinct from and infinitely surpassing one's own forgiving love of other people. It involves the direct intrinsic evaluation of intrinsic values (God transvaluing us, transforming us and our values from within), not simply the intrinsic evaluation of systemic values (us transvaluing received doctrines).

Wesley thought that *assurance* comes mainly from the *direct witness* of God's presence and communication within us, where each of us literally becomes a temple of God, or "temple of the Holy Ghost,"[145] and consciously so. It *also* comes partly from our own direct witness to ourselves. "There is in every believer," he wrote, "both the testimony of God's Spirit, and the testimony of his own, that he is a child of God."[146] The "own spirit" part is spelled out most clearly in his sermon on "The Witness of Our Own Spirit." The new birth affords new self-knowledge and knowledge of a new self. Specifically, the second-born have an awareness of their own deep sinfulness and guilt. They also know themselves as being forgiven and transformed internally and externally, and as now living in harmony with, and not contrary to, God's will, rules, principles, commandments, and laws. Thus, Christians also have an "*indirect witness*," which is "a *good conscience*," an easy conscience before God, or as St. Paul said, "a conscience void of offense toward God, and toward men." "A good conscience," Wesley wrote, "brings a man the happiness of being consistent with himself."[147] Of this, too, Christians have "an inward perception" or "inward impression."[148] Guilt is gone, peace with God and others is present, and this is experienced through the inward spiritual senses.

Assurance from the witness of God's Spirit, registered by a highly personal sense of and response to God's actual presence within, was what Wesley himself experienced at Aldersgate in 1738. Here is how he described it.

> In the evening I went very unwillingly to a society in Aldersgate Street, where one was reading Luther's preface to the Epistle to the Romans. About a quarter before nine, while he was describing the change which God works in the heart through faith in Christ, I felt my heart strangely warmed. I felt I did trust in Christ, Christ alone, for salvation; and an assurance was given me that He had taken away my sins, even mine, and saved me from the law of sin and death.[149]

Before Aldersgate, Wesley tried to save himself through good works, but works-righteousness gave him no assurance and left him with much guilt. Salvation by faith through grace did give both assurance and forgiveness. Wesley wrestled with whether assurance is absolutely necessary for being a real Christian and finally concluded that it is not. Assurance is highly desirable but not absolutely essential. Faith and grace do not always give instant assurance, even if usually so, Wesley came to believe.

More Perceived Religious Affections

In his *Journal* entry for the day and night of Aldersgate, Wesley said that he did not immediately feel *joy* and *peace* in this *assurance*, but he did receive such religious affections in due time. As he often stressed, the sanctified life of faith working through love is a *joyful* life filled with *delight*. "What we love we delight in,"[150] he wrote. Saints find lasting happiness in God and divine things, and "The Christian 'rejoiceth always'."[151] There is a "joy in the Lord which accompanies that witness of his Spirit."[152] Sinners are restored to "joy unspeakable, to real, substantial happiness."[153] Those who love God find that "Their delight is in him. He is the joy of their heart."[154] Being a Christian is delightful, joyful, and happy! On that also, Wesley and Jonathan Edwards agreed.

In the sanctified life, the saints also find or experience *peace*. Wesley asked and answered, "And what is this peace, the peace of God, but that calm serenity of soul, that sweet repose in the blood of Jesus, which leaves no doubt of our acceptance in him? Which excludes all fear but the loving, filial fear of offending our Father which is in heaven?"[155] It is the peace of forgiveness and release from both the burden of sin itself and the misery of sinful dispositions and affections like guilt, malice, hatred, envy, jealousy, and revenge.

All the religious affections are *aroused and intensified* once the spiritual senses begin to function, as perceived by enhanced inner awareness. According to Wesley, "By the same means [inner consciousness] you cannot but perceive if you love, rejoice, and delight in God."[156] But the religious affections (assurance, love, hope, joy, peace, trust, confidence, gratitude, etc.), usually do not come all at once in all their glory. Typically, they develop slowly and gradually. Not every Christian is perfected instantly in his or her religious tempers, so Christians grow in such spiritual perfections.

Wesley had a mean streak of perfectionism within himself, and, like all perfectionists, he really knew how to make himself and others miserable! In his perfectionistic, systemic, "all or nothing" moods, he frequently expressed serious doubt that he was a Christian at all, even after Aldersgate—because he was not a *perfect* Christian, as he very well knew.[157] Wesley's original and most extreme perfectionism was developed under the influence of those Moravians whose systemic religious outlook was totally black or white, all or nothing, and admitted no degrees of anything spiritual. To them, perfect faith, sinlessness, salvation, assurance, joy, peace, gratitude, and holiness all went hand in hand, and anything short of being an "altogether" Christian was not Christian at all. Extreme perfectionism can be just another way of being "under the law" and being condemned by it. Wesley wrestled with having it all versus getting it only by degrees, but he finally decided that real Christians can be on the right road without having arrived at the final destination; they can be completely justified and forgiven without being completely sanctified. They can be assured that God loves them even while they are yet imperfect, while sin remains but does not completely reign. Conversion may be sudden, but sanctification usually increases by degrees and takes a whole lifetime and beyond.

Do *only* born-again protestant Christians experience the religious affections? Is the affective line separating once-born from twice-born souls absolute, or are there affective continuities between them? What about persons outside the Christian fold altogether? Have they no significant degrees of love, hope, joy, peace, trust, confidence, gratitude, and other virtuous spiritual dispositions? To these questions, posed earlier, we now return. Wesley admitted that non-Christians and pre-Christians have religious affections to some degree due to prevenient grace.

> There may be foretastes of joy, of peace, of love—and those not delusive, but really from God—long before we have the witness in ourselves, before the Spirit of God witnesses with our spirits that we have 'redemption in the blood of Jesus, even the forgiveness of sins.' Yea, there may be a degree of long-suffering, of gentleness, of fidelity, meekness, temperance (not a shadow thereof, but a real degree, by the prevenient grace of God) before we are 'accepted in the beloved,' and, consequently, before we have a testimony of our acceptance. But it is by no means advisable to rest here.[158]

By prevenient grace, pre-Christians and non-Christians don't seem to be nearly as bad as "total depravity" declares them to be! Many such people have very good moral and spiritual affections, but they could still be better and do better.

Enhanced Discernment of Good and Evil

The spiritual senses, as Wesley understood them, also produce a greater capacity for "discerning spiritual good and evil." This capacity is intensified and reinforced as sanctification proceeds. Wesley did not explain exactly what intensified "discerning of spiritual good and evil" means, but it definitely goes beyond what comes before conversion. So what does come before? Here are some educated axiological answers or conjectures.

Most people, worldly people for instance, are very good at discerning *practical* good-making or bad-making properties in material things, physical processes, sensory objects, the things of the world, useful human behaviors, and social rankings within the world. They are skilled at applying "better" and "worse" to extrinsically valuable things, objects, processes, and actions. They value well when good-making properties are external sensory properties. They can be very competent at sorting out extrinsically better things from those less desirable. But they are weak and relatively insensitive with respect to internal good-making or bad-making moral and spiritual properties. Spiritually transformed people, by contrast, become more aware of:

- intrinsic value-making properties (individuated consciousness or inwardness and its capabilities),
- good-making moral properties (conscience, moral virtues, obeying the moral commandments, loving our neighbors, doing justice, loving others, practicing mercy, etc.),
- good-making spiritual properties (all the religious affections, faith, hope, peace, joy, repentance, forgiveness, and properly loving God and divine things),
- God himself and all other "divine things."

Over time, by the grace of God, sanctifying souls get better and better at recognizing and appreciating moral and spiritual good-making properties and standards, and at applying them to particular beliefs, people, practices, and social situations and institutions. Their capacity for intrinsic values and evaluations increases. They grow inwardly in grace. They strive for and actually move toward moral and spiritual perfection. Gradually, through God's power working with and within them, and through their own cooperation with God's initiatives, they approach genuine fulfillment more and more. They gradually acquire the good-making properties that match the highest ideals or standards of Christian goodness or saintliness. With God's help, they approach perfection. They become good Christians, not just fair, average, or poor Christians. They receive and give forgiveness. They begin to have a clear conscience before God, a conscience void of offense.

This does not mean that people in non-Christian cultures, or that worldly or skeptical people within the "Christian dispensation," are entirely without morality or moral conscience and the ability to discern intrinsic good and evil. The augmented discernment of good and evil just described can occur outside of distinctively Christian contexts. Wesley agreed that conscience is a "natural" or universal human endowment of God's prevenient grace. Recall, though, that the natural is the prevenient, and the prevenient is the natural, so God is always there. Worldly people are never totally worldly, heartless, or immoral. Nor are wicked people ever totally wicked. Everyone has some ability to evaluate within all three dimensions of value. Through conscience, God gives "the law" to everyone the world over, just as Saint Paul said. By nature (prevenient grace), even "the gentiles" have a basic knowledge of good and evil, right and wrong. Many know "the law" by revelation as well and understand that the law is fulfilled by love. All human beings have a "heart" as well as a "head," even those predominately hard-hearted and/or hard-headed.

Choosing between moral and spiritual good and evil presupposes knowing what they are, so the "First step," in God's plan for human beings "is to enlighten the understanding by that general knowledge of good and evil."[159] Sinners, including worldly people, can tell the difference between good and bad sense objects and processes. To some degree, they can also distinguish between moral and spiritual goodness and badness. They don't live as they should, but they know how they should live, at least dimly. People dominated by extrinsic values and evaluations also embrace some systemic and intrinsic values and evaluations. The spiritual senses enliven, expand, and properly prioritize what all people already have and are able to sense or intuit, even before they are born again.

As a good empiricist, Wesley officially renounced rationally intuited "innate ideas," or "self-evident truths," but many basic structures, beliefs, and contents of consciousness and conscience do seem to be inherent and inborn, akin to our capacity to learn a language. By degrees, we are by nature (or prevenient grace) disposed almost instinctively to believe in God, in the existence of other minds, in the reality of the past, in an objectively existing physical world, in the uniformity of nature, in the general reliability of our sensory and cognitive capacities, in the astonishing relevance and applicability of math and logic, and in morally sensed right and wrong, good and evil.[160] The most basic and inevitable of these beliefs cannot be proved to be true without logical circularity, that is, without presupposing or appealing to the very things we are trying to prove. As explained earlier, even Wesley, like many other empiricists (e.g., Locke), finally got around to making a place for "self-evident truths." Human nature, we now realize, is never a complete "*tabula rasa*" or blank tablet on which nothing is originally written by nature, despite the dogmas of extremist empiricism. All rational thinking must start somewhere, for there can be no infinite regress of proofs of proofs of proofs. Being rational, being a reasonable person, just means accepting some such beliefs as axiomatic, that is, without further non-circular evidential proof. That is how God created us. The inborn, foundational, natural, (or prevenient) beliefs and moral propensities of consciousness and conscience are only latent in newborns and very young children, and they may be almost unconscious, asleep, or dormant in mature adults, but they can be brought into the full light of immediate awareness.

Eating of the tree of good and evil means that our latent intuitive structures and forms of value gradually emerge into wakeful awareness. In that sense, eating of this tree is a good thing, not a bad thing. Wesley thought that being born-again accelerates this process dramatically. But almost everyone, sociopaths excepted perhaps, has an innate capacity for discerning moral and spiritual good and evil, right and wrong, just as everyone has an innate capacity for learning and speaking a language, counting, or thinking logically. Value capacities, like our capacities for language, are hard-wired into our genes. The trouble is, though we are hard wired for moral *knowing*, we are only soft wired (for freedom's sake) for *doing* the right thing! Some people never learn to speak or think very well. Some never seem to learn to discern moral good and evil, right and wrong, very well. Most of us, like Saint Paul, consistently do what we clearly know we ought not to do and neglect what we know we ought to do. Some experience dramatic enhancements of conscience-awareness at crisis or conversion points in moral and spiritual development. In others, this happens only gradually. Some, by God's grace, fully awaken their value sensitivities in all value dimensions and live accordingly. A few people (the true saints of God) activate all their evaluational capacities and learn to speak, think, feel, and act exceptionally well. Sleepers awake!

A New Appreciation for Old Beliefs

Wesley identified yet another function of the spiritual senses: they produce a deeper understanding of and appreciation for Christian doctrines "not by a chain of *reasoning* but by a kind of *intuition*, by a direct view."[161] Some things we just know directly or experientially without further proofs, arguments, or evidence. Supposedly, there is nothing historically new in these beliefs. Quoting the scriptures to find illustrations, Wesley wrote of a deeper discernment "that 'God was in Christ, reconciling the world to himself'.... 'We know that we are of God,' children of God by faith, 'having redemption through the blood of Christ, 'even the forgiveness of sin.' 'Being Justified by faith, we have peace with God through our Lord Jesus Christ...'"[162]

To repeat what was summarized earlier, the spiritual senses give a new understanding and appreciation of such religious beliefs as:

"the exceeding greatness" of God's power, and that
God loves "them that believe,"
God is merciful to *myself* in particular,
God's love is reconciling and pardoning,
God enlightens with 'the knowledge of the Glory of God in the face of Jesus Christ.'[163]
"what the peace of God is,"
"what is joy in the Holy Ghost,"
"what the love of God" is.[164]

These affirmations reflect the doctrinal presuppositions that Wesley brought with him into his interpretation of the "direct witness" experience. This experience may directly confirm *something*, but all these beliefs, Wesley realized, are also *given antecedently* in the Scriptures, mainly in the New Testament. The spiritual senses may actually give *us* very little novel cognitive or doctrinal knowledge or information, even if it was novel or original to some of our spiritual ancestors. Even "God loves and accepts us" is nothing new, but the "direct witness" experience gives it an experiential vivacity, validity, and confirmation that goes beyond its foundation in scripture and tradition. Wesley well understood this. Contemporary Christians may receive "inspirations," but these are not new revelations, he firmly believed. He was just as suspicious as anyone of those enthusiasts who claimed to receive new doctrinal disclosures directly from God. He regularly insisted that all alleged inspirations be checked by the fruit they bear, and by their agreement with the Scriptures, Reason, Tradition, and other Experiences. Like Jonathan Edwards, Wesley wanted enlightened heat or zeal, but not heat or zeal without light.

Wesley thought that the spiritual senses vitalize a newborn person's appropriation of old cognitive revelations or beliefs. Wesley, like Jonathan Edwards, insisted that the spiritual senses do not give any new revelations. They give no new doctrinal knowledge, information, truths, or beliefs; they merely give us a renewed appreciation for the old truths of the Scriptures and how they apply to us personally. In one of his most widely acclaimed sermons, Edwards called the inner spiritual senses the "Divine and Supernatural Light." He was as much concerned to explain *what this light is not* as *what it is*. One of his main negative accounts was this.

> This spiritual light is not the suggesting of any new truths, or propositions not contained in the Word of God. This suggesting of new truths or doctrines to the mind, independent of any antecedent revelation of those propositions, either in word or writing, is inspiration; such as the prophets and apostles had, and such as some enthusiasts pretend to. But this spiritual light that I am speaking of, is quite a different thing from inspiration: it reveals no new doctrine, it suggests no new proposition to the mind, it teaches no new thing of God, or Christ, or another world, not taught in the Bible; but only gives a due apprehension of those things that are taught in the Word of God.[165]

Echoing Jonathan Edwards, Wesley said that the spiritual senses are "a kind of spiritual *light* exhibited to the soul, and a supernatural *sight* or perception thereof."[166] This negative feature of the spiritual senses—no new revelations—was vitally important to both of them. Protestant ministers and theologians of that era were acutely attuned to and dead set against all claims to new (non-biblical) revelations, lest Roman Catholic innovations that go far beyond biblical religion—like "Popish indulgences"[167]—be admitted into the ranks of revealed truths. They were convinced that once the Protestant Bible (minus the *Apocrypha*, which is present in the Catholic and Jewish Scriptures) was finalized, God had absolutely nothing new to say to anybody after that. They branded as heretics and enthusiasts anyone who claims to have new revelations from God. Such people were ostracized, exiled, and sometimes tortured, hanged, or burned at the stake. John Wesley was not about to make that mistake! He wrote that "Whatever doctrine is *new* must be wrong; for the *old* religion is the only *true one*."[168]

He didn't write it, but Wesley would have agreed with "Give Me that Old Time Religion." A word of caution, however: just what any given individuals identify as the "Old Time Religion" depends heavily on their preconceptions, reflections, and values, plus their situation in human society, culture, and history. According to Wesley himself, "the plain, old Christianity"[169] was the religion of love—the very stuff you have been reading about thus far in this book (and not the religion of predestination and divine election of the few, not a worldly religion, and not a religion of mere "opinions"). Not everyone, not every Christian, agreed then or agrees today. The cognitive disclosures of the spiritual senses that Wesley identified were heavily doctrinal; in theory it was all old stuff, newly appreciated, enlivened, re-evaluated, and re-affirmed. His new "experience" or "sense" of the truth of certain fundamental Scriptural beliefs seemed to be just an intense, heartfelt, intrinsic re-evaluation of selected but already-given systemic religious values. Before conversion, perhaps they are unknown, or perhaps they hardly valued at all, or maybe they are only valued with academic impersonal (systemic) detachment. New birth transforms them into live options.

An Awareness of God's Presence or Omnipresence in All Creation

Experiencing God's *special presence,* as just discussed, is different from being keenly aware of God's *omnipresence*, even if they are somehow closely related. God's special presence is with particular people at special times and places in human history. Omnipresence is God's presence absolutely everywhere at all times. Sanctified souls can sense or experience both God's special presence and God's universal presence. Atheists and agnostics may be skeptical about this inner awareness of God's presence, but the saints are not.

By tying its interpretation to specific Christian doctrines, Wesley gave his account of the *special experience* of God's *special presence* a distinctively Christian flavor. Yet, he did not deny that God was and is present in special ways with special people *before* and *outside* the Christian era, arena, or dispensation. The Bible at its best, including the pre-Christian Old Testament, is largely the story of how God was experienced by and interacted with particular existing individuals in special historical circumstances. The special presence of God, and human sensitivity to it, are not limited only to born-again doctrinal Christians. Even non-Christians may sense, in their own way, God's presence witnessing to their spirits about God's acceptance, mercy, and love. Today, within and without Christendom, many saintly and non-saintly people seem to have a keen sense of the special presence of God guiding, nurturing, comforting, forgiving, and assuring them. Sensing God's special presence is always sporadic, unpredictable, transient, historical, and not under the immediate willful control of those who have such experiences. God sometimes seems to make special efforts to be known and experienced in ways that go beyond his general presence everywhere.

Does God's unpredictable presence to particular people in special times and places have an intelligible connection with God's universal presence? Maybe God is *always* trying to be specially present with everyone everywhere, but only a few people are sufficiently advanced spiritually to be sensitive, attuned, or responsive to God's ubiquitous self-communications, which only *seem* to happen sporadically. Or maybe God really does make special efforts at special times to manifest himself in special ways to particular people in specific circumstances. Maybe a belief in God's omnipresence is a kind of inductive generalization based on increasing spiritual sensitivity. We may never know how God himself understands the relation between his special presence and his omnipresence. Maybe there are special as well as general gifts and communications from God. That seems to be the story of biblical religion.

Many morally and spiritually undeveloped people are just plain insensitive to God's universal presence because their spiritual sensitivities are not yet awakened, because their souls are so poorly developed morally and spiritually, because they have not accepted and grown in grace. As Wesley described this insensitivity, the "natural man" (or natural woman)

> has scarce any knowledge of the invisible world, as he has scarce any intercourse with it. Not that it is afar off: no: he is in the midst of it; it encompasses him round about. The *other world*, as we usually term it, is not far from every one of us: it is above, and beneath, and on every side. Only the natural man discerneth it not; partly because he has no spiritual senses, whereby alone we can discern the things of God; partly because so thick a veil is interposed as he knows not how to penetrate.[170]

If God is *universally present everywhere*, spiritually advanced people may be more attuned to this, as well as to God's special presence *within* their own souls. Can we make any sense of this? Perhaps, but first we must try to understand *omnipresence* as one of God's value-laden attributes or perfect-making predicates. This must be explained in two steps, first in terms of metaphysical omnipresence, then as devotional sensitivity and inner responsiveness to God's omnipresence.

God's Metaphysical Omnipresence

Where is God? God is everywhere. Yet, God has no body, so God is nowhere. How can this be? What sense does this make? Wesley wanted to have it both ways, but can we? Let's first try to understand Wesley's position, then figure out where we might go from there.

Wesley affirmed that we exist in the "spiritual" image of God, by which he usually meant the "immaterial"[171] or "incorporeal" image of God. Wesley was a Platonic/Cartesian mind/matter dualist. Both we and God are immaterial spirits, but *we* are embodied spirits, whereas *God* is not. As Wesley explained, "God's image upon man, consists, in his nature, not that of his body, for God has not a body, but that of his soul. The soul is a spirit, an intelligent, immortal spirit, an active spirit, herein resembling God, the Father of spirits, and the soul of the world."[172] We are the immaterial souls of and in our bodies, yet embodied. God is the immaterial omnipresent soul of the world, yet not embodied, Wesley believed. This is a puzzle, to say the least! Getting to the bottom of it requires a brief metaphysical detour into what is traditionally called the "mind/body problem."

We exist in the spiritual image of God, but what did Wesley mean by "spirit"? Occasionally he equated being spiritual with being non-worldly, with not being dominated by "the flesh," that is, by "its affections and lusts," and by extrinsic sensory goods and pleasures.[173] However, Wesley also gave "spirit" a distinctively metaphysical meaning, drawn from Platonic/Cartesian mind/matter dualism; and this dualism is the ultimate philosophical root of the above puzzle.

From this dualistic perspective, *matter*, by definition, has spatial properties, whereas mind (or soul or spirit) does not. Descartes' "All bodies are (spatially) extended" is the very definition of material or physical reality, as universally accepted to this day. Bodies have spatial extension but no thinking; minds have thinking but no spatial extension, Descartes proclaimed. Wesley accepted or assumed this definition: "It may be observed of them all, that they are extended, solid, divisible, figured, and capable of motion. We cannot conceive any body that is not extended, or composed of several parts."[174] Presumably, Wesley agreed with this dualism as expressed in Charles Bonnet's *Compendium of Natural Philosophy*, which he rewrote and published in his own name. In his own sermon "On Dissipation," Wesley said "that intelligence is as essential to spirits as extension is to matter."[175] Like Descartes, Wesley meant far more by "thinking" than mere cognition or reasoning. In "What is Man?" after affirming that the body is composed of the "four elements," Wesley wrote, "But beside this strange compound of the four elements earth, water, air, and fire, I find something in me of a quite different nature, nothing akin to any of these. I find something in me that *thinks*, which is neither earth, water, air, fire, nor any mixture of them can possibly do. Something which see, and hears, and smells, and tastes, and feels, all which are so many modes of thinking;" and he adds that his (and every) mind judges, reasons reflects and has imagination, memory, and liberty of choice.[176] He further explains that "This inward principle, wherever it is lodged, is capable not only of thinking, but likewise of love, hatred, joy, sorrow, desire, fear, hope, etc., and a whole train of other inward emotions which are called 'passions' or 'affections'. They are styled by a general appellation, 'the will'."[177]

Cartesian dualists (like Wesley) affirm that *minds* (or souls, or spirits) have many *psychological properties,* but they have *no spatial properties*. "I think, therefore I am," and "I love, therefore I am," are supposedly very different from, "My brain weighs three pounds, therefore I am." Physical bodies, whether living or dead, have size, shape, resistance, weight, motion, and position in our common world of space and time. Minds have none of these properties, dualists suppose; they are "of a quite different nature," as Wesley put it. Thus, Wesley claimed, "I am something distinct from my body."[178] Of course, minds may have an infinitesimally small spatial position or location in the pineal gland or somewhere in the brain, as Descartes suggested. Wesley himself was never sure that he agreed with this, or that he understood the precise location of immaterial or spiritual souls within the body, but they are located or positioned *somewhere*.[179] Even so, they have no additional physical or spatial properties of their own—no size, shape, velocity, weight, mass, etc., just as matter has no psychological properties.

Anticipating quantum and many-worlds theories when discussing the infinite divisibility of matter, Wesley said (through Bonnet), "There is no such thing, strictly speaking, as parts infinitely small."[180] He affirmed the infinite extent of spacetime, and what is today called "many worlds," conjecturing "that our solar system is but one of innumerable systems; that the universe is of infinite extension, and occupied by an infinite multitude of worlds."[181] Neither then nor now can this conjecture be verified, especially so if "worlds" means "universes" and not just "galaxies," of which Wesley did not know. By "an infinite multitude of worlds," Wesley probably had in mind only inhabited planets both with within and beyond our own solar system, but existing in a single universe of "infinite extension." He was convinced that our moon has no atmosphere and is thus not inhabited, but he thought that other planets in our solar system might be.[182]

Wesley did not view the existence of innumerable other worlds as an obstacle to believing that God loves and acts in special ways upon us and within this world, just as Christianity proclaims. Wesley sometimes doubted that other worlds were actually inhabited, but he wrote in one of his own sermons, "Suppose there were millions of worlds, yet God may see, in the abyss of his infinite wisdom, reasons that do not appear to us why he saw good to show this mercy to ours in preference to thousands or millions of other worlds."[183] Of course, if God is as we think he is, he doubtless loves, cares for, and acts upon and within all worlds (planets? galaxies?) or universes other than our own.

In Platonic/Cartesian dualism, the defining property of "body" is spatial "extension," and the defining property of minds is non-spatial "thinking." Minds as such are incorporeal. With Descartes Wesley agreed, "That the soul is immaterial, is clear from hence, that it is a thinking substance."[184] Wesley agreed with Jesus that "God is a spirit," but he interpreted the meaning of "spirit" in ways completely unknown to Jesus, who never said anything about whether spirits do or do not have spatial properties. Wesley accepted Platonic/Cartesian body/mind dualism and, like many others, he imposed it upon the Bible. He knew that Descartes thought that the immaterial mind (having no spatial properties) is located in the pineal gland, but he was not sure about its precise location, other than somewhere in the head.[185] He thought that no one really knows where it is located or how it is coupled to the body,[186] but he clearly presumed that thinking minds, as well as their functions and contents, have no spatial size, shape, weight, resistance, and motion, whereas bodies do. That is what he meant metaphysically by "spirit" (and what Jesus never affirmed). Our minds or souls, Wesley thought, share this immaterial "spiritual" image of God. Wesley extended his Platonic/Cartesian dualism to the God/world relation. Both divine and human souls are "immaterial" spirits that have no physical properties. The puzzle is, why are we embodied, whereas God is not?

Philosophers ask many tough questions about mind/body dualism. One of the toughest is this. How can minds, whether human or divine, ever act on bodies, or bodies act on minds, when they have absolutely nothing in common? How does one ever "get a grip" on the other when one has spatial properties but the other absolutely does not? *Idealists* like Malebranche and Berkeley say that this really is not a problem because matter exists only in our minds or experiences but not in itself. *Materialists* say that this really is not a problem because minds don't exist at all.

Wesley reject both of these deviant extremes in favor of Cartesian *dualism*, but he knew that he did not know how immaterial minds and material bodies can interact.[187] No dualist can explain this.

Cartesian dualism is not the only way to preserve all the properties that we know from experience that minds and bodies have without reducing them to one another. Contemporary Process Thinkers and Non-reductive Physicalists[188] think that *both* minds and bodies *have both spatial properties* and *psychological properties*; and this makes the problem of their interaction easier to resolve because they have much in common from the very outset.

In theology, metaphysical Platonic/Cartesian dualism generates serious difficulties for understanding God's omnipresence. How can an "immaterial" God be everywhere in space while possessing no spatial properties at all? This dilemma is inherent in Wesley's view of God's omnipresence. On the one hand, he insisted, God is not an embodied spirit; we are embodied, but God is not. On the other hand, he clearly said that God is "the soul of the universe" or "of the world"[189] and that "God is in this and every place."[190] Let's consider more carefully Wesley's explanation of God's ubiquitous presence, first in biblical terms, then in his own more technical or philosophical language.

In his sermon "On the Omnipresence of God," Wesley cited the key biblical verses that affirm God's omnipresence, all of which associate God's presence with space. The first below was his sermon text.

Do not I fill heaven and earth? (Jeremiah 23:24)

Whither shall I go from thy spirit? Or whither shall I flee from thy presence? If I ascend up to heaven, thou art there: if I make my bed in hell, behold thou art there. If I take the wings of the morning, and dwell in the uttermost parts of the sea, even there shall thy hand lead me, and thy right hand shall hold me. (Psalms 139:7–10)

For in him we live, and move, and have our being. (Acts 17:28)

Him that filleth all in all. (Ephesians 1:23)

Philosophically understood, according to Wesley, all these texts mean that "There is no point of space, whether within or without the bounds of creation, where God is not," and that "The universal God dwelleth in universal space."[191] Many (but not all) of today's astrophysicists postulate the reality of an infinite superspacetime that contains our own natural world or universe but also much more—many "other worlds" or "parallel universes." We cannot empirically verify the existence of any of them—so this is highly speculative metaphysics or pseudo-theology rather than real natural or empirical science, even if offered by professional scientists. Wesley, ahead of his time, conjectured in his "On the Omnipresence of God" that "space exists beyond the bounds of creation" and that God is present even there[192] in "the whole universe, the whole extent of space, space created and uncreated, and all that is therein" in "extramundane space."[193] By *"uncreated"* space, he may have meant the "superspacetime" of heaven. Wesley assumed that heaven, "beyond the bounds of creation," is spatiotemporally ordered. As noted, Wesley linked God's presence everywhere and in everything to other divine attributes like omnipotence and omniscience. In order to know and to influence everything everywhere, God has to be present in everything everywhere.[194]

Did Wesley emphasize God's omnipresence in *time* as well as in *space*? All of time is timelessly present in God's eternity, he thought, but is the everlasting God present in and with all of time and history as they happen? His view of God's eternity as utterly timeless may have obscured his understanding of God's omnipresence in time as well as space. However, he did appreciate the value of time from a human perspective and advocated "being deeply sensible of the value of time, of every precious, fleeting moment."[195] To escape "Satan's Devices," we must "redeem the time. Improve the present moment. Buy up every opportunity of growing in grace, or of doing good."[196] Christianity "leaves no time upon our hands. It fills up all the blank spaces of life."[197] Wesley's take on "Sufficient for the day is the evil thereof" was, "Sufficient for the day is the grace thereof."[198] He also spoke often of God in temporalistic terms without the qualification, "speaking only in the manner of men," despite his official view of God as timeless. For example, in his sermon, "On Divine Providence" he wrote that "Scripture is *the history of God*,"[199] "He is present at all times, in all places,"[200] "He is concerned every moment for what befalls every creature on earth;"[201] and God "is continually employed in managing all the affairs of creation for the good of all his creatures....His power, being equal to his wisdom and goodness, continually co-operates with them."[202] Wesley's *eternal* God has no temporal perspective, only an "all at once" perspective; but Wesley's *everlasting* God could "continually" have an endless or everlasting temporal encounters and perspectives, so that, as Wesley said, "God's time is always the best time."[203] Today's Temporalistic Theologians emphasize God's temporal as well as spatial presence with us everywhere and in every precious fleeting moment as they happen, and not all at once. Wherever and whenever there is time and space, God is then and there. An omnipresent God is both everywhere and everywhen, but future "whens" do not yet exist to accommodate is presence.

The most serious puzzle about omnipresence is this. How can God be present everywhere, thus having all the properties of space, or the properties of all space, while being present nowhere, thus having no spatial properties or embodiment at all? Claiming that God exists at every point in space, yet God has no body at all, seems logically incoherent. Viewing the universe, or some universe—or even the superspacetime of heaven—as aspects of God's body would remove this incoherence, but Wesley resisted, out of deference to dualistic philosophical and theological traditions. Many modern Process Thinkers take two interesting steps to resolve this difficulty.

First, they suggest, *the universe (or some universe) is God's body*, so God, like us, is embodied. They agree with Wesley that God is the soul of the universe, but they add that this implies that the universe is the body of God. All souls, including God, are embodied souls. Since the universe is not shaped like a human body, God does not have a humanoid body, but God is embodied all the same. All psychological properties, including God's, also have physical (spatial) properties. God is necessarily embodied in *some* world, though not necessarily *this* world. God may be embodied in many created and uncreated worlds, perhaps in infinite supertime, perhaps in infinite superspace, or what Wesley called "uncreated" space. Process thinkers do not speculate much about the spacetime of heaven, but they could (and perhaps should) hold that God is embodied everlastingly (or infinitely) in the superspacetime of heaven ("Our Father, who art in heaven") and finitely in the spacetime of our created universe (which is only around 13.5 billion years old). Maybe "heaven" refers to what Wesley called "uncreated" space. Wesley did not know the real age of our universe and thought it was only 4,000 years old (following Newton),[204] or maybe 6,000 (following Bishop James Ussher);[205] but he was confident that God created it *out of nothing*,[206] *ex nihilo*.

Many Process Theologians today think that God created our universe *out of something*, some antecedently exiting universe located within an infinite series of expanding and collapsing universes. Wesley was probably right about the creation of *our* universe *ex nihilo*, though not about its age. This point will not be further argued here, though this author has thoroughly explained and defended creation *ex nihilo* elsewhere.[207] Our universe could have been created out of nothing, even if, as most current Biblical scholars acknowledge, the authors of Genesis and the rest of the Bible knew nothing of creation *ex nihilo*. In Genesis 1, unknown to Wesley, a pre-existent chaos or formless void already exists when God begins to create, and God only orders it. In Genesis, God is only a world-designer, not a creator out of nothing, but Wesley did not realize this. In his day, biblical scholarship had not advanced quite that far.

Second, *all souls are spatially extended* and exist like or as *energy fields* that surround and pervade our human brains, or, in God's case, as an omni-field (like invisible gravity) that pervades and encompasses all of heaven and creation.[208] This does not turn embodied or spatially extended spirits into particles or collections of particles, for we now know of the existence of physical or spatially located and extended realities that are not particulate, for example gravity itself, which was recognized by the Newtonian physics of Wesley's day, or waves and fields, as recognized by today's non-Newtonian physicists. Today, space itself is thought of as a real something with physical properties of its own; space is not just a totally empty container or "void" that holds "matter" or particles in motion. And just below the surface of everywhere lies a domain of potential or virtual particles writhing to be born. Some cosmologists identify this with God's potential creative energy.

Energy fields—gravitational, electromagnetic, psychic, etc.,—are all invisible, not directly sensed, just as Wesley[209] and the Cartesians thought minds to be, *but they are spatially extended*. We detect them only through their effects. But they do exist in, pervade, and organize regions of space. They endure for a time, have spatial and causal properties, influence their contents, and are influenced by them—which is just what souls and bodies need to do in order to interact. Some (if not all) spatially extended fields (e.g., of consciousness) have psychological properties as well as spatial properties. Thus, minds and bodies can interact because each is both spatial and psychical. Today, powerful brain-scanning devices reveal which parts of our brains light up (burn energy) as we think, feel, love, enjoy, suffer, choose, remember, sense, etc. Now we can see from the outside, if only dimly, what those inner psychical structures, fields, and processes look like when externally observed. Neither Descartes nor Wesley knew or dreamed of anything like that. Brain scanners give us an external perspective on the spatiotemporal internalities of consciousness, but immediate self-awareness is still required for knowing what inwardness looks like from within. There is nothing bad or undesirable about this, about being embodied. Being spatially extended is not a bad, inferior, or undesirable thing, despite what dualists assert. The philosophical commonplace that ideas, feelings, and other mental contents have no size, shape, or other spatial properties now seems to be wrong empirically, as well as based on an unfounded prejudice against (disvaluation of) spatial extension.

Wesley refused to think of any space as "empty space," for all space is filled with God, if with nothing else.[210] One of Wesley's favorite and often cited texts declares that God is the one "in whom we live and move and have our being." Jonathan Edwards also loved this text, and so do today's Temporalistic Theologians. It suggest, at least analogically, that God is something like a container, receptacle, or whole—an infinite whole—that includes us and all else within Godself. Such an all-inclusive God is not an empty or vacuous container or void. God is "all things in all things," just as Wesley said.[211] Space is not a void of emptiness; God fills heaven, our heavens, and our earth. Temporalistic Theology avoids pantheism by offering a panentheistic interpretation of all of this: God includes all without being perfectly identical with all, because God grants fleeting moments of independence and self-determination to all creatures.

The upshot is, the paradox of God's being everywhere without being anywhere can be resolved. "God is everywhere" means just what it says, that God really is everywhere—"at every point in space," just as Wesley said. If we and God are embodied souls having spatial properties as well as psychological properties, we can better comprehend how our own souls can influence and be influenced by our bodies, and how God's soul can pervade, influence, and be influenced by us and all of creation. If we can influence our bodies without violating the physical laws of nature, God should be able to do the same. Also, God can have a direct, first-hand, or first-person knowledge or experience of what it is like to grow and suffer as an embodied conscious reality only if God is himself embodied. As Wesley insisted, God has to be everywhere in order to know everything, and we now can see that God has to be embodied in order to know embodiment.

Based on Wesley's major premises, "There is no point of space, whether within or without the bounds of creation, where God is not," "The universal God dwelleth in universal space,"[212] and even "infinite space is full of God,"[213] consider this argument for God's embodiment in the universe. If God fills all of space and is located at every point of space, finite or infinite, then God has all the spatial properties of everything in the universe (and beyond). If having spatial properties is the defining characteristic of "body," then God has a body, the created universe. God's body may also extend beyond created space into "uncreated" space, as Wesley put it. God's superspacetime is not limited to our finite spacetime system, to our created universe.

God is "at every point in space;" yet, Wesley cautioned, we should think of God as "strongly and sweetly influencing all, and yet without destroying the liberty of his rational creatures."[214] So how can God be all in all without determining all? Jonathan Edwards thought that this is not possible. Does *deterministic pantheism* have the last word? How can we affirm that God is all in all without lapsing into a pantheistic determinism like that of Jonathan Edwards?

The Process or Temporalistic solution is *panentheistic pluralism*. God *includes* all and *becomes* all without *being* all or *determining* all, and *time* (not space) makes freedom possible. In every present occasion of our existence, we enjoy a fleeting instant or duration of independence, freedom, and limited self-creativity, before our present moments perish, become past occasions, and are immortalized in God's everlasting and faultless memory or "consequent nature." Eventually, God *becomes* all, and we become a part of God, but only after we have made our own fleeting, free, and co-creative efforts and decisions. In relating our fleeting present moments of relative independence to God, we should think of God as *passively and receptively present* in us, aware of us, valuing us, and gently influencing and being influenced by us *without actively determining or controlling* us. Some mainstream Process Theologians hold that God is *totally absent* from our *present* moments of limited self-creativity, and God receives temporal occasions into himself and knows them only as or after they completely perish to themselves. They think that all introspective experience, even God's, is really only retrospective experience of immediately past experiences. However, God's passive or receptive presence in and immediate awareness of all present moments or occasions is a better solution to this and many other related issues, including the "direct witness" experience. Otherwise, God misses the immediate inner intrinsic reality, self-enjoyment, self-creativity, and value of all of creation's present moments—and even of God's own transcendent present moments. Either way, in every momentary choice and self-initiative, we are limited co-creators with the God of grace in whom we live and move and have our being, and who has both the power and the will to share his power and will with us. For brief moments of time, we and the events of our world transcend God's control, but God with his infinite and enduring aspects, attributes, or "perfections" transcends us and our world forever.

The Devotional Significance of God's Omnipresence

Both metaphysically and systemically or conceptually, God is all in all. Only the saints are profoundly sensitive to this and experience and value God as all in all. Some people may just pay lip service to God's omnipresence, and others may have a merely systemic understanding of its metaphysical meaning, without fully grasping or participating profoundly in its intrinsic devotional significance. Devotionally and intrinsically, God is reverentially experienced and adored as all in all; and all things are valued for, in, and because of God's relations to and presence within them. Wesley believed that those who are loving and pure in heart can *sense God's presence in all good things*. At times, anything and everything can be a sacrament, a thin place where the "veil is lifted" and God's presence breaks through. Using our threefold classification of goodness, this means first that saintly people are sensitive to God's presence in intrinsically good things like people and animals.[215] Second, they sense God's presence in systemically good things like divine laws, ordinances, beliefs, and formal means of grace.[216] Third, they are even aware of God's presence in extrinsically good sensory objects, structures, actions, and processes within the world.[217] With Brother Lawrence, who he admired, Wesley believed in practicing or "exercising" the presence of God. Wesley concluded his sermon "On the Omnipresence of God" with "Spare no pains to preserve always a deep, a continual, a lively, and a joyful sense of his gracious presence."[218] Sanctified souls see or sense "that every creature is God's, and he is everywhere present, in all, and over all....He is as intimately present in earth as in heaven."[219] Following the theme of God-in-all-space, let's further consider "sensing" God in the world, that is, "in earth as in heaven."

> They [the pure in heart] now see him by faith (the veil of flesh being made, as it were, transparent), even in these his lowest works, in all that surrounds them, in all that God has created and made. They see him in the height above, and in the depth beneath; they see him filling all in all.
>
> The pure in heart see all things full of God. They see him in the firmament of heaven; in the moon, walking in brightness; in the sun, when he rejoiceth as a giant to run his course. They see him 'making the clouds his chariots, and walking upon the wings of the wind.' They see him 'preparing rain for the earth', 'and blessing the increase of it'; 'giving grass for the cattle, and green herb for the use of man'. They see the Creator of all wisely governing all, and 'upholding all things by the word of his power'. 'O Lord, our Governor, how excellent is Thy name in all the world!'[220]

Sensitivity to God's presence within the world was also beautifully expressed by Jonathan Edwards in his *Personal Narrative*. He described a spiritual experience in which he found himself "wrapt and swallowed up in God," then further explained how this direct and immediate encounter with God later affected his ordinary perception of mundane things.

After this my sense of divine things gradually increased, and became more and more lively, and had more of that inward sweetness. The appearance of everything was altered: there seemed to be, as it were, a calm, sweet cast, or appearance of divine glory, in almost everything.

God's excellency, his wisdom, his purity and love, seemed to appear in everything; in the sun, moon and stars; in the clouds, and blue sky; in the grass, flowers, trees; in the water, and all nature; which used greatly to fix my mind. I often used to sit and view the moon, for a long time; and so in the daytime, spent much time in viewing the clouds and sky, to behold the sweet glory of God in these things: in the meantime, singing forth with a low voice, my contemplations of the Creator and Redeemer. And scarce anything, among all the works of nature, was so sweet to me as thunder and lightning. Formerly, nothing had been so terrible to me. I used to be a person uncommonly terrified with thunder: and it used to strike me with terror, when I saw a thunderstorm rising. But now, on the contrary, it rejoiced me. I felt God at the first appearance of a thunderstorm. And used to take the opportunity at such times, to fix myself to view the clouds, and see the lightnings play, and hear the majestic and awful voice of God's thunder: which often times was exceeding entertaining, leading me to sweet contemplations of my great and glorious God. And while I viewed, used to spend my time, as it always seemed natural to me, to sing or chant forth my meditations; to speak my thoughts in soliloquies, and speak with a singing voice.[221]

The *Gospel of Thomas* had not been rediscovered during the days of Wesley and Edwards, but they probably would have appreciated the following, from *saying 77*, where Jesus says: "I am the light which is on them all. I am the All, and the All has gone out from me and the All has come back to me. Cleave the wood: I am there; lift the stone and thou shalt find me there!"

Amazingly, *sanctified souls value the things of the world even more than worldly people do!* In fact they value *everything* more than worldly people do because their evaluational capacities and sensitivities are so much more developed. Worldly souls may value extrinsically good things intrinsically with all their hearts, but they have very small hearts. Dogmatists may value systemic goods intrinsically with all their hearts, but they also have very small hearts. Saintly souls, with much bigger or richer hearts and souls, that is, with much more advanced evaluational and spiritual capacities, *impose additional layers of value and evaluation upon their perception, understanding, and evaluation of everything, including the world.* They value God's own evaluation of and presence in intrinsically, extrinsically, and systemically good things. They see and value all things in God, and God in all things. They *sense* the infinite within and behind the finite. They locate the finite within the infinite. Their doors of spiritual perception have been opened. They passionately value extrinsically good things, not just for their general usefulness and pleasantness, but for their holiness or sacredness. They sense and understand that God is the necessary condition for or cause of everything that is, that all depends on God, and that God pervades, sustains, and interpenetrates all. For them, all things are experienced as holy, all objects are sanctified, everything declares the glory of God, and God is all in all. Like Jesus, they sense God's presence in the sparrows, the birds of the air, and in the lilies of the field. We live in a sacramental universe where anything can be a sacrament, a means of grace, a thin place through which God's reality, love, and purposes shine. The saints sense every day as a holy day, all space as sacred space.

Saints experience all of reality as sacred, including the sensory world, and for this they are profoundly grateful. Worldly souls just don't get it. They are spiritually impoverished, blind, or asleep. They do not live in or with this abundance of spiritual goodness. By contrast, as Wesley said, sanctified and purified souls believe and perceive that

> God is in all things, and that we are to see the Creator in the glass of every creature; that we should use and look upon nothing as separate from God, which indeed is a kind of practical Atheism; but, with a true magnificence of thought, survey heaven and earth, and all that is therein, as contained by God in the hollow of His hand, who by His intimate presence holds them all in being, who pervades and actuates the whole created frame, and is, in a true sense, the soul of the universe.[222]

(If you haven't noticed, this has been quoted more than once before.) Sanctified souls can and often do value the world in all the ways that non-sanctified souls do, but even more so, because, for them, God pervades and penetrates everything. Systemic values and evaluations have less worth than extrinsic and intrinsic values and evaluations, so they are listed third in the summary below. In the order of human development our practical values tend to develop first.

1. The saints are perfectly capable of extrinsically valuing sensory objects, processes, and structures for their general usefulness. Valuing other things more need not mean that they value physical things any less than usual or appropriate. At times, like many non-saints, they may be impractical and out of touch with what is commonly called "the real world," but they do not have to be. They can and should be as wise as serpents while remaining as innocent and harmless as doves.[223] They can properly value *things* without overvaluing or undervaluing them, without abusing the world, and without exploiting the environment, people, animals, and God in order to gain the world for themselves. According to Wesley, we cannot "say that one perfected in love would be incapable of marriage or of worldly business—if he were called thereto, he would be more capable than ever; as being able to do all things without hurry or carefulness, without any distraction of spirit."[224]

2. The saints are also perfectly capable of recognizing and valuing sense objects for their specific pleasure-producing effectiveness. They can rejoice and delight in the beauty of the earth, the glory of the skies, the grandeur of nature, the magnificence of the arts, and even the ecstasies of sex, properly constrained. According to Wesley, the saints can enjoy "any pleasure of sense," although "(1) They need none of these things to be happy; for they have a spring of happiness within. They see and love God. Hence they rejoice evermore, and in everything give thanks. (2) They may use them, but they do not seek them. (3) They use them sparingly, and not for

the sake of the thing itself." Thus, any Christian "may smell a flower, or eat a bunch of grapes, or take any other pleasure which does not lessen but increase his delight in God."[225]

Wesley's Puritanical asceticism may at times have prevented him from enjoying all of God's creation, including nature and the arts, as he might have. With God in them, the saints do need sensory goods, can seek and co-create or construct them, and can rejoice in their givenness and abundance. Wesley had little interest in and appreciation for aesthetics, as evinced perhaps in his general hostility toward "diversions"[226] or "dissipations."[227] In his frequent discussions of the "pleasures of the imagination," he was generally hostile toward the arts, (despite the fact that an omnipresent and creative God surely must be there too). Yet, he well and correctly understood that the arts may be served and overvalued idolatrously, unduly. He may have interfered inordinately with the enjoyment of natural creation and the human arts by others, but at least he acknowledged that Christians *can* do it, for "It is possible to *use* without *abusing* them."[228] Søren Kierkegaard well understood that the aesthetic stage along life's way can be taken up into the religious stage, and Wesley may have come close to this insight. Did he not recognized that some harmless pleasures of sense can be taken up into profound spirituality and thereby sanctified? His belief in the omnipresence of God definitely allows for this. To repeat a critical quote, he wrote, "The man who loves God feels that 'God hath given him all things richly to enjoy.' He delights in his works, and surveys with joy all the creatures which God hath made. Love increases both the number of his delights, and the weight of them, a thousandfold. For in every creature he sees as in a glass the glory of the great Creator."[229] Affirming this, he also saw a danger in "Every creature of God is Good, and nothing to be rejected." It could just be just a lame excuse for evading "Give all you can," that is, for buying and wearing gold, silver, precious stones, beautiful things, and "gay and costly apparel" instead of helping others in desperate need.[230]

3. Without ranking them as highly as love to God and others, the saints can and often do highly value knowledge, common sense, science, philosophy, theology, and all other conceptual formalities or systemic value-objects. They understand that conceptual truth can set them free. They are not afraid of truth and the advance of human knowledge—scientific, philosophical, theological, or otherwise. Without ceasing to be saints, they can see, understand, appreciate, and find meaning within the systemic structures around and within them, and they bring belief systems (hopefully, spiritual and truthful ones) to bear upon their interpretations of all experiences. Reality is conceptually *meaningful* to them, though non-saints may find it to be meaningless. The world makes sense to saints.

Worldly people can go only as far as 1. and 2. above. They usually overvalue extrinsically good things at the expense of systemically and intrinsically good things. They are often very shallow both intellectually and intrinsically. They gain the world but not themselves, other souls, or the spirit, mind, and reality of God. Worldly people may fail to gain deep systemic knowledge of or insight into many important things. Ideologists, dogmatists, authoritarians, and intellectuals are good at systemics, but they tend to overvalue conceptually good things, and they may be fairly incompetent in managing their practical affairs, social intimacies, and interpersonal relations. They may gain knowledge, but not themselves, or others, or God, and they may not cope well with the world because they are "out of touch" with it.

Worldly people and ideologists do not use all their brains. In our most common human "natural state," we do not love or intrinsically evaluate conscious individuals as we should. We now know that our systemic and extrinsic value capacities are located largely (though not entirely) in our left brains, and our intrinsic value capacities are located largely (though not entirely) in our right and mid brains. Extremely worldly people and ideologists use only half of their brains. Saints have it all; they use all their brains! Saintly people at their best are competent evaluators in every level or dimension of value, without overvaluing or undervaluing anything. They bring additional layers of value and evaluation to bear upon their experience of the world and everything else, as next explained.

4. Saintly people love God and their neighbors, human and sub-human, more than they love extrinsic or systemic value objects. Yet, they can and do love extrinsic and systemic value objects. They value intrinsically good things first, extrinsically good things next, and systemically good things last of all, while identifying fully, passionately, and intrinsically with them all when properly ordered in a reasonable, moral, and spiritually adequate hierarchy of value. They love and identify themselves with everything, with all that is, but without losing their perspectives on priorities. They bring their advanced intrinsic sensitivities (their religious affections and spiritual senses) to bear upon their evaluation of the sensory or natural world, the intellectual world, the social world, themselves, and all else, including God.

5. Saintly people bring their essential spiritual beliefs, their systemic religious value-objects, to bear upon their experience of the world and all that dwell therein, and this affects their spiritual sensitivities and insights. They see all sensory things, all ordered structures, and all their human and non-human neighbors, as meaningful, created, sustained, and loved by God. They see and value all things as effects of God's creative activity, as sustained by God's ongoing support, as ordered and directed by God's laws, as valued and loved by God, as interacting with God, and as manifesting Gods omnipresence. They value all things as "sub-species of eternity," as this is sometimes expressed, (usually in Latin). This applies to people, to all sentient creatures great and small, to the mindless things of the world, and to mind itself (thoughts and beliefs). They are committed to creation care. If God is omnipresent, then God looks back at us through the eyes of every human being, of every animal, and of every conscious being. God looks at the world through our own eyes; through all other eyes God looks back at us. Yet, when everything is valued intrinsically within God, people are still more valuable than animals and mere things, and things are more valuable than mere ideas of things, people, or animals.

6. Saintly people are grateful. Gratitude is an important religious affection, another intrinsic evaluation capacity through which we can identify fully with all goodness and with the proximate and ultimate sources thereof. Saintly people are grateful, not only for all of the positive values we have considered, but also for being delivered, at least in part, from obstacles (like bondage to sin and guilt) that interfere with properly valuing (loving) all that is.[231] They once were blind, but now they see. They are grateful for and rejoice in small mercies, blessings, and gifts, as well as for large ones. As the world measures triviality and greatness, they can get more out of simple things than worldly people get out of great or extravagant things! They are grateful for God's goodness to themselves; they are grateful for God's goodness to others. They are constantly grateful and joyful, thus prayerful, without ceasing.

Spiritual growth involves moving all the way through the preceding stages or dimensions of value and evaluation. This does not happen all at once, but it can and does happen gradually by degrees. For most Christians, ultimate or "entire" sanctification is a process and a goal, not an accomplished fact. We *strive* for and *go on* toward perfection in values and evaluations. As we gradually achieve the holiness of *faith that works through love*, we live more and more abundantly.

Abundant Life

As people grow in grace and sanctification proceeds, their lives get better and better, more and more fulfilled, richer in inner and outer goodness. They begin to live more and more abundantly. Their lives become more and more valuable to God, to other people, to all other creatures great and small, and to themselves. By identifying intrinsically with all in all, they take all goodness into themselves and make all good-making properties their own, but not in a selfish way, for they are no longer selfish selves. Our love to others increases our value to and for them, but this section will concentrate on *how moral and spiritual growth increases our own value to and for ourselves*. We can be self-interested without being selfish; we can love ourselves as well as our neighbors and God. Loving all is the essence of abundant living. Jesus said that he came that we might have life and have it more abundantly (John 10:10). Surprisingly, Wesley's brief remarks about this verse in his *Explanatory Notes Upon the New Testament* make no reference at all to abundant life, and he seldom if ever directly comments on it anywhere else. The list of his sermons by textual scripture reference does not include this chapter or verse from the gospel of John. Wesley's remarks on happiness, earlier discussed, certainly have a strong bearing, but perhaps much more can be said.

Almost Heaven on Earth

Charles Wesley accented "heaven begun upon earth; 'a kingdom of God within thee',"[232] and John would have agreed, for he thought that finding one's soul affords "a foretaste of heaven now."[233] As sanctification (moral and spiritual development) proceeds, unique and intrinsically valuable human souls become more and more valuable, not only to God and others, but also internally to, in, and for themselves. By degrees, abundant life (salvation) is something that sanctified persons have here and now as well as in the future. Unsanctified or unholy persons do not live as abundantly. Abundant life in this world should eventually approach or approximate a kind of heaven on earth, a kingdom of God within that manifests itself without. What sense can we make of this?

Abundant living must occur within the context of being fully aware of and realistic about evil in the world and within ourselves. Wesley was not oblivious to "natural evil" and tended to give a "soul-making" explanation for it.[234] Without overcoming evil, we could not grow in goodness, he argued. However, soul-making really doesn't explain everything bad that happens to good or innocent people, especially to infants who suffer and die before any soul-making occurs. So this can be only a small part of an adequate theodicy[235] that effectively reconciles God's power and knowledge with his goodness. Heaven on earth is always "almost."

As our desirable compassion increases, our otherwise undesirable suffering also increases when we begin to sympathize with and bear the burdens of others and take their sufferings and losses into ourselves.[236] We share their pains as well as their joys. Christian happiness or well-being includes the cross, a tragic sense of life, and suffering with those who suffer; and it should include a hard-headed realism about evils in nature, in ourselves, and in other people. The Christian's joy is always mixed with an awareness of and a sadness for the sins of the "natural man" and the evils and perils in the natural world. Since most of us are never fully developed morally and spiritually, internal and external sinfulness always hold us back. Yet, sinfulness can be overcome more and more with God's help, which is what happens as sanctification proceeds and abundant living increases.

Living in moral and spiritual abundance does not guarantee our external safety, or exempt us from the sometimes ruthless laws and accidents of nature, or spare us from external natural evils like earthquakes, hurricanes, diseases, calamities, or death. Such evils are not just punishments for sins, as Jesus well understood (Luke 13:1–5 and John 9:1–2). But why doesn't God work miracles abundantly to deliver us from all evils? Like most others before and since, Wesley stoutly defended miracles as deviations from or suspensions of the general laws of nature.[237] The contemporary Christian philosopher, Alvin Plantinga,[238] has demonstrated quite conclusively that God's intervention in and special action upon the world need not be so conceived. Even the laws of classical physics apply only to causally closed systems, but if God acts on the world, or even if there is free choice within the world, says dualist Plantinga, then the physical world just isn't a causally closed system, and no natural laws whatsoever would be violated either by special acts of God or by free and originative choices. That the universe is an absolutely closed causal system (that all causes are natural causes[239]) is not a verified or verifiable conclusion of, or even a logical presupposition of, empirical natural science. It is an unverified and unverifiable postulate of metaphysical naturalism, not a scientific finding or truth. In fact, none of the central claims of naturalism have been or can be verified using empirical scientific method, the only method naturalists themselves recognize as legitimate.[240] To do their work, scientists need only the imperative, "Look for natural causes;" they do not need an *a priori* metaphysical guarantee that they will always find them, or that they are somehow there even if they can't find them.

Still, if we believe in miracles as special acts of God upon the world that deviate from its normal regularities, we must acknowledge from experience that highly noticeable instances very rare. Unpredictable miracles don't happen very often. With God (and with quantum physics), all logically consistent things are equally possible, but they are not all equally probable. The world usually functions predictably as a *relatively* closed causal system in accord with the statistical laws of nature, so bad things frequently happen to good people, and good things often happen to bad people, as Jeremiah lamented and Jesus acknowledged when he said that the sun shines and the rain falls on both the good and the bad, the just and the unjust (Matthew 5:25). We know that we cannot normally count on special acts of God to get us out of every jam, or to save us from every natural catastrophe, or to deliver us from all or great moral evil. Miracles are rare indeed, and we must be realistic about this.

Nevertheless, good people usually do live more abundantly. As Wesley insisted, religious people do not have to choose to be miserable now for the sake of bliss hereafter; their real choice is between misery here and hereafter, versus happiness here and hereafter.[241] He regularly insisted that Christians are happy people. Value theory can help us understand *what is involved in abundant living*. An abundant life is a value-filled life, a good life, a meaningful life, a worthwhile life, a saved and transformed better life. Our lives grow in abundance as they are enriched with positive values, with good-making properties, and as disvalues are somehow diminished, transcended, or overcome. *The most abundant life of which we can conceive is the one than which none richer in good-making properties is possible.* Only God has a maximally abundant life, and even that is constantly being enriched by God's ongoing creativity and interactions with his creatures. In God's own abundant living, God is everlastingly self-surpassing in new and creative experiences, in *created goodness*, though God's uncreated *moral and spiritual goodness* are always the same and unchanged. God's goodness never fails, but in God's changing experiences there are spoilers and crosses as well as joys and triumphs. God identifies with us, so vicarious suffering makes perfectly good sense. God compassionately suffers with us as we suffer and is hurt by all the hurts we inflict on others and ourselves. The life and death of Jesus show us that God, too, is vulnerable. We hurt (offend and wound) God when we sin and hurt others or ourselves. In these ways, evil is in God, not as intended by God, but as inflicted on and suffered by God. God is our fellow sufferer. God understands. God takes the evils as well as the goodness of the world into and upon himself, and by his stripes we are healed. There is great consolation in the assurance that God suffers with us in and through everything.

Positively considered, God constantly exceeds or surpasses himself, not in abstract moral and spiritual goodness, but by being perpetually enriched by newly created concrete valuers and values, so Temporalistic Theologians say. Finite goodness is constantly being created, and by taking it all into himself faithfully, intrinsically, lovingly, and compassionately, God incessantly surpasses himself in value-richness. Jesus came to share abundant living (salvation and sanctification) with us, to show us the way, to help us to become more Godlike, more constantly and consistently inclusive of goodness, just as God is. To the degree that we identify with God, God's triumphs become our triumphs, God's goodness becomes our goodness. As we grow experientially, morally, and spiritually, our lives become richer and richer in good-making properties. "Abundance" means "richness in good-making properties." This comes in and by degrees.

Without speaking directly of "abundant life," Wesley wondered how the lives of saintly persons become more and more valuable in, to, and for themselves (as well as in, to, and for God). He explicitly answered, as earlier indicated, in terms of increasing *happiness*. He often conceived of happiness in purely hedonic terms—as sustained pleasure and as little pain as possible over extended time. As indicated already, he did not hesitate to meet hedonists on their own grounds. He argued that in both this world and the next, sanctified people experience more happiness, more pleasure and less pain, than sinners over the long run.[242] Wesley insisted "that religion is happiness, that wickedness is misery."[243] But he could have gone further, and perhaps he did when he linked "superior holiness" with "superior happiness."[244] What might this mean? Holiness is more than happiness; it is faith that worketh through love, but holiness makes us happy. Our present and ultimate well-being include both holiness and happiness and thus transcend the limits of hedonism.

For hedonists, *pleasure is the only good-making property that really counts, the only thing that is intrinsically good*, and *happiness consists by definition of much pleasure and little or no pain over extended time*. Wesley emphasized the goodness of happiness, but he held that *in addition to pleasure, other good-making properties really count* and have a vital place in an abundant life. Only individual souls are intrinsically good, but both happiness and many other good-making properties are *good for us*, even if they are not *intrinsically good* (in isolation from us and all else).

Let's ignore for the moment our value to God, other people, and other sentient beings—the very heart of true religion—and concentrate only on our value to ourselves. Loving ourselves as we love others has an important place in profound spirituality. In explaining how individual sanctified souls are more valuable in, to, and for themselves than sinful souls, Wesley could have and should have argued as follows, and implicitly perhaps he did.

- A plurality of good-making properties really count, not pleasure alone.
- None of these properties are good "in themselves" (intrinsically); they are only good "for us."
- Increasing or actualizing any or all of these good-making properties makes our lives better.
- Saintly or holy souls tend to be richer in good-making properties than sinful souls.
- Only conscious individuals have intrinsic worth; other good-making properties like pleasure are just intrinsic-value enrichers or enhances—good for us, but not good in themselves.

Yes, there is such a thing as *Christian self-realization* or self-fulfillment, but the Christian self is not a selfish self, and there is far more to Christian self-realization than pleasure.

Pluralistic Goodness

In explaining why saintly or holy lives are better than sinful lives, Wesley focused almost exclusively on happiness, understood hedonistically as optimum pleasure and minimal pain over the long run. This does not mean that Wesley simply accepted the hedonistic answer to "What things are intrinsically good?" Hedonists say that pain is the only bad-making property that really counts (the only thing that is *intrinsically bad,* they have said) and pleasure is the only good-making property that really counts (that is *intrinsically good,* they have said). However, such properties are not really intrinsically good or bad, that is, valuable *in themselves*; they are only good or bad *for, in, and to us.* Wesley did concede to the hedonists that pleasure is *good for us* in the sense that it directly increases our value to, for, and in ourselves; correspondingly, pain is bad for us in that it diminishes our value to, for, and in ourselves. But, as we saw, Wesley explicitly called other things intrinsically good besides pleasure or hedonistic happiness—specifically, faith,[245] as well as spiritual growth in holy dispositions and religious affections.[246] Thinking positively and pluralistically, Wesley insisted that our well-being consists in pleasure *plus* many other self-enriching properties, especially all those included in holiness (faith working by love). Many pluralistic non-hedonic qualities are good for us and directly increase our value to, for, and in ourselves. Wesley implicitly adopted a pluralistic or *eudaimonistic* understanding of what is fundamentally good for, in, and to us, *not* a narrowly *hedonistic* view.[247] One place to look for this is in the seriousness with which Wesley took *all of our human image of God properties.*

When discussing the image of God in us, Wesley didn't say that all that matters is that since God is happy, we should be happy. He did say that God "knew there was but one way for man to be happy like himself, namely, by being like him in holiness."[248] But holiness is far richer in good-making properties than mere happiness, hedonistically understood. Holiness consists in having a faith that works through love. Wesley identified *many God-like qualities* in us, including holiness, all of which are good-making properties, all of which are good for us, all of which enrich and make our souls or lives better to, for, and in themselves (as well as to, for, and in God and others). Wesley edged toward a broad *eudaimonistic understanding of happiness or well-being* when he wrote, "As our knowledge and love of him [God] increase, by the same degrees, and in the same proportion, the kingdom of an inward heaven must necessarily increase also;...when we are 'filled with him';...When we dwell in Christ, and Christ in us, we are one with Christ and Christ with us, then we are completely happy."[249]

Recall that some of our image of God properties are preveniently natural or common, that is, universally human. Others are available ("restored," Wesley would say) through special saving grace at their more advanced levels. We may not know exactly where to draw the line between them.

As explained already, according to Wesley, our human image of God or resemblance to God good-making properties are:

1. embodied spirituality or ensoulment,
2. self-motion, or being self-starting,
3. reason or understanding, the ability to inquire and know,
4. will, that is, desires, feelings, affections, emotions,
5. liberty (free choice), a capacity for making or originating our own choices,
6. imagination,
7. memory,
8. sentience, our five "external senses"
9. consciousness (awareness) and self-consciousness (inner awareness),
10. conscience, the capacity for discerning good and evil, right and wrong,
11. general moral laws "written in our hearts,"
12. moral and spiritual sensitivities, affections, dispositions, and virtues, in various degrees of activation or actualization, and
13. a "capacity for God."

Wesley regarded *all of these shadows and images of divine things as good-making properties, as good for, to, and in us*, not just pleasure or hedonic happiness alone. Our lives or souls are better in, to, and for themselves to the extent that *all* of these good-making properties are actualized. Hedonic-happiness is included, but human well-being and abundant living encompass so much more than sustained pleasures alone.

Actualizing our Good-making Properties

All of our image or likeness of God capacities exists in us in various stages of realization or actualization. What is often called "self-realization" consists in working with and actualizing the potentialities given to us "by nature" or "by prevenient grace," plus those added "by saving grace," recognizing that there is no such thing as nature apart from grace. Spiritual self-realization is further expanded by sanctification, by growing in special grace, holiness, and goodness. *Growing* in value involves every grace and every Godlike property, and it happens effectively only when God is and acts with us and within us. Our lives get better and better, richer and richer in good-making properties, to the extent that we actualize *each* of our image or likeness of God potentials. Abundant living consists in constructively actualizing as many of our positive human capacities as possible. This whole process, Wesley insisted, is empty or "without value" unless and until our intrinsic value capacities are developed under, within, and before God. As holiness increases, our souls grow richer and richer in goodness, thus more and more abundant in good-making-properties. As salvation is "worked out," our Godlike (image of God) properties are actualized within us, especially our capacities for intrinsic values and evaluations, without which sin prevails.

Through it all, we are at liberty to cooperate with God or to choose against God; we can choose to frontslide or to backslide at any point, though "frontslide" makes it sound too easy. Godliness requires constant vigilance and effort; no grace is irresistible or guaranteed forever without our ongoing efforts, commitment to, and cooperation with God. Every day is a renewal day. In this world, there is no such thing as Calvinistic "eternal security," meaning, "once saved, always saved" and guaranteed perseverance. To the degree that we choose against God, we fail to live abundantly and to respond to prevenient and saving grace. To the extent that we live "according to God's plan," we do live abundantly—but there is far more to this than just being hedonically happy. A great deal of thought, effort, guidance, help from, and intimacy with God must go into actualizing our Godlike potentials. Proper self-realization must take place in harmonious and rightly prioritized ways, where self-enrichment is not selfish, self-destructive, or other-destructive, and is not in conflict with itself or the life-enrichment of others. To the degree that our inescapable finitude permits, sanctification or growth in holiness increases our own internal inherent goodness and approximates or imitates the internal inherent goodness of God. Such internal goodness expresses itself in external goodness, in good works, in works of piety, love, and mercy. Intrinsic evaluation without extrinsic evaluation is dead. Intrinsic evaluation without systemic evaluation is blind. Spiritual self-realization is informed (given form) by having within ourselves the mind of Christ and the heart of Christ, and it is expressed by doing the deeds of Christ lovingly. Faith must work by love. "The mind of Christ," Wesley thought, "may be taken in a far more extensive sense, so as to include the whole disposition of his mind, all his affections, all his tempers, both toward God and man."[250]

Christians strive to become more Godlike or Christlike, to imitate Christ, to walk in his steps, to have his mind and heart within us, to love as he loved, to help as he helped, to serve as he served. Despite his mistaken apocalyptic belief in the immanent end of the world, Jesus is the very best human image of Godlike moral and spiritual self-realization that we have. He is the best image we have of what it is like to actualize our good-making human capacities in constructive, harmonious, rightly prioritized, and Godlike ways. For Christians, Jesus is the way, the truth, and the life. To best realize the human potentials that are really good for us, we must constantly ask: What would Jesus think? What would Jesus do? Who and what would Jesus love? Then live accordingly. Quoting his own grandfather, Wesley advised, "Think, and speak, and do what you are persuaded Christ himself would do in your case, were he on earth."[251] Elsewhere he wrote, "Glorify Christ by imitating Christ in all things, by walking as he walked."[252] Walking "in his steps" was nothing new to Wesley. That is the best way for Christians to actualize their truly fulfilling good-making potentials. We must "walk the walk" as well as "talk the talk."

There is *nothing selfish* about *saintly self-realization*, for the self being realized at the spiritual stage of saintliness is no longer an exclusively or a primarily selfish self which, by definition, excludes the interests of others from its own interests except as means to its own once-born ends. Its interests now include the well being of others for their sakes. The saintly self is a new self, a born-again self, a twice-born self that to a degree has outgrown or overcome the extravagantly self-interested sensuality of worldliness and/or the excessive narrow intellectualism of ideology and dogmatism. This new self is deeply concerned for the well-being of others. It finds its satisfaction in the satisfaction of others. It aims at the happiness and more inclusive well being of others, and its own happiness and well being are indirect serendipity effects of loving and serving others. As Wesley said, we are commanded "to desire and pursue their [human] happiness as sincerely and steadily as our own; but also to love many of his [non-human] creatures in the strictest sense."[253] Christian unselfishness does not exclude self-interest, what Wesley here calls "our own;" but it is incompatible with *exclusive* self-interest, "only our own." There is nothing selfish about satisfying our desires if and when our desires are for the well being of other people, all creation, and God. "Getting what we want" for sanctified souls is radically different from "getting what we want" for sinful egoistic souls. Their wants are very different because their souls are very different. Saintly souls are partly self-interested or self-loving, but they are significantly devoted also to the well-being and best interests of others. They love others as they love themselves. They love themselves as they love others.

Sanctified Souls are Better

In another very significant way, saintly souls are different from sinful souls, and this also affords them a better life, a more abundant life, one far richer good-making properties. Let's reconsider our capacity for identifying ourselves with others. This happens in profound experiences of love, empathy, compassion, consolation, intimacy, concentration, creativity, etc. Only a few saintly souls can do this constantly, but almost everyone has rudimentary identification-with-others capacities. Those who cannot identify with all in all can still identify with their jobs, their athletic teams and sports activities, their country right or wrong, their families and friends, their religious groups and denominations, etc. But not with "universal being," as Jonathan Edwards might say.

When we identify ourselves with others, the differences between us and them just disappear psychologically and valuationally. We achieve a profound psychological and valuational union with them. Existentially, our differences still exist, but they do not matter much any more spiritually, and we may pay very little if any attention to them. In *identification spirituality* we become one with others in such a way that their goodness becomes our goodness, (and their badness, suffering, and burdens becomes our badness, suffering, and burdens). Concentrating on goodness, when we fully identify ourselves with others, their good-making properties become our good-making properties, become part of our egos (our individuated consciousness), but we are no longer purely selfish egos or exclusively self-interested selves. Their happiness becomes our happiness; their desires and interests become our desires and interests, their fulfillment becomes our fulfillment, their well-being becomes our well-being. What happens to and within them also happens to and within ourselves. When they are winners we are winners; when they are losers we are losers; it all feels just the same. What is good (or bad) for them is good (or bad) for us. Their enrichment or diminishment in good-making properties becomes our own enrichment or diminishment. We rejoice as they rejoice and weep as they weep. As we grow experientially, morally, and spiritually, our lives become richer and richer in good-making properties—their properties. "Abundance" just means "rich in good-making properties." "More abundant" just means "richer." Identification with others accomplishes just this. Identifying intrinsically *with all* takes *all goodness* into ourselves, makes all and everyone's good-making properties our own. God does this, and we can by approximation. "Identifying with others" means that for psychological, evaluational, and spiritual purposes, all good-making properties in everyone and everything become our own good-making properties. Thereby we do indeed live more abundantly, but not in a selfish way, for the self that identifies with others has been reborn and greatly magnified; it is no longer a small, narrow, and selfish self.

Saintly souls live more abundantly than sinful souls because their lives are richer in good-making properties, and these are properly ordered. "Better" just means "richer in good-making properties." According to Albert Outler, Christian salvation/sanctification is a journey from the *barely* human, to the *truly* human, to the *fully* human.[254] Such an insight has now been explained axiologically, that is, in terms of growth in internal intrinsic and systemic goodness that is expressed in external extrinsic goodness—faith working through love. Value enrichment as we move from the barely human to the fully human is a helpful and illuminating account of what it means to live more abundantly and experience salvation *today*. As Wesley said, "The state of love, being attending with 'joy unspeakable and full of glory,' with rest from the passions and vanities of man, with the integrity of an

250 *John Wesley's Values—And Ours*

unchangeable judgment, and an undivided will, is, in a great measure, its own reward: yet not so as to supersede the desire of another world."[255]

Stars in Our Crowns

The Philosopher Francis Hutcheson shocked and irked John Wesley by arguing that Christianity is just another manifestation of egoism or selfishness in disguise because Christians expect to be more than amply rewarded in heaven, if not on earth, for all the crosses, sufferings, sacrifices, and inconveniences that they bear in this life. Christianity is just *very* long range egoism or selfishness, Hutcheson contended, or so Wesley misunderstood him to say. Our gratitude to God can be and sometimes is unselfish, Hutcheson realized; but sometimes (and Wesley thought that he meant "always") it is for nothing more than trying to gain God's benefits to and for ourselves.[256] To some extent, Wesley played into his hands, but not completely so. We have seen how this works with respect to *almost heaven on earth*. Let us now consider *the rewards of heaven*.

Wesley's sermon on "God's Love to Fallen Man" is an extended argument for the conclusion that good people are rewarded both on earth and in heaven for their good works. Here and hereafter, good people are happier [and live more abundantly] than bad people. Wesley definitely believed that people are *rewarded in heaven* according to their good works, even though they are not and cannot be *saved* by their good works.[257] Once saved by grace, Wesley thought, we can then rack up higher and higher rewards in both heaven and on earth through good works. Both Wesley and Jesus believed this. Jesus said that the "Son of man" will "reward every man according to his works," (Matthew 16:27; compare Luke 6: 35 and 23:41). Other New Testament writers affirm this; compare Rev. 20:11–12, cited by Wesley.[258] Presumably Jesus included both this world and the next, but his views were somewhat ambivalent. His parable of the workers in the vineyard (Matthew 20:1–16) seems to say that no matter how long and hard we work, we will all get the same rewards, equal rewards, in the end. Part of our problem today is not being sure about exactly what the "historical Jesus" really said or meant, but maybe this doesn't really matter very much as long as we have our values straight.

Many younger Christians today have never heard it, but most of us old-timers will remember the song titled "Stars in My Crown." We may recall singing it in church or youth groups, or we may remember it as featured in the 1950 movie, *Stars In My Crown*, starring Joel McCrea, Ellen Drew, and Dean Stockwell. The song itself was composed around 1897 (over a century after Wesley's death in 1791), with words by Eliza E. Hewitt and music by John R. Sweney. Here is the first verse and the refrain.

> I am thinking today of that beautiful land
> I shall reach when the sun goeth down;
> When through wonderful grace by my Savior I stand,
> Will there be any stars in my crown?

> Refrain
> Will there be any stars, any stars in my crown
> When at evening the sun goeth down?
> When I wake with the blest in the mansions of rest
> Will there be any stars in my crown?

John Wesley never saw the movie or heard the song, but he knew the thought or the phrase, and he applied it to rewards in heaven.[259] He repeatedly affirmed that Christians will be rewarded there according to their works. In "The Wisdom of Winning Souls," Wesley specifically linked stars in our crown to winning souls.[260] In "The More Excellent Way," he distinguished between "two orders of Christians." One group takes the low road and makes some progress toward sanctification while still "being in most things like their neighbors;" the other group takes the high road and walks "in every point, as their beloved Master."[261] In some sermons, those on the low road are called mere "servants;" those on the high road are adopted "sons" or "children."[262] About the rewards of those belonging to the two orders, Wesley wrote,

> I do not affirm that all who do not walk in this [higher or better] way are in the high road to hell. But this much I must affirm; they will not have so high a place in heaven as they would have if they had chosen the better part. And will this be a small loss? The having so many fewer stars in your crown of glory? Will it be a little thing to have a lower place than you might have in the kingdom of your Father?[263]

Is there any way to bring Jesus' "equal" rewards" any closer to Wesley's "greater" rewards? In heaven, or in an ideal heaven on earth, it could be that everyone would equally have all the *external* basics, whatever they might be, including being equally loved and respected by all others, including God; but people who are more advanced morally and spiritually could still have more *internal* goodness because they are richer, deeper, more complex, more developed souls. Is there a way to understand this that makes sense, and also avoids the egoism in disguise with which Frances Hutcheson and other critics charge Christians?

It all depends on what we mean by "the basics" and "having more." Very often the "rewards" of heaven are conceived of in very extrinsic or external and worldly ways. Some people believe in a very worldly heaven, a literal heaven of sensual gold, silver, pearls, diamonds, mansions, ivory palaces (poor elephants!), stars in our crowns, and social honor and glory. "Greater rewards," on this view, would just consist in having more toys, more gold, silver, ivory, diamonds, stars, a bigger mansion, and more social deference and esteem from one's "inferiors," for example, sitting on Jesus' right hand rather than his left. Worldly inequality in heaven as it is on earth!

However, "stars in our crowns" could and probably should be construed metaphorically and intrinsically, not literally and extrinsically. It could refer to something internal and private, not to something external and public. Wesley himself wrote of "an inward heaven"[264] that consists of developing and exercising one's spiritual affections and virtues. Literalists are stuck with and in a worldly sensual language. Literalism seems to be a product of worldly religion! Neither the rewards of heaven, nor of heaven-on-earth, have to be understood literally, externally, or extrinsically. "Stars in our crowns" can be understood metaphorically, internally, and intrinsically, or even as intrinsic/extrinsic/systemic combinations. Perhaps Wesley tried to have it both ways, perhaps not, but exclusive emphasis on external stars in our crowns can be avoided by emphasizing internal intrinsic enrichment. In a sermon that he preached and rewrote but did not originally write, he said, "More glorious stars" means "that the most heavenly bodies will be given to the most heavenly souls."[265] This reference to "more heavenly bodies" (better or improved resurrected bodies?) echoes worldly religion if taken in the sense in which the handsomest, most beautiful, most accomplished, and sexiest people are said to have "heavenly bodies" here and now.

However, in another sermon that he did write, in explaining I. Corinthians 15:40–42, Wesley interpreted heavenly well-being much more internally and intrinsically. We should "Remember the observation of the Apostle: As 'one star differeth from another star in glory, so also is the resurrection of the dead.' The most glorious stars will undoubtedly be those who are the most holy; who bear most of that image of God wherein they were created." After reviewing the internal "holy tempers" that constitute their holiness, Wesley added, "And on account of this superior holiness they will then enjoy superior happiness."[266] Here, the "rewards of heaven" are internal, intrinsic, soul-enriching rather than external, public, and extrinsic. He explicitly denied that finding our happiness in God involves earthly or earth-like pleasures.[267] He wrote, "The end of every rational creature is God: the enjoying him in time and in eternity. The best, indeed the only, means of attaining this end, is 'the faith that worketh by love'."[268]

One plausible solution to the "rewards" problem would be this: everyone in heaven, or in heaven on earth, loves and respects everyone else equally, as do true saints on earth, while ever growing internally in their ability to love and in the scope of those loved. Equal basic love for all prevails socially; but, along with that, some people might be more advanced inwardly than others in actualizing their internal intrinsic Godlike properties. At one level, in relation to external others, all workers in God's vineyard are equally loved and thus receive the same wages; but in their internal self-relations or self-development, some might be more abundantly enriched than others in internal goodness or good-making properties. Even if everyone gets equal love and respect externally from God and others, some souls could still be internally richer and more advanced than others in their good-making Godlike properties, if for no other reason than they have been at it longer. Time constantly adds good-making properties (e.g., desirable new experiences and enhanced virtues) to our total property inventories; so it may be also in heaven as on earth.

Physically and psychologically, in this world there are definite upper limits to moral, spiritual, and internal growth; death guarantees our finitude. Beyond that, everything is in God's hands, and God's will, will be done. Our present limitations differ for each of us in kind and extent. In terms of logical possibilities, however, there are no upper limits to our internal personal growth in Godlikeness, just as God himself can be infinitely creative and loving. Wesley insisted that even after attaining moral and spiritual perfection (after becoming completely sinless and all-loving), saintly souls still grow and somehow get better—even in heaven.

This is a very puzzling claim; how can you improve on perfection? Well, maybe this means that saintly souls are not always exactly equal in the degree to which they have internally actualized all of their Godlike properties. To the question, "Can those who are perfect grow in grace?" Wesley answered, "Undoubtedly they can; and that not only while they are in the body, but to all eternity."[269] He explained more specifically that the Christian "still grows in grace, in the knowledge of Christ, in the love and image of God; and will do so, not only till death, but to all eternity."[270] Sanctification takes forever! *Gradual internal intrinsic value enrichment* could be *endless after death* in the superspacetime or "uncreated space" of heaven. In still other Godlike ways, postmortem growth might be endless. Wesley conjectured that people in paradise and heaven will retain "all their faculties," including memory and understanding, and these abilities will be "inconceivably strengthened."[271] So, another way we might continue to grow in heaven would be in knowledge, with strengthening systemic and cognitive capacities.

The purpose of this book is not to speculate about what will in fact happen after death; it is to consider the respective *values and evaluations* that might prevail then, and their relevance to *what and how we value here and now*. A vision of what the other world might be like can shed much light on what this world ought to be like, on what we ought to be like in this world—on earth as in heaven. If endless loving, learning, helping, and intellectual and aesthetic creativity and expression are exceedingly worthwhile hereafter, their finite counterparts should be very worthwhile in this life. And vice versa. Wesley explicitly suggested that hereafter opportunities for *learning and systemic value enrichment (e.g., conversing)* might be endless, as would opportunities for *extending the scope of who we love to those never previously met*. In "On the Discoveries of Faith" and "On Faith," Wesley described *temporalistically* the activities of the Christian in "the delights of paradise, the garden of God," (despite saying that "Time vanishes away").

> He converses, not only with his former relations, friends, and fellow-soldiers, but with the saints of all nations and all ages, with the glorious dead of ancient days, with the noble army of martyrs, the Apostles, the Prophets, the Patriarchs, Abraham, Isaac, and Jacob: Yea, above all this, he shall be with Christ, in a manner that could not be while he remained in the body.[272]

Billy Graham wrote in one of his newspaper articles that he looked forward to dying so that he could go to heaven and meet Elvis Presley! Well, think about it anyway. Who would you like to meet and talk with in heaven? Will things (e.g., meeting new people, conversing with them) happen successively there? If so, not our time, but a heavenly time or succession of events, will be there. Heaven will be everlasting time, not all of time all at once.

Since there will be bodies-in-space-and-time in heaven—resurrected bodies—possibilities for rewarding *extrinsic aesthetic experience, creativity, enjoyment, and enrichment* might also be inexhaustible. There would be space as well as time both in Wesley's intermediate paradise and in the finality of heaven; things happen sequentially there, first involving disembodied souls and finally resurrected bodies. Heaven requires its own superspacetime, but not the spacetime of our own created universe. Wesley neglected this theme, but not completely.[273] Resurrected bodies require a physical or sensory environment, so the spacetime of paradise/heaven should be exquisitely and aesthetically beautiful, and we could be endlessly active, creative, expressive, and helpful in it. We will continue to grow in all graces and "holy tempers," and presumably we will take endless aesthetic delight in its "astonishing scenes," its environmental and artistic forms and out exquisite extrinsic surroundings. Wesley argued that we will not have *bodily senses* in heaven, because our earthly bodies will be left behind, but *something akin to them, yet superior to them, would be available.*[274]

The essential thought is that in heaven our general capacities for intrinsic, extrinsic, and systemic values and evaluations would still be intact, but much improved; our values and evaluations would be properly ranked; and growth in values and valuations could continue forever. Presently exercising our value capacities makes life worthwhile, abundantly so, here and now. So, why not then and there? And if there and then, why not here and now?

Finally, can the rewards of heaven be understood in a non-egoistic way. Do our good works here and now aim selfishly at the rewards of heaven? As rewards are on earth, so those of heaven can be understood in a non-egoistic way. Understanding what and how we might value in heaven can illuminate what and how we value on earth, and vice versa, so thinking about heaven is worthwhile even from our earthly perspective. Spiritually advanced persons now live more abundantly and have more value to, in, and for themselves by finding lasting self-realization and fulfillment in the well-being of others, and this could be true in both time and eternity. Both now and then, redeemed souls are no longer selfish selves dominated by narrowly self-centered interest, feelings, and desires. Their well-being and self-fulfillment consist in identifying with the well-being and self-fulfillment of others, and finally with all in all. The barriers that separate souls psychologically and evaluationally can gradually break down and would ultimately no longer exist or matter, even if all souls continue as unique and intrinsically valuable individuals with their own personal histories and powers.

In an ideal spacetime system, each individual fully identifies with every other, just as Jesus fully identified with God, and God fully identified with Jesus—who was thus both fully human and fully divine. Identification spirituality can shed some light on how Jesus could be fully God and fully man; he was the man, completely a man, who fully identified himself with God; and God fully identified himself with this man. They were one, yet more than one. In heaven, the saints would be axiologically and psychologically one with all, one with and within God, having transcended selfishness, and one in love with all of "the least of these," as Jesus was—yet still retain their individuality. May that kingdom come soon on earth! In God's kingdom, we are one but distinctly many, just as the church is one body with distinctly many members who are evaluationally and spiritually members of one another. In God's kingdom, God is metaphysically, evaluationally, and spiritually all in all, yet each is uniquely himself or herself. May John Wesley's values, our values, and God's values soon and finally become one.

Notes

1. Rem B. Edwards, *The Essentials of Formal Axiology*. (Lanham, MD: University Press of America, 2010). Rem B. Edwards and John W. Davis, eds., *Forms of Value and Valuation: Theory and Applications*. (Lanham, MD: University Press of America, 1991).

2. Thomas Jay Oord, ed., *Divine Grace and Emerging Creation: Wesleyan Forays in Science and Theology of Creation*. (Eugene, Oregon: Pickwick Publications, 2009).

3. William R. Cannon, *The Theology of John Wesley*. (Lanham, MD: University Press of America, 1974).

4. John B. Cobb, Jr., *Grace and Responsibility: A Wesleyan Theology for Today*. (Nashville: Abingdon Press, 1995).

5. Kenneth J. Collins, *The Theology of John Wesley: Holy Love and the Shape of Grace*. (Nashville: Abingdon Press, 2007).

6. Richard P. Heitzenrater, *Wesley and the People Called Methodists*. (Nashville: Abingdon Press, 1995).

7. Randy L. Maddox, *Responsible Grace: John Wesley's Practical Theology*. (Nashville: Kingswood Books, 1994).

8. Ted Runyon, *The New Creation: John Wesley's Theology Today*. (Nashville: Abingdon Press, 1998).

9. Robert G. Tuttle, Jr., *Mysticism in the Wesleyan Tradition*. (Grand Rapids, MI: Francis Asbury Press, 1989).

10. J. Gregory Crofford, *Streams of Mercy: Prevenient Grace in the Theology of John and Charles Wesley*. (Lexington, KY: Emeth Press, 2010).

11. Manfred Marquardt, *John Wesley's Social Ethics: Praxis and Principles*. (Nashville: Abingdon Press, 1992).

12. For a much more profound and detailed analysis of Wesley as a practical theologian see Randy L. Maddox, "John Wesley: Practical Theologian?" in the *Wesleyan Theological Journal*, 1998, 23, 122–147.

13. Richard B. Steele, *"Gracious Affection" and "True Virtue" According to Jonathan Edwards and John Wesley*. (Metuchen, NJ: Scarecrow Press, Inc., 1994); Richard E. Brantley, "The Common Ground of Wesley and Edwards," *Harvard Theological Review*, July, 1990, 83:3, 271–303.

14. Steele, 237.

15. Philip Clayton and Arthur Peacocke, eds., *In Whom We Live and Move and Have Our Being: Panentheistic Reflections on God's Presence in a Scientific World*. (Grand Rapids, MI: William B. Eerdmans Publishing Co., 2004).

16. Open Theology is represented now in many publications. A good place to begin is with Clark H. Pinnock, et al., eds, *The Openness of God: A Biblical Challenge to the Traditional Understanding of God*. (Downers Grove, IL: InterVarsity Press, 1994).

17. Paul R. Sponheim, *Speaking of God: Relational Theology*. (St. Louis: Chalice Press, 2006)

18. Albert Outler, "An Editorial Comment," *The Bicentennial Edition of the Works of John Wesley*, ed. Albert C. Outler. (Nashville: Abingdon Press, 1985), 2:349.

Chapter One

1. John Wesley, Sermon 91, "On Charity," II, 6–7, *The Bicentennial Edition of the Works of John Wesley*, ed. Albert C. Outler. (Nashville: Abingdon Press, 1986), 3:297–298.
2. John Wesley, Letter to John Smith, June 25, 1746, *The Bicentennial Edition of the Works of John Wesley*, ed. Frank Baker. (Nashville: Abingdon Press, 1987), 26:202.
3. John Wesley, Sermon 15, "The Great Assize," II, 5–9, *The Bicentennial Edition of the Works of John Wesley*, ed. Albert C. Outler. (Nashville: Abingdon Press, 1984), 1:361–364.
4. *Ibid.*, II, 7, 1:363.
5. John Wesley, Sermon 33, "Upon Our Lord's Sermon on the Mount, XIII," II, 8, *Works*, 1:697.
6. The sinlessness of Jesus has actually become a matter of theological discussion and controversy. See the references in Clayton and Peacocke, eds., *In Whom We Live and Move and Have Our Being: Panentheistic Reflections on God's Presence in a Scientific World*, 288, n. 184.
7. John Wesley, Sermon 45, "The New Birth," III, 1, *Works*, 2:194–195.
8. John Wesley, *A Survey of the Wisdom of God in the Creation: A Compendium of Natural Philosophy*. (New York: The Methodist Episcopal Church, 1823), 2:170.
(Hereafter, *A Compendium of Natural Philosophy*.) Available on line at: http://books.google.com/books?ei=LUr9TLroHcWblgew-ImYBQ&ct=result&dq=John%20Wesley%2C%20A%20Survey%20of%20the%20Wisdom%20of%20God%20in%20the%20Creation%3A%20A%20Compendium%20of%20Natural%20Philosophy.%20%28New%20York%3A%20The%20Methodist%20Episcopal%20Church%2C1823%29%2C&q=but%20I%20have%20found%20occasion&id=4RpMAAAYAAJ&ots=JrgSxwRtWt&output=text&pg=PR4.
For summary accounts of the sources and contents for Wesley's survey, read Randy L. Maddox, "Wesley's Engagement with the Natural Sciences" in Randy L. Maddox and Jason E. Vickers, eds., *The Cambridge Companion to John Wesley*. (Cambridge: University Press, 2010), 160–175. In Thomas Jay Oord, ed., *Divine Grace and Emerging Creation*. (Eugene, OR: Pickwick Publications, 2009) see Laura B. Felleman, "Degrees of Certainty in John Wesley's Natural Theology," 58–80 and Marc Otto and Michael Lodahl, "Mystery and Humility in John Wesley's Narrative Ecology," 81–105.
9. Wesley, *A Compendium of Natural Philosophy*, 2:iii.

Chapter Two

1. Ted Runyon, *The New Creation: John Wesley's Theology Today*. (Nashville: Abingdon Press, 1998), 95, 110.
2. John Wesley, *A Compendium of Logic*, in *The Works of the Reverend John Wesley, A.M.*, ed. John Emory. (New York: The Methodist Episcopal Church, 1831), 7:609–625.
3. John Wesley, "Remarks upon Mr. Locke's *Essay on Human Understanding*," *The Works of the Reverend John Wesley, A.M.*, ed. John Emory. (New York: The Methodist Episcopal Church, 1831), 7:455–464.
4. John Wesley, "Upon Our Lord's Sermon on the Mount, XIII," II, 2, *The Bicentennial Edition of the Works of John Wesley*, ed. Albert C. Outler. (Nashville: Abingdon Press, 1984), 1:692.
5. John Wesley, Sermon 16, "The Means of Grace," *Works*, 1:378–397.

6. John Wesley, Sermon 29, "Upon Our Lord's Sermon on the Mount, IX," 5. *Works*, 1:635.

7. John Wesley, Sermon 30, "Upon Our Lord's Sermon on the Mount, X," 2, *Works*, 1:651.

8. John Wesley, "A Plain Account of Genuine Christianity," III, 10, *John Wesley*, ed. Albert C. Outler. (New York: Oxford University Press, 1964), 194.

9. John Wesley, Sermon 60, "The General Deliverance," I, 2, *The Bicentennial Edition of the Works of John Wesley*, ed. Albert C. Outler. (Nashville: Abingdon Press, 1985), 2:439.

10. Wesley, "Upon Our Lord's Sermon on the Mount, X," 2, *Works*, 1:651.

11. John Wesley, Sermon 44, "Original Sin," I, 3, *Works*, 2:173.

12. Albert C. Outler, Chair, "An Interim Report to the General Conference," in *The Theological Study Commission on Doctrine and Doctrinal Standards*. (The United Methodist Church, 1970), 7–8; Albert C. Outler, "The Wesleyan Quadrilateral in Wesley," *Wesleyan Theological Journal*, 1985, 20:7–18.

13. Wesley, "A Plain Account of Genuine Christianity," III, 11–12, Outler, *John Wesley*, 195–196.

14. John Wesley, Sermon 55, "On the Trinity," 1, *Works*, 2:375; John Wesley, Sermon 104, "On Attending Church Service," 15, *The Bicentennial Edition of the Works of John Wesley*, ed. Albert C. Outler. (Nashville: Abingdon Press, 1986), 3:470.

15. These attributes or perfections of God are abstracted from John Wesley, Sermon 26, "Upon Our Lord's Sermon on the Mount, VI," III, 4–7, *Works*, 1:578–581. He discussed God's attributes in many other places, for example, John Wesley, Sermon 114, "The Unity of the Divine Being," *The Bicentennial Edition of the Works of John Wesley*, ed. Albert C. Outler. (Nashville: Abingdon Press, 1987), 4:61–71. For a detailed Wesleyan account of God's attributes, see Kenneth J. Collins, *The Theology of John Wesley: Holy Love and the Shape of Grace*. (Nashville: Abingdon Press, 2007), Ch. 1.

16. John Wesley, Sermon 39, "Catholic Spirit," 12, *Works*, 2:81–82.

17. Wesley, "Original Sin," I, 3, *Works*, 2:175.

18. Wesley, *A Compendium of Natural Philosophy*, 2:433.

19. *Ibid.*

20. Wesley's most detailed argument for the inseparability of God's attributes may be found in his "Predestination Calmly Considered," XXIX–LX, Outler, *John Wesley*, 438–456.

21. *Ibid.*, LIII, 451.

22. John Wesley, Sermon 127, "On the Wedding Garment," 15, *Works*, 4:146.

23. Wesley, "Predestination Calmly Considered," XLVII–XLVIII, Outler, *John Wesley*, 447–448.

24. *Ibid.*, XC, 472.

25. John Wesley, "Thoughts Upon Necessity," III, 8, Outler, *John Wesley*, 485.

26. *Ibid.*, III, 9, 486. See also John Wesley, Sermon 57, "On the Fall of Man," *Works*, 2:400–401.

27. John Wesley, Sermon 62, "The End of Christ's Coming," I, 4, *Works*, 2:475.

28. Wesley, "Predestination Calmly Considered," LII, Outler, *John Wesley*, 450.

29. John Wesley, "A Thought on Necessity," V, 1, *The Works of the Reverend John Wesley, A.M.*, ed. John Emory. (New York: The Methodist Episcopal Church, 1831), 6:214.

30. Wesley, "The End of Christ's Coming," I, 4, *Works*, 2:475.

31. Wesley, "Predestination Calmly Considered," XXIII, Outler, *John Wesley*, 435.

258 *John Wesley's Values—And Ours*

32. John Wesley, Sermon 77, "Spiritual Worship," I, 1–10, 3:90–95; John Wesley, Sermon 117, "On the Discoveries of Faith," 7, *Works*, 4:31.

33. Sidney Norton Deane, ed. *St. Anselm* (La Salle, IL: Open Court Publishing Co., 1954), 190.

34. *Ibid.*, 13–14.

35. Collins, 143–144.

36. John B. Cobb, Jr., *Grace and Responsibility: A Wesleyan Theology for Today*. (Nashville: Abingdon Press, 1995), 66.

37. Randy L. Maddox, *Responsible Grace: John Wesley's Practical Theology*. (Nashville: Kingswood Books, 1994), 31.

38. Wesley, "The Unity of the Divine Being," 8, *Works*, 4:63.

39. John Wesley's abridgment of William Tilly's sermon (also preached by Wesley), "On Grieving the Holy Spirit," I, 1, *The Works of the Reverend John Wesley, A.M.*, ed. John Emory, 2:515.

40. Wesley, "Upon Our Lord's Sermon on the Mount, II," I, 5, *Works*, 1:490.

41. John Wesley, Sermon 36, "The Law Established Through Faith, II," II, 3, *Works*, 2:39.

42. John Wesley, Sermon 103, "What is Man?" 6, *Works*, 3:460.

43. John Wesley, Sermon 51, "The Good Steward," I, 2, *Works*, 2:284.

44. Wesley, "The New Birth," I, 1, *Works*, 2:188.

45. John Wesley, Sermon 67, "On Divine Providence," 15, *Works*, 2:540–541.

46. John Wesley, Sermon 141, "The Image of God," I, 2, *Works*, 4:294.

47. Wesley, "The New Birth," I, 1, *Works*, 2:188.

48. Maddox, *Responsible Grace: John Wesley's Practical Theology*, 276, n. 23.

49. Wesley, "Heavenly Treasure in Earthen Vessels," II, 7, *Works*, 4: 167.

50. John Wesley, Sermon 58, "On Predestination," 5, *Works*, 2:417.

51. From Wesley's comments on Romans 8.28 and 11:2 in his *Explanatory Notes Upon the New Testament*.

52. Wesley, "On the Unity of the Divine Being," 2, 21, *Works*, 4:61 and 69; Wesley, "On Eternity," 1–3, *Works*, 2:358–360.

53. John Wesley, Sermon 69, "On the Imperfections of Human Knowledge," I, 3, *Works*, 2:570; Wesley, "On Predestination," 5, 7, 15, *Works*, 2:417, 418, and 420.

54. Wesley, "Thoughts Upon Necessity," Outler, *John Wesley*, III, 1, 481.

55. *Ibid.*, III, 2–3, 481–482.

56. Wesley, "On Predestination," 5, *Works*, 2:417.

57. Jonathan Edwards, "Freedom of the Will," II, 12 in *The Works of Jonathan Edwards*, ed. Paul Ramsey. (New Haven: Yale University Press, 1957), 1:257–258, 264–269.

58. Wesley, Sermon 70, "The Case of Reason Impartially Considered," I, 1, *Works*, 2:590.

59. Wesley, *A Compendium of Natural Philosophy*, 2:440.

60. John Wesley, Sermon 118, "On the Omnipresence of God," II, 1, Works, 4:42.

61. John Wesley, Sermon 56, "God's Approbation of His Works," I, 14, *Works*, 2:396–397.

62. Thomas Jay Oord, *The Nature of Love: A Theology*. (St. Louis, MO: Chalice Press, 2010), 50–60.

63. Wesley, "The General Deliverance," I, 2, *Works*, 2:439.

64. Wesley, "Upon Our Lord's Sermon on the Mount, VI," II, 2, *Works*, 1:576; Wesley, "On the Discoveries of Faith," 6, *Works*, 4:31.

65. John Wesley, Sermon 17, "The Circumcision of the Heart," I, 7, *Works*, 1:405; Wesley, "Journal," 24 May, 1738, *Works*, 18:250; Wesley, "Original Sin," III, 3, *Works*, 2:184; Wesley, "What is Man?" II, 7, *Works*, 3:460–461, Wesley, "Spiritual Worship," II, 5, *Works*, 3:96; Wesley, "On the Discoveries of Faith," 14, *Works*, 4:36, and in many other writings.

66. Wesley, "A Plain Account of Genuine Christianity," I, 14, Outler, *John Wesley*, 187; Wesley, "On Eternity," 20, *Works*, 2:372.

67. John Wesley, Sermon 94, "On Family Religion," II, 2, *Works*, 3:337.

68. Wesley, "What is Man?" II, 5, *Works*, 3:460. Compare the discussion in John Wesley, Sermon 142, "The Wisdom of Winning Souls," I, *Works*, 4:308, lines 15–29.

69. G. E. Moore, *Principia Ethica*. (Cambridge: The University Press, 1903), 91; see also 93, 95, 187, and 197.

70. Wesley, "Upon Our Lord's Sermon on the Mount, IX," 5, *Works*, 1:635.

71. Wesley, "The Love of God," II, 6, *Works*, 4:337–338.

72. *Ibid.*, 4:335.

73. Wesley, "The Circumcision of the Heart," I, 12, *Works*, 1:408.

74. *Ibid.*, II, 10, 1:413–414.

75. Oord, *The Nature of Love*, 64–65.

76. Wesley, "The Love of God," I, 6, *Works*, 4:334; Wesley, "The Circumcision of the Heart," 11–13, *Works*, 1:407–409.

77. Wesley, "The Love of God," I, 6, *Works*, 4:334.

78. John Wesley, Sermon 18, "The Marks of the New Birth," III, 3, *Works*, 1:426.

79. Wesley, *Explanatory Notes Upon the New Testament*, I. John, 4:19.

80. Wesley, "Catholic Spirit," I, 17, *Works*, 2:89; John Wesley, "The Character of a Methodist," 9, *The Bicentennial Edition of the Works of John Wesley,* ed. Rupert E. Davies. (Nashville: Abingdon Press, 1989), 9:38; John Wesley, Sermon 52, "The Reformation of Manners," 7, *Works*, 2:321.

81. J. Gregory Crofford, *Streams of Mercy: Prevenient Grace in the Theology of John and Charles Wesley*. (Lexington, KY: Emeth Press, 2010), 140.

82. Jonathan Edwards, "A Treatise Concerning Religious Affections," Part III, Second Sign, *The Works of Jonathan Edwards*, ed. John E. Smith. (New Haven: Yale University Press, 1959), 2:240–253.

83. *Ibid.*, 2:246.

84. *Ibid.*, 2:245, 242–243.

85. Richard B. Steele, *"Gracious Affection" and "True Virtue" According to Jonathan Edwards and John Wesley*. (Metuchen, NJ: Scarecrow Press, Inc., 1994), xvi, 91, 228–230, 338–339.

86. Wesley, "The Circumcision of the Heart," II, 3, *Works*, 1:410.

87. John Wesley, Sermon 34, "The Original, Nature, Properties, and Use of the Law," II, 5, III, 5–12, *Works*, 10, 12–15.

88. Wesley, "Upon Our Lord's Sermon on the Mount, VI," 1, *Works*, 1:572–573.

89. Wesley, "A Plain Account of Genuine Christianity," III, 10, Outler, *John Wesley*, 194.

90. John Wesley, Sermon 7, "The Way to the Kingdom," I, 4, *Works*, 1:219.

91. Wesley, "Upon Our Lord's Sermon on the Mount, VI," 1, *Works*, 1:573.

92. John Wesley, Sermon 123, "On Knowing Christ After the Flesh," 14, *Works*, 4:105; John Wesley, Sermon 129, "Heavenly Treasure in Earthen Vessels," 2, *Works*, 4:162.

93. Wesley, "On Divine Providence," 11, *Works*, 2:539.

94. John Wesley, Sermon 149, "On Love," II, *Works*, 4:382–385.
95. Wesley, *A Compendium of Natural Philosophy*, 2:432, 434.
96. Wesley, "The General Deliverance," I, 1, *Works*, 2:438–439. These features of the image of God are discussed elsewhere, for example, Wesley, "The End of Christ's Coming," I, 3–8, *Works*, 2:474–475; Wesley, "The Good Steward," I, 2–3, *Works*, 2:284–285; Wesley, "On the Fall of Man," II, 6 *Works*, 2:409–410; Wesley, "The New Birth," I, 1, *Works*, 2:188.
97. Wesley, "The Image of God," I,1–3, *Works*, 4:293–295; Wesley, "Heavenly Treasure in Earthen Vessels," I, 1, *Works*, 4:163; Wesley, "On the Fall of Man," I, 1 and II, 6, *Works*, 2:400–401, 409–410; Wesley, "On Divine Providence," 15, *Works*, 2:540–541, Wesley, "The End of Christ's Coming," I, 3–8, *Works*, 2:474–476.
98. Wesley, "Upon Our Lord's Sermon on the Mount, IX," 6, *Works*, 1:636; Wesley, "The New Birth," I, 1, *Works*, 2:188; Wesley, "The Image of God," *Works*, 4:294.
99. Wesley, "The Good Steward," I, 3, III, 3, *Works*, 2:285–286, 293–294.
100. Wesley's positive appreciation of the senses comes through in John Wesley, Sermon 19, "The Great Privilege of Those That are Born of God," I, 3–5, *Works*, 1:432–433.
101. Wesley, "The Good Steward," I, 4, III, 4, *Works,* 2:285, 294–295.
102. Wesley, "The Imperfection of Human Knowledge," I, 2, *Works*, 2:570. See also *Works*, 1:276–277, n. 46.
103. John Wesley, Sermon 12, "The Witness of Our Own Spirit," 4, *Works*, 1:301.
104. John Wesley, Sermon 105, "On Conscience," I, 1, 3, *Works*, 3:481. Wesley, "Heavenly Treasure in Earthen Vessels," I, 1, *Works*, 4:163.
105. Wesley, "The Witness of Our Own Spirit," 5, *Works*, 1:302.
106. Wesley, "On Conscience," I, 3, *Works*, 3:481.
107. *Ibid.*, I, 5, 3:482.
108. John Wesley, Sermon 85, "On Working Out Our Own Salvation," III, 4, *Works*, 3:207; John Wesley, Sermon 43, "The Scripture Way of Salvation," I, 2, *Works*, 2:156.
109. Wesley, "Heavenly Treasure in Earthen Vessels," I,1, *Works*, 4:163.
110. Wesley, "The Original, Nature, Properties, and Use of the Law," *Works*, 2:4–19; Wesley, "The Witness of Our Own Spirit," 6, *Works*, 1:302.
111. For example, Umphrey Lee and Kenneth J. Collins; see Collins, 74.
112. Wesley, "On Working Out Our Own Salvation," III, 4, *Works*, 3:207.
113. Umphrey Lee, *John Wesley and Modern Religion*. (Nashville: Cokesbury Press, 1936), 124–125.
114. Collins, 73–82; Maddox, 83–93; Crofford, 70–71.
115. Randy L. Maddox, "Wesley as Theological Mentor: The Question of Truth or Salvation through Other Religions," *Wesleyan Theological Journal*, 1992, 27, 13.
116. John Wesley, Sermon 23, "Upon Our Lord's Sermon on the Mount, III," I, 11, *Works*, 1:516–517.
117. Wesley, "Heavenly Treasure in Earthen Vessels," 2, *Works*, 4:162; John Wesley, "On Knowing Christ After the Flesh,"14, *Works*, 4:105.
118. Wesley, "On Working Out Our Own Salvation," III, 7, *Works*, 3:208.
119. John Wesley, Sermon 86, "A Call to Backsliders," *Works*, 3:210–226.
120. Steele, 309.
121. Edwards, *Freedom of the Will*, Part I, Section 1 in *Works*, 1:139–140.
122. Steele, 310–311.
123. Wesley, "Thoughts Upon Necessity," III, 8, 9, Outler, *John Wesley*, 485, 486.
124. *Ibid.*, III, 7, 485.
125. John Wesley, Sermon 116, "What is Man," 11, *Works* 4:23–24.

126. Edwards, *Freedom of the Will*, Part I, Section 2, *Works*, 1:141–143.
127. Wesley, "Thoughts Upon Necessity," IV, 3, Outler, *John Wesley*, 489.
128. *Ibid.*, IV, 3, 489–490.
129. Edwards, *Freedom of the Will*, Part II, Section 7, *Works*, 1:203–212.
130. Wesley, "The Image of God," I, 3, *Works* 4:295.
131. Edwards, *Freedom of the Will*, Part II, Section 1, *Works*, 1:173–174.
132. *Ibid.*, Part II, Sections 2 and 3, 1:175–185.
133. *Ibid.*, Part I, Sections 4 and 5, 1:186–194.
134. Wesley, "On Divine Providence," 15, *Works*, 2:540–541; Wesley, "The End of Christ's Coming," I, 6, *Works*, 2:475.
135. Edwards, *Freedom of the Will*, Part IV, Sections 7, 9, and Conclusion, *Works*, 1:375–414, 430–439.
136. See Rem B. Edwards, *What Caused the Big Bang?* (Amsterdam – New York: Rodopi, 2001), 253–257. See also the books written or edited by Tom Oord cited in other endnotes.
137. I defended a free choice position against these and a vast number of other objections in my doctoral dissertation (1962), which was later published as Rem B. Edwards, *Freedom, Responsibility, and Obligation*. (The Hague: Martinus Nijhoff, 1969). I am still prepared to defend it against all comers! My book did not deal directly with Edwards and Wesley. It dealt mainly with those then-contemporary British philosophers who were still bickering over their issues.
138. John Wesley, Sermon 2, "The Almost Christian," I, 1–8, *Works*, 1:131–134.
139. William R. Cannon, *The Theology of John Wesley: With Special Reference to the Doctrine of Justification*. (Lanham, MD: University Press of America, 1974), 212, n. 53.
140. For details on Wesley's eschatology, see Maddox, *Responsible Grace*, 247–256.
141. John Wesley, Sermon 64, "The New Creation,"17, *Works*, 2:509.
142. Wesley, "The General Deliverance," 1, *Works*, 2:437.
143. Wesley, "The Imperfection of Human Knowledge," I, 12, *Works*, 2:576.
144. Wesley, "The General Deliverance," III, 10, *Works*, 2:449.
145. Wesley, "Upon Our Lord's Sermon on the Mount, III," I, 11, *Works*, 1:516–517.
146. Wesley, "The General Deliverance," *Works*, 2:437.
147. Wesley, "The General Deliverance," III, 5, 9, *Works*, 2:447, 449.
148. Wesley, "God's Approbation of His Works," I, 2–9, *Works*, 2:389–393.
149. *Ibid.*, I, 11–13, 2:393–394.
150. Wesley, "On the Fall of Man," *Works*, 2:400.
151. A very important exception is Craig A. Boyd, "The Goodness of Creation and the Openness of God," in Thomas Jay Oord, ed., *Creation Made Free: Open Theology Engaging Science*, 111–124.
152. Wesley, "The General Deliverance," II, 2–5, *Works*, 2:442–444.
153. *Ibid.*, II, 6, 2:444–445.
154. *Ibid.*, III, 1–4, 2:445–447.
155. *Ibid.*, I, 1, 2:438–439; Wesley, "On the Fall of Man," II, 6, *Works*, 2:409–410; Wesley, "The Image of God," I, 1–3, *Works*, 4:293–295.
156. Wesley, "The General Deliverance," I, 4, *Works*, 2:440–441.
157. Wesley, *A Compendium of Natural Philosophy*, 2:466–467.
158. Wesley, "The Imperfection of Human Knowledge," I, 12, *Works*, 2:576.
159. Wesley, "The General Deliverance," I, 5, *Works* 2:441.
160. *Ibid.*, I, 2, 2:439.

262 *John Wesley's Values—And Ours*

161. *Ibid.*, I, 5, III, 9, 2:441 and 449.
162. *Ibid.*, I, 5, 2:441.
163. Stephen R. L. Clark, *The Nature of the Beast*, (Oxford: Oxford University Press, 1984); S. F. Sapontzis, *Morals, Reason, and Animals.* (Philadelphia: Temple University Press, 1987); Franz de Waal, *Good Natured: The Origins of Right and Wrong in Humans and Other Animals.* (Cambridge: Harvard University Press, 1996); Franz de Waal, *Primates and Philosophers: How Morality Evolved.* (Princeton, NY: Princeton University Press, 2006); Franz de Waal, *The Age of Empathy: Nature's Lessons for a Kinder Society.* (New York: Harmony Books, 2009); D. Katz, ed., *Evolutionary Origins of Morality: Cross-Disciplinary Perspectives.* (Bowling Green, OH: Imprint Academic, 2000); Marc Bekoff and Jessica Pierce, *Wild Justice: The Moral Lives of Animals.* (Chicago: The University of Chicago Press, 2009).
164. Wesley, "The General Deliverance," I, 6, *Works*, 2:441–442.
165. *Ibid.*, III, 5, 2:447–448.
166. *Ibid*, 5, 2:447.
167. *Ibid*, III, 6, 2:448.
168. Randy L. Maddox, "John Wesley's Precedent for Theological Engagement," Thomas Jay Oord, ed., *Divine Grace and Emerging Creation."* (Eugene, OR: Pickwick Publications, 2009), 34.
169. *Ibid.*, III, 10, 2:449.
170. Wesley, "On Love," II, 3 and 6, *Works*, 4:383 and 384; Wesley, "The Love of God," III, 6, *Works*, 4:343.
171. John Wesley, Sermon 95, "On the Education of Children," 25, *Works*, 3:360.

Chapter Three

1. John Wesley, Sermon 90, "An Israelite Indeed," II, 4, *Works*, 3:286.
2. John Wesley, "Cautions and Directions Given to the Greatest Professors in the Methodist Societies," II, A, Albert C. Outler, *John Wesley.* (New York: Oxford University Press, 1964), 300.
3. John Wesley, "The Scripture Way of Salvation," I, 2, *Works*, 2:156.
4. Wesley, "The Means of Grace," I, 1, *Works*, 1:378.
5. *Ibid.*, II, 1, 1:381.
6. Wesley, "On Zeal," II, 5, III, 7–10, *Works*, 3:313–314, 318–320; Wesley, "The Scripture Way of Salvation," III, 9–10, *Works*, 2:166.
7. Wesley, "The Scripture Way of Salvation, III, 10, *Works*, 2:166.
8. John Wesley, Sermon 98, "On Visiting the Sick," II, 4, *Works*, 3:391.
9. Wesley, "The Scripture Way of Salvation, III, 10, *Works*, 2:166.
10. Wesley, "The Means of Grace," I, 1, *Works*, 1:381.
11. *Ibid.*
12. *Ibid.*
13. *Ibid.*, II, 2, 1:381.
14. *Ibid.*, V, 4, 1:396–397.
15. Wesley, "The New Birth," IV, 1, *Works*, 2:196.
16. *Ibid.*, IV:1, 2:196–197.
17. Wesley, "The Means of Grace," II, 3, *Works*, 1:382.
18. *Ibid.*
19. *Ibid*, II, 5, 1:383.

20. John Wesley, "Popery Calmly Considered," IV, 5, *The Works of the Reverend John Wesley, A.M.*, ed. John Emory. (New York: The Methodist Episcopal Church, 1831), 5:811. See also Article XVIII of Wesley's Twenty Four Articles of Religion. See also John Wesley, Sermon 101, "The Duty of Constant Communion," I, 2, *Works*, 3:429.

21. Wesley, "The New Birth," IV, 1, *Works*, 2:196.

22. Wesley, "The Marks of the New Birth," IV, 3, *Works*, 1:429.

23. Wesley, "The New Birth," IV, 2, *Works*, 2:197.

24. Wesley, "The Means of Grace," IV, 4, *Works*, 1:391–392; John Wesley, "Journal," December 31, 1739, *The Bicentennial Edition of the Works of John Wesley*, eds. W. Reginald Ward and Richard P. Heitzenrater. (Nashville: Abingdon Press, 1990), 19:132–33.

25. Wesley, "The Means of Grace," II, 3, 1:382.

26. *Ibid.*

27. John Wesley, Sermon 27, "Upon Our Lord's Sermon on the Mount, VII," 4, *Works*, 1:593–594.

28. Wesley, "The Means of Grace," V, 1, *Works*, 1:394.

29. John Wesley, Sermon 37, "The Nature of Enthusiasm," 39, *Works*, 2:59–60.

30. Wesley, "Upon Our Lord's Sermon on the Mount, IV," III, 6, *Works*, 1:545.

31. Wesley, "An Israelite Indeed," II, 4, *Works*, 3:286.

32. Wesley, "The Nature of Enthusiasm," 27, 39, *Works*, 2:56, 59; John Wesley, *A Plain Account of Christian Perfection*, Q. 33, *The Works of the Reverend John Wesley, A.M.*, ed. John Emory, 6:521.

33. Wesley, "Catholic Spirit," II, 1, *Works*, 3:89–90.

34. John Wesley, "On Visiting the Sick," II, 1–4, *Works*, 3:389–391.

35. Abraham H. Maslow, "A Theory of Human Motivation." *Psychological Review*, 1943, 50:4, 370–396; Abraham Maslow, *Motivation and Personality*. (New York: Harper, 1954).

36. John Wesley, Sermon 9, "The Spirit of Bondage and of Adoption," I, 1–8, *Works*, 1:251–255.

37. Wesley, "On Divine Providence," 8, *Works*, 2:537–538; Wesley, "God's Approbation of His Works," especially 1–2, *Works*, 2:387–388; John Wesley, Sermon 68, "The Wisdom of God's Counsels," 2, *Works*, 2:552; John Wesley, Sermon 109, "The Trouble and Rest of Good Men," first sentence, *Works*, 3:533.

38. John Wesley, *Explanatory Notes Upon the Old Testament*, Genesis 1.

39. John Wesley, Sermon 147, "Wiser than the Children of Light," IV, 1, *Works*, 4:366–367.

40. John Wesley, Semen 116, "What is Man?" 8, *Works*, 4:22–23.

41. John Wesley, "The Promise of Understanding," I, 1, *Works*, 4:283.

42. Isaac Newton, *Philosophical Writings*. Andrew Janiak, ed. (Cambridge: Cambridge University Press, 2004), 21.

43. Wesley, "Upon Our Lord's Sermon on the Mount, VI," III, 7, *Works*, 1:581; Wesley, "Spiritual Worship," I, 5–6, *Works*, 3:92–93; Wesley, "God's Approbation of His Works," I, 1, *Works*, 2:388.

44. Wesley, "Upon Our Lord's Sermon on the Mount, VI," III, 7, *Works*, 1:581; Wesley, "Spiritual Worship," I, 6, *Works*, 3:92–93; Wesley, "What is Man?" 8, *Works*, 4:23.

45. Wesley, "Thoughts Upon Necessity," I, 2, II, 1, Outler, *John Wesley*, 475, 479.

46. Wesley, "On Divine Providence," 8, *Works*, 2:537–538.

47. On the Big Bang and its significance for theism, see Rem B. Edwards, *What Caused the Big Bang?* (Amsterdam – New York: Rodopi, 2001).

48. Wesley, *A Compendium of Natural Philosophy*, 2:448.
49. John Wesley, Sermon 71, "Of Good Angels," I, 3, II, 7, *Works*, 3:8, 13.
50. See Karen Strand Winslow, "The Earth is Not a Planet," in Thomas Jay Oord, ed., *Creation Made Free: Open Theology Engaging Science*. (Eugene, OR: Pickwick Publications, 2009), 13–27.
51. Wesley, "The New Creation," 10–13, *Works*, 2:504–506; Wesley, "God's Approbation of His Works," I, 3–6, *Works*, 2:389–391; Wesley, "What is Man?," 2, 5, *Works*, 4:20–21.
52. Wesley, "The Imperfection of Human Knowledge," *Works*, 2:573, n. 26.
53. John Wesley, Sermon 54, "On Eternity," 7, *Works*, 2:362–363.
54. Wesley, "God's Approbation of His Works," II, 1, *Works*, 2:397.
55. *Ibid.*, I, 12, 2:395.
56. Richard N. Jostling, "The Search for the Historical Adam," *Christianity Today*, 55:6, June 2011, 23–27.
57. Wesley, "The Love of God," II, 5, *Works*, 4:337; Wesley, "Of the Church," I, 12, *Works*, 3:50; Wesley, "Upon Our Lord's Sermon on the Mount, I," 6, *Works*, 1:473; Wesley, "A Call to Backsliders," I, 4, *Works*, 3:215.
58. Wesley, "Upon Our Lord's Sermon on the Mount, X," 7, *Works*, 1:653.
59. John Wesley, Sermon 28, "Upon Our Lord's Sermon on the Mount, VIII,"11, *Works*, 1:618–619.
60. John Wesley, Sermon 78, "Spiritual Idolatry," I, 17, *Works*, 3:110.
61. Wesley, "Upon Our Lord's Sermon on the Mount, IX," 4, *Works*, 1:634.
62. John Wesley, Sermon 87, "The Danger of Riches," I, 6, *Works*, 3:232.
63. Wesley, "Upon Our Lord's Sermon on the Mount, I," I, 3, *Works*, 1:476.
64. John Wesley, Sermon 50, "The Use of Money," 2, *Works*, 2:268.
65. *Ibid.*, I, 1–8, 2:268–273.
66. *Ibid.*, II, 1–8, 2:273–276.
67. Wesley, "The Imperfection of Human Knowledge," I, 2, *Works*, 2:570.
68. Wesley, "The Use of Money," 2, *Works*, 2:268
69. John Wesley, Sermon 84, "The Important Question," *Works*, 3:183–198.
70. *Ibid.*, I, 3:183–185.
71. John Wesley, Sermon 41, "Wandering Thoughts," II, 1, *Works*, 2:129. On Worldliness as idolatry see Wesley, "Spiritual Idolatry," *Works*, 3:103–114.
72. Wesley, "The Unity of the Divine Being," 12–13, *Works*, 4:65–66.
73. Wesley, "Wandering Thoughts," I, 2, *Works*, 2:127.
74. Wesley, "The Spirit of Bondage and of Adoption, I, 5, *Works*, 1:253.
75. *Ibid.*, IV, 1, 1:264.
76. Wesley, "Upon Our Lord's Sermon on the Mount, IX," 8–11, *Works*, 1:636–637.
77. Charles Wesley, Sermon 3, "Awake, Thou that Sleepest," in John Wesley, *Works*, 1:142–158. See also Wesley, "The Spirit of Bondage and of Adoption," I, 1, *Works*, 1:251; John Wesley, Sermon 25, "Upon Our Lord's Sermon on the Mount, V," III, 9, *Works*, 1:560; John Wesley, "On Charity," III, 11, *Works*, 3:306; Wesley, "The Way to the Kingdom," II, 1, *Works*, 1, 225, and elsewhere.
78. Wesley, "The Important Question," I, 2, *Works*, 3:183.
79. Wesley, "Original Sin," II, 9, *Works*, 2:180; Wesley, "A Plain Account of Genuine Christianity," I, 10, Outler, *John Wesley*, 186.
80. *Ibid.*

81. Wesley, "Spiritual Idolatry," I, 5, *Works*, 3:106; Wesley, "The First-fruits of the Spirit," I, 2, *Works*, 1:235.
82. Wesley, "The Way to the Kingdom," I, 10–12, *Works*, 1:223–224.
83. Wesley, "An Earnest Appeal to Men of Reason and Religion," 16, *Works*, 11:50.
84. Wesley, "Original Sin,: I, 6, *Works*, 2:185.
85. Wesley, "The Circumcision of the Heart," I, 12, *Works*, 1:408.
86. John Wesley, "Letter to Mr. Fleury," 9, *Works*, 9:393.
87. Wesley, "Spiritual Idolatry," I, 4–18, *Works*, 3:105–111; Wesley, "An Israelite Indeed," I, 1, *Works*, 3:282–283; Wesley, "The Important Question," I, 3–5, III, 7–10, *Works*, 3:183–185, 192–194; Wesley, "The Circumcision of the Heart," I, 13, *Works*, 1:409; Wesley, "Original Sin," II, 9–11, *Works*, 2:179–182; Wesley, "The Unity of the Divine Being," 12, *Works*, 4:65–66; John Wesley, Sermon 14, "The Repentance of Believers," I, 5–7, *Works*, 1:338–339; Wesley, "On the Education of Children," 8, 19, 21, *Works*, 3:350–351, 356–357, 358–359; Wesley, "The Use of Money," II, 1–7, *Works*, 2:273–276; Wesley, "The Wisdom of God's Counsels," 16, *Works*, 2:560–561.
88. Wesley, "An Israelite Indeed," I, 1, *Works*, 3:282; Wesley, "Spiritual Idolatry," I, 7–8, *Works*, 3:106–107; Wesley, "Original Sin," II, 10, *Works*, 2:181.
89. Wesley, "The Wisdom of God's Counsels, 16, *Works*, 2:561.
90. Wesley, "Original Sin," II, 11, *Works*, 2:182.
91. John Wesley, Sermon 88, "On Dress," 11, *Works*, 3:252.
92. Wesley, "The Important Question," II, 2, *Works*, 3:185.
93. The debate about and the distinctions between quantitative versus qualitative hedonism were carefully examined in Rem B. Edwards, *Pleasures and Pains: A Theory of Qualitative Hedonism*. (Ithaca, NY: Cornell University Press, 1979).
94. John Wesley, Sermon 79, "On Dissipation," 18, *Works*, 3:123.
95. Wesley, "Spiritual Idolatry," II, 1, *Works*, 3:111.
96. Wesley, "Spiritual Worship," III, 8, *Works*, 3:101.
97. Wesley, Sermon 136, "On Mourning for the Dead," 8, *Works*, 4:239.
98. Wesley, "Spiritual Idolatry," III, 7, *Works*, 3:100.
99. John Wesley, "On Love," III, 4, *Works*, 4:386.
100. Wesley, "The Danger of Riches," I, 15, *Works*, 3:235.
101. John Wesley, Sermon 6, "The Righteousness of Faith," II, 9, *Works*, 1:213–214.
102. Wesley, "The Important Question," III, 3, *Works*, 3:189.
103. Edwards, *Pleasures and Pains: A Theory of Qualitative Hedonism*, 84–92.
104. Wesley, "Self-Denial, *Works*, 2:238–252.
105. *Ibid.*, I, 7, 2:243.
106. Wesley, "The Important Question," III, 6, *Works*, 3:191–192.
107. Wesley, "A Plain Account of Genuine Christianity," I, 11, Outler, *John Wesley*, 186.
108. Wesley, "The Important Question," III, 10, *Works*, 3:194.
109. Wesley, "On Love," III, 1, *Works*, 4:386.
110. Wesley, "The New Birth," III, 3, *Works*, 2:195–196.
111. Wesley, "The Means of Grace," V, 4, *Works*, 1:396, Wesley, "Spiritual Worship," III, 1, *Works*, 3:97.
112. Wesley, "Spiritual Idolatry," II, 2, *Works*, 3:112.
113. Wesley, "A Call to Backsliders," 2–5, *Works*, 3:21–213.
114. Wesley, "A Plain Account of Genuine Christianity," I, 10, Outler, *John Wesley*, 185–186.

115. Wesley, "The Important Question," III, 15, *Works*, 3:197.
116. Wesley, "Heavenly Treasure in Earthen Vessels," II, 1–4, *Works*, 4: 164–167.
117. Wesley, "On the Fall of Man," II, 2. *Works*, 2:405–406.
118. Wesley, "Thoughts Upon Necessity," IV, 2, Outler, *John Wesley*, 487; Wesley, "Wandering Thoughts," I, 3 and IV, 3–4, *Works*, 2:127–128 and 135; Wesley, "Heavenly Treasure in Earthen Vessels," II, 1, *Works*, 4:165.
119. Wesley, "The Image of God," II, *Works*, 4:296.
120. Wesley, "What is Man?" 10, *Works*, 4:23.
121. John Wesley, "On the Resurrection of the Dead," II, 1, *Sermons on Several Occasions*. (New York, J & J Harper, 1831), 3:345. This sermon was originally written by another minister, Benjamin Calamy, but Wesley re-wrote it, preached it, and it was published it as his own. Even if he did not originally write every word in it, he presumably agreed with its contents as we now have it.
122. John Wesley, Sermon 115, "Dives and Lazarus," I, 3, *Works*, 4:7.
123. Wesley, "The Good Steward," *Works*, 2:281–298; John Wesley, Sermon 132, "On Faith," 4:187–200.
124. Wesley, "On the Resurrection of the Dead," II, 3, 3:348.
125. Wesley, *Explanatory Notes Upon the New Testament*, I. Corinthians 15:42–44.
126. Wesley, "The Great Assize," I, 1, *Works*, 1:358.
127. Wesley, "What is Man?" 10, *Works*, 4:23; Wesley, "On Faith," 6, *Works*, 4:191.
128. Wesley, "On The Resurrection of the Dead," II, 3, 4, 3:345–346.
129. Wesley, "On the Fall of Man," II, 2–5, *Works*, 2:405–408.
130. John Wesley, *Primitive Physick, or An Easy and Natural Method of Curing Most Diseases*, available on line at: http://new.gbgm-umc.org/umhistory/wesley/primitive-physick. See also Deborah Madden, "Wesley as Adviser on Health and Healing," in Randy L. Maddox and Jason E. Vickers, eds., *The Cambridge Companion to John Wesley*. (Cambridge: University Press, 2010), 176–189.
131. Wesley, "Upon Our Lord's Sermon on the Mount, VII," IV, 4, *Works*, 1:609.
132. Wesley, "Upon Our Lord's Sermon on the Mount, III," II, 5–6, *Works*, 1:519.
133. Wesley, "Upon Our Lord's Sermon on the Mount, IV," III, 7, *Works*, 1:546.
134. John Wesley, Sermon 38, "A Caution against Bigotry," I, 14, *Works*, 2:68.
135. Wesley, "On Working Out Our Own Salvation," III, 2, *Works*, 3:206.
136. Wesley, "Upon Our Lord's Sermon on the Mount, V," IV, 11, *Works*, 1:568.
137. John Wesley, "The Nature, Design, and General Rules of the United Societies," *Works,* 1989, 9:67–73.
138. Wesley, "Dives and Lazarus," II, 15, *Works*, 4:15.
139. Wesley, "Upon Our Lord's Sermon on the Mount, IV," III, 4, *Works*, 1:544.
140. John Wesley, "A Letter to the Rev. Mr. Horne," *The Works of John Wesley, Bicentennial Edition*, ed. Gerald R. Cragg. (Nashville: Abingdon Press, 1989), 11:444–458; John Wesley, Sermon 150, "Hypocrisy in Oxford [English]," I, 5–7, *Works*, 4:395–398.
141. John Wesley, Sermon 35, "The Law Established Through Faith, I," II, 6 and all of II, *Works*, 2:26–29. See Articles IX and X of Wesley's Twenty Five Articles of Religion.
142. Wesley, "The Nature of Enthusiasm," 23, *Works*, 2:54–55.
143. John Wesley, Sermon 5, "Justification by Faith," III, 5–6, *Works*, 1:192. The Jackson version cited here is significantly different from the *Bicentennial Edition* version.
144. Wesley, "Upon our Lord's Sermon on the Mount, IV," *Works*, 531–549.
145. Wesley, "Justification by Faith," III, 5–6, *Works*, 1:192; Wesley, "A Letter to the Rev. Mr. Horne," II, 7, *Works*, 11:455

146. Wesley, "Journal," December 31, 1739, *Works*, 19:132–133; and September 3, 1741, *Works*, 19:211–224.
147. Wesley, "The Law Established Through Faith, I," II, 2, *Works*, 2:26.
148. Wesley, "Cautions and Directions Given to the Greatest Professors in the Methodist Societies," III, A, Outler, *John Wesley*, 302.
149. Wesley, "Upon Our Lord's Sermon on the Mount, IV," 3, *Works*, 1:532.
150. *Ibid.*, 5, 1:533.
151. John Wesley, Sermon 99, "The Reward of the Righteous," I, 3, *Works*, 3:403; Wesley, "Journal," December 31, 1739, *Works*, 19:132–133.
152. Wesley, "The Law Established Through Faith, I," II-III, *Works*, 2:26–32.
153. Wesley, "Cautions and Directions Given to the Greatest Professors in The Methodist Societies," VI, Albert Outler, *John Wesley*, 303.
154. Wesley's much abbreviated version of Edwards' *A Treatise Concerning Religious Affections* is available on line from the Wesley Center. Go to:
http://wesley.nnu.edu/john_wesley/christian_library/vol30/CL30Part8.htm, and to http://wesley.nnu.edu/john_wesley/christian_library/vol30/CL30Part9.htm.
155. Jonathan Edwards, "A Treatise Concerning Religious Affections," *Works*, 2:409–410.
156. *Ibid.*, 2:383.
157. John Wesley, Sermon 32, "Upon Our Lord's Sermon on the Mount, XII," III, 1–4, *Works* 1:680–681.
158. Wesley, "A Plain Account of Genuine Christianity," I, 9, Outler, *John Wesley*, 185.
159. Wesley, "Original Sin," II, 8–11, *Works*, 2:179–182.
160. Wesley, "The Way to the Kingdom," II, 1, *Works*, 1:226.
161. Wesley, "On Dissipation," 9, *Works*, 3:119.
162. Wesley, "Original Sin," II, 9, *Works*, 2:179–180.
163. *Ibid.*, 3, 2:173.
164. Wesley, "The Image of God," II, *Works*, 4:296. Compare Wesley, "On the Fall of Man," I, 1, *Works*, 2:401–402, where he speaks of "the tree of knowledge," but does not add "of good and evil."
165. Wesley, "On the Fall of Man," II, 3, *Works*, 2:406–407.
166. John Wesley, *Explanatory Notes Upon the Old Testament*, Genesis 2:17.
167. Wesley, "Thoughts Upon Necessity," I, 1, Outler, *John Wesley*, 475.
168. Wesley recited the Adam and Eve story and their original perfection in many sermons: Wesley, "On the Fall of Man," *Works*, 2:400–412. Wesley, "Original Sin," *Works*, 2:172–185; Wesley, "The General Deliverance," *Works*, 2:437–450; Wesley, "Justification by Faith," I, *Works*, 1:184–187; Wesley, "The End of Christ's Coming," I, *Works*, 2:473–477; Wesley, "The Image of God," II, *Works*, 4:292–303.
169. Wesley, *A Compendium of Natural Philosophy*. See Randy L. Maddox, "Wesley's Engagement with the Natural Sciences" in Randy L. Maddox and Jason E. Vickers, eds., *The Cambridge Companion to John Wesley*. (Cambridge: University Press, 2010), 160–175.
170. Wesley, *A Compendium of Natural Philosophy*, Part V.
171. Wesley, "Original Sin," II, 2, *Works*, 2:176.
172. See all of "Original Sin" for details.
173. *Ibid.*, I, 4, 2:175.
174. Lee, 124–125.
175. For Wesley's views on war, see Manfred Marquardt, *John Wesley's Social Ethics: Praxis and Principles*. (Nashville: Abingdon Press, 1992), 128–130.

176. For Wesley's views on poverty and sustained efforts to alleviate it, see Marquardt, Ch. II.

177. Wesley, "Self-Denial," I, 1, *Works*, 2:240.

178. Randy L. Maddox, *Responsible Grace: John Wesley's Practical Theology*. (Nashville: Kingswood Books, 1994), 74–81.

179. *Ibid.*, as quoted by Maddox, 78, from *Works*, 26:519.

180. *Ibid.*, 179.

181. Irenaeus, "Against Heresies", 4:38.1 in Alexander Roberts and James Donaldson, eds., *The Ante-Nicene Fathers*. (New York: Charles Scribner's Sons, 1903), 1:521.

182. Maddox, 87; Marquardt, 169, note 33.

183. J. Gregory Crofford, *Streams of Mercy: Prevenient Grace in the Theology of John and Charles Wesley*. (Lexington, KY: Emeth Press, 2010), 192.

184. John Wesley, "On the Holy Spirit," originally written by John Gambold, I, *The Works of the Reverend John Wesley, A.M.*, ed. John Emory. (New York: The Methodist Episcopal Church, 1831), 2:532.

185. Wesley, *Explanatory Notes Upon the New Testament*, on John 6:44.

186. John Wesley, "A Farther Appeal to Men of Reason and Religion," Part I, III, 2, (3), *Works*, 11:120; Wesley, "The Unity of the Divine Being," 16, *Works*, 4:66–67.

187. John Wesley, Sermon 22, "Upon Our Lord's Sermon on the Mount, II," II, 4, *Works*, 1:496–497.

188. *Ibid.*

189. *Ibid.*, II, 6, 1:498.

190. Wesley, "Spiritual Worship," III, 8, *Works*, 3:101.

191. John Wesley, "On a Single Eye," III, 5, *Works*, 4:128.

192. Wesley, "The Wisdom of Winning Souls," II, *Works*, 4:313–314.

193. Joel Osteen, *Your Best Life Now*. (New York: Faith Worlds, 2004), 5.

194. *Ibid.*, 257.

195. Randal J. Stephens, "The Holiness/Pentecostal/Charismatic Extension of the Wesleyan Tradition," in Randy L. Maddox and Jason E. Vickers, eds., *The Cambridge Edition to John Wesley* (Cambridge: University Press, 2010), 278–279.

196. John Wesley, Sermon 121, "Prophets and Priests," 8, *Works*, 4:77.

197. Wesley, "The More Excellent Way," 2, *Works*, 3:263; John Wesley, Sermon 102, "Of Former Times," 16, *Works*, 3:450; John Wesley, Sermon 61, "The Mystery of Iniquity," 27, *Works*, 2:463.

198. Wesley, "The Wisdom of God's Counsels," 8-12, *Works*, 2:555–559.

199. Wesley, "The Danger of Riches," II, *Works*, 3:236–246.

200. *Ibid.*, II, 5–8, 3:237–239; Wesley, "The Wisdom of God's Counsels," 16, *Works*, 2:560–561; Wesley, "Causes of the Inefficacy of Christianity," 8–9, 16–18, *Works*, 4: 91–92.

201. John Wesley, Sermon 80, "On Friendship with the World," 8, *Works*, 3:130–131.

202. John Wesley, Sermon 63, "The General Spread of the Gospel,"19, *Works*, 2:494.

Chapter Four

1. Wesley, "The Imperfection of Human Knowledge," 1, *Works* 2:568.
2. Wesley, "On Charity," II, 2, *Works*, 3:299.
3. Wesley, Monday, June 15, 1741, *Works*, 19:201.
4. Gerald R. Cragg, "Introduction," Wesley's *Works*, 11:14.

5. John Wesley, "A Letter to the Rev. Dr. Rutherford," March 28, 1768, III, 4, *Works*, 9:382.

6. For details, see Marquardt, *John Wesley's Social Ethics: Praxis and Principles*, Ch. 4.

7. Wesley, "On the Education of Children," 15, *Works*, 3:353–354, but see the whole sermon, 347–360. Wesley gives Susanna's written perspective on educating children in his Journal; see *Works*, 19:286–291.

8. Take a look at the very high standards of cognitive development in many fields of learning that he set for his ministers, as expressed in John Wesley, "An Address to the Clergy," I, 1–2, II, 1, *The Works of the Reverend John Wesley, A.M.*, ed. John Emory. (New York: The Methodist Episcopal Church, 1831), 6:217–221, 223–224.

9. Wesley, "Men of Reason ands Religion, Part III," *Works*, 11:295 n. 2.

10. Wesley, "God's Approbation of His Works," 2, *Works*, 2:387.

11. Wesley, "The Imperfection of Human Knowledge," *Works*, 2:568–586.

12. Wesley, "A Farther Appeal to Men of Reason and Religion, Part III, III, 28, *Works*, 11:310.

13. Collins, *The Theology of John Wesley: Holy Love and the Shape of Grace*, 1–5, 327–331.

14. Ted A. Campbell, *Wesleyan Beliefs: Formal and Popular Expressions of the Core Beliefs of Wesleyan Communities*. (Nashville, TN: Abingdon Press, 2010).

15. Values in heaven will be discussed later. For Wesley's views of the disvalues of hell, see John Wesley, Sermon 73, "Of Hell," *Works*, 3:31–44.

16. John Wesley, Sermon 1, "Salvation by Faith," I, 1, *Works* 1:119.

17. *Ibid.*, I, 4, 1:120.

18. Wesley, "Upon Our Lord's Sermon on the Mount, V," III, 9, *Works*, 1:559–560.

19. Wesley, "Predestination Calmly Considered," XIII, LIV, Outler, *John Wesley*, 432, 452; John Wesley, Sermon 13, "On Sin in Believers," II, *Works*, 1:319; Wesley, "An Earnest Appeal to Men of Reason and Religion," 12, 18, *Works*, 11:49, 50.

20. John Wesley, "The Case of Reason Impartially Considered," I, 6, *Works*, 2:589.

21. John Wesley, Sermon 75, "On Schism," 3, *Works*, 3:60.

22. Wesley, "The Case of Reason Impartially Considered," I, 2, *Works*, 2:590.

23. John Locke, *Essay Concerning Human Understanding*, Vol. II, Book IV, Ch. VII.

24. Consider "We hold these truths to be self-evident" in the *Declaration of Independence*.

25. John Wesley, *A Compendium of Logic*, Bk. II, Ch. 1, Sects. ii and iv, *The Works of the Reverend John Wesley, A.M.*, ed. John Emory, 7:621, 622.

26. Wesley, "The Case of Reason Impartially Considered," I, 6, *Works*, 2:591.

27. *Ibid.*, I, 6–7, 2:591–592.

28. Wesley, "Salvation by Faith," I, 1, *Works* 1:119.

29. Wesley, "An Earnest Appeal to Men of Reason and Religion," 30, *Works*, 11:56.

30. *Ibid.*, II, 10, 2:598. See all of Section II, 593–600.

31. Wesley, "The Case of Reason Impartially Considered," II, 1, *Works*, 2:593.

32. Wesley, "A Farther Appeal to Men of Reason and Religion, Part II," III, 21-23, *Works*, 11:268–270.

33. Wesley, "An Earnest Appeal to Men of Reason and Religion," 32-34, *Works*, 11:56–57.

34. Wesley, "The Circumcision of the Heart," II, 2, *Works*, 1:410.

35. Wesley, "An Earnest Appeal to Men of Reason and Religion," 35, *Works*, 11:57.

270 *John Wesley's Values—And Ours*

36. *Ibid.*, 20–22, 11:51–53.
37. Wesley, "Upon our Lord's Sermon on the Mount, V," IV, 10, *Works*, 1:567.
38. Wesley, "The Original, Nature, Properties, and Uses of the Law," IV, 8, *Works*, 2:18.
39. Wesley, "Predestination Calmly Considered," XIII, LIV, Outler, *John Wesley*, 432, 452.
40. John Wesley, Sermon 119, "Walking by Sight, and Walking by Faith," 18, *Works*, 4:57.
41. John Wesley, Sermon 112, "On Laying the Foundations of the New Chapel," II, 9, *Works*, 3:588.
42. Wesley, "Predestination Calmly Considered," XIII, LIV, Outler, *John Wesley*, 432, 452, where Wesley uses the expression "true believers" a number of times.
43. Wesley, "The Mystery of Iniquity," 13, *Works*, 2:456.
44. Wesley, "A Plain Account of Genuine Christianity," II, 5, Outler, *John Wesley*, 189.
45. John Wesley, Sermon 106, "On Faith," I, 9-10, *Works*, 3:496–497.
46. John Wesley, Sermon 4, "Scriptural Christianity," 5, *Works*, 1:161.
47. Wesley, "The Unity of the Divine Being," 15, *Works*, 4:66.
48. *Ibid.*, I, 2, 1:161–162.
49. John Wesley, Sermon 125, "On Living Without God," 15, *Works*, 4:175.
50. For example, see: John Wesley, Sermon 107, "On God's Vineyard," I, 1–9, *Works*, 3:504–508; John Wesley, "A Letter to a Roman Catholic," 6-11, Outler, *John Wesley*, 494–496; John Wesley, Sermon 122, "Causes of the Inefficacy of Christianity," 6, *Works*, 4:89.
51. Wesley, "A Plain Account of Genuine Christianity," II, Outler, *John Wesley*, 188–191.
52. Wesley, "Salvation by Faith," I, 4, *Works*, 1:120.
53. *Ibid.*
54. Wesley, "The Marks of the New Birth," I, 2, *Works*, 1:418.
55. "Wesley, "The Scripture Way of Salvation," II, 3, *Works*, 2:161.
56. *Ibid.*, II, 2-3, 2:161-162; Wesley, "The Marks of the New Birth," II, 2, 3, *Works*, 1:423.
57. Wesley, "The Way to the Kingdom," II,10, *Works*, 1:230; Wesley, "The Marks of the New Birth," I, 3, *Works*, 1:418–419; John Wesley, "The Principles of a Methodist," 8, *Works*, 9:52–53.
58. Wesley, "An Earnest Appeal to Men of Reason and Religion," 57-58, *Works*, 11:67–68; Wesley, "Upon Our Lord's Sermon on the Mount, IX," 4-6, *Works*, 1:635–636.
59. Wesley, "The Marks of the New Birth," I, 3, *Works*, 1:418–419; Wesley, "The Principles of a Methodist," 9, *Works*, 9:53; John Wesley, "Advice to the People Called Methodists," 5, *Works*, 9:124.
60. Wesley, "The Law Established Through Faith, II," II, 1, *Works*, 2:38.
61. Wesley, "To John Smith, June 25, 2007," section 9, *Works*, 26.
62. Wesley, "The Law Established Through Faith," II, 2, *Works*, 2:39.
63. *Ibid.*, II, 6, 2:40–41.
64. Wesley, "On Charity," *Works*, 3:292–307.
65. John Wesley, "Of True Christian Faith," 2, 129.
66. David Hume, *A Treatise of Human Nature*. (Oxford: The Clarendon Press, 1958), 269.
67. Wesley, "The Way to the Kingdom," I, 5, *Works*, 1:220.
68. Wesley, "Salvation by Faith," III, 1, *Works*, 1:125.
69. Wesley, "Upon Our Lord's Sermon on the Mount, V," III, 9, *Works*, 1:559–560.

70. Wesley, "Upon Our Lord's Sermon on the Mount, IV," II, 2, *Works*, 1:539–540.
71. Wesley, "Preface" to his sermons, *Works*, 1:106; "On Charity," III, 11, *Works*, 3:306, Wesley, "On the Wedding Garment," 17, *Works*, 4:147, Wesley, "The End of Christ's Coming," III, 6, *Works*, 2:483, and in many other sermons.
72. Wesley, "Upon Our Lord's Sermon on the Mount, IV," III, 4, *Works*, 1:544.
73. Wesley, "The Law Established Through Faith, II," II, 1, *Works*, 2:38.
74. Wesley, "Preface" to his sermons, *Works*, 1:107.
75. Wesley, "On Living Without God," 15, *Works*, 4:175.
76. Wesley, "Salvation by Faith," I, 2, *Works*, 1:119-120; Wesley, "The Way to the Kingdom," I, 6 and II, 10, *Works*, 1:220 and 230; Wesley, "The Marks of the New Birth," I, 2, *Works*, 1:418; Wesley, "The Almost Christian," II, 4, *Works*, 1:4:138–139; Wesley, "On Faith," I, 9, *Works*, 3:497; Wesley, "On the Wedding Garment," 15, *Works*, 4:146.
77. Wesley, "The Almost Christian," II, 1-3, *Works*, 1:137–138.
78. Wesley, "The Way to the Kingdom," I, 6, *Works*, 1:220.
79. Wesley, "Catholic Spirit," 3, *Works*, 2:82.
80. Wesley, "On Attending the Church Service," 33, *Works*, 3:478.
81. Wesley, "Catholic Spirit," 3, *Works*, 2:4, 82.
82. *Ibid.*, 2:5, 82.
83. Wesley, "Upon our Lord's Sermon on the Mount, XIII," III, 12, *Works*, 1:698.
84. Wesley, "Catholic Spirit," I, 3, *Works*, 2:83.
85. *Ibid.*, III, 1, 2:92.
86. *Ibid.*, I, 12-18, 2:87–89.
87. *Ibid.*, II, 1, 2:89.
88. Wesley, "On the Trinity," 2, *Works*, 2:376.
89. *Ibid.*, 1, 2:374.
90. *Ibid.*, 4, 2:377–378.
91. *Ibid.*, 14, 2:383.
92. *Ibid.*, 15, 2:384. See also Wesley's discussion of the Trinity in *A Compendium of Natural Philosophy*, 2:451–454.
93. *Ibid.*, 3–4, 2:376–378.
94. Wesley, "A Caution against Bigotry," II, 1-3, *Works*, 2:69–70.
95. *Ibid.*, IV, 1, 2:76.
96. *Ibid.*, IV, 4, 2:77.
97. *Ibid.*, IV, 5, 2:77.
98. Wesley, "On Faith," 2 and I, 6, *Works*, 3:492, 495.
99. *Ibid.*, I, 1–8, 3:493–496.
100. *Ibid.*, I, 4, 3:494–495.
101. Wesley, "On Living Without God," 14, *Works*, 4:174.
102. Wesley, "On Charity," II, 4, *Works*, 3:295–296.
103. Wesley, "Predestination Calmly Considered," XLIII, Outler, *John Wesley*, 445.
104. Wesley, "On Divine Providence," 16, *Works*, 2:542.
105. Wesley, "On Living Without God," 14, *Works*, 4:174.
106. John Wesley, *Explanatory Notes Upon the New Testament*, Acts 10:35.
107. John Wesley, "To Thomas Whitehead," Feb 10, 1748, *Works*, 26.
108. Wesley, "The Mystery of Iniquity," 3–6, *Works*, 2:452–453.
109. Wesley, "Upon Our Lord's Sermon on the Mount, XII," III, 1–3, *Works*, 1:680.
110. Wesley, "On Attending the Church Service," 33, *Works*, 3:478.
111. John Wesley, Sermon 110, "Free Grace," 26, *Works*, 3:556.

272 *John Wesley's Values—And Ours*

112. *Ibid.*, 25, 3:555.
113. Wesley, "Predestination Calmly Considered," XVI and XVII, Outler, *John Wesley*, 433; Wesley, "On Predestination," 5, *Works*, 2:417
114. Wesley, "Free Grace," 29, *Works*, 3:558.
115. Maddox, *Responsible Grace: John Wesley's Practical Theology*. (Nashville: Kingswood Books, 1994), 36–38.
116. John Wesley, Sermon 74, "Of the Church," I, 12, *Works*, 3:50.
117. Wesley, "The Love of God," II, 5, *Works*, 4:337. See also Wesley, "Upon our Lord's Sermon on the Mount, I," 6, *Works*, 1:473; Wesley, "A Call to Backsliders," I, 4, *Works*, 3:215.
118. Wesley, "Upon Our Lord's Sermon on the Mount, I," I, 3, *Works*, 1:476.
119. Wesley, "Popery Calmly Considered," IV, 5, *The Works of the Reverend John Wesley, A.M.*, ed. John Emory, 5:811. This sermon may have been written by someone else besides Wesley, but he would have agreed.
120. John Wesley, "On Working Out Our Salvation," II, 2, 204.
121. John Wesley, *A Compendium of Natural Philosophy*, Part V, Chapter II, "Of the Heavenly Bodies in Particular," 2:114–170.
122. Wesley, "The Great Assize," I, 2, *Works*, 1:358–359.
123. *Ibid.*, II, 2, 1:360.
124. Wesley, "On Predestination," 5, *Works*, 2:417.
125. *Ibid.*, 15, 2:420–421.
126. John Wesley, *Explanatory Notes Upon the Old Testament*, Exodus 33:22–23.
127. Wesley, *A Compendium of Natural Philosophy*, 2:437.
128. Wesley, "The New Birth," II, 3, *Works*, 2:191–192.
129. Wesley, "Free Grace," 20, *Works*, 3:552.
130. Wesley, "The Means of Grace," III, 8, *Works*, 1:388.
131. Wesley, "Free Grace," 20, *Works*, 3:552.
132. John Wesley, Sermon 139, "On the Sabbath," II, 1, *Works*, 4:272–273; Wesley, "Self-Denial, I, 13–14, *Works*, 2:245; Wesley, "The Important Question," I, 1, *Works*, 3:183; Wesley, "The Reward of the Righteous," 4, *Works*, 4:402; Wesley, "A Call to Backsliders," II, 2, (4), *Works*, 3:215; John Wesley, "Of the Church," 20, *Works*, 3:53; Wesley, "On Knowing Christ After the Flesh," 3, 99; Wesley, "The New Creation," 17, *Works*, 2:508–509; Wesley, "The Great Assize," I, 2, *Works*, 1:358–359; II, 2; John Wesley, Sermon 81, "In What Sense We Are To Leave the World," 4, *Works*, 3:145. For other instances, search Wesley's *Works* for "absurdity," "in the manner of men," "figurative," "analogical," and related terminology.
133. Wesley, "On Charity," *Works*, 3:292.
134. Wesley, "On Laying the Foundations of the New Chapel," II, 8, *Works*, III, 587–588.
135. Maddox, n. 57, 291.
136. Marquardt, 164, n. 35.
137. Wesley, "The Nature, Design, and General Rules of the United Societies," *Works*, 9:70–71, n. 11.
138. Cynthia Lynn Lyerly, *Methodism and the Southern Mind, 1770–1810*. (New York and Oxford: Oxford University Press, 1998).
139. John Wesley, "Thoughts Upon Slavery," *The Works of the Reverend John Wesley, A.M.*, ed. John Emory, 6:278–293. See also Marquardt, Ch. V.
140. Wesley, "Thoughts Upon Slavery," IV, 1; V, 6, 6:286, 292–293.

141. *Ibid.*, IV, 2–4 and V, 3, 6, 6:286–287, 291, 292–293.

142. John Wesley, "Thoughts Upon Liberty," 16, *The Works of the Reverend John Wesley, A.M.*, ed. John Emory, 6:263; Wesley, "An Earnest Appeal to Men of Reason and Religion," 17, *Works*, 11:50.

143. Wesley, "Thoughts Upon Slavery," V, 3, 7, 6:291, 293.

144. Heitzenrater, 235–237, 247–248, 276, 298,

145. Maddox, 72.

146. Wesley, "On Visiting the Sick," III, 7, *Works*, 3:396.

147. Wesley, "A Farther Appeal to Men of Reason and Religion, Part I," VII, 4, *Works*, 11:189.

148. *Ibid.*, VII, 5, 11:190.

149. Wesley, "The Good Steward," IV, 2–3, *Works*, 2:297.

150. John Wesley, Sermon 92, "On Zeal," I, 1, *Works*, 3:311.

151. *Ibid.*, I, 2, 3:311–312.

152. Wesley, "On Charity," I, 1, *Works*, 3:293–294.

153. Wesley, "On Zeal," I, 3, *Works*, 3:312.

154. *Ibid.*, II, 1, 3:312

155. Wesley, "An Israelite Indeed," II, 2–3, *Works*, 3:284–286.

156. *Ibid.*, II, 3, 3:286.

157. Wesley, "On Zeal," II, 4, *Works*, 3:313.

158. *Ibid.*, II, 5, 3:313–314.

159. *Ibid.*, III, 7, 3:318.

160. *Ibid.*, II, 5–6, 3:313–314. Wesley repeats and further explains this hierarchy at least three other times in this sermon; see: III, 7, 9, and 12, 3:318–319, 319, 320–321.

161. *Ibid.*, III, 5, 3:317.

162. Wesley discussed whether ecclesiastical vestments and other churchly ornaments and properties had to be properly "consecrated" in "Thoughts on the Consecration of Churches and Burial Grounds," 1, 2, *Works*, 9:531–532. He thought that insisting on this was "flatly superstitious," section 5, 532.

163. *Ibid.*, III, 6, 3:317.

164. Maddox, *Responsible Grace: John Wesley's Practical Theology* 41. Randy L. Maddox, "John Wesley's Precedent for Theological Engagement," in Oord, ed., *Divine Grace and Emerging Creation,* 24–25.

165. Wesley, "The Character of a Methodist," 1, *Works*, 9:34.

166. *Ibid.*, 5–18, 9:35–42.

167. Wesley, "Free Grace," 26, *Works*, 3:556.

168. Wesley, "On Zeal," II, 9, *Works*, 3:314.

169. John Wesley, "Advice to the People Called Methodists," 23, *Works*, 9:130.

170. John Wesley, "Preface" to his *Sermons on Several Occasions, 1746*, 10, *Works*, 1:107.

171. Wesley, "On Charity," II, 6–7, *Works*, 3:300.

172. *Ibid.*, III, 6, 3:303–304.

173. Wesley, "On the Trinity," 1, *Works*, 2:374.

174. Wesley, "The Spirit of Bondage and of Adoption," IV, 1–4, *Works*, 1:263–266. Outler traces this distinction back at least as far as St. Augustine, 1:248.

175. *Ibid.*, IV, 2, 1:264–265.

176. *Ibid.*, II, 1–10, 1:255–260.

177. Wesley, "The Original, Nature, Properties, and Use of the Law," II, 1, IV, 4, *Works*, 2:8, 17.

178. Wesley, "Upon Our Lord's Sermon on the Mount, V," I,1, *Works*, 1:551.

179. Wesley, "The Way to the Kingdom," I, 4, *Works*, 1:219.

180. Wesley, "The Important Question," III, 1, *Works*, 3:189.

181. Wesley, "On the Wedding Garment," 14, *Works*, 4:145.

182. Wesley, "The Important Question," III, 2, *Works*, 3:189; Wesley, "The Unity of the Divine Being," 16, *Works*, 4:66–67.

183. Wesley, "The Circumcision of the Heart," I, 11, *Works* 1:407.

184. John Wesley, "Advice to the People Called Methodists," 23, *Works*, 9:130.

Chapter Five

1. John Wesley, *A Plain Account of Christian Perfection* in *The Works of the Reverend John Wesley, A.M.*, ed. John Emory. (New York: The Methodist Episcopal Church, 1831), 6:483–531. See also Wesley, "Christian Perfection," *Works*, 2:99–124 and John Wesley, "On Perfection," Sermon 76, *Works*, 3:71–87.

2. Wesley, "Christian Perfection," *Works*, 3:71.

3. Wesley, "On Working Out Our Own Salvation," II. 1, *Works*, 3:203–204; John Wesley, Sermon 10, "The Witness of the Spirit, I," II, 3–5, *Works*, 1:277–279.

4. Wesley, "The Scripture Way of Salvation," III, 16, *Works*, 2:168.

5. Wesley, "The Way to the Kingdom," I, 1–2, *Works*, 1:218.

6. Wesley, "The Scripture Way of Salvation," I, 1, *Works*, 2:156.

7. Wesley, "A Farther Appeal to Men of Reason and Religion," Part I, I, 3, *Works*, 11:106.

8. Look at his description of this revivalistic oversimplification in Runyon, *The New Creation: John Wesley's Theology Today*. (Nashville: Abingdon Press, 1998), 246, n. 57.

9. Wesley, "Upon Our Lord's Sermon on the Mount, V," III, 9, *Works*, 1:560.

10. Wesley, "On God's Vineyard," I, 5, *Works*, 3:505.

11. Wesley, "The Scripture Way of Salvation," I, 3–4, *Works*, 2:157–158.

12. *Ibid.*, I, 8, 2:160; Wesley, "On God's Vineyard," I, 6–7, *Works*, 3:506–507.

13. Maddox, *Responsible Grace: John Wesley's Practical Theology*. (Nashville: Kingswood Books, 1994), 151–156.

14. Jonathan Edwards, "A Treatise Concerning Religious Affections," Part II, Eighth "False Sign," *Works*, 2:151–163.

15. Wesley, "On God's Vineyard," I, 6, *Works*, 3:506; Wesley, "On Living Without God," 12–14, *Works*, 4:173–174.

16. *Ibid.*, I, 7, 3:508.

17. Wesley, "On Living Without God," 14, *Works*, 4:174–175.

18. Wesley, "The Spirit of Bondage and of Adoption," IV, 3, *Works*, 1:265–270.

19. Wesley, "The Unity of the Divine Being," 18–20, *Works*, 4:67–69.

20. Wesley, "The Almost Christian," I, 1–3, *Works*, 1:132.

21. Wesley, "On Working Out Our Own Salvation," II, 1, *Works*, 3:203–204.

22. *Ibid.*, II, 1–2, 3:203–205.

23. Wesley, "Christian Perfection," II, 2, 21, *Works*, 2:105, 117.

24. Wesley, "Justification by Faith," I, 1–6, *Works*, 1:184–185.

25. Wesley, "The Great Privilege of Those That are Born of God," I, 3, *Works*, 1:433.

26. Wesley, "Original Sin," III, 5, *Works*, 2:185.

27. Wesley, "The New Birth," I, 1, *Works*, 2:188; Wesley, "The End of Christ's Coming," I, 3–7, *Works*, 2:474–476.

28. Wesley, "The Marks of the New Birth," I, 4–5, *Works*, 1:419–421.

29. Wesley, "Christian Perfection," I, 1–9, *Works*, 2:100–105.

30. Wesley, "A Plain Account of Christian Perfection," *The Works of the Reverend John Wesley, A.M.*, ed. John Emory, 6:490.

31. *Ibid.*, 6:487.

32. *Ibid.*, 6:489. See also Wesley, "The Marks of the New Birth," I, 5, *Works*, 1:420–421.

33. Wesley, "On Zeal," III, 2, *Works*, 3:316; Wesley, "The Scripture Way of Salvation," III, 6, *Works*, 2:165.

34. Wesley, "On Sin in Believers," V, 1, 2, *Works*, 1:332–333.

35. Wesley, "The Repentance of Believers," *Works*, 1:335–352.

36. Wesley, *Explanatory Notes Upon the Old Testament*, comments on verse 28 of Genesis 1.

37. St. Augustine, *The City of God*. (New York: The Modern Library, 1950), 407.

38. Anton C. Pegis, ed., *Basic Writings of Saint Thomas Aquinas*. (New York: Random House, 1945), 1:27.

39. John Calvin, *Commentary on Genesis*. (England: Calvin Translation Society, 1847), 1:28.

40. John Wesley, Sermon 146, "The One Thing Needful," II, 2, *Works*, 4:355.

41. Wesley, "The New Birth," I, 1, *Works*, 2:188.

42. Wesley, "Upon Our Lord's Sermon on the Mount, IX," 6, *Works*, 1:636.

43. Wesley, "The Righteousness of Faith," I, 5, *Works*, 1:205.

44. Wesley, "On Laying the Foundation of the New Chapel," 17, *Works*, 3:592.

45. Wesley, "On Love," II, 2, *Works*, 4:383.

46. Wesley, "Upon Our Lord's Sermon on the Mount, IX," 5, *Works*, 1:635.

47. Wesley, "On Charity," *Works*, 3:295.

48. Wesley, "The Almost Christian," II, 1, *Works*, 1:137. Compare also the similar discussion in Wesley, "The Circumcision of the Heart," I, 12, *Works*, 1:408.

49. Wesley, "The Almost Christian," II, 1, *Works*, 1:137.

500. John Wesley, "Brief Thoughts on Christian Perfection," *The Works of the Reverend John Wesley, AM.*, ed. John Emory, 6:531.

51. Wesley, "On Perfection," I, 4, *Works*, 3:74.

52. Wesley, "Upon Our Lord's Sermon on the Mount, IV," III, 1, *Works*, 1:541.

53. Wesley, "The Circumcision of the Heart," I, 12, *Works*, 1:408.

54. For the details see the excellent study of Wesley's involvement with and rejection of mysticism by Robert G. Tuttle, Jr., *Mysticism in the Wesleyan Tradition*. (Grand Rapids, MI: Francis Asbury Press, 1989), especially Chapter I.

55. John Wesley, Sermon 40, "The Wilderness State," III, 8–9, and 12, *Works*, 2:217–218; John Wesley, Sermon 47, "Heaviness Through Manifold Temptations," III, 7–8, *Works*, 2:229–230.

56. Wesley, "The Wilderness State," III, 10, 12, *Works*, 2:218–220.

57. John Wesley, January 24, 1738, 5, *Works*, 19; Wesley, "Upon Our Lord's Sermon on the Mount, IV," III, *Works*, 1:541–547.

58. Wesley, "Upon Our Lord's Sermon on the Mount, IV," I, 2, *Works*, 1:532.

59. *Ibid.*, III, 2–3, 1:542–543.

60. Wesley, January 9, 1738, *Works*, 18.

61. John Wesley, August 8, 1740, *Works*, 26:14–15.
62. Wesley, "The Wilderness State," III, 12 *Works*, 2:219–220; Wesley, "Heaviness Through Manifold Temptations," III, 8, 9, *Works*, 2:230–231.
63. Wesley, "An Earnest Appeal to Men of Reason and Religion," 30–31, *Works*, 11:55–56; Wesley, "Journal," June 15, 1741, *Works*, 19:201.
64. Evelyn Underhill, *Mysticism*. (Oxford: Oneworld Publications, 1993), 370–372,
65. *Ibid*., 400.
66. John Wesley, "A Second Letter to the Author of the Enthusiasm of Methodists, Etc.," 38, *Works*, 11:416.
67. Underhill, *Mysticism*, 420–426.
68. Critiqued by Tuttle, 167–183.
69. John Wesley, "A Letter to the Right Reverend The Lord Bishop of Gloucester," I, 15, *Works*, 11:481.
70. Walter T. Stace, *The Teachings of the Mystics*. (New York: New American Library, 1960); Robert Forman, ed., *The Problem of Pure Consciousness, Mysticism and Philosophy*, (New York and London: Oxford University Press, 1993).
71. Tuttle, 132.
72. John Wesley, Letter to Ann Bolton, March 25, 1772. Available at: http://wesley.nnu.edu/john-wesley/the-letters-of-john-wesley/wesleys-letters-1772.
73. Wesley, "Upon Our Lord's Sermon on the Mount, IV," I, 1, *Works*, 1:533–534
74. Wesley, "On the Discoveries of Faith,"16, *Works*, 4:37.
75. Wesley, "The New Creation," 18, *Works*, 2:509–510.
76. Wesley, "On Love," II, 3, *Works*, 4:383.
77. Wesley, "The Way to the Kingdom," I, 8, *Works*, 1:221.
78. Wesley, "On Love," II, *Works*, 4:382–385. Compare also the detailed description of love in Wesley, "Upon Our Lord's Sermon on the Mount, II," III, *Works*, 1:499–509.
79. Wesley, "On Family Religion," 4, *Works*, 3:335.
80. I explain "identification spirituality" in much greater depth in Chapter Seven of *Developing Your Christian Values*, which I co-authored with David and Vera Mefford. At present, this is available only on line as an e-book at: http://www.christianvaluesprofile.com.
81. Jonathan Edwards, "The Nature of True Virtue," I, Paul Ramsey, ed., *The Works of Jonathan Edwards, Ethical Writings*, (New Haven: Yale University Press, 1989), 8:540.
82. *Ibid*., V, 8:589.
83. Wesley, "Scriptural Christianity," III, 4, *Works*, 1:171.
84. Wesley, "Upon Our Lord's Sermon on the Mount, II," III, 1, *Works*, 1:499; Wesley, "Upon Our Lord's Sermon on the Mount, VI," III, 14, *Works*, 1:587; Wesley, "A Plain Account of Genuine Christianity," I, 7, Outler, *John Wesley*, 185.
85. Wesley, "Upon Our Lord's Sermon on the Mount, II," III, 1, *Works*, 1:499; Wesley, "The Almost Christian," I, 5, *Works*, 1:139; Wesley, "The Repentance of Believers," I, 11, *Works*, 1:341 and the more detailed discussion of the Golden Rule in Wesley, "Upon Our Lord's Sermon on the Mount, X," 21–26, *Works*, 1:660–662.
86. Wesley, "Upon Our Lord's Sermon on the Mount, X," 24, *Works*, 1:661.
87. Wesley, "The Way to the Kingdom," I, 8. *Works*, 1:221–222.
88. Wesley, "A Plain Account of Genuine Christianity," I, 5, Outler, *John Wesley*, 184.
89. Wesley, "The Love of God," III, 6, *Works*, 4:343.
90. Jonathan Edwards, "The Nature of True Virtue," *Works*, 8:621.
91. *Ibid*., 554.
92. *Ibid*., 555.

93. Wesley, "A Plain Account of Genuine Christianity," I, 5, Outler, *John Wesley*, 184.
94. Wesley, "Catholic Spirit," I, 17, *Works*, 2:89; John Wesley, "The Character of a Methodist," 9, *Works*, 9:38; Wesley, "The Reformation of Manners," 7, *Works*, 2:321.
95. Wesley, "The Good Steward," IV, 2–3, *Works*, 2:297.
96. John Wesley, *A Compendium of Natural Philosophy*, 2:431.
97. Wesley, "On the Discoveries of Faith," 1, *Works*, 4:29.
98. Wesley, "Walking by Sight, and Walking by Faith," 7 *Works*, 4:51; Wesley, "On Faith," 18, *Works*, 4:200.
99. Wesley, *A Compendium of Natural Philosophy*, 2:432.
100. Wesley, "On the Discoveries of Faith," 1–4, *Works*, 4:29–30.
101. *Ibid.*, 4:431. Wesley was much influenced by Browne. Peter Browne's book, *The Procedure, Extent, and Limits of Human Understanding*, was published in 1728. A reprint of it is available through New York: Garland, 1976. Wesley included his own edited version of it in his *Christian Library*. Browne was the original author of the highly edited "Appendix" to the *Compendium of Natural Philosophy*.
102. Albert Outler, "Introduction," *Works*, 1:59, n. 15.
103. John Locke, *An Essay Concerning Human Understanding*, Book II, Chapter I, 4.
104. *Ibid.*, Book II, Chapter VI.
105. *Ibid.*, Book II, Chapter XXIII, 30.
106. *Ibid.*, Book II, Chapter I, 2.
107. John Wesley, "Remarks upon Mr. Locke's *Essay on Human Understanding*," *The Works of the Reverend John Wesley, A.M.*, ed. John Emory, 7:455.
108. Wesley, "An Earnest Appeal to Men of Reason and Religion," 32, *Works*, 11:56.
109. Wesley, *A Compendium of Natural Philosophy*, 2:442.
110. Wesley, "An Earnest Appeal to Men of Reason and Religion," 6–7, 32–34, *Works*, 11:46–47, 56–57.
111. *Ibid.*, 11:30–31, 55–56.
112. William Alston, *Perceiving God; The Epistemology of Religious Experience*. (Ithaca: Cornell University Press, 1991; Alvin Plantinga, *Warranted Christian Belief*. New York: Oxford University Press, 2000, Chs. 6, 9, 10.
113. Wesley, "The Great Privilege of Those that are Born of God," I, 6, *Works*, 1:433–434.
114. *Ibid.*, I, 8, 1:435; Wesley, "The Witness of Our Own Spirit," 18, *Works*, 1:311; Wesley, "On Living Without God," 11, *Works*, 4:173.
115. Wesley, "The Great Privilege of Those that are Born of God," I, 9, *Works*, 1:435.
116. *Ibid.*, I, 10, 1:435.
117. Wesley, "The Spirit of Bondage and Adoption," III, 3, *Works*, 1:261.
118. Wesley, "The Witness of the Spirit, I," I, 7, *Works*, 1:274.
119. Wesley, "The Great Privilege of Those that are Born of God," I, 6, *Works*, 1:433–434.
120. *Ibid.*, I, 7–8, 1:434.
121. Wesley, "An Earnest Appeal to Men of Reason and Religion," 61, *Works*, 11:70.
122. Maddox, *Responsible Grace*, 129.
123. John Wesley, Sermon 11, "The Witness of the Spirit, II," V, 1, *Works*, 1:296.
124. William James, *The Varieties of Religious Experience*. (New York: The Modern Library, 1902), 372.
125. Wesley, "The Great Privilege of Those that are Born of God," I, 8, *Works*, 1:434–435.

126. Wesley, "On Zeal," II, 5, III, 7-10, *Works*, 3:313–314, 318–320; Wesley, "The Scripture Way of Salvation," III, 9–10, *Works*, 2:166.

127. Ralph Waldo Emerson, "The Over-soul," second paragraph.

128. David R. Griffin, "Panentheism: A Postmodern Revelation," in Philip Clayton and Arthur Peacocke, eds., *In Whom We Live and Move and Have Our Being: Panentheistic Reflections on God's Presence in a Scientific World.* (Grand Rapids, MI: William B. Eerdmans Publishing Co., 2004), 36–47.

129. Wesley, "An Earnest Appeal to Men of Reason and Religion," 7, *Works*, 11:47.

130. Wesley, "Of the Church," 22, *Works*, 3:53–54.

131. Wesley, "A Plain Account of Genuine Christianity," I, 3, Outler, *John Wesley*, 184.

132. Wesley, "The Nature of Enthusiasm," 18–28, *Works*, 2:52–57.

133. Wesley, "The Witness of the Spirit, II," II, 1, *Works*, 1:286.

134. Jonathan Edwards, "A Treatise Concerning Religious Affections," I, 2, *Works*, 2:95.

135. *Ibid.*, I, 2, 10–11, 2:116–117.

136. Wesley, "On Charity," III, 12, *Works*, 3:306.

137. Wesley," On Zeal, III, 1–6, *Works*, 3:315–318.

138. *Ibid.*, II, 5, 10, 11, and III, 11, 3:313–315, 320.

139. Jonathan Edwards, "A Treatise Concerning Religious Affections," I, II, 5, *Works*, 2:107–108.

140. Wesley, "A Plain Account of Genuine Christianity," I, 7, Outler, *John Wesley*, 185.

141. Wesley, "The Unity of the Divine Being," 16, *Works*, 4:66–67.

142. Wesley, "Upon Our Lord's Sermon on the Mount, X," 15, *Works*, 1:656.

143. Wesley, "The Law Established Through Faith, II," *Works*, 2:33–43; Wesley, "The Nature of Enthusiasm," *Works*, 2:46–60.

144. Wesley, "The Witness of the Spirit, I," I, 7, *Works*, 1:274.

145. Wesley, "The Marks of the New Birth," IV, 2, *Works*, 1:428.

146. Wesley, "The Witness of the Spirit, I," I, 1, *Works*, 1:271.

147. John Wesley, "On the Holy Spirit," I, *The Works of the Reverend John Wesley, A.M.*, ed. John Emory, 2:533; Wesley, "Sermon on the Mount, IX," 13, *Works*, 1: 638.

148. Wesley, "The Witness of Our Own Spirit," 7, *Works*, 1:304; Wesley, "The Witness of the Spirit, II," V, 1, *Works*, 1:296.

149. John Wesley, "Journal," May 24, 1738, *The Bicentennial Edition of the Works of John Wesley*, eds. W. Reginald Ward and Richard P. Heitzenrater. (Nashville: Abingdon Press, 1988), 18:250.

150. Wesley, "Original Sin," II, 5, *Works*, 2:178.

151. Wesley, "The Witness of Our Own Spirit," 17, *Works*, 1:310.

152. Wesley, "The Witness of the Spirit, I," II, 6, *Works*, 1:279; Wesley, "The Marks of the New Birth," II, 5, *Works*, 1:424–425.

153. Wesley, "The End of Christ's Coming," III, 2, *Works*, 2:481.

154. Wesley, "The Marks of the New Birth," III, 1, *Works*, 1:425; Wesley, "The Way to the Kingdom," 1, 7, *Works*, 1:221.

155. Wesley, "Upon Our Lord's Sermon on the Mount, I," I, 11, *Works*, 1:481.

156. Wesley, "The Witness of the Spirit, I," I, 5, 11, *Works*, 1:273, 275–276.

157. See Kenneth J. Collins, "Twentieth-Century Interpretations of John Wesley's Aldersgate Experience: Coherence or Confusion," *Wesleyan Theological Journal*, 24, 1988, 18–31. See Wesley's self-doubts in Wesley, January 4, 1739, *Works*, 19:29–31.

158. Wesley, "The Witness of the Spirit, II," V, 4, *Works*, 1:298.

159. Wesley, "Predestination Calmly Considered," LII, Outler, *John Wesley*, 450.

160. Such basic beliefs are heavily emphasized by Alvin Plantinga throughout his two books: *Warranted Christian Belief,* and *Where the Conflict Really Lies: Science, Religion, & Naturalism,* (Oxford, New York: Oxford University Press, 2011). Of course, Plantinga has not convinced everyone that belief in God belongs in this list of inescapable basic beliefs.

161. Wesley, "The End of Christ's Coming," III, 1, *Works*, 2:481.

162. *Ibid.*

163. Wesley, "The Great Privilege of Those that are Born of God," I, 9, *Works*, 1:435.

164. *Ibid.*, I, 10, 1:435.

165. Jonathan Edwards, "The Divine and Supernatural Light," I, 3, *The Works of Jonathan Edwards,* ed. Mark Valeri. (New Haven, Yale University Press, 1999), 17:412.

166. Wesley, "The Scripture Way of Salvation," II, 1, *Works*, 2:160.

167. John Wesley, "On Conscience," I, 19, (5), *Works*, 3:489

168. Wesley, "On Sin in Believers," III, 9, *Works*, 1:324.

169. Wesley, "The Character of a Methodist," 17, *Works*, 9:41.

170. Wesley, "The Great Privilege of those that are Born of God," I, 7, *Works* 1: 434.

171. Wesley, "Heavenly Treasure in Earthen Vessels," I, 1, *Works*, 4:163.

172. Wesley, *Explanatory Notes Upon the Old Testament*, Genesis 1:28; Wesley, "The Unity of the Divine Being," 8, *Works*, 4:63.

173. John Wesley, Sermon 8, "The First-Fruits of the Spirit," I, 3, *Works*, 1:236.

174. Wesley, *A Compendium of Natural Philosophy*, 2:170.

175. Wesley, "On Dissipation," 4, *Works*, 3:117.

176. Wesley, "What is Man?" 5, 11, *Works*, 4:21, 23–24.

177. *Ibid.*, 7, 4:22.

178. *Ibid.*, 10, 4:23.

179. *Ibid.*, 6, 4:21–2; Wesley, "The Imperfection of Human Knowledge," I, 13, *Works*, 2:576

180. Wesley, *A Compendium of Natural Philosophy*, 2:171.

181. *Ibid.*, 2:112.

182. Wesley, "What is Man?" II, 9–11, *Works*, 3:461–462.

183. *Ibid.*, II, 8, 3:461. See Outler's note 46 on that page.

184. Wesley, *A Compendium of Natural Philosophy*, 2:433, 189, 467.

185. Wesley, "What is Man?," 6, *Works*, 4:21–22.

186. Wesley, "The Imperfections of Human Knowledge," I, 13, *Works*, 2:576.

187. Wesley, "The Promise of Understanding," I, 2, *Works*, 4:283.

188. Non-reductive physicalism is explained, developed, and effectively related to morality and religion by the contributors to Warren S. Brown, Nancey Murphey, and H. Newton Maloney, eds., *Whatever Happened to the Soul? Scientific and Theological Portraits of Human Nature.* (Minneapolis: Fortress Press, 1998).

189. Wesley, "Upon Our Lord's Sermon on the Mount, III," I, 11, *Works*, 1:517; Wesley, *Explanatory Notes Upon the Old Testament*, comments on Genesis 1:28; Wesley, "An Earnest Appeal to Men of Reason and Religion,"19, *Works*, 11:51.

190. Wesley, "On the Omnipresence of God," 3, *Works*, 4:41.

191. *Ibid.*, I, 1–2, 4:42.

192. *Ibid.*, II, 3, 4:44.

193. *Ibid.*, II, 5, 7, 4: 44–45; Wesley, "On Eternity," 1, 5, *Works* 2:358, 360.

194. *Ibid.*, I, 1, II, 6 and II, 2–4, 4:41–42, 44, 43–44.

195. Wesley, "The Law Established Through Faith, I," III, 6, *Works*, 2:30.
196. John Wesley, Sermon 42, "Satan's Devices," II, 7, *Works*, 2:151.
197. Wesley, "An Earnest Appeal to Men of Reason and Religion," 45, *Works*, 11:62.
198. Wesley, "Satan's Devices," II, 7, *Works*, 2:151.
199. Wesley, "On Divine Providence," 4, *Works*, 2:536.
200. *Ibid.*, 10, 2:538.
201. *Ibid.*, 13, 2:540.
202. *Ibid.*, 14, 2:540.
203. Wesley, "Satan's Devices," II, 2, *Works*, 2:148.
204. Wesley, *A Compendium of Natural Philosophy*, 2:448.
205. Wesley, "Of Good Angels," I, 3, II, 7; *Works*, 3:8, 13.
206. Wesley, "On Divine Providence," 8, *Works*, 2:537.
207. Rem B. Edwards, *What Caused the Big Bang?*, Ch. 4 (a critique of antecedent universes cosmologies) and 257–274 on "How Process Theology Can Affirm Creation *Ex Nihilo*."
208. Rem B. Edwards, "Process Thought and the Spaciness of Mind." *Process Studies*, 1990, 19:156–166.
209. Wesley, "On the Omnipresence of God," II, 8, *Works*, 4:45.
210. *Ibid.*, II, 3, 4:43–44.
211. *Ibid.*, II, 4, 4:44.
212. *Ibid.*, I, 1–2, 4:42.
213. Wesley, "The Imperfection of Human Knowledge," I, 1, *Works*, 2:569.
214. Wesley, "On the Omnipresence of God," II, 1, *Works*, 4:42–43.
215. Wesley, "Upon Our Lord's Sermon on the Mount, III," I, 7, *Works*, 1:514.
216. *Ibid.*, I, 8–10, 1:514–516.
217. *Ibid.*, I, 6, 1:513–514.
218. Wesley, "On the Omnipresence of God," III, 6, *Works*, 4:47.
219. Wesley, "Upon Our Lord's Sermon on the Mount, III," I, 9, *Works*, 1:515.
220. *Ibid.*, I, 6, 1:513–514.
221. Jonathan Edwards, "Personal Narrative," *The Works of Jonathan Edwards*, ed. George S. Claghorn. (New Haven: Yale University Press, 1998), 16:793–794.
222. Wesley, "Upon Our Lord's Sermon on the Mount, III," I, 11, *Works*, 1:516–517.
223. Wesley, "The Reformation of Manners," IV, 4, *Works*, 2:318.
224. John Wesley, *A Plain Account of Christian Perfection* in The Works of the Reverend John Wesley, A.M., ed. John Emory, 6:483–531.
225. *Ibid.*
226. John Wesley, Sermon 89, "The More Excellent Way," V, *Works*, 3:272–274.
227. Wesley, "On Dissipation." *Works*, 3:116–125.
228. Wesley, "Spiritual Idolatry," I, 14, *Works*, 3:109.
229. Wesley, "The Love of God," III, 6, *Works*, 4:343.
230. Wesley, "On Dress," *Works*, 3:247–261, especially 3, 248–249.
231. Wesley, "On The Discoveries of Faith," 16–17, *Works*, 4:37–38.
232. Charles Wesley, "Awake, Thou That Sleepest," II, 10, John Wesley's *Works*, 1:150.
233. Wesley, "The Important Question," III, 14, *Works*, 3:197.
234. John Wesley, Sermon 59, "God's Love to Fallen Man," I, 8–9, *Works*, 2:429–430.
235. For a much richer and more adequate theodicy see: Rem B. Edwards, *What Caused the Big Bang?*, 295–310.
236. Wesley, "Of the Church," II, 26, *Works*, 3:55.

237. Wesley, "On Divine Providence," 20–22, *Works*, 2:545–546.
238. Plantinga, *Where the Conflict Really Lies: Science, Religion, & Naturalism*.
239. See my discussion of "All events have natural causes" in Edwards, *What Caused the Big Bang?*, 34–36, 48, 58–59
240. *Ibid.*, Ch. 2.
241. Wesley, "The Important Question," III, 15, *Works*, 3:197.
242. Wesley, "God's Love to Fallen Man," I, 9–10, II, 11, *Works*, 2:430–432.
243. *Ibid.*, III, 14, 3:197; Wesley, "Spiritual Worship," III, 4–102, *Works*, 3:99–102.
244. Wesley, "God's Love to Fallen Man, II, 11, *Works*, 2:432.
245. Wesley, "A Plain Account of Genuine Christianity," III, 10, Outler, *John Wesley*, 194.
246. Wesley, "Upon Our Lord's Sermon on the Mount, X," 2, *Works*, 1:651.
247. According to Randy Maddox, 243, Albert Outler characterized Wesley as an eudaimonist, but Outler seems to have equated eudaimonist with the hedonistic view that happiness is sustained pleasure without pain. "Eudaimonist" is occasionally used that way, but in this book it is used in the more common way to refer to the pluralistic alternative to hedonism, which says that other properties in addition to pleasure are intrinsically good or constitute human well-being.
248. Wesley, "The Duty of Constant Communion," II, 5, *Works*, 3:432.
249. Wesley, "Spiritual Worship," II, 6, *Works*, 3:96–97.
250. Wesley, "On Perfection," I, 5, *Works*, 3:74.
251. Wesley, "On Conscience," I, 19 (10), *Works*, 3:489.
252. John Wesley, "A Blow at the Root, or Christ Stabb'd in the House of His Friends," 11, Outler, *John Wesley*, 383.
253. Wesley, "On Love," II, 3, *Works*, 4:383.
254. Albert C. Outler, "Pastoral Care in the Wesleyan Spirit," *The Perkins School of Theology Journal*, 1971, 25:10.
255. Wesley, "On the Holy Spirit," *The Works of the Reverend John Wesley, A.M.*, ed. John Emory, 2:536.
256. Wesley, "On Conscience," I, 11, *Works*, 3:485; Wesley, "The Unity of the Divine Being," 18 and note 55, *Works*, 4:68; Wesley, "An Israelite Indeed," 1, *Works*, 3:279.
257. Wesley, "God's Love to Fallen Man," I, 9, II, 1, *Works*, 2:430–431, 431–432; Wesley, "The Good Steward," III, 6, *Works*, 2:296; Wesley, "The Wisdom of Winning Souls," I, *Works*, 4:310–311.
258. Wesley, "The Important Question," II, 6, *Works*, 3:187.
259. Wesley, "The More Excellent Way," 5, 8, *Works*, 3:265–266, 266. See Wesley, "On the Fall of Man," II, 8, *Works*, 2:411, for "adding so many stars to that crown which is reserved in heaven for us." See Wesley, "God's Love to Fallen Man," II, 11, *Works*, 2:431–432; "The most glorious stars will undoubtedly be those who are the most holy;" for their good works "Innumerable stars will be added to their eternal crowns."
260. Wesley, "The Wisdom of Winning Souls," I, *Works*, 4:311.
261. Wesley, "The More Excellent Way," 5, *Works*, 3:265–266.
262. Wesley, "On Faith," I, 10–13, *Works*. 3:497–498; John Wesley, "On the Discoveries of Faith," 13–14, *Works*, 4:35–36; Wesley, "Walking by Sight and Walking by Faith," 1, *Works*. 4:49.
263. Wesley, "The More Excellent Way," 8, *Works*, 3:266.
264. Wesley, "Spiritual Worship," II, 6, *Works*, 3:96; Wesley, "Satan's Devices," 2, *Works*, 2:139.

265. John Wesley, "On the Resurrection of the Dead," II, 1, *Sermons on Several Occasions*. (New York, J & J Harper, 1831), III, 2, 3:348.

266. Wesley, "God's Love to Fallen Man," II, 11, *Works*, 2:431–432

267. Wesley, "An Israelite Indeed," I, 1, *Works*, 3:282–283.

268. *Ibid.*, II, 4, 3:286; Wesley, "The Unity of the Divine Being," 17, *Works*, 4:67; Wesley, "The End of Christ's Coming," III, 6, *Works*, 2:483; Wesley, "Spiritual Worship," II, 6, *Works*, 3:96–97.

269. Wesley, *A Plain Account of Christian Perfection*, in *The Works of the Reverend John Wesley, A.M.*, ed. John Emory, 6:505.

270. *Ibid.*

271. Wesley, "The Good Steward," II, 8, *Works*, 2:289–290; Wesley, "On Faith," 6–7, 11–12, *Works*, 4:191–193, 195–198.

272. Wesley, "On the Discoveries of Faith," 8, *Works*, 4:32–33; Wesley, "On Faith," 11, *Works*, 4:193–197.

273. Wesley, "On Faith," 7, 11, *Works*, 4:192–193, 195–197.

274. Wesley, "The Good Steward," II, 6, *Works*, 2:288–289; Wesley, "On Faith," 7, *Works*, 4:192.

Index

abundant life, 9, 12, 62, 179, 182, 241–244, 248
Adam and Eve, 36, 50, 63, 76, 94, 108, 118–120, 127–129, 159, 187, 192
aesthetic, 239, 253, 254
Aldersgate, 51, 112, 184–186, 220, 221
analogy, 39, 43–44, 160–161
animals, 7, 8, 18, 20, 24, 36, 50, 53, 54, 58, 59, 73–83, 91–93, 96–98, 102, 103, 106–108, 118, 119, 123, 127, 146, 156, 161, 165, 167, 173, 185, 192, 200, 202–205, 236, 238, 240, 257
Anselm, 37, 39, 42, 43, 45
Aquinas, 43, 78, 81, 139, 192
Aristotelian, 35, 209
Aristotle, 42, 52, 78, 135
Arminian, 64, 135, 136
assurance, 9, 142–145, 186, 195, 196, 211, 212, 214, 215, 217, 219–221, 244
atonement, 137, 142, 152, 156, 186, 195
Augustine, 50, 54, 65, 105, 175, 192, 218
axiological, 11, 17, 21, 31, 36, 54, 59, 97, 102, 123, 168, 170, 197, 198, 205, 222, 257–258

bad-making, 19, 32, 44, 222, 245
baptism, 28, 84–88
beliefs, 8, 9, 15, 18–21, 23–25, 28, 33, 35, 37, 81, 86, 87, 97, 107, 119, 124, 126, 127, 135–138, 140–149, 151, 152, 155–157, 165–167, 169, 171, 172, 174–177, 189, 199, 201, 203, 204, 210–212, 216, 219, 220, 223–227, 236, 240
believe, 14, 27, 29, 35, 38, 51, 66, 69, 75, 76, 78, 84, 88, 90, 93, 120, 122, 123, 125, 128, 130, 132, 133, 135, 137, 139, 143, 144, 147–150, 152–155, 158, 161, 171, 174, 182, 186, 190, 205, 211, 215, 218, 221, 224, 225, 238, 243, 251
believer, 8, 136, 137, 141, 145, 148, 149, 169, 216, 220
Big Bang, 72, 93, 233, 242, 258
body of God, 198, 199, 233
Bonnet, Charles, 35, 39, 49, 229

born again, 125, 129, 160, 186, 224 155, 188, 222, 224, 227, 248

Calvin, John 119, 192
Calvinist, 37, 42, 181
capable of God, 78, 80
Cartesian, 74, 109, 110, 228–231
Christ, 23, 25, 27–30, 35, 38, 51, 56, 65, 86–88, 108, 112, 115, 116, 130, 132, 135, 142–145, 149, 151, 154–156, 161, 163, 166, 169, 180–183, 185, 190, 195, 198, 199, 204, 211, 219, 220, 225, 226, 246–248, 253
Christian, 7, 8, 11, 12, 15–17, 21–24, 26–30, 33, 36, 37, 41, 42, 46, 52, 56, 60, 63, 65, 73, 81, 84, 86, 88–90, 95, 103, 104, 106–109, 111–113, 115, 116, 131, 133–156, 161–174, 179, 180, 182–187, 189, 190, 194–196, 199, 200, 202–204, 209–211, 216–227, 238, 239, 242, 245, 249, 253, 258
Christian Library, 65, 116, 135, 136, 209, 219
Christian Values, 7, 8, 11, 12, 15–17, 106, 135–137, 140–142, 165–167, 169–173, 202, 258
Christlike, 29, 146, 148, 166, 188, 189, 203, 247
Cobb, John B., Jr., 13, 43, 46
Collins, James, 13, 38, 43, 62, 63, 137, 221
commandments, 22, 32, 33, 113, 115, 116, 140, 146, 148, 165, 173, 175, 177, 182, 186, 189, 192, 220, 223
comparative value, 146, 168–170, 173
compassion, 19, 36, 42–45, 47, 76, 79, 81, 98, 104, 107, 113, 114, 119, 129, 134, 141, 162, 166, 171, 180, 184, 186, 192, 198, 201–203, 213, 214, 217, 218, 242–244, 248
conscience, 59–61, 63, 64, 96, 106, 113, 119, 122, 123, 126, 129, 130, 137, 139, 151, 161–164, 166, 184, 188, 203, 206, 209, 210, 216, 217, 220, 223, 224, 226, 246, 248, 250

284 *John Wesley's Values—And Ours*

consciousness, 9, 59, 61, 78, 85, 86, 96, 106, 124, 126, 164, 175, 188, 196–198, 209–213, 223, 224, 234, 246, 249
Constantine, 133
conversion, 25, 62, 73, 113–115, 129, 155, 175, 180–186, 188–190, 210, 222, 224, 227
Copernicus, 93, 119, 159
created, 14, 26, 30, 38, 39, 41, 44, 45, 47, 50, 51, 57, 58, 63, 66, 68, 73, 75, 78, 81, 92, 93, 128, 146, 191, 192, 197, 224, 231, 233, 235, 236, 238, 240, 243, 244, 252–254
creation, 9, 12–14, 26, 27, 35, 39, 44, 51, 52, 58, 63, 72–74, 76, 77, 80, 81, 93, 94, 107, 108, 124, 137, 156, 159, 161, 165, 172, 181, 189, 192, 194, 199, 200, 227, 231–234, 239, 240, 248
creation care, 76, 124, 240

Darwin, Charles, 76, 78, 79, 120
Darwinian, 77, 93, 119, 159
death, 27, 35, 76, 77, 79, 84, 87, 93, 94, 108, 109, 118, 119, 127, 128, 133, 142, 154, 155, 180, 181, 183, 187, 202, 217, 220, 242, 243, 250, 253
delight, 30, 81, 95, 99, 101, 102, 104, 148, 193, 202, 221, 238, 239, 254
development, 12, 13, 16, 29, 36, 62, 65, 119, 129, 130, 136, 182, 183, 186, 187, 210, 224, 238, 242, 252
devils, 141, 142, 144, 145, 150, 153
direct witness, 215, 220
disinterested, 19, 140–142, 218
dominant, 130, 134, 178, 183
dominate, 121, 123, 185, 188
dualism, 109, 110, 228, 229–231, 242

Eden, 108, 118, 128
education, 13, 60, 81, 101, 124, 135, 136, 140, 258
Edwards, Jonathan, 11, 11, 14–15, 48, 55, 58, 65–73, 90, 93, 102, 104, 116, 165, 181, 183, 202, 206, 208, 210, 217–219, 221, 226, 233–237, 242, 249
Edwards, Rem B., 16, 255, 261, 263, 265, 280, 291–292

elect, 40, 41, 52, 65, 67, 71, 73, 90, 116, 125, 149, 219
embodied, 27, 51, 58, 61, 106, 107, 109, 187, 228, 230–234, 246
empirical, 30, 70, 120, 121, 127, 130, 186, 231, 242, 243
empiricism, 209, 210, 224
empiricist, 139, 208–210, 224
ends in themselves, 18, 23, 33, 50, 53, 56, 99, 100
enthusiasm, 89, 90, 113, 165, 195, 196, 215, 216, 219
equals, 35, 61, 77, 80, 130, 164, 179, 232, 250, 252, 253
essential doctrines, 142, 152
eternal, 48, 49, 55, 99, 108, 154, 181, 216, 232, 251
eternity, 7, 14, 38, 44–49, 51–53, 68, 69, 93, 101, 108, 110, 133, 151, 158, 160, 232, 240, 252–254
evil, 9, 17, 25, 30, 44, 55, 59–61, 66, 72, 76, 95–97, 99, 106, 107, 111, 118, 120, 126–131, 133, 151, 153–155, 159, 166, 168, 179, 188–191, 200–204, 207, 211, 212, 216–218, 222–224, 232, 242, 243, 246
extrinsic evaluation, 19, 247
extrinsic value, 8, 50, 83, 93, 94, 97, 167, 169, 170, 173, 240

faith that works by love, 25, 90, 138, 141, 145–148, 182, 244, 252
feelings, 7, 19, 28, 42–44, 48, 58, 59, 61, 66, 67, 73–75, 96, 100, 102, 106, 107, 140, 165–167, 187, 188, 195, 199, 203, 210, 217–219, 234, 246, 254
fields, 76, 233, 238
flesh, 27, 56, 65, 88, 99, 100, 105, 107–109, 117, 137, 152, 161, 190, 204, 228, 236
follow nature, 127, 164
foreknowledge, 46, 49, 160
formalities, 18, 19, 28, 87, 88, 131, 141, 167, 174–176, 239
free choice, 41, 48, 58, 61, 64–71, 73, 77–78, 96, 116, 187, 216, 242, 246
fruits, 90, 100, 112, 113, 116, 156, 216, 218, 219, 228

fundamentals, 142

God
    attributes of, 32, 37–51, 58, 137, 139, 152, 158, 168, 172, 194, 196, 228, 232, 235, 261
    creator, 28, 38, 42, 44, 48, 54, 58, 75, 79, 117, 192, 205, 218, 233, 236–239
    eternity, 14, 38, 44-49, 151, 158, 160, 232
    feelings or affections, 42–45
    immaterial, 58, 96, 191, 228–231
    loving, 40–43, 45, 51, 65, 72, 75, 157 191–192, 204
    necessary existence, 49
    omniscience, 38, 45–49, 196, 132
    omnipotence, 38, 40–42, 47, 49, 72, 232
    omnipresence, 38, 49, 57, 75, 92, 189, 197, 215–216, 228–241
    Trinity, 37, 38, 143, 151, 152, 175
Godlike, 29, 44, 51, 57–59, 63, 75, 78, 81, 166, 187–189, 191, 202, 203, 244, 247, 248, 252, 253
Godly, 59, 116, 133, 140
God's enemies, 55, 151, 154
Golden Rule, 81, 203, 289
good and evil, 9, 44, 55, 59–61, 66, 72, 96, 106, 118, 128, 129, 179, 188, 189, 211, 216, 217, 222–224, 246
good works, 8, 21, 28, 83, 107, 111–113, 115, 116, 131, 136, 147, 166, 167, 169, 170, 172, 180, 195, 219, 220, 247, 250, 251, 254
good-making, 7–9, 18–21, 31, 36, 37, 39, 41, 43–45, 49, 51–53, 57, 61–66, 73, 74, 77, 78, 80, 96, 106, 113, 114, 129, 134, 148, 167, 168, 172, 174, 176, 178, 179, 183, 185, 187, 188, 193, 194, 196–199, 202, 208, 222, 223, 241, 243–249, 252
greed, 27, 55, 59, 66, 77, 78, 92, 97, 105, 109, 116, 122, 123, 159, 162, 181, 190, 193, 206, 210, 217–219, 221, 223, 226, 229, 230, 241
    growing in grace, 65, 182, 185, 194, 208, 232, 241, 253

growth, 12, 13, 15, 36, 75, 88, 107, 112, 129, 171, 180, 182, 183, 186, 199, 241, 245, 247, 249, 253, 254

heaven, 9, 38, 40, 45, 71, 73–75, 77, 80, 104, 109, 115, 137, 146, 177, 181, 182, 221, 231–234, 236, 238, 241, 242, 246, 250–255
hedonism, 101–102, 104, 244, 245, 257
Heitzenrater, Richard P., 13, 89, 163, 220
hell, 40, 41, 71, 105, 109, 122, 137, 154, 155, 177, 181, 231, 251
hermeneutics, 8, 155–157, 159, 161, 165, 166, 168, 171, 172, 216
hermeneutics of love, 8, 155–157, 159, 161, 165, 168, 171, 172, 216
hierarchy of Christian value, 8, 169
hierarchy of value, 8, 20, 21, 83, 97, 167, 169, 240
holiness, 25, 38, 56, 65, 86, 88, 112, 113, 133, 138, 147–150, 157, 181, 182, 185, 200, 217, 221, 237, 241, 244, 245, 247, 252
holy tempers, 113, 169, 170, 183, 218, 219
human nature, 42, 50, 60, 61, 63, 64, 104, 109, 117, 129, 130, 147, 224, 231
Hume, David, 147

identification spirituality, 25, 202, 249, 254
identify with, 19, 25, 99, 106, 194, 201, 205, 244, 248
image of God, 7, 44, 49, 51, 52, 57, 58, 60, 64–66, 70, 78, 80, 103, 108, 118, 163, 172, 180, 181, 185, 187, 188, 191–193, 196, 199, 201, 228, 230, 245–247, 252, 253
immaterial, 58, 96, 191, 228–231
immortality, 51, 73, 74, 78, 79, 109, 163
isolation, 42, 52–53, 96, 244
individuals, 14, 23, 24, 26, 27, 33, 50–53, 56, 61, 83, 122, 157, 195, 197, 199, 200, 204, 208, 212, 244, 254
individuated, 56, 124, 223, 249
internal, 24, 31, 58, 71, 85–87, 90, 100, 101, 106, 111, 114, 139, 146, 176, 189, 191, 202, 208–210, 219, 222, 242, 247, 249, 251–253

interpretation, 40, 42, 81, 152, 155–162, 165, 172, 100, 212–213, 215–216, 221, 225, 227, 234, 239
intrinsic faith, 8, 142–147
intrinsic value, 28, 36, 56, 81, 83, 86, 87, 106, 124, 167, 169, 170, 185, 189, 223, 240, 247, 253
intrinsically good, 7, 18, 31, 33, 35, 36, 50, 51, 53, 56, 57, 62, 65–66, 73-74, 95–97, 106–107, 164, 167, 179, 223, 228, 236, 239, 240, 244, 245
Irenaeus, 118, 128, 129

James, William, 71, 214
Jesus, 22, 23, 25, 28–30, 32, 33, 35, 38, 42, 44, 54–56, 94, 116, 130, 137, 139, 141, 143–145, 151, 154, 155, 157, 160, 172, 174, 176, 177, 181, 183, 186, 195, 203, 204, 211, 219, 221, 222, 225, 230, 237, 238, 241–244, 247, 248, 250, 254, 255
Jews, 153, 154, 168, 186
joy, 44, 99, 100–102, 104, 106, 140, 144, 145, 196, 198, 202, 203, 205, 211, 212, 217, 221–223, 225, 229, 236, 239, 241–242
justice, 27, 28, 40, 42, 44, 72, 73, 79, 112, 113, 119, 125, 148, 151, 158, 161, 162, 164, 171, 181, 184, 192, 198, 217, 219, 223
justification, 73, 112, 113, 137, 142, 180, 182, 190, 195

Kierkegaard, Søren 135, 239
Kingdom of God, 23, 28, 29, 33, 134, 181, 241, 242

Lee, Unphrey, 62, 120
legal state, 175, 185
liberty, 7, 41, 44, 48, 58, 61, 64–68, 71, 74, 78, 96, 106, 108, 162, 163, 187, 188, 191, 229, 235, 246, 247
literal, 8, 39, 43, 45, 119, 120, 127, 158–161, 251
Locke, John, 15, 35, 100, 138, 208–210, 224
logic, 19, 28, 35, 39, 43–45, 47, 49, 62, 72, 93, 104, 112, 113, 120, 127, 136, 138, 139, 160, 161, 187, 188, 210, 224, 232, 234, 242, 243, 253
Lord's Supper, 84–88, 90, 131, 159, 170
love the Lord, 22, 32, 54, 146, 192
love your neighbor, 22, 54, 200
Luther, Martin, 119, 135, 182

Maddox, Randy L., 13, 27, 43, 44, 63, 64, 74, 81, 110, 119, 128, 129, 133, 137, 158, 162, 163, 172, 183, 213, 245
Mahometan, 153, 154
Marquardt, Manfried, 13, 122, 129, 136, 162
matter, 25, 26, 33, 43, 58, 72, 93, 102, 107–110, 123, 124, 127, 134, 138, 141, 143, 144, 150, 153, 161, 164, 168, 176, 178, 181, 185, 187, 191, 195, 202–204, 228–230
means of grace, 8, 28, 35, 83–90, 101, 105, 110, 115, 132, 149, 161, 169, 182, 195, 214, 236, 238
means to ends, 18, 19, 26, 34, 50, 53, 56, 83–85, 90, 99, 101
mercy, 13, 27–29, 36, 40, 42–44, 55, 72–76, 81, 84, 88, 95, 101, 112, 113, 119, 130, 141, 144, 145, 148, 151, 154, 157, 158, 161, 164, 169–172, 181, 184, 192, 204, 213, 214, 216, 217, 219, 223, 227, 230, 247
metaphysics, 9, 72, 103, 160, 195, 228–231, 236, 243, 255
Methodist, v, 11, 14, 17, 27, 35, 37, 41, 43, 46, 55, 73, 84–86, 88, 115, 116, 130, 133, 136, 144, 145, 162, 172, 180, 186, 207, 226, 257, 258
mirror neurons, 79, 81, 201
money, 28, 95, 97–99, 101, 123–125, 159
Moore, G. E., 52, 53
mystical, 87, 195–199
mysticism, 13, 87, 194–199, 200, 215

natural man, 62, 120, 184, 212, 228
natural philosophy, 27, 39, 49, 57, 78, 93, 119, 136, 140, 152, 159, 160, 172, 209, 210, 229, 230, 233
natural science, 119, 136, 147, 156, 165, 242
natural state, 73, 98, 185, 206

neighbor, 22, 54, 69, 131, 146, 172, 194, 200, 204, 206, 218
new birth, 25, 44, 54, 58, 86–88, 105, 112, 113, 143–145, 150, 160, 180, 182, 183, 185, 188–190, 192, 211, 220, 221, 227
Newton, Isaac, 59, 92, 93, 231, 233
Newtonian, 159, 233
non-Christian, 138, 153, 154, 179, 186, 223

once-born, 183, 185, 211, 222, 248
Oord, Thomas J., 72, 255, 256, 258, 259, 261, 262, 266, 273
opinion, 141, 150, 151, 153, 165, 175
original perfection, 63, 76, 94, 118, 159, 187
original sin, 8, 50, 83, 116–120, 127, 129, 137
other world, 123, 181, 186, 228, 253
Outler, Albert, 15, 22, 24, 35–38, 40–42, 48, 52, 56, 66, 67, 84, 93, 100, 104, 106, 108, 115, 116, 118, 136, 138, 140–143, 154, 158, 175, 203, 204, 207, 209, 216, 218, 223, 245, 248, 249
overvalue, 83, 84, 87–89, 91, 97, 116, 136, 140, 174, 239, 240
own sake, 12, 23, 34–36, 50–55, 86, 95, 99, 100, 103, 142, 164, 193, 197

pain, 8, 42, 74–79, 81, 96, 100, 101, 104, 105, 108, 119, 126, 134, 196, 209, 244, 245
panentheism, 14, 282
parents, 81, 126, 130, 136, 201
Paul, St., 14, 21, 25, 27–29, 33, 34, 48, 94, 139, 143, 159, 162, 163, 172, 175, 181, 190, 202, 220, 223, 224
perfect, 29, 30, 32, 36–42, 45, 47, 53, 76, 78, 93, 108, 115, 118, 119, 128, 153, 157, 166, 172, 185, 187, 189, 190, 194, 196, 221, 228, 253
perfection, 7, 9, 36, 38, 39, 45–47, 57, 61, 63, 73, 76, 79, 90, 93, 94, 114, 115, 118, 120, 128, 130, 137, 159, 176, 180, 181, 185–187, 189, 190, 192, 194, 200, 223, 238, 241, 247, 253

philosophy, 11–13, 35, 57–58, 93, 103, 119, 136, 138, 140, 147, 159, 172, 209, 239, 257–258
Plantinga, Alvin, 210, 224, 242
Plato, 42, 46, 52
pleasure, 8, 54, 59, 60, 74, 75, 77–79, 95, 96, 98–103, 105, 117, 132, 134, 209, 238, 239, 244–246
politics, 121, 124–126, 165, 187, 207
predestination, 37, 42, 46–48, 64, 67, 71, 72, 116, 157, 158, 160, 161, 226
presence, 9, 14, 25, 38, 46, 56, 61, 64, 70, 75, 87, 89, 101, 130, 138, 148, 184, 188, 189, 195, 197, 211–217, 220, 227, 228, 231, 232, 235–238
prevenient grace, 13, 55, 57, 60–64, 73, 77, 98, 106, 115, 119–120, 136, 177–180, 183, 185, 187–188, 205, 210, 222–224, 247
Process Theology, 14, 72, 199, 215, 233, 235, 284
preventive grace, 179
priorities, 13, 20, 97, 129, 161, 167, 183, 240
prosperity, 23, 92, 102, 105, 107, 123, 125, 132, 133, 174, 205
prosperity gospel, 132
Protestant, 15, 37, 43, 62–64, 84, 85, 137, 142, 145, 154, 155, 180, 182, 185, 186, 215, 222, 226

Quadrilateral, 37, 135, 136

ranking, 8, 15, 17, 20, 22, 31–34, 83, 106, 132–133, 138, 149, 150, 167, 170–174, 239
realities, 62, 95, 97, 100, 124, 142–146, 149, 167, 175, 177, 205, 209, 210, 233
reality, 14, 21, 24, 25, 29, 30, 38, 45, 47, 50–52, 90, 106, 110, 118, 130, 142–144, 148, 151, 195, 197, 198, 211, 220, 224, 229, 231, 234, 235, 238, 239
reason, 14, 37, 39–41, 49, 52, 53, 55, 58, 61, 63, 64, 66, 74, 78, 79, 89, 93, 96, 101, 105, 106, 116, 117, 120, 131, 135, 136, 138–140, 144, 152, 153, 155, 157, 159, 161–164, 166, 172, 177, 181, 182, 187, 188, 190–192,

288 *John Wesley's Values—And Ours*

196, 209, 210, 213, 215, 216, 219, 224, 226, 231, 232, 240, 246, 252, 257
reciprocal altruism, 102, 103, 107, 114, 121, 132
rejoice, 111, 124, 151, 157, 193, 203, 218, 221, 238, 239, 241, 249
religious affections, 9, 15, 29, 36, 43, 44, 51, 55, 56, 113, 116, 131, 144, 145, 183, 188, 191, 209, 212, 217–219, 221–223, 240, 245
religious experience, 156, 165, 194, 195, 199, 200, 210, 211, 214, 215
restored, 41, 57, 60–65, 77, 78, 109, 136, 180–181, 186–187, 192, 205, 213, 221
resurrection of the body, 27, 100, 109, 110
revelation, 139, 145, 146, 159, 215, 223, 226
Roman Catholic, 63, 85, 88, 142, 145, 153, 163, 171, 186, 191, 192, 195, 226
Runyon, Ted, 13, 35, 181

salvation, 8, 13, 23–25, 40, 41, 55, 60, 62, 64, 65, 84, 85, 87, 111–113, 115, 116, 137, 143, 145, 146, 153–155, 159, 180–184, 186, 188, 190, 191, 195, 198, 199, 215, 219–221, 226, 242, 244, 247, 249
sanctification, 8, 24, 25, 62, 65, 68, 112, 113, 137, 180–186, 188–192, 194, 200, 208, 222, 241, 242, 244, 247, 249, 251, 253
saving grace, 41, 61–63, 79, 178, 179, 184, 246, 247
scientific, 12, 14, 25, 93, 119, 120, 124, 136, 147, 156, 159, 165, 172, 215, 224, 231, 239, 243, 258
scripture, 60, 84, 85, 88, 89, 116, 136, 143, 155, 157, 158, 160–162, 164, 165, 172, 180–182, 190, 193, 195, 215, 216, 219, 225, 226, 241
selfish, 98, 100, 102, 106, 114, 116, 119, 121–123, 129, 205, 241, 245, 247–249, 254
self-evident, 70, 71, 138, 139, 208
self-motion, 58, 61, 74, 78, 96, 106, 187, 246
sentient, 59, 61, 74, 75, 96, 106, 188, 246

sin, 8, 9, 14, 20, 21, 24, 25, 29, 37–39, 50–52, 57, 59, 62, 72, 73, 76, 83, 87, 93, 94, 97, 100–102, 105–108, 114–120, 125–127, 129–131, 133, 137–139, 144, 147, 148, 153–155, 160, 164, 170, 172, 175, 177, 180–182, 185, 187–191, 195, 196, 200, 206, 216, 220–222, 225, 226, 233, 241–243, 245, 247, 248, 254, 258
sinner, 24, 25, 84, 117, 142, 208
slavery, 13, 162–163
social religion, 115, 198
Southern Baptists, 163
special grace, 62, 129, 188, 247
special presence, 227, 228
spiritual goods, 106, 211, 212, 222–224
spiritual growth, 12, 15, 36, 88, 129, 171, 241, 245
spiritual light, 226
spiritual union, 194, 197, 198, 200, 215
stars in our crowns, 9, 52, 237, 250–252
status, 57, 101, 102, 164, 185, 205
Steele, Richard B., 14, 55, 65–67
success, 103, 107, 132, 133, 174
suffer, 25, 42, 45, 74, 76, 77, 104, 107, 127, 155, 173, 234, 242, 243
systemic evaluation, 19, 247
systemic goods, 28, 33, 56, 237
systemic value, 30, 31, 86, 124, 138, 141, 142, 167, 168, 173, 239, 240, 253
systemically good, 18, 28, 31, 33, 149, 236, 237, 240

tempers, 25, 44, 56, 59, 99, 105, 113, 144, 149, 150, 169, 170, 181, 183, 188, 192, 194, 212, 218, 219, 221, 247, 254
temples of God, 27, 51, 108, 110, 220
Temporalistic Theology, 46, 47, 234
Ten Commandments, 32, 33, 116, 182
theoretical construct, 63, 187
total depravity, 62, 120
totally depraved, 73, 119, 120, 130, 136
tradition, 13, 14, 22, 23, 37, 40, 45, 46, 71, 84, 85, 127, 128, 133, 143–145, 147, 155, 157, 181, 190, 191, 195, 208, 210, 214–216, 219, 225, 226, 228
Trinity, 37, 38, 143, 151, 152, 175

true religion, 50, 55, 56, 116, 138, 148, 153, 157, 166, 175–177, 193, 196, 217–219
true virtue, 202, 206
Tuttle, Robert G., Jr., 13, 195–197
twice-born, 183, 185, 222, 248

undervalue, 83, 84, 87, 89, 91, 92, 140, 174
union in love, 197, 198
union with God, 9, 189, 191, 194, 196, 198–201
Ussher, Bishop James, 233

value combinations, 30, 31, 33, 52, 87
vice, 58, 72, 108, 114, 184, 253, 254
virtue, 52, 57, 58, 72, 113, 114, 133, 137, 139, 154, 184, 191, 202, 206

war, 77, 122, 123, 125, 162
Wesleyan, 11–13, 15, 16, 22, 37, 38, 43, 47, 50–52, 64, 72, 73, 76, 81, 129, 130, 133, 135–138, 165, 166, 176, 190, 194, 195, 199, 200, 202, 206, 219, 221, 249
Whitefield, George, 40, 58, 72, 162
women, 73, 98, 100, 125, 158, 161–164
works of love, 28, 29, 84, 112, 113, 141, 147, 170, 171, 214, 219
works of mercy, 27, 84, 95, 112, 169, 170, 172, 216
works of piety, 84, 85, 88, 170, 172, 216, 247
world, 8, 14, 19, 21, 24–32, 45, 47, 50–52, 58–60, 62, 63, 72, 73, 76, 83, 85, 90–103, 106–109, 111, 115–117, 120, 121, 123, 125–129, 131–134, 137, 143, 144, 149, 151, 154, 159, 161, 164–168, 173, 174, 176, 181–187, 190, 191, 195–197, 207, 209, 214–216, 222–226, 228–231, 233, 235–244, 247, 250, 253
worldliness, 8, 26, 29, 83, 97–100, 102, 104, 107, 116, 117, 133, 185, 188, 248
worldly, 8, 26, 83, 92, 95, 97–106, 115, 117, 120, 122–124, 126, 127, 129, 131–134, 139, 140, 164, 174, 175, 178, 179, 185, 191, 205, 222–224, 226, 228, 237–241, 251, 252
worldly goods, 8, 92, 97, 133
worldly religion, 8, 83, 131–133, 164, 174, 226, 252
zeal, 8, 84, 166–172, 190, 215, 218, 219, 226

About the Author

REM B. EDWARDS, Ph.D., grew up in the small town of Crawfordville, GA. He attended Emory at Oxford, then graduated as a Philosophy major from Emory University with an A.B. degree in 1956. There he was elected to Phi Beta Kappa. Throughout graduate school, he was a Danforth Graduate Fellow. He received a B.D. degree from Yale University Divinity School (YDS) in 1959 and a Ph.D. in Philosophy from Emory University in 1962, where he studied under Charles Hartshorne. While at YDS, during the summer of 1958 he was the minister at the Old Brick Church Congregational in Clarendon, VT. After finishing YDS, he served for a year as the minister of Dixie Methodist Church in La Grange, GA. After completing his Ph.D. at Emory, he taught for four years at Jacksonville University in Florida, moved from there to the University of Tennessee in 1966, and retired from there partly in 1997 and partly in 1998. He kept an office on the University campus until the end of May, 2000. He was a U. T. Chancellor's Research Scholar in 1985 and a distinguished Lindsay Young Professor between 1987–1998. He continues to be professionally active.

His areas of specialization are Philosophy of Religion, American Philosophy, Medical Ethics, and Ethical Theory, with a special focus on Mental Health Care Ethics, Ethics and Animals, and Formal Axiology.

He is the author and/or editor of twenty other books including *Reason and Religion* (New York: Harcourt, 1972 and Lanham, MD: University Press of America, 1979); *Pleasures and Pains: A Theory of Qualitative Hedonism* (Ithaca: Cornell University Press, 1979); with Glenn Graber, *BioEthics* (San Diego: Harcourt, 1988); with John W. Davis, *Forms of Value and Valuation: Theory and Applications* (Lanham, MD: University Press of America, 1991); *Formal Axiology and Its Critics* (Amsterdam – Atlanta: Rodopi, 1995); *Violence, Neglect, and the Elderly*, co-edited with Roy Cebik, Glenn Graber, and Frank H. Marsh (Greenwich, CT: JAI Press, 1996); *New Essays on Abortion and Bioethics*, (Greenwich, CT: JAI Press, 1997); *Ethics of Psychiatry: Insanity, Rational Autonomy, and Mental Health Care*, (Buffalo, NY: Prometheus Books, 1997); *Values, Ethics, and*

Alcoholism, co-edited with Wayne Shelton, (Greenwich, CT: JAI Press, 1997); *Bioethics for Medical Education*, co-edited with Dr. Edward Bittar, (Stamford, CT: JAI Press, 1999); *Dialogues on Values and Centers of Value* (Amsterdam – New York: Rodopi, 2001), co-authored with Thomas M. Dicken; and *What Caused the Big Bang?* (Amsterdam – New York: Rodopi, 2001). *What Caused the Big Bang* received the "Best Book of 2001" award from the Editors of the Value Inquiry Book Series. His *The Essentials of Formal Axiology* was published in 2010 by the University Press of America. Awaiting publication by Emeth Press are his *Developing Your Christian Values*, co-authored with David Mefford and Vera Mefford, and his own *Spiritual Values and Evaluations*. Edwards has also authored over eighty articles and reviews.

He is an Associate Editor with the Value Inquiry Book Series, published by Rodopi, where he is responsible for the Hartman Institute Axiological Studies special series. For a number of years he was co-editor of the Advances in Bioethics book series published by JAI Press. He also did significant editorial work on the following books published in Rodopi's Hartman Institute Axiological Studies: Frank G. Forrest, *Valuemetrics: The Science of Personal and Professional Ethics*, 1994; Robert S. Hartman, *Freedom to Live: The Robert Hartman Story*, 1994; Armando Molina, *Our Ways: Values and Character*, 1997; Gary Acquaviva, *Violence, Values, and Our Future*, 2000; Robert S. Hartman, *The Knowledge of Good*, 2002, co-edited with Arthur Ellis; Leon Pomeroy, *The New Science of Axiological Psychology*, 2005; Gary Gallopin, *Beyond Perestroika: Axiology and the New Russian Entrepreneurs*, 2009. In 2008, Edwards became the senior editor of the new *Journal of Formal Axiology: Theory and Practice*.

Edwards has been the President of the Tennessee Philosophical Association (1973–74), the Society for Philosophy of Religion (1981–82), and the Southern Society for Philosophy and Psychology, (1984–85). He is a Charter Member and Fellow of the Robert S. Hartman Institute for Formal and Applied Axiology and has served on its Board of Directors since 1987. In 1989 he became its Secretary/Treasurer; after October of 2007, he continued as its Secretary until October, 2009 and is now the Contact Secretary. He is a Webmaster for the website of the Robert S. Hartman Institute at: http://www.hartmaninstitute.org. He is a lifelong Methodist.

www.ingramcontent.com/pod-product-compliance
Lightning Source LLC
Chambersburg PA
CBHW030337240426
43661CB00052B/1658